DOGS
UNLEASHED

DOGS
UNLEASHED

TAMSIN PICKERAL

Thunder Bay
P·R·E·S·S

SAN DIEGO

Thunder Bay Press
An imprint of the Baker & Taylor Publishing Group
10350 Barnes Canyon Road, San Diego, CA 92121
www.thunderbaybooks.com

Moseley Road Inc, www.moseleyroad.com
Publisher: Sean Moore
Editorial Director: Damien Moore
Production Director: Adam Moore
General Manager: Karen Prince

Editorial: Lesley Malkin
Design: Philippa Baile, www.oiloften.co.uk
Mark Johnson Davies, www.bannau.com
Kate Stretton @ KatieLoveDesign

Library of Congress Cataloging-in-Publication Data

Dogs unleashed.
    pages cm
 ISBN 978-1-62686-068-1 (hardcover)
1. Dog breeds. 2. Dogs.
 636.7--dc23
                        2014015942

Printed in China.
1 2 3 4 5 18 17 16 15 14

CONTENTS

INTRODUCTION

DOG LOVERS

There are about 400 recognized dog breeds today and a great number of new breeds in development. There is truly a dog to fit every requirement for size, color, skill, adaptation, character, and more. There are dog hotels, dog vacations, dog whisperers, dog doctors—the list goes on. Dogs today are a multi-billion-dollar industry. The bottom line is that (generally) people love dogs and, in return, dogs (generally) love people. They are surely the most loyal, devoted, forgiving, affectionate, and nonjudgmental companions, although they may not be the cleanest, most obedient, or quietest!

Dogs Unleashed presents a selection of the best-loved, rarest, fastest, slowest, biggest, smallest, hairiest, baldest, and most beautiful breeds. The breeds are categorized into groups depending on their specific specializations or shared origins. From sleek sight hounds to agile and intelligent sporting dogs, from imposing guard dogs to super-sensitive scent hounts, from spitz breeds that endure the world's harshest climates to terriers that are characteristically small but feisty, from affectionate and hugely popular companion dogs to fashionable designer breeds. Each group exhibits some similar physical and character traits—scent hounds, for example, have an extraordinary heightened ability to track smells. Every breed is described in detail, and each includes photographs to illustrate key characteristics. Side panels provide at-a-glance information on important criteria such as exercise requirements and temperament. These ratings are designed to help readers understand the key traits of the breed, although it must be remembered that there are always exceptions!

When dealing with dogs there are two rules that should never be broken. First, while some breeds are more suitable for families than others, no dog should ever be left unattended with small children. Second, it is essential that a puppy is always seen in its home environment with its mother before being purchased to be sure that it is being sold by a responsible breeder.

There are a few hereditary health issues that are more commonly associated with specific purebred animals, including hip dysplasia, patellar luxation, and epilepsy. The health information included here is to be a guide only, and it is recommended that all puppies, as well as their parents, are thoroughly checked by a reputable veterinary practitioner.

Several breeds traditionally have cropped ears or docked tails. This is common in the United States but illegal in many other countries, including much of Europe and Australia. There is rarely a good reason to alter a dog's natural appearance (other than to occasionally clip the coats of certain breeds).

Above all, *Dogs Unleashed* is a celebration of humanity's oldest and most faithful friend in all its delightful and astonishing diversity.

THE WOLF WITHIN

Dogs are members of the large Canidae family, which is divided into *Canini* (related to wolves) and *Vulpini* (related to foxes), all of which share some basic behaviors. Wolves, jackals, and coyotes are the domestic dogs' closest relatives, and they are all members of the genus *Canis*; they all share the same number of chromosomes and are able to interbreed. Genetic evidence indicates that our modern dogs, in all their incredible variety, trace back to the Gray Wolf, *Canis lupus*, although there is continuing debate over precisely how, where, when, and why domestic dogs evolved from these wild relatives.

Three main areas—Southeast Asia, the Middle East, and Europe—are all cited as the "birthplace" of the dog, each with supporting evidence. Fossil remains found in the Goyet Cave, Belgium, and dated to around 30,000 BCE are more dog-like than wolf-like, and are thought to represent an evolutionary stage between the two. Currently, the date of actual domestication is put at about 12,000–13,000 BCE based on the study of mitochondrial DNA in dogs worldwide.

Wolves are opportunists and are thought to have followed early tribes of hunter gatherers, staying close to their campsites and scavenging for food. It is speculated that wolf cubs, particularly sociable wolves, or possibly even the weakest of the pack, allowed themselves to be gradually tamed and raised in the domestic environment. Over millennia, the animals' jaws and teeth changed, there was a reduction in overall body size, and they modified their behavior. By 4,000 BCE, artistic, literary, and archaeological evidence from ancient cultures in the Middle East and Europe indicated that not only were dogs firmly within the domestic forum, but also exhibited clear types, such as sight hounds, mastiffs, and spitz.

ABOUT BREEDS

The oldest dog types are thought to have developed as early tribal groups migrated from central and eastern Asia, taking their dogs with them. The dogs evolved in response to their geographic environments and new functions. Although no written records exist from these early times, people probably began to breed their dogs for certain characteristics such as hunting ability, guarding ability, herding skills, and even companionship. This gave rise to early types like the Molosser, ancestor to the mastiff breeds and famed for its use in warfare.

Early hunting types developed: the slender sight hound and a heavier framed hound that hunted by scent and was probably the ancestor to modern scent hounds. Other early hunting types were the old pointers and the spaniel group, which gave rise to the setters and even the tiny lap dog, favored for companionship and vermin control. Sight hounds are one of the earliest types of dog and represent the fastest breeds in the world. They are instantly recognizable with their long legs and sleek bodies, and they hunt by sight on open terrain, usually singly or in pairs. Historically, sight hounds were considered the noblest of all dogs and belonged to royalty. They are noted for their excellent temperament, intelligence, and independence, and are considered superb companions. They will always retain a strong instinct to hunt small prey, however, so care should be taken around cats and even small dogs.

Herding and guardian breeds are extremely versatile and historically had to perform a range of roles on farms and small holdings. Livestock-guardian breeds and general guardians share the same qualities and similar histories. Many of these developed from early mastiff-types, and they all exhibit a strong protective instinct.

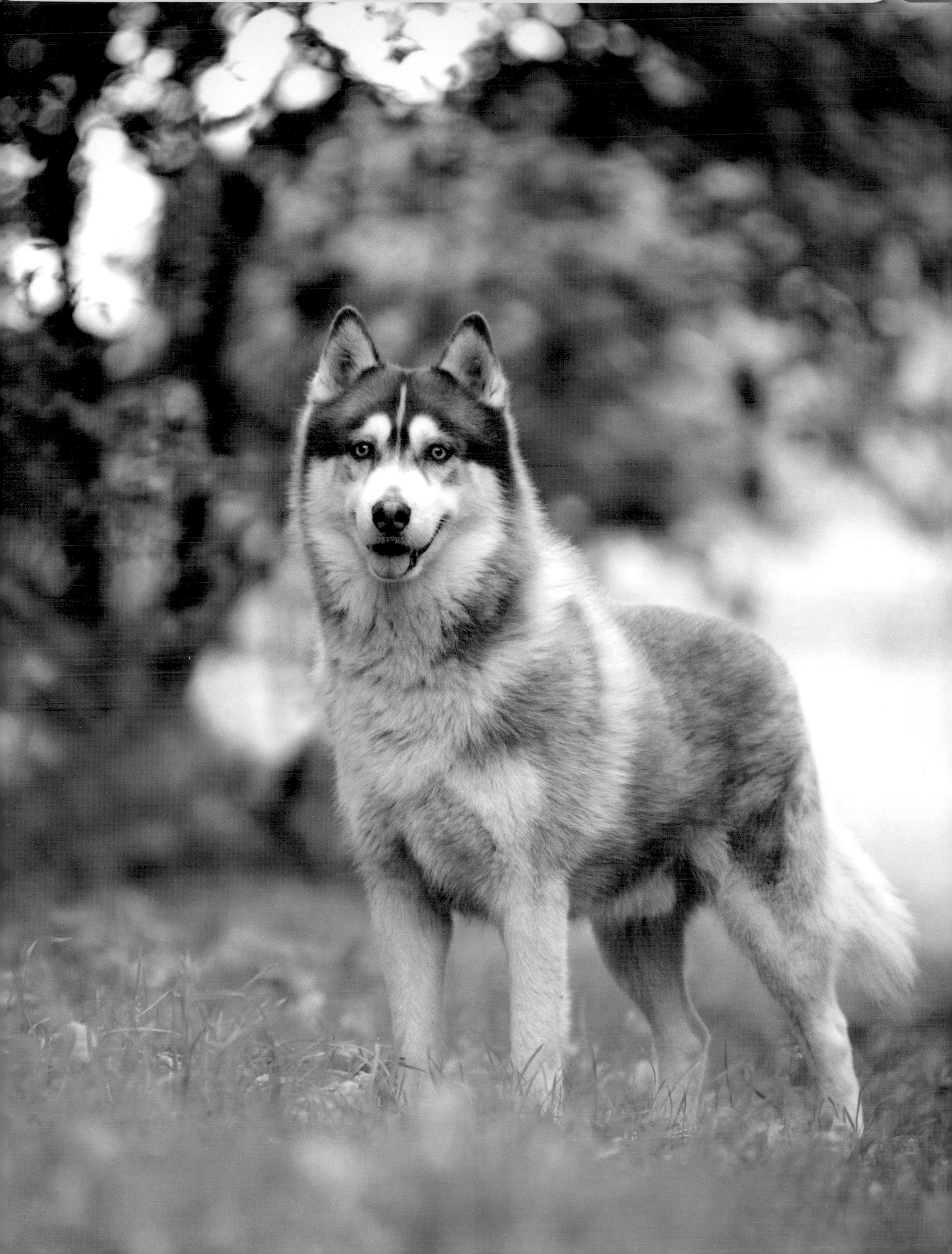

Livestock guardians are independent, brave, and clever. Their protective instincts are applied to their families and homes when they are companion animals.

Herding breeds are agile, tough, and obedient. Some are more suited to small stock such as sheep and goats, whereas others will work cattle. Some of these dogs are "heelers" and work behind the animal; others are "headers" and work in front of the animal. All these breeds exhibit strong herding instincts and can even try to herd children and other animals in the domestic environment! Herding and guarding breeds can have high energy levels and exercise requirements.

Scent hounds hunt by ground scent and are "hot nosed," meaning they follow a fresh trail at speed, or "cold nosed," meaning they follow an older trail, slowly and methodically. They generally have long, hanging, or pendent, ears that stir up air currents and help them detect smells. Scent hounds also "give voice" when hunting. The level and tone of their barks and baying alert the hunters to the location of the prey and how close they are to catching it. Scent hounds normally live and work in packs, so they tend to get along with other dogs. They generally have affable temperaments and are good with children, but are happiest in a working environment.

The spitz group of dogs represents some of the oldest dog breeds: the Shiba Inu, Shar-Pei, Akita, and Chow Chow. These were fundamental to the lives of people in the Arctic Circle, where they were used for hunting, herding, and draft work. They are perfectly adapted to life in the very harshest environments and are among the strongest, toughest, most enduring dogs in the world. Spitz typically have pricked, triangular ears, thick coats, and curved, bushy tails. They generally have affectionate temperaments but can be aggressive with other dogs. Many spitz breeds,

particularly the larger ones, have extremely high exercise requirements. They can be strong on a lead (their instinct is to pull), they dig, they can bark, and they can be difficult to train—but for the right, active home, they can make great companions.

Terriers take their name from the Latin *terra*, meaning "earth," and they were developed to dig into burrows and holes and bring out (and sometimes kill) prey such as fox or badger. They are tenacious, brave beyond their size, determined, and relentless when it comes to hunting. They are lively, highly intelligent, and occasionally stubborn. Some can be aggressive with other dogs. They tend to have enormous characters and can make wonderful, humorous companions, but can be inclined to nip, dig, and bark.

Then there are those dogs that were bred specifically as companion animals. "Lapdogs" were among the earliest companion dogs. Evidence of tiny dogs traces back at least 2,500 years to Asia and the Mediterranean. The primary function of these small, charming dogs was companionship, although they also served as watch dogs and rodent hunters. Historically, companion dogs were the preserve of the wealthy, since having a dog that performed no working function was a luxury most people could not afford. They are widespread today, though, and are found in every shape and size in almost every culture and country across the world.

Although people have selectively bred dogs for specific characteristics throughout history, it is only in the last 300 years that this has become formalized. This period of "modern dog history" represents the greatest explosion of dog breeds, which is still ongoing, most notably in the creation of hybrid "designer" breeds.

The term "designer" has been applied to a new group of companion "breeds" that are the result of crossing established breeds to create a new hybrid breed, such as the Labrador and Poodle cross, which produced the Labradoodle. Poodles, with their woolly, non-shedding coats, are often used in these crosses to produce dogs that are more suitable for allergy sufferers.

Last but not least, there is the humble "mutt," distinguished by the fact that it is not a breed at all, but of mixed or unknown origin. Mutts have the advantage of being unique and tend to be hardy animals. Even if the mutt's heritage is not documented, it is often clear from the dog's physical appearance that it is a composed of certain types. The "lurcher-type," for instance, is a sight hound-terrier cross. A mutt's likely ancestry is worth exploring because the dog will still exhibit behavior traits typical of the major breeds in the mix.

KENNEL CLUBS AND BREED STANDARDS

By the 1800s, it had become fashionable to own dogs of specific breeds, even though the term "breed" was still used loosely. The first official dog show was held in Birmingham, England, in 1859, with classes for pointers and setters. The same year, another was held that included spaniels, and the following year, hounds were added. At this time, there was still no formalized way of judging a dog, and no breed standards.

The first standard was drawn up in 1865 and was based on a pointer named Major, allocating marks for different parts of the body—this was a ground-breaking moment. In 1873 the British Kennel Club was established and produced the first studbook with the pedigrees of about 4,000 dogs divided into 40 breeds. Shortly afterward, breed clubs began to be established and to produce breed standards, with the Bulldog Club and the Dandie Dinmont Terrier Club both founded in England in 1875. In 1880 the Kennel Club decreed that only dogs registered with the club could be shown under club rules; this was the second milestone moment in dog-breeding history, as it defined a breed based on the Kennel Club's categorization. The American Kennel Club (AKC) was established in 1884, and the second-largest and second-oldest U.S. club, the United Kennel Club (UKC), was founded in 1898. The International Federation of Kennel Clubs, or the *Fédération Cynologique Internationale* (FCI), was founded in Europe in 1911.

Many modern breeds have changed significantly in appearance since the development of standards, and standards have been revised. These changes are based largely on the production of a "show" animal, rather than a "working" breed. The Bulldog, for example, was bred so far away from its original athletic, fighting frame that the breed began to suffer health issues. Likewise, some breeds are bred specifically for show or working lines, with working Cocker Spaniels differing greatly from those on the show bench. Some breeds, particularly gun dogs and working livestock dogs, have a system of field trials and testing, to keep emphasis on working ability.

Breed standards can differ from country to country and between clubs. This is particularly noticeable in sizes and weights between American and English standards. Also, different clubs categorize their breeds into different groups. In *Dogs Unleashed*, all the heights and weights are averages, and all physical descriptions are general and not allied to any one kennel club.

Now that breeders have a greater understanding of genetics, it is possible to selectively breed to reduce hereditary diseases and disorders. There are a number of tests available to determine if a dog will be predisposed to a disorder, and if so, it should not be used to breed new animals.

Thomas Gainsborough's *Portrait of Miss Robinson* shows an aristocratic lady and her dog. Companion dogs were once the preserve of the wealthy, but today in the United States alone, there are an estimated 80 million domestic dogs with more than 35 percent of households owning at least one dog.

DOGS AND PEOPLE

Dogs are the world's oldest domesticated pet and have shared human cultural development and change for thousands of years—they also share our hearths, sofas, armchairs, and beds. We can only guess at what the original ground rules were for this long and extraordinary relationship, and certainly the "rules" have changed. Early dogs were an essential part of life in many cultures, providing guardianship, hunting, transport, herding, vermin control, and companionship—through time, they have formed the fabric of myths, legends, and spiritual beliefs. They have been traded as commodities, eaten, revered, gifted among royalty, used in sport, lavished, abused, and even charged with crimes. They have appeared in artwork for more than 5,000 years and still appear in literature, movies, and advertising.

In modern times, the role of dogs has largely changed, and for the most part, they have shifted from being valued working stock to companions. The therapeutic value of loving a dog is not to be underrated. In simple terms, dogs make people feel good—and in turn, they generally enjoy the interaction we provide. Studies have shown that stroking a dog can lower blood pressure, slow heart rate, and diminish anxiety. Dog owners are also usually more active, more confident, and more healthy than people who don't own dogs.

Scientists at the University of Veterinary Medicine in Vienna, Austria, have established that the bond between an owner and his or her dog shares many similarities to that between a parent and child. It is worth bearing in mind before considering dog ownership, however, that dogs are also a huge commitment. Sharing life with a dog is good for the body and the soul, but is it always good for the dog? The majority of dog breeds are historically working, hunting, or sporting breeds. These dogs can make superb companion animals, but they also have requirements that have to be met for their health and happiness. These requirements primarily include adequate mental and physical stimulation—some dogs are simply happier when they have a job to do, whatever that job might be.

DOGS IN FASHION

The old adage "all men are equal, but some are more equal than others" could well be applied to dogs. Throughout history, there have been some breeds or types that have stood apart from the others. Among the most notable were the sight hounds. Historically, Greyhounds and other "elite" sight hounds were wholly the preserve of the most important members of society. They were highly prized for hunting (Alexander the Great liked them because they could keep up with his horse), and unlike most other hunting dogs, the sight hounds were not kept in kennels; instead, they were afforded lavish treatment and typically kept indoors. Of course, it helped that they are renowned for their affectionate temperament. They were so respected that they were given as diplomatic gifts to dignitaries across Europe; and they were especially popular in Spain, Italy, and France, where they changed hands for vast sums of money. In the eleventh century, it was made illegal for "commoners" in England to own them.

There has been a long tradition of European royalty setting trends for breeds. Perhaps most famously, the dog-loving British queen Victoria owned Greyhounds, Collies, Cavalier King Charles Spaniels, Pomeranians, a Skye Terrier, and more. The current British monarch, Queen Elizabeth II, is famous for her love of Corgis. Historically, monarchies in England and continental Europe have sparked trends among the aristocracy for a variety of breeds that remain hugely popular today, including Pugs, Cavalier King Charles Spaniels, and Papillons.

In the United States, trends have similarly followed presidential pooches and movie-star "royalty." In modern times, Hollywood and advertisers have had much to do with breed popularity, with Siberian Huskies, for example, surging after the release of films like *Snow Dogs* and *Eight Below*. This type of craze for a breed is not always in the breed's best interest, however, as the cute factor can overshadow the realities of the breed requirements. Huskies, for example, are not adapted for life in Florida! Currently trends lean toward the novel and often non-shedding "designer" breeds such as the Schnoodle, which is a cross between the Poodle and Schnauzer.

Stamps from the United Kingdom show dog portraits by artist George Stubbs. Today, dogs regularly appear in movies, often as the stars. Popular breeds have also been used in advertising to sell everything from pet products to paint and even toilet tissue.

WORKING DOGS

Dogs are generally intelligent, interactive, and sensitive to their human companions, which has made them ideal for a range of working roles, including traditional ones such as guarding, herding, hunting, and draft, and more recent roles in policing, military work, assistance, and therapy. Some breeds, such as Komondors or Great Pyrenees, are independent thinkers that can work on their own and make decisions. This is essential for livestock guardians that are left unsupervised for long periods protecting their herds from predators. Other breeds, such as the bright Border Collie, German Shepherd, and Poodle, have high problem-solving skills, combined with a particularly keen desire to please. This makes them trainable, obedient, and valuable for a range of services. Of course, being an independent thinker or a problem solver can have downsides if the dog decides to do things its own way!

Many breeds are naturally protective and have been used for guarding since ancient times. Guard dogs will protect their territories and families, and have the courage and capability to use physical force, which distinguishes them from "watch dogs" that tend to sound a vigorous alarm but don't necessarily follow through with defensive action. The guard-dog instincts of the German Shepherd make them hugely popular for a variety of roles in the police and military. They have to be extremely disciplined, obedient, and brave, and prepared to tackle a criminal on command. Police and military dogs have proven invaluable over the years. Many are used for tracking fugitives and victims, or for drug, bomb, and firearm detection. An American Bloodhound named Nick Carter is the most famous tracker of all time. He has brought about 600 convictions!

Historically, thousands of dogs have been used in warfare, and many are still deployed today. They have been used for carrying messages, locating injured soldiers, packing supplies, keeping rodents at bay, improving troop morale, and a range of other roles.

The value of dogs for boosting morale is also demonstrated by "pet therapy." Therapy dogs, which can be any breed depending on their temperament, visit a range of places including hospitals, hospices, and nursing homes, bringing comfort and affection to people with physical and mental ailments.

Assistance dogs, those that aid the blind and deaf, display an astonishing level of intelligence, obedience, and sensitivity. Herding and gun-dog breeds tend to be the most suited to assistance training because of their high intelligence. In 1819 Austrian educator Johann Wilhelm Klein published a guide on training guide dogs and recommended using German Shepherds. The German government began the guide dog movement after World War I to help troops blinded in action. By 1930 a similar program had started in England. Other popular assistance dogs for the blind include Labrador Retrievers, Golden Retrievers, Smooth Collies, and Australian Shepherds. Similarly, assistance dogs for the deaf range widely in breed types, but many are smaller breeds such as Cocker Spaniels, Poodles, Corgis, and Cavalier King Charles Spaniels.

SPORTING DOGS

All breeds have different activity needs, but all—from the smallest to the largest—require some degree of exercise and play. Sporting events provide a lot of exercise and are great for dog/owner bonding. Above all, they are fun. There are a multitude of events available that test the natural instincts and abilities of different breeds.

Sheep-dog trials, for example, began in the nineteenth century in New Zealand to test the working ability of sheep dogs, and to aid their training. They have since become highly competitive and spread internationally. Many breeds compete, and all demonstrate superb obedience, intelligence, and agility. Gun-dog working tests, hunt tests, field trials, and other events also developed to perpetuate the qualities of the many gun-dog breeds. These competitions vary from country to country; in some tests, dogs compete against each other, whereas in others they are judged against a written standard. These trials test the dog's ability to find and retrieve game (or dummies), and to work closely or at a distance.

There are also a number of high-octane sports to which some of the spitz breeds are particularly suited, including sledding, dry-land mushing, and weight pulling. Dog skijoring involves a cross-country skier pulled by up to three dogs at high speed. Bikejoring is a similar event that uses bikes instead of skis. Another exciting sporting event is canicross, which is popular in Europe. This competition involves cross-country running with one or two dogs attached to the runner via a belt and bungee-cord system, any dog breed and any owner can take part—provided that all participants are extremely fit! These are thrilling events to participate in or watch, and best of all, the dogs love it.

Agility, flyball, and disc dog (Frisbee) are all popular events suitable for virtually any breed, as are obedience competitions. Most competitions are organized into levels ranging from novice to advanced. New sports continue to be developed that provide plenty of opportunities for dog owners to have great fun with their dogs, which after all, should be what life with a dog is all about.

PRIMITIVE DOGS
AND SIGHT HOUNDS

CIRNECO DELL'ETNA : ITALY

This elegant ancient breed of dog is native to Sicily and can be found all over that small island, particularly around Mount Etna. These are tough, rugged dogs that thrive in the hot climate of their home country and are able to hunt across the harsh volcanic terrain surrounding the mountain. Historically they were widely used for hunting rabbits— a task at which they still excel today. However, these smart, lively dogs also make good companions for active homes.

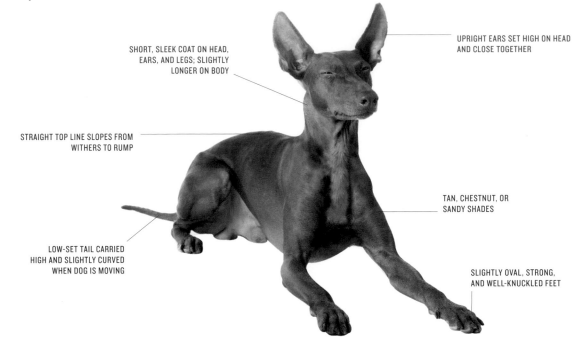

SHORT, SLEEK COAT ON HEAD, EARS, AND LEGS; SLIGHTLY LONGER ON BODY

UPRIGHT EARS SET HIGH ON HEAD AND CLOSE TOGETHER

STRAIGHT TOP LINE SLOPES FROM WITHERS TO RUMP

TAN, CHESTNUT, OR SANDY SHADES

LOW-SET TAIL CARRIED HIGH AND SLIGHTLY CURVED WHEN DOG IS MOVING

SLIGHTLY OVAL, STRONG, AND WELL-KNUCKLED FEET

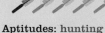
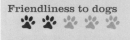
NEW GUINEA SINGING DOG : NEW GUINEA

These "foxy" looking dogs were once found wild all across New Guinea, although wild populations are now thought to be extinct. They are an ancient and genetically pure breed related to the Australian Dingo. Although with time and training they make great companions, they do retain elements of their wild heritage, and careful consideration should be made before taking one on. Their name comes from the tonal howl they produce, which sounds a lot like singing.

SMALL, ERECT, TRIANGULAR EARS SET WIDE APART WITH TIPS TILTING OUTWARD

WEDGE-SHAPED HEAD WITH PROMINENT STOP

THICK BRUSH TO UNDERSIDE OF TAIL

SHORT, THICK COAT WITH A PLUSH FEEL

COLORS INCLUDE RED, BLACK AND TAN; CAN HAVE WHITE MARKINGS

SMALL, NEAT, CAT-LIKE FEET

AT A GLANCE

Size: medium

Exercise needed:

Grooming needed:

Aptitudes: watchdog, service, assistance, companion

Height: 19–24 in.

Weight: 35–55 lb.

Average life expectancy: 12–13 yrs

AKC: herding

CHARACTER

Affection
🐾 🐾 🐾 🐾 🐾

Playfulness
🐾 🐾 🐾 🐾 🐾

Friendliness to dogs
🐾 🐾 🐾 🐾 🐾

Friendliness to strangers
🐾 🐾 🐾 🐾 🐾

Ease of training
🐾 🐾 🐾 🐾 🐾

CANAAN DOG : ISRAEL

This breed traces back to prehistory and was used by the ancient Israelites to guard their camps and herd their livestock. Canaan Dogs were unknown in the West until 1934 when Austrian animal behaviorist Rudolphina Menzel began training the dogs for the Israeli Defense Forces. These tough, feral dogs were the only breed able to cope with the harsh climatic conditions. Canaan Dogs are affectionate, loyal, eager to please, and very trainable. They are naturally protective of their families and can make superb companions for an active home.

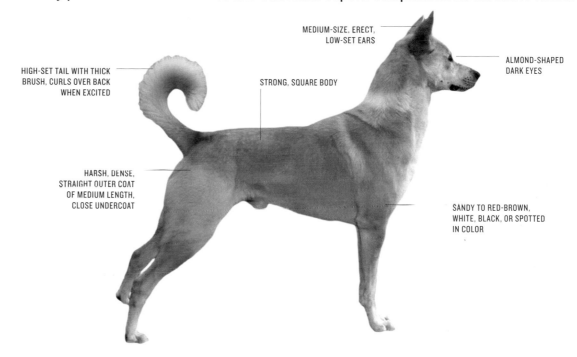

MEDIUM-SIZE, ERECT, LOW-SET EARS

ALMOND-SHAPED DARK EYES

HIGH-SET TAIL WITH THICK BRUSH, CURLS OVER BACK WHEN EXCITED

STRONG, SQUARE BODY

HARSH, DENSE, STRAIGHT OUTER COAT OF MEDIUM LENGTH, CLOSE UNDERCOAT

SANDY TO RED-BROWN, WHITE, BLACK, OR SPOTTED IN COLOR

AT A GLANCE

Size: medium-small

Exercise needed:

Grooming needed:
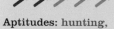

Aptitudes: hunting, coursing, companion

Height: 17–20 in.

Weight: 30–44 lb.

Average life expectancy: 12–14 yrs

AKC: not recognized

CHARACTER

Affection
🐾 🐾 🐾 🐾 🐾

Playfulness
🐾 🐾 🐾 🐾 🐾

Friendliness to dogs
🐾 🐾 🐾 🐾 🐾

Friendliness to strangers
🐾 🐾 🐾 🐾 🐾

Ease of training
🐾 🐾 🐾 🐾 🐾

CAROLINA DOG : UNITED STATES

Carolina Dogs were discovered living wild in parts of South Carolina and Georgia in the 1970s, and since then, much research has been undertaken to uncover their origins. The remoteness of their home area allowed the dogs to develop naturally and with little influence from other breeds. The Carolina Dog shares many characteristics with the Australian Dingo and other primitive breeds, suggesting a shared ancient ancestry; it also has a similar bone structure to the remains of neolithic dog bones from Native American burial sites dating back several thousand years. Carolina Dogs are now bred domestically and can make good companion animals, provided that they are very well socialized with people and other animals.

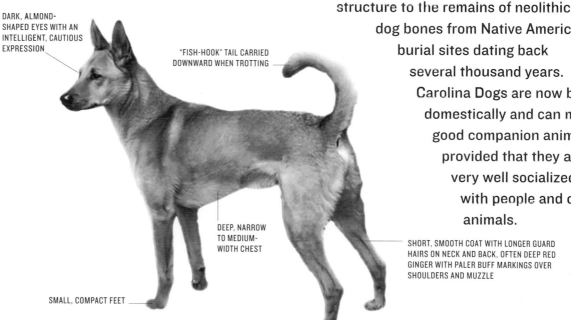

DARK, ALMOND-SHAPED EYES WITH AN INTELLIGENT, CAUTIOUS EXPRESSION

"FISH-HOOK" TAIL CARRIED DOWNWARD WHEN TROTTING

DEEP, NARROW TO MEDIUM-WIDTH CHEST

SHORT, SMOOTH COAT WITH LONGER GUARD HAIRS ON NECK AND BACK, OFTEN DEEP RED GINGER WITH PALER BUFF MARKINGS OVER SHOULDERS AND MUZZLE

SMALL, COMPACT FEET

Size: large

Exercise needed:

Grooming needed:

Aptitudes: hunting, coursing, companion

Height: 24–28 in.

Weight: 50–60 lb.

Average life expectancy: 11–13 yrs

AKC: hound

CHARACTER

Affection

Playfulness

Friendliness to dogs

Friendliness to strangers

Ease of training

+ HEALTH +

Afghans are prone to cataracts and often suffer from the lung disease chylothorax. They can also be sensitive to anesthesia.

AFGHAN HOUND : AFGHANISTAN

One of the world's oldest breeds, Afghan Hounds were originally employed as hunters and guardians in their native Afghanistan. They have distinctive personalities and are often aloof, almost haughty, around people they don't know. They are exceptionally regal and elegant dogs and with their gorgeous (extremely high maintenance) coats could be considered the "supermodels" of the dog world. Once they have accepted you into their inner circle, Afghan Hounds can be rewarding, playful companions.

TRIANGULAR-SHAPED DARK EYES

LOW-SET TAIL WITH DISTINCTIVE CURL

At birth, Afghan puppies have short noses, legs, and hair—very different from the adult dogs!

COMMON COAT COLORS

RED/GOLD   CREAM   DOMINO   BLUE   BRINDLE

All coat colors are allowed with color combinations considered particularly desirable. Common colors include red, cream, domino, blue, brindle, and black and tan.

HISTORY

The Afghan Hound is an ancient and rugged breed with a glamorous appearance. Returning army officers took sight hounds from Afghanistan, India, and Iran to the United Kingdom early in the 1900s. The most famous dog was Zardin, imported from India in 1907, and the first breed standard was based on him. In the 1920s, two types of Afghan were imported to the United Kingdom and formed the basis for the breed development there. The breed made it to the United States in 1922, with breeding kennels established on the East Coast. Zeppo Marx, youngest of the Marx brothers, famously imported two Afghans in 1931.

LOW-SET EARS COVERED WITH LONG, SILKY HAIR

MEDIUM-LENGTH BACK

WELL-SPRUNG RIBS

MUSCULAR FRONT END WITH DEEP CHEST

STRAIGHT, STRONG, AND LONG FORELEGS

LARGE FEET WITH WELL-ARCHED TOES, COVERED IN LONG, THICK FUR

COAT CLOSE-UP

The Afghan hound's coat is thick and silky. It is long over the hindquarters, flanks, ribs, forequarters, and legs. The fur is shorter and smooth along the back. Afghans have a topknot of long, silky hair on the tops of their heads.

SILKY & SMOOTH

AZAWAKH : MALI

These ancient African sight hounds take their name from the Azawakh Valley in the Niger Basin. They are elegant, angular, and graceful, and were used for hunting gazelles in packs. Sensitive, aloof, and haughty with strangers, they bond closely with their families and are loyal to loved ones. They retain a strong "hunt-on-sight" instinct, though, and while they might be fine with cats and small critters in an enclosed space, if they see those animals run, their hunting instinct will take over and a chase will be on.

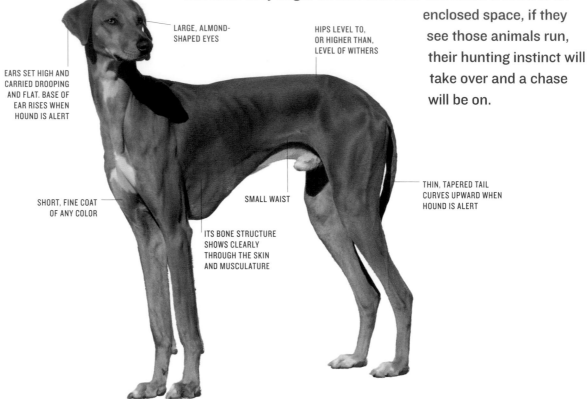

LARGE, ALMOND-SHAPED EYES

HIPS LEVEL TO, OR HIGHER THAN, LEVEL OF WITHERS

EARS SET HIGH AND CARRIED DROOPING AND FLAT. BASE OF EAR RISES WHEN HOUND IS ALERT

THIN, TAPERED TAIL CURVES UPWARD WHEN HOUND IS ALERT

SHORT, FINE COAT OF ANY COLOR

SMALL WAIST

ITS BONE STRUCTURE SHOWS CLEARLY THROUGH THE SKIN AND MUSCULATURE

KANNI : INDIA

The Kanni is a rare breed of sight hound that was traditionally given as a gift by a bride to her groom; *kanni* translates as "maiden" in the classical language Tamil. The dogs are still highly prized by families and still generally given as gifts, not bought or sold. Like all sight hounds, they are accomplished at hunting small game and deer, and are particularly fast and strong. They are also affectionate and loyal to their families but can be shy with strangers.

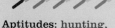
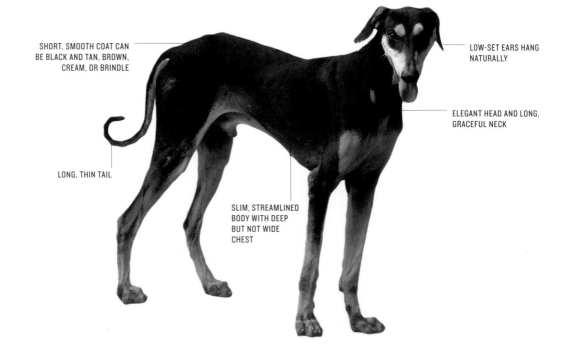

SHORT, SMOOTH COAT CAN BE BLACK AND TAN, BROWN, CREAM, OR BRINDLE

LOW-SET EARS HANG NATURALLY

ELEGANT HEAD AND LONG, GRACEFUL NECK

LONG, THIN TAIL

SLIM, STREAMLINED BODY WITH DEEP BUT NOT WIDE CHEST

BASENJI : DEMOCRATIC REPUBLIC OF THE CONGO

Basenjis are fascinating and rewarding dogs that bond strongly with their owners and can be extremely playful. They are independent and inquisitive, noted for their problem-solving abilities. They are unusual in that they are barkless, although they do vocalize through a range of yodels, and are sometimes described as "cat-like" in some of their behavior.

ALMOND-SHAPED, "FAR SEEING," DARK EYES

"NOBLE"-LOOKING HEAD WITH DISTINCTIVE WRINKLED BROW

SHORT, LEVEL BACK

LONG LEGS IN RELATION TO BODY

SMALL, OVAL, AND COMPACT FEET WITH WELL-ARCHED TOES AND THICK PADS

Basenji puppies have characteristic wrinkles on their face that give them a particularly endearing look. These wrinkles diminish as the dog grows up.

HISTORY

Recent genetic testing has discovered that these intelligent dogs are among the oldest type in the world and, as such, are an important link to ancient history. Their name means "wild dog from the bush," and it was in the remote bushlands of Africa that they developed their unique characteristics. The breed was not discovered by westerners until the nineteenth century. Two were exhibited at Crufts in London in 1895, but tragically both died from distemper shortly afterward. Basenjis arrived in the United States in 1937, and in 1944 the American Kennel Club recognized the breed.

COMMON COAT COLORS

Chestnut red, black, tricolor, or brindle are the Basenji's coat colors. All dogs have white feet, chests, and tail tips. White legs, blazes, and collars are also seen.

CHESTNUT RED   BLACK   TRICOLOR   BRINDLE

MAGYAR AGÁR : HUNGARY

The Magyar Agár, also called the Hungarian Greyhound, was bred to accompany hunters on horseback and is, therefore, capable of traveling long distances at speed. Traditionally, they were owned by the nobility, and their history stretches back more than 1,100 years; the working classes kept a smaller version of the dog, which is not around today. These are exceptionally hardy dogs that make good companions for active homes, requiring extensive exercise and balanced, consistent training.

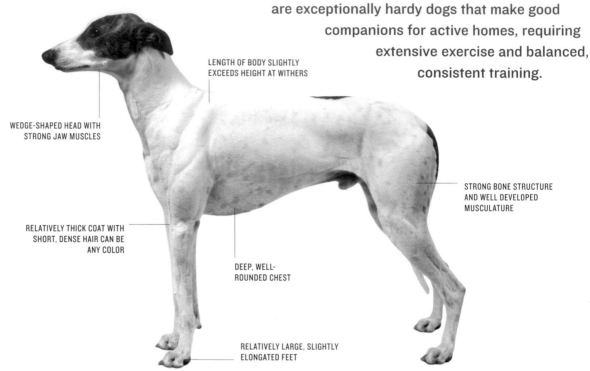

LENGTH OF BODY SLIGHTLY EXCEEDS HEIGHT AT WITHERS

WEDGE-SHAPED HEAD WITH STRONG JAW MUSCLES

STRONG BONE STRUCTURE AND WELL DEVELOPED MUSCULATURE

RELATIVELY THICK COAT WITH SHORT, DENSE HAIR CAN BE ANY COLOR

DEEP, WELL-ROUNDED CHEST

RELATIVELY LARGE, SLIGHTLY ELONGATED FEET

AT A GLANCE

Size: large

Exercise needed:

Grooming needed:

Aptitudes: hunting, coursing, companion

Height: 25–27 in.

Weight: 50–70 lb.

Average life expectancy: 12–14yrs

AKC: not recognized

CHARACTER

Affection

Playfulness

Friendliness to dogs

Friendliness to strangers

Ease of training

SLOUGHI : MOROCCO

The elegant and regal Sloughi was originally used primarily for coursing and hunting small game. They still excel in this respect, but are now typically kept as companions. They do make rewarding companion dogs but require a lot of exercise, particularly a good off-leash run in a safe environment. Given their sight-hound heritage, they will naturally chase small, furry creatures. Generally, the breed is aloof with strangers but affectionate and loyal to its family. They are also sensitive dogs that need to be trained with lots of positive reinforcement.

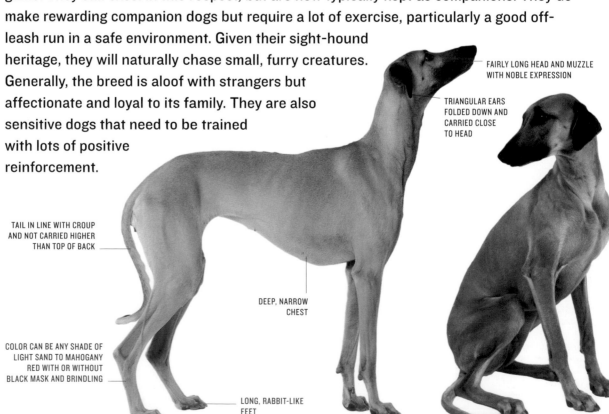

FAIRLY LONG HEAD AND MUZZLE WITH NOBLE EXPRESSION

TRIANGULAR EARS FOLDED DOWN AND CARRIED CLOSE TO HEAD

TAIL IN LINE WITH CROUP AND NOT CARRIED HIGHER THAN TOP OF BACK

DEEP, NARROW CHEST

COLOR CAN BE ANY SHADE OF LIGHT SAND TO MAHOGANY RED WITH OR WITHOUT BLACK MASK AND BRINDLING

LONG, RABBIT-LIKE FEET

AT A GLANCE

Size: large

Exercise needed:

Grooming needed:

Aptitudes: hunting, coursing, companion

Height: 24–29 in.

Weight: 40–62 lb.

Average life expectancy: 12–16 yrs

AKC: FSS

CHARACTER

Affection

Playfulness

Friendliness to dogs

Friendliness to strangers

Ease of training

AT A GLANCE

Size: large

Exercise needed:

Grooming needed:

Aptitudes: hunting, coursing, companion

Height: 24–28 in.

Weight: 50–60 lb.

Average life expectancy: 12–15 yrs

AKC: not recognized

CHARACTER

Affection

Playfulness

Friendliness to dogs

Friendliness to strangers

Ease of training

GALGO ESPAÑOL : SPAIN

The Galgo Español, or Spanish Greyhound, is an ancient breed that is not well known outside Spain. Galgos are robust, lively dogs with wonderful temperaments and can make excellent companions in active homes. In Spain they are still widely used for coursing and compete for the prestigious annual prize, the *Copa de Su Majestad el Rey*, or the King's Cup.

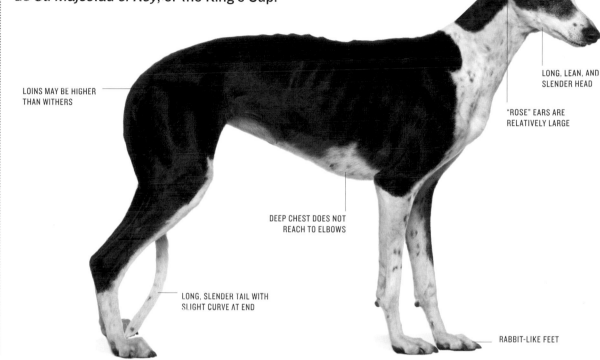

LONG, LEAN, AND SLENDER HEAD

"ROSE" EARS ARE RELATIVELY LARGE

LOINS MAY BE HIGHER THAN WITHERS

DEEP CHEST DOES NOT REACH TO ELBOWS

LONG, SLENDER TAIL WITH SLIGHT CURVE AT END

RABBIT-LIKE FEET

AT A GLANCE

Size: medium-large

Exercise needed:

Grooming needed:
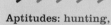

Aptitudes: hunting, companion

Height: 22–30 in.

Weight: 60–66 lb.

Average life expectancy: 10–12 yrs

AKC: not recognized

CHARACTER

Affection

Playfulness

Friendliness to dogs

Friendliness to strangers

Ease of training

RAMPUR GREYHOUND : INDIA

The Rampur Greyhound is native to the Rampur region of Northern India and was bred by Ahmed Ali Khan Bahadur in the eighteenth century. Bahadur is said to have crossed fierce hounds from Afghanistan with Greyhounds to create a superior hunting dog. These hounds were used for hunting wild boar, jackal, and even lions and tigers. When hunting was curtailed in India, the breed began to diminish and today is found only in small numbers. These dogs are brave and tenacious; they bond well with their family but are wary of strangers and make excellent guard dogs.

RELATIVELY BROAD HEAD WITH FLAT SKULL AND POINTED MUZZLE

VERY STRONG JAWS

SHORT COAT; BRINDLE, GRIZZLE, MOUSE-GRAY, PARTI-COLOR, OR BLACK IN COLOR

SOLID AND MUSCULAR FRAME

DEEP CHEST

LARGE, RABBIT-LIKE FEET WITH WEBBING BETWEEN VERY FLEXIBLE TOES

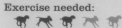
CHARACTER

Affection

Playfulness

Friendliness to dogs

Friendliness to strangers

Ease of training

✚ HEALTH ✚

Whippets are generally exceptionally healthy dogs.

WHIPPET : ENGLAND

Whippets are charismatic and highly intelligent dogs that make great companions and are suitable for homes with other pets and children as long as they get the right introduction, socialization, and supervision. Whippets are active dogs that thrive on interacting with their families; they make good agility dogs, love to go jogging with their owners, and are very obedient with correct and sensitive training. They are sight hounds, though, and will naturally chase small, furry things that move. One of the biggest causes of fatality in the breed is being hit by cars, so it is essential to provide a properly enclosed area for their exercise.

As well as being adorable, Whippet puppies are really smart and learn quickly.

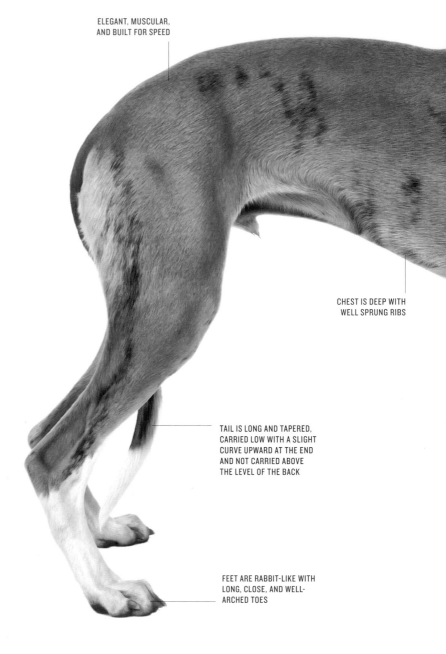

ELEGANT, MUSCULAR, AND BUILT FOR SPEED

CHEST IS DEEP WITH WELL SPRUNG RIBS

TAIL IS LONG AND TAPERED, CARRIED LOW WITH A SLIGHT CURVE UPWARD AT THE END AND NOT CARRIED ABOVE THE LEVEL OF THE BACK

FEET ARE RABBIT-LIKE WITH LONG, CLOSE, AND WELL-ARCHED TOES

COMMON COAT COLORS

BRINDLE & WHITE

FAWN

PARTI-COLORED

BLUE

BLACK

Whippets' coats can be any color.

COAT UP-CLOSE

The coat is short, close, smooth, and firm.

VERY DARK, OVAL EYES WITH
AN INTELLIGENT EXPRESSION

SMALL, FINELY
TEXTURED, ROSE
EARS SET FAIRLY WIDE
APART ON THE HEAD

BACK HAS A
NATURAL ARCH

HISTORY

The exact origin of the Whippet is unknown, although other small dogs of this type trace back to ancient times. The modern history of the Whippet begins in the nineteenth century in northern England where the small, sporty dogs became popular with factory workers and miners. Sometimes called "the poor man's Greyhound," Whippets were cheaper and easier to keep, but just as fun to race. Poachers also favored Whippets for catching their ill-gotten gains, and could hide the dogs in their coats if necessary. An early blood sport was testing how many rabbits a Whippet could "snap up" and kill in an enclosure; this led to the breed's nickname "snap dogs." Whippet racing became popular too, with the dogs encouraged by their owners waving pieces of rag, earning them the nickname "rag dogs." Whippets came to the United States with immigrants, particularly mill operators in the Massachusetts area, but the dog's popularity quickly spread to Baltimore, Maryland—home of the prestigious Green Spring Valley racing track. The American Kennel Club recognized the breed in 1888, but the Whippet was not accepted by the British Kennel Club until 1891.

Whippets exercise often but in energetic bursts, characteristically running around their owners in wide circles at tremendous speed. Although they are very much built for speed, they also enjoy comfort and, with sufficient exercise, will happily curl up and sleep for much of the day.

AT A GLANCE

Size: small

Exercise needed:
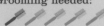

Grooming needed:

Aptitudes: companion

Height: 13–15 in.

Weight: 7–14 lb.

Average life expectancy:
12–15 yrs

AKC: toy

CHARACTER

Affection

Playfulness

Friendliness to dogs

Friendliness to strangers

Ease of training

✚ HEALTH ✚

Generally a very healthy breed, but they can be prone to teeth and gum problems, idiopathic epilepsy, hypothyroidism, and progressive retinol atrophy.

COAT CLOSE-UP

SATIN-LIKE

The coat is short, glossy, and satin-like.

ITALIAN GREYHOUND : ITALY

The Italian Greyhound is a charming companion animal that thrives on attention and affection. These are playful and lively little dogs that, despite their small size, still need a fair amount of exercise. As with all breeds, they should be well socialized as puppies and will generally get along with other dogs, pets, and children if properly introduced and supervised.

SMALL, FINE EARS USUALLY FOLDED BACK, RAISED AND FOLDED WHEN ALERT

BACK CURVED AND DROOPING DOWN OVER HINDQUARTERS

MEDIUM-SIZE, DARK, BRIGHT EYES WITH AN INTELLIGENT LOOK

LONG, GRACEFUL, AND SLENDER NECK

TAIL SET AND CARRIED LOW, AND REACHES TO HOCKS

RABBIT-LIKE FEET WITH ARCHED TOES

HISTORY

These racy little dogs trace back to Roman times and possibly even earlier; depictions from Ancient Rome and on Egyptian tombs show tiny Greyhound-like dogs that were the ancestors of the modern Italian Greyhound. Although they were undoubtedly bred as pets, it is likely that they were also useful in vermin control and they retain these sight-hound qualities. They became popular in England by the sixteenth century and were frequently found in aristocratic homes. In 1886 the first Italian Greyhound was registered in the United States with a breed club formed in 1951.

Puppies need lots of attention, diversions, and moderate exercise, to prevent destructive behavior.

COMMON COAT COLORS

Italian Greyhounds can be any color except brindle, and they never have tan markings.

CHOCOLATE   **RED FAWN**   **BLUE**

CHARACTER

Affection

Playfulness

Friendliness to dogs

Friendliness to strangers

Ease of training

✚ HEALTH ✚

Borzois tend to be a healthy breed but can suffer from gastric torsion, hip and shoulder dysplasia, and progressive retinol atrophy.

COAT CLOSE-UP

WAVY   **CURLY**

The coat is long and silky and either flat, wavy, or rather curly, shorter on head and ears and longer on body.

BORZOI : RUSSIA

The Borzoi's graceful appearance belies its incredible strength, speed, and tenacity, all qualities that should be considered before taking one on as a pet. Like most sight hounds, Borzois require a very particular and dedicated home environment, especially one that allows for proper, safe exercise in an enclosed area. Provided that they are socialized with other people and other animals, Borzois can make excellent companions, but they will retain their strong "hunt-on-sight" instinct, and small dogs, cats, and other critters seen at a distance can be at risk; it is best to keep Borzois on a leash when in public parks. Borzois generally have wonderful temperaments, although they can be somewhat stubborn. They are sensitive dogs and respond to lots of positive reinforcement.

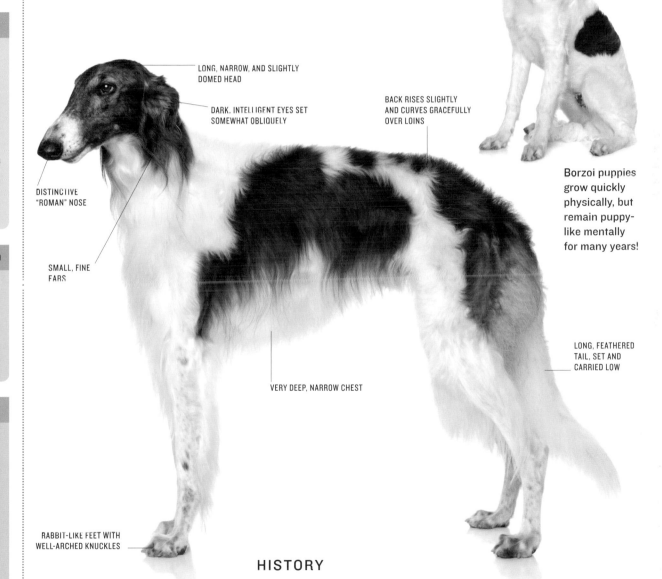

LONG, NARROW, AND SLIGHTLY DOMED HEAD

DARK, INTELLIGENT EYES SET SOMEWHAT OBLIQUELY

DISTINCTIVE "ROMAN" NOSE

SMALL, FINE EARS

BACK RISES SLIGHTLY AND CURVES GRACEFULLY OVER LOINS

LONG, FEATHERED TAIL, SET AND CARRIED LOW

VERY DEEP, NARROW CHEST

RABBIT-LIKE FEET WITH WELL-ARCHED KNUCKLES

Borzoi puppies grow quickly physically, but remain puppy-like mentally for many years!

HISTORY

These elegant dogs were originally bred for hunting wolves and hares in Russia and are also known as Russian Wolfhounds. The breed is believed to have developed through crossbreeding ancient sight hounds such as the Saluki with heavier native Russian dogs. Some of the earliest references to "hare-coursing dogs" date to 1260 at the court of the Grand Duke of Novgorod, and there are records of a special breeding station for these sight hounds at the Imperial Czar's kennels in Gatchina in 1613. The breed was first imported to the United States in 1888, and the American Kennel Club registered the breed in 1892. By this date, the breed had also become popular in the United Kingdom aided by Kathleen, Duchess of Newcastle, who established breeding kennels and raised a number of champion dogs.

COMMON COAT COLORS

Common colors include white and fawn, black and tan, and white.

WHITE & FAWN   **BLACK & TAN**   **WHITE**

AT A GLANCE

Size: large

Exercise needed:
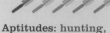

Grooming needed:

Aptitudes: hunting, coursing, racing, companion

Height: 27–30 in.

Weight: 60–70 lb.

Average life expectancy: 10–13 yrs

AKC: hound

CHARACTER

Affection

Playfulness

Friendliness to dogs

Friendliness to strangers

Ease of training
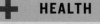

✚ HEALTH ✚

Normally very healthy dogs, Greyhounds can suffer from bone cancer, gastric torsion, poor teeth, and corns.

GREYHOUND : ENGLAND

Despite being bred for speed for so many years and excelling in this department, Greyhounds are also noted for their wonderful temperaments. These large dogs are generally calm and quiet around the house, needing short but vigorous bouts of exercise. They are loyal, friendly, affectionate, and typically good with children, as long as they are properly socialized. Greyhounds make excellent companions, but retain their instincts to hunt on sight, so small furry critters, including other dogs, are not always safe around them.

DARK, OVAL EYES WITH AN INTELLIGENT EXPRESSION

SMALL, FINE EARS FOLDED BACK BUT SEMI-PRICKED WHEN ALERT

POWERFUL AND FINELY CHISELED JAWS

LONG, NARROW HEAD, FAIRLY WIDE BETWEEN EARS

DEEP CHEST

In the British Isles, about 25,000 Greyhound pups are registered each year. However, thousands of dogs have to be rescued or are euthanized when they fail to make the grade as racing dogs.

COMMON COAT COLORS

Greyhounds can be any color, including fawn, brindle, parti-colored, and gray.

FAWN

BRINDLE

PARTI-COLORED

GRAY

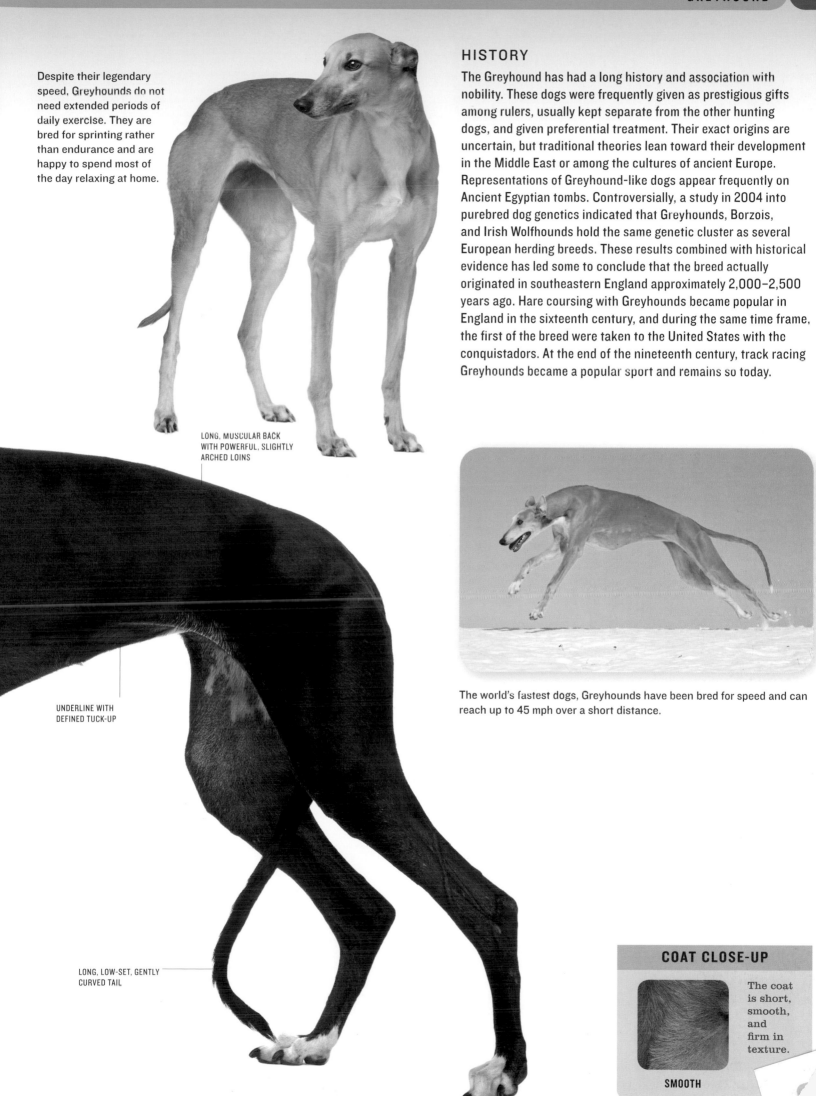

Despite their legendary speed, Greyhounds do not need extended periods of daily exercise. They are bred for sprinting rather than endurance and are happy to spend most of the day relaxing at home.

HISTORY

The Greyhound has had a long history and association with nobility. These dogs were frequently given as prestigious gifts among rulers, usually kept separate from the other hunting dogs, and given preferential treatment. Their exact origins are uncertain, but traditional theories lean toward their development in the Middle East or among the cultures of ancient Europe. Representations of Greyhound-like dogs appear frequently on Ancient Egyptian tombs. Controversially, a study in 2004 into purebred dog genetics indicated that Greyhounds, Borzois, and Irish Wolfhounds hold the same genetic cluster as several European herding breeds. These results combined with historical evidence has led some to conclude that the breed actually originated in southeastern England approximately 2,000–2,500 years ago. Hare coursing with Greyhounds became popular in England in the sixteenth century, and during the same time frame, the first of the breed were taken to the United States with the conquistadors. At the end of the nineteenth century, track racing Greyhounds became a popular sport and remains so today.

LONG, MUSCULAR BACK WITH POWERFUL, SLIGHTLY ARCHED LOINS

The world's fastest dogs, Greyhounds have been bred for speed and can reach up to 45 mph over a short distance.

UNDERLINE WITH DEFINED TUCK-UP

LONG, LOW-SET, GENTLY CURVED TAIL

COAT CLOSE-UP

The coat is short, smooth, and firm in texture.

SMOOTH

AT A GLANCE

Size: small

Exercise needed:

Grooming needed:

Aptitudes: companion

Height: 21–25 in.

Weight: 45–55 lb.

Average life expectancy: 11–14 yrs

AKC: hound

CHARACTER

Affection

Playfulness

Friendliness to dogs

Friendliness to strangers

Ease of training

✛ HEALTH ✛

Normally healthy and robust dogs, Pharaoh Hounds can suffer in very cold climates, where their thin ears are prone to frostbite.

PHARAOH HOUND : MALTA

The elegant and powerful Pharaoh Hound has a noble bearing and is one of the oldest domesticated breeds. It takes its name from its resemblance to images from Ancient Egypt painted as many as 5,000 years ago. Pharaoh Hounds are versatile, intelligent, sensitive, and rewarding dogs that make excellent companion animals for the right home environment. A unique and endearing breed characteristic is their "blush"—when they are excited, their noses and ears turn a deep rose.

MOBILE EARS SET MEDIUM-HIGH ON HEAD, PRICKED WHEN ALERT

BODY SLIGHTLY LONGER THAN TALL

LONG, SLOPING SHOULDERS

OVAL, AMBER EYES WITH INTELLIGENT EXPRESSION

SHORT, GLOSSY COAT WITH WHITE "STAR" ON CHEST

MODERATELY DEEP CHEST

HISTORY

The Pharaoh Hound has changed little in appearance from its depiction on Ancient Egyptian tombs and is a breed with a long history. Although its origins trace to the Middle East, it was in Malta that the breed was preserved, taken there by the Phoenicians who settled the region in the seventh century BCE. The Maltese treasured their dogs, which they used for hunting, for guarding, and as companions. Today, the Pharaoh Hound is recognized as the national dog of Malta.

Pharaoh Hounds are extremely active, and their lively, inquisitive nature becomes evident at an early age.

COMMON COAT COLORS

Pharaoh Hounds are shades of red, ranging from tan to chestnut.

RED

COAT CLOSE-UP

The coat is fine and short, often with a silky texture.

SHORT & GLOSSY

PODENCO CANARIO : SPAIN

The Podenco Canario is an ancient breed found throughout the Canary Islands. The dogs are believed to have been taken there from Egypt, the Middle East, and possibly Africa by early settlers, including the seafaring Phoenicians. Pondenco Canarios are still used for hunting rabbits on the islands, and are known for their durability and toughness. They are high-energy dogs that require an active home with plenty of diversions and lots of socialization, but are also very loyal.

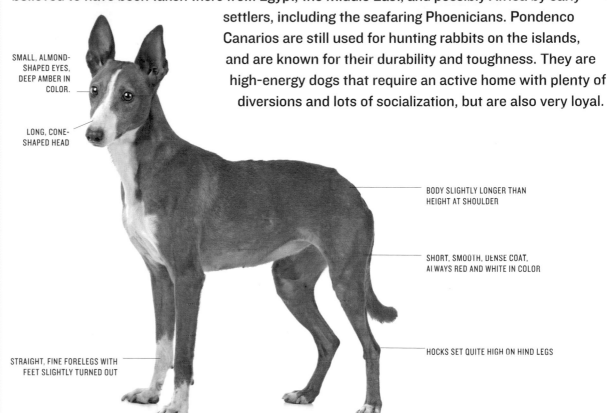

SMALL, ALMOND-SHAPED EYES, DEEP AMBER IN COLOR.

LONG, CONE-SHAPED HEAD

STRAIGHT, FINE FORELEGS WITH FEET SLIGHTLY TURNED OUT

BODY SLIGHTLY LONGER THAN HEIGHT AT SHOULDER

SHORT, SMOOTH, DENSE COAT, ALWAYS RED AND WHITE IN COLOR

HOCKS SET QUITE HIGH ON HIND LEGS

AT A GLANCE

Size: medium

Exercise needed:

Grooming needed:

Aptitudes: hunting, companion

Height: 21–25 in.

Weight: 45–55 lb.

Average life expectancy: 10–12 yrs

AKC: not recognized

CHARACTER

Affection

Playfulness

Friendliness to dogs

Friendliness to strangers

Ease of training

POLISH GREYHOUND : POLAND

Also known as the Chart Polski, these dogs differ from Greyhounds in that they are heavier, stronger, and not directly related. They are thought to have developed from Asian sight hounds such as the Saluki and are relentless, brave, and determined hunting dogs with great speed and agility. Typically they form strong bonds with their owners and, as such, can be territorial and make good guard dogs. They can be reserved with strangers and require consistent socialization with people and other dogs. Although they can be stubborn, Polish Greyhounds are generally obedient and thrive in active, experienced homes.

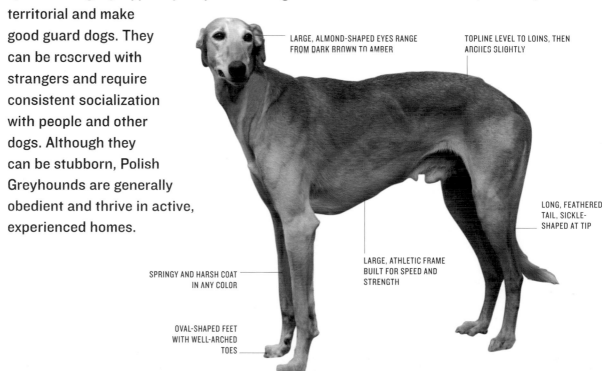

LARGE, ALMOND-SHAPED EYES RANGE FROM DARK BROWN TO AMBER

TOPLINE LEVEL TO LOINS, THEN ARCHES SLIGHTLY

LONG, FEATHERED TAIL, SICKLE-SHAPED AT TIP

LARGE, ATHLETIC FRAME BUILT FOR SPEED AND STRENGTH

SPRINGY AND HARSH COAT IN ANY COLOR

OVAL-SHAPED FEET WITH WELL-ARCHED TOES

AT A GLANCE

Size: very large

Exercise needed:
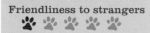

Grooming needed:

Aptitudes: racing, coursing, hunting, companion

Height: 26–31 in.

Weight: 65–95 lb.

Average life expectancy: 10–13 yrs

AKC: not recognized

CHARACTER

Affection

Playfulness

Friendliness to dogs

Friendliness to strangers

Ease of training

AT A GLANCE

Size: small, medium, and large

Exercise needed:
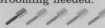

Grooming needed:

Aptitudes: hunting, companion

Height: pequeno 8–12 in./medio 16–22 in./grande 22–28 in.

Weight: pequeno 9–13 lb./medio 35–44 lb./grande 44–66 lb.

Average life expectancy: 14–16 yrs

AKC: FSS

CHARACTER

Affection

Playfulness

Friendliness to dogs

Friendliness to strangers
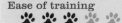

Ease of training

✚ HEALTH ✚

Generally healthy, but problems can include Legg-Calves-Perthes disease and luxating patella.

COAT CLOSE-UP

SMOOTH   WIRE

All three types have two coat varieties: smooth and wire. The smooth coat is short and dense with an undercoat present. The wire coat is rough, harsh, not as dense as the smooth, and without an undercoat. Wire coats will have a beard.

PORTUGUESE PODENGO : PORTUGAL

The breed is found in three sizes; some classify the smallest, the pequeno, as a separate breed rather than a size variation. Each of the three is found as either smooth or wire-coated, and all three share the same general appearance, character, and qualities. These are sporty, lively, intelligent dogs that thrive in an environment with plenty of diversions, and they hunt using sight, scent, and sound. They retain a strong hunting instinct, but are generally obedient and easily trained, making them good agility candidates. They can also compete effectively in lure coursing.

MODERATELY HIGH-SET TAIL, THICK AT BASE

PODENGO GRANDE

LONG, ERECT, TRIANGULAR EARS

ALMOND-SHAPED, EXPRESSIVE EYES

STRAIGHT, STRONG, WELL-MUSCLED NECK

MEDIUM-WIDTH CHEST REACHES TO ELBOW

SOLID, STRONG BODY WITH SLIGHTLY TUCKED-UP UNDERLINE

PODENGO MEDIO

HISTORY

Tracing their history back to at least the time of Ancient Rome, Portuguese Podengos were taken to the Iberian Peninsula by Romans and Phoenician seafarers. The dogs adapted to hunting different-sized game from large, aggressive wild boar to deer and rabbit. There are three sizes of the Portuguese Podengo which are classified by their Portuguese terms: *grande*, *medio*, and *pequeno*; each type excelled at hunting different quarry. The grande was favored by the Portuguese and Spanish nobility and was noted for its bravery and tenacity during the hunt. The medio and pequeno were popular with farmers and commoners, able to hunt all day and travel long distances through difficult terrain. Today, the Portuguese Podengo is one of Portugal's national dogs and is becoming better known outside its homeland.

PODENGO PEQUENO

COMMON COAT COLORS

YELLOW & WHITE   DARK FAWN

Portuguese Podengos can be yellow and white, fawn and white, shades of black or brown with white patches, or white with patches of black or brown.

IBIZAN HOUND : SPAIN

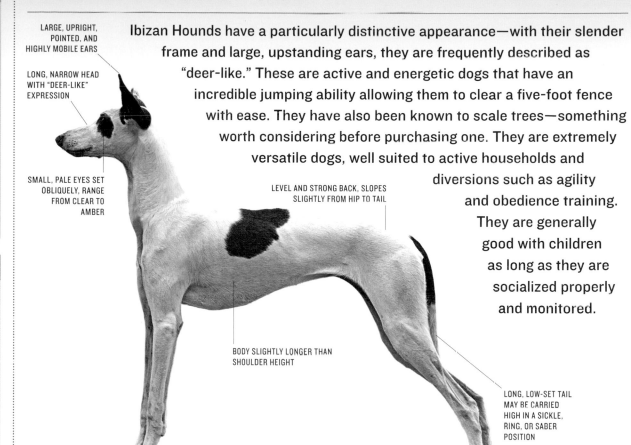

LARGE, UPRIGHT, POINTED, AND HIGHLY MOBILE EARS

LONG, NARROW HEAD WITH "DEER-LIKE" EXPRESSION

SMALL, PALE EYES SET OBLIQUELY, RANGE FROM CLEAR TO AMBER

LEVEL AND STRONG BACK, SLOPES SLIGHTLY FROM HIP TO TAIL

BODY SLIGHTLY LONGER THAN SHOULDER HEIGHT

LONG, LOW-SET TAIL MAY BE CARRIED HIGH IN A SICKLE, RING, OR SABER POSITION

Ibizan Hounds have a particularly distinctive appearance—with their slender frame and large, upstanding ears, they are frequently described as "deer-like." These are active and energetic dogs that have an incredible jumping ability allowing them to clear a five-foot fence with ease. They have also been known to scale trees—something worth considering before purchasing one. They are extremely versatile dogs, well suited to active households and diversions such as agility and obedience training. They are generally good with children as long as they are socialized properly and monitored.

THAI RIDGEBACK : THAILAND

Little is known about the origin of this rare breed found mainly in eastern Thailand, but it is one of only three breeds that exhibit an unusual ridge of hair along the spine; the others are the South African Rhodesian Ridgeback and the little-known Phu Quoc Ridgeback from Vietnam. Thai Ridgebacks are tough, loyal dogs that are used as guard dogs, for hunting, and as companions. They are active and intelligent, and they make good companions for experienced owners. But they can be wary with strangers and overly territorial if they are not properly socialized.

TRIANGULAR EARS SET ON SIDES OF SKULL

WRINKLES ON FOREHEAD VISIBLE WHEN DOG IS ALERT

WEDGE-SHAPED MUZZLE

STRONG, LEVEL BACK

RED, BLACK, BLUE, OR LIGHT-FAWN COAT

UNDERLINE SHOWS DEFINITE TUCK-UP

AT A GLANCE

Size: large

Exercise needed:

Grooming needed:

Aptitudes: hunting, guarding, companion

Height: 22–27 in.

Weight: 70–85 lb.

Average life expectancy: 10–12 yrs

AKC: hound

CHARACTER

Affection

Playfulness

Friendliness to dogs

Friendliness to strangers

Ease of training

✚ HEALTH ✚

Generally a very healthy breed, these dogs can sometimes develop hip or elbow dysplasia, dermoid sinus, and gastric torsion.

RHODESIAN RIDGEBACK : ZIMBABWE

Despite its history of hunting big game, the Rhodesian Ridgeback can make a wonderful family pet as long as it is properly socialized. These large dogs are protective and territorial, making them useful guard dogs, but they are also affectionate and loyal to their families. When introduced correctly, they are good with other dogs, animals, and children—though small children should always be supervised with any breed of dog. Their versatility is reflected in their popularity and high breed numbers in the United States and the United Kingdom.

ROUND EYES, SET MODERATELY FAR APART, WITH AN INTELLIGENT EXPRESSION

MEDIUM-SIZE EARS WITH ROUNDED TIPS, SET HIGH AND CARRIED CLOSE TO HEAD

STRONG, ATHLETIC BODY

LONG NECK

STRAIGHT FORELEGS WITH SOLID, HEAVY BONES

CHEST NOT TOO WIDE, BUT VERY DEEP

TAIL TAPERS TO TIP, USUALLY CARRIED IN GENTLE CURVE

COMPACT FEET WITH ARCHED TOES AND PROTECTIVE HAIR BETWEEN TOES AND PADS

Ridgeback puppies can be very lively and mischievous if they get bored!

COMMON COAT COLORS

LIGHT WHEATEN   **RED WHEATEN**

Rhodesian Ridgebacks range in color from light wheaten to red wheaten.

COAT CLOSE-UP

GLOSSY   **RIDGE OF HAIR**   **WHORLS OF HAIR**

The coat is short, dense, sleek, and glossy. A distinctive ridge of hair runs along the backbone. It forms because some of the hair grows in the opposite direction. The ridge should have two identical whorls of hair (crowns).

HISTORY

The unique ridge along the Rhodesian Ridgeback's spine would suggest a shared ancestry with the other two breeds that exhibit it: the Thai Ridgeback and the Phu Quoc Ridgeback. These two ancient Asian breeds may have influenced the development of the Rhodesian Ridgeback when prehistoric people moved from central Asia outward, reaching Africa and taking their dogs with them. Native dogs of the South African Khoekhoen people developed specific adaptations to their environment: they were semi-wild and extremely tough, durable, and self-sufficient. During the seventeenth century, European settlers moved to South Africa and took their dogs—Mastiffs, Great Danes, Greyhounds, and Bloodhounds—which interbred with the native dogs, eventually giving rise to various types, including what became the Rhodesian Ridgeback. The dogs were bred specifically to hunt big game such as lions, most notably by early breeder Cornelius von Rooyen, and became known for their unrivaled bravery and tenacity. They were also colloquially called "lion dogs."

The Rhodesian Ridgeback has an intelligent expression with dark brown or amber eyes.

The breed's characteristic feature is the ridge of hair running along its back in the opposite direction of the rest of its coat. The ridge is more than an inch wide for most of its length and tapers toward the tail.

CHARACTER

Affection

Playfulness

Friendliness to dogs

Friendliness to strangers

Ease of training

✚ HEALTH ✚

Generally a very healthy breed, but problems can include gastric torsion, bone cancer, heart problems, and hip or elbow dysplasia.

IRISH WOLFHOUND : IRELAND

The tallest of the hound breeds, the Irish Wolfhound is something of a couch potato and loves nothing better than to lie around for most of the day in the most comfortable spot. These dogs have superb temperaments, are calm when indoors, and are generally easygoing, making them excellent companions for people who have large houses. They are huge dogs, and although their energy levels are low, they do require a lot of space and daily exercise.

LONG HEAD, NOT TOO BROAD

LONG, STRONG, MUSCULAR NECK

LONG BACK WITH ARCHED LOINS

LONG EYEBROWS AND A BEARD

DEEP, BROAD CHEST

LONG, GENTLY CURVED TAIL

MODERATELY LARGE, ROUND FEET

Wolfhound puppies initially grow very quickly and will be large by six months of age. However, they continue to grow slowly for several more years and are not fully matured until they are at least three years old.

HISTORY

Irish Wolfhounds have been highly valued from Roman times as guardians, hunters, and companions. Despite their delightful temperaments now, Irish Wolfhounds were known historically for being ferocious and fearless, used to hunt wolves as their name suggests. The coat of arms of early Irish kings bore an image of the Irish Wolfhound and the words "gentle when stroked, fierce when provoked."

COMMON COAT COLORS

GRAY

BLACK

WHITE

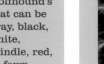

BRINDLE

The Irish Wolfhound's coat can be gray, black, white, brindle, red, or fawn.

COAT CLOSE-UP

WIRY

The coat is rough and wiry.

SCOTTISH DEERHOUND : SCOTLAND

Scottish Deerhounds are superbly designed to hunt fast animals for long periods over difficult terrain. They are in a sense the 4x4 vehicle of the dog world. Like many sight hounds, the Deerhound has a wonderful temperament—calm and affectionate in the home and happy to lie about on a couch for much of the day. Scottish poet Sir Walter Scott described them as "the most perfect creature in heaven," and people who own them surely agree! Scottish Deerhounds are very large dogs, but for the right family, they make truly wonderful companions.

BROAD AND POWERFUL HINDQUARTERS

BLACK OR DARK-COLORED EARS

SLOPED SHOULDERS

GOOD MOUSTACHE AND BEARD OF SILKY HAIR

GENERAL APPEARANCE OF GREYHOUND, BUT HEAVIER IN BUILD WITH WIRY COAT

LONG, TAPERING TAIL, REACHES BELOW HOCKS

SALUKI : MIDDLE EAST

These lithe sight hounds with their slender frames and regal appearance might look fragile, but they are tough and resilient dogs with tremendous stamina and capable of great bursts of speed. Like many of the sight hounds, Salukis are extremely loyal and affectionate to their families, but can be wary and aloof with strangers. They are charismatic, independent dogs, best suited to experienced homes with a fenced yard.

LARGE, OVAL EYES, DARK BROWN TO HAZEL IN COLOR, WITH A BRIGHT EXPRESSION

FAIRLY BROAD BACK AND LOINS

LONG EARS, COVERED IN LONG, SILKY HAIR, HANG CLOSE TO SKULL

STRAIGHT FORELEGS, LONG FROM ELBOW TO KNEE

FEET FEATHERED BETWEEN TOES

FEATHERED TAIL WITH SILKY HAIR

PERUVIAN INCA ORCHID : PERU

These charismatic dogs are known by a number of different names including the Moonflower Dog and are distinctive by their hairlessness, although they can also have some fur—usually on the head, tail, and feet—or even a full coat (although the coated variety is not used as a show dog). The skin of the hairless variety requires some care to prevent sunburn, injury, and skin conditions such as dryness. On the plus side, they are exceptionally clean dogs, free from most odor, and can be suitable for people with allergies.

AT A GLANCE

Size: small, medium, and large

Exercise needed:

Grooming needed:

Aptitudes: companion

Height: small 9–15 in./ medium 15–19 in./ large 19–25 in.

Weight: small 8–17 lb./ medium 17–26 lb./ large 26–55 lb.

Average life expectancy: 11–12 yrs

AKC: FSS

CHARACTER

Affection

Playfulness

Friendliness to dogs

Friendliness to strangers

Ease of training

+ HEALTH +

The genes that cause hairlessness often result in the breed having fewer or more teeth than other dogs. They often lack molars and premolars.

COAT CLOSE-UP

HAIRLESS

The Peruvian Inca Orchid may have hair on top of its head, on its feet, and on the tip of its tail.

Smaller dogs seem to be more sensitive to the cold than larger ones, and Peruvian Inca Orchid puppies get chilled easily.

LOW-SET TAIL, THICK AT BASE AND TAPERING TO TIP, CARRIED IN A CURVE ABOVE THE BACK LINE WHEN DOG IS EXCITED

CONE-SHAPED HEAD

DISTINCTIVE TRIANGULAR EARS, PRICKED WHEN ALERT

SLIGHTLY ALMOND-SHAPED EYES RANGE FROM BLACK TO BROWN TO YELLOW

SLENDER BUT MUSCULAR FRAME

SKIN CAN BE ANY COLOR, WITH OR WITHOUT MOTTLING

COMMON COLORS

BROWN

MOTTLED

Brown, gray, copper, or mottled. These dogs can be a solid color or one color with pink spots or patches.

AT A GLANCE

Size: small, medium, and medium-large

Exercise needed:

Grooming needed:

Aptitudes: companion, guard

Height: toy 10–14 in./ miniature 14–18 in./ standard 18–23 in.

Weight: toy 5–15 lb./ miniature 15–30 lb./ standard 25–40 lb.

Average life expectancy: 13–15 yrs

AKC: non-sporting

CHARACTER

Affection

Playfulness

Friendliness to dogs

Friendliness to strangers

Ease of training

✚ HEALTH ✚

Generally very robust, however all hairless dogs need regular bathing and moisturizing to prevent skin problems. They are not suited to cold climates.

COAT CLOSE-UP

HAIRLESS

The xoloitzcuintli may have hair on top of its head, on its feet, and on the tip of its tail.

XOLOITZCUINTLI : MEXICO

This breed is also known as the Xolo or Mexican Hairless and is a national treasure in its home country. The breed is ancient, appearing in artworks and on pots from the Mayan and Colima cultures, dating back about 3,000 years, and in many works from the Aztecs. Since then, there has been virtually no change in the dogs' physical appearance. Originally used as guard dogs and companions, Xolos also had strong magical and spiritual healing associations: the Aztecs considered them to be sacred and believed a master's soul needed his dog to help him safely through the underworld. Today, Xolos are still used as guard dogs but excel as companions. There is also a coated variety of the breed.

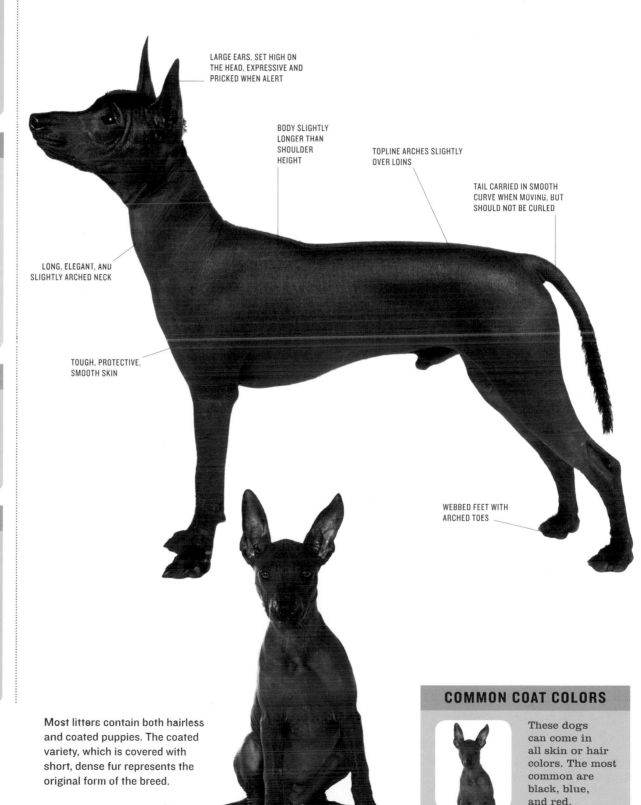

LARGE EARS, SET HIGH ON THE HEAD, EXPRESSIVE AND PRICKED WHEN ALERT

BODY SLIGHTLY LONGER THAN SHOULDER HEIGHT

TOPLINE ARCHES SLIGHTLY OVER LOINS

TAIL CARRIED IN SMOOTH CURVE WHEN MOVING, BUT SHOULD NOT BE CURLED

LONG, ELEGANT, AND SLIGHTLY ARCHED NECK

TOUGH, PROTECTIVE, SMOOTH SKIN

WEBBED FEET WITH ARCHED TOES

Most litters contain both hairless and coated puppies. The coated variety, which is covered with short, dense fur represents the original form of the breed.

COMMON COAT COLORS

These dogs can come in all skin or hair colors. The most common are black, blue, and red.

BLUE

SPORTING DOGS

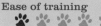
COCKER SPANIEL : UNITED STATES

The Cocker Spaniel, or American Cocker Spaniel as they are also known, is the smallest of the sporting dogs and a truly compact athlete. These are working dogs, but they are also extremely popular as family pets and excel in this capacity. Cockers are generally friendly, cheerful, and lively companions that require vigorous daily exercise.

DOMED HEAD WITH BROAD, DEEP MUZZLE AND MODERATE STOP

ROUND, DARK EYES WITH AN INTELLIGENT AND SOFT EXPRESSION

SHOULDERS WELL LAID BACK

STURDY, COMPACT BODY; TOPLINE SLOPES SLIGHTLY TO REAR

LOBULAR, LONG, WELL-FEATHERED EARS

LARGE, COMPACT, ROUND FEET

COMMON COAT COLORS

BLACK

BLACK & TAN

CREAM

BROWN

PARTI-COLOR

Any solid color, including black, cream, and brown. Any of these colors may appear on a white base as a parti-color, ticked, or roan.

CHAMPION OBO II
Whelped August 7, 1882.   A.K.C. No. 4911.   Black

HISTORY

The spaniel family is large and very old. The first spaniel arrived in the United States on board the *Mayflower* in 1620. Historically these active dogs were divided into land and water spaniels, and in the nineteenth century, they were categorized as the breeds we recognize today. Given their small size, Cocker Spaniels were first used for flushing woodcock, hence their name, and later for flushing and retrieving. Today, they are also popular field trial dogs. Although the breed originated in England, by the twentieth century distinct differences could be seen between the English-bred and American-bred cockers. Today, they are recognized as different breeds.

Cocker Spaniel puppies are virtually full-grown by six months of age.

The American Cocker is one of the most popular breeds in the United States and is divided into three color varieties: black, ASCOB (any solid color other than black), and parti-color. Cockers bred for the show ring tend to have longer, fuller coats and can be slightly heavier in frame

COAT CLOSE-UP

The medium-length, silky coat is shorter on the head. It can be flat or slightly wavy, with an undercoat.

SILKY & WAVY

AMERICAN WATER SPANIEL : UNITED STATES

This rare breed of gun dog was developed in the United States in the early 1900s and recognized by the American Kennel Club in 1940. Always brown in color, these active, personable animals make excellent gun dogs and are particularly suited to water retrievals and upland flushing. They also double as wonderful companions.

SOLIDLY BUILT, SLIGHTLY LONGER THAN TALL

WELL-DEVELOPED HIPS AND THIGHS

LONG, LOBULAR, WIDE EARS SET SLIGHTLY ABOVE EYE LINE

COLOR RANGES FROM LIVER TO BROWN TO DARK CHOCOLATE

MEDIUM-LENGTH, STRAIGHT FORELEGS

COAT RANGES FROM WAVY TO CURLED, WITH UNDERCOAT

ARIEGE POINTER : FRANCE

This French breed with its excellent sense of smell was developed in the nineteenth century in the Ariege area of the Pyrenees Mountains primarily as a pointing dog, although they are also useful retrievers. They are active, powerful dogs rarely seen outside their homeland, and are typically used for hunting partridge and hare. They are relatively sociable and thrive when working, but are not generally used solely as companion dogs.

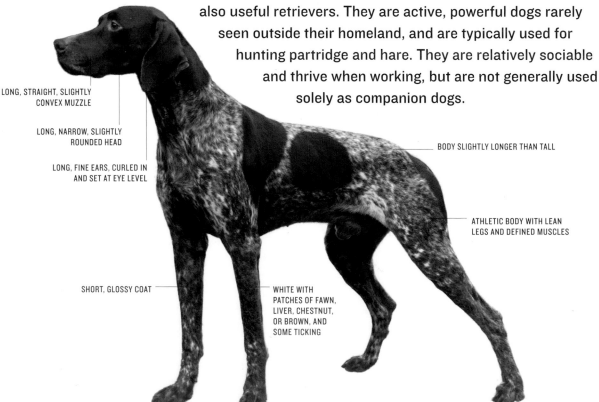

LONG, STRAIGHT, SLIGHTLY CONVEX MUZZLE

LONG, NARROW, SLIGHTLY ROUNDED HEAD

LONG, FINE EARS, CURLED IN AND SET AT EYE LEVEL

BODY SLIGHTLY LONGER THAN TALL

ATHLETIC BODY WITH LEAN LEGS AND DEFINED MUSCLES

SHORT, GLOSSY COAT

WHITE WITH PATCHES OF FAWN, LIVER, CHESTNUT, OR BROWN, AND SOME TICKING

BARBET : FRANCE

This rare French breed is believed to trace back to the fourteenth century when it was developed primarily for hunting water game. These dogs are superb hunters with a highly refined sense of smell that allows them to find game hidden in vegetation and along river banks. They are used for pointing, flushing, and retrieving and are particularly hardy dogs able to withstand cold and cold water due to their distinctive coats. Their thick, water-resistant coats form a beard on their chins—the French word *barbe*, meaning "beard," giving rise to their name. They have excellent temperaments and can make great companions, though they thrive when working and need plenty of exercise and diversions.

ROUND, DARK EYES

SQUARE MUZZLE

LONG, FLAT, WIDE EARS, SET LOW, COVERED IN LONG HAIR HANGING IN STRANDS

DISTINCTIVE, LONG BEARD

LONG, WOOLLY, CURLY COAT

BROWN, BLACK, GRAY, FAWN, WHITE, OR PIEBALD COAT COLOR

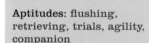
BOYKIN SPANIEL : UNITED STATES

Described as the "dog that doesn't rock the boat," the Boykin Spaniel was developed in the 1900s as a small, robust duck-hunting dog that could fit into duck boats and blinds. They were bred by South Carolina hunters in the Wateree River Swamp area and are thought to have Springer Spaniel, Cocker Spaniel, American Water Spaniel, and Chesapeake Bay Retriever in their heritage. These are true dual-purpose dogs bred for flushing and retrieving, but they also make wonderful family companions.

MEDIUM-SIZE, OVAL EYES IN SHADES OF BROWN

MUZZLE APPROXIMATELY SAME LENGTH AS SKULL

SLIGHTLY ARCHED NECK

WELL BALANCED AND SOLIDLY BUILT

RICH LIVER, BROWN, OR DARK CHOCOLATE COLOR

MEDIUM-LENGTH COAT RANGES FROM FLAT TO SLIGHTLY WAVY AND HAS UNDERCOAT

BRACCO ITALIANO : ITALY

More hound-like in appearance than gun dog, the Bracco Italiano is an ancient breed tracing back to at least the fourth and fifth centuries. They were bred by noble Italian families such as the Gonzagas and Medicis, and were so revered they were given as diplomatic gifts to visiting royalty and dignitaries, particularly during the Renaissance. Although probably derived from ancient Egyptian hounds and mastiff-types, they developed in Italy from pointing dogs from the Piedmontese and Lombardy areas. They are highly regarded in Italy as hunt, point, and retrieve gun dogs, and although they can make good companions, they thrive in a working environment.

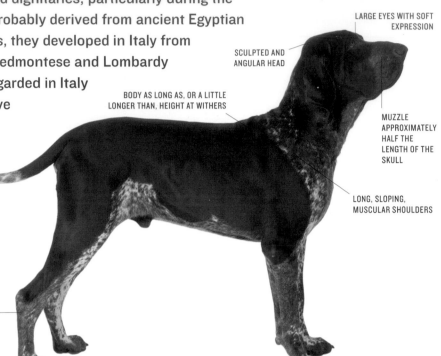

LARGE EYES WITH SOFT EXPRESSION

SCULPTED AND ANGULAR HEAD

BODY AS LONG AS, OR A LITTLE LONGER THAN, HEIGHT AT WITHERS

MUZZLE APPROXIMATELY HALF THE LENGTH OF THE SKULL

LONG, SLOPING, MUSCULAR SHOULDERS

WHITE, WHITE WITH PATCHES OF AMBER, WHITE SPECKLED WITH PALE ORANGE, WHITE SPECKLED WITH CHESTNUT

BRAQUE D'AUVERGNE : FRANCE

This ancient breed of pointing dogs developed in the Cantal region of France and takes its name from the French word *braquer*, meaning to aim or point. As with many breeds, Braque d'Auvergne numbers were decimated during World War II, and they were threatened with extinction until breeder Andre de Tournay and his wife found about twenty of the dogs after the war. The modern Braque is descended from these. Braques did not arrive in the United States until the latter half of the twentieth century, and their numbers there remain low. The breed excels at hunting and trials as well as making a suitable companion for the right, active home.

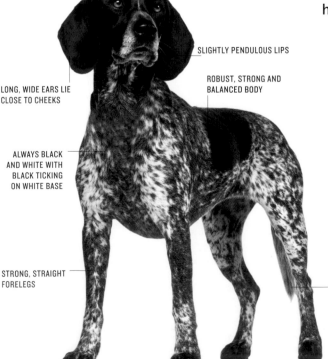

SLIGHTLY PENDULOUS LIPS

ROBUST, STRONG AND BALANCED BODY

LONG, WIDE EARS LIE CLOSE TO CHEEKS

ALWAYS BLACK AND WHITE WITH BLACK TICKING ON WHITE BASE

STRONG, STRAIGHT FORELEGS

TAIL TAPERS SLIGHTLY TO TIP AND IS CARRIED HORIZONTALLY

BRAQUE DU BOURBONNAIS : FRANCE

In France the different pointing dogs are known for their area of origin, but all share some similar characteristics, particularly their efficiency at hunting, pointing, and retrieving. These dogs are thought to descend from the ancient Spanish pointing dogs early in history, with the Bourbonnais first mentioned in the 1500s. Historically Bourbonnais pointers were born tail-less or with a very short tail and with a white coat covered in fawn or liver ticking or fine lines. This was called *lie de vin*, wine dregs, or *fleur de peche*, peach blossom. Breeding for these traits instead of performance was detrimental to the dogs, and the standard has since been changed to address the problem. These are versatile hunting dogs that work on land and in water.

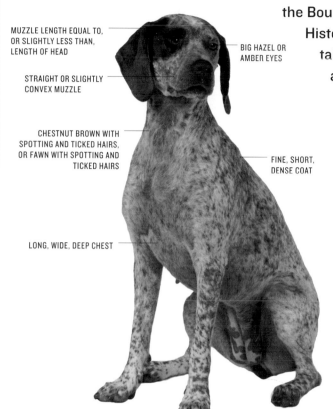

MUZZLE LENGTH EQUAL TO, OR SLIGHTLY LESS THAN, LENGTH OF HEAD

BIG HAZEL OR AMBER EYES

STRAIGHT OR SLIGHTLY CONVEX MUZZLE

CHESTNUT BROWN WITH SPOTTING AND TICKED HAIRS, OR FAWN WITH SPOTTING AND TICKED HAIRS

FINE, SHORT, DENSE COAT

LONG, WIDE, DEEP CHEST

CHARACTER

Affection

Playfulness
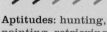

Friendliness to dogs

Friendliness to strangers

Ease of training

BRAQUE SAINT-GERMAIN : FRANCE

This versatile hunting breed was developed in the 1830s at the royal kennels at Compiègne, northern France, before being moved down to Saint Germain en Laye on the outskirts of Paris, from where it takes its name. English Pointers and different regional French pointing breeds were used to produce the Saint-Germain, which was initially favored for the show ring rather than as a working breed. These dogs became popular in France in the 1860s and were the most-shown pointing breed. Despite this, the Saint-Germain is valued as a good working gun dog.

SLIGHTLY ROUNDED HEAD

WHITE WITH FAWN MARKINGS, SOME TICKING, AND FAWN EARS

BROAD, PINK NOSE

HEAVY BONED WITH STRONG MUSCULATURE

LONG, DEEP, BROAD CHEST

LONG FEET WITH TIGHT TOES

CHARACTER

Affection

Playfulness

Friendliness to dogs

Friendliness to strangers

Ease of training

BRITTANY : FRANCE

Once known as the Brittany Spaniel, but now simply the Brittany, these are busy, lively, intelligent, personable, and highly skilled hunting dogs. They have spaniel-like characteristics, particularly in their appearance, but when working, they behave more like pointers. These small, compact, leggy dogs are capable of covering a lot of ground, but they work best in a smaller range than pointers. They are excellent at pointing and holding game and retrieving on land and water. They are highly energetic and thrive when working or exercising, but also make superb companions for the right, active home.

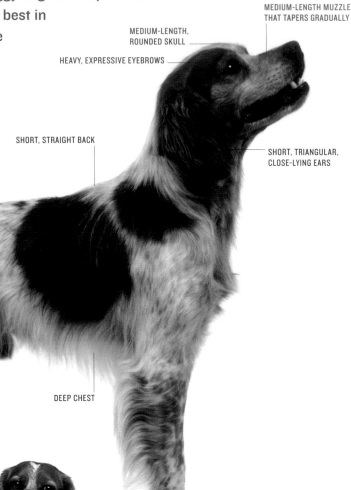

MEDIUM-LENGTH MUZZLE THAT TAPERS GRADUALLY

MEDIUM-LENGTH, ROUNDED SKULL

HEAVY, EXPRESSIVE EYEBROWS

SHORT, TRIANGULAR, CLOSE-LYING EARS

SHORT, STRAIGHT BACK

TOPLINE SLOPES SLIGHTLY TO TAIL

POWERFUL HINDLEGS

DEEP CHEST

AT A GLANCE

Size: medium-small

Exercise needed:

Grooming needed:

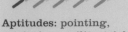

Aptitudes: pointing, retrieving, agility, trials, companion

Height: 17–20 in.

Weight: 30–40 lb.

Average life expectancy: 14–15 yrs

AKC: sporting

CHARACTER

Affection

Playfulness

Friendliness to dogs

Friendliness to strangers

Ease of training

✚ HEALTH ✚

Generally healthy, but some hereditary problems can include hip dysplasia and epilepsy.

COAT CLOSE-UP

FLAT   WAVY

Medium length, dense, flat, or wavy.

Brittanys are one of a handful of breeds that are born naturally bob tailed (short tailed). Breed standards require the tail to be no longer than 4 inches.

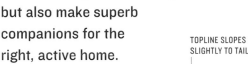

HISTORY

The Brittany, like other bird dogs, derives from ancient stock. There is no documentation surrounding its origins, but paintings from the seventeenth century include dogs with similar characteristics. They are most associated with Brittany, in France, hence their name, and are believed to derive from English Setters and small spaniel-types. The earliest records date to the 1800s, to the town of Pontou. Although bred by the wealthy for hunting woodcock and other small game, they were also popular with poachers due to their small size and the ease with which they could be hidden if necessary. The breed arrived in United States in the early twentieth century and has since become one of the most popular breeds in pointing field trials.

COMMON COAT COLORS

ORANGE & WHITE   LIVER & WHITE   TRICOLOR

Dogs can be orange and white, liver and white, or tri-color. Black is allowed in countries other than the United States.

CHESAPEAKE BAY RETRIEVER : UNITED STATES

The Chesapeake Bay Retriever has been bred over the last 200 years as a working gun dog, and there are few breeds that surpass it in water-retrieving abilities. However, Chesapeakes also combine their brilliant working skills with a loyal, affectionate nature and can make superb family companions; they also excel at agility and working trials. They are intelligent and lively, requiring an active home, and can be independent, although with early training this can be overcome. The Chesapeake Bay Retriever was declared Maryland's official state dog in 1964.

BROAD, ROUND SKULL

SMALL EARS SET HIGH ON HEAD, HANGING LOOSELY

SHORT, POWERFUL BACK, SLIGHTLY HIGHER AT HINDQUARTERS THAN WITHERS

MEDIUM-LENGTH TAIL CARRIED LEVEL OR SLIGHTLY ABOVE BACK LINE

MEDIUM-LARGE, CLEAR, AMBER EYES WITH AN INTELLIGENT EXPRESSION

TAPERED MUZZLE, EQUAL IN LENGTH TO SKULL

POWERFUL SHOULDERS

DEEP, WIDE CHEST

WELL-WEBBED, RABBIT-LIKE FEET

Chessies have large litters with the average size being nine puppies.

AT A GLANCE

Size: large

Exercise needed:
🐎🐎🐎🐎🐎

Grooming needed:
🪮🪮🪮🪮🪮

Aptitudes: retrieving, working trials, agility, companion

Height: 21–26 in.

Weight: 55–79 lb.

Average life expectancy: 9–12 yrs

AKC: sporting

CHARACTER

Affection
🐾🐾🐾🐾🐾

Playfulness
🐾🐾🐾🐾🐾

Friendliness to dogs
🐾🐾🐾🐾🐾

Friendliness to strangers
🐾🐾🐾🐾🐾

Ease of training
🐾🐾🐾🐾🐾

✚ HEALTH ✚

Generally healthy, but some hereditary problems can include hip dysplasia, cancer, and progressive retinol atrophy.

COAT CLOSE-UP

OILY & HARSH

Double-coated, short, thick waterproof coat. Outercoat is oily, harsh, and often wavy over shoulders, neck, back, loins. Undercoat is dense, woolly, and oily.

COMMON COAT COLORS

Any shade of brown, "dead grass," tan, ash, or sedge.

RED BROWN   SEDGE

HISTORY

The breed's origins are partly documented in a letter written by George Law in 1845. Law describes how he rescued two puppies from a floundering English brig heading from Newfoundland to England. The puppies are described as Newfoundlands, but could have been the smaller, now extinct St. John's Water Dogs. Law returned to the United States with the puppies, the male Sailor and female Canton. Sailor found a home in eastern Maryland and bred to a variety of dogs, including Irish Water Spaniels, setters, and various retrievers. Canton went to western Maryland and bred with various hunting and retrieving dogs. Sailor and Canton's progeny all shared similar characteristics, including great skill at duck hunting, leading to the eventual recognition of a true type.

CLUMBER SPANIEL : ENGLAND

By far the stockiest of the spaniel breeds, the Clumber traces back to at least the eighteenth century. A painting from 1788 depicts the Duke of Newcastle with several lemon-and-white dogs that appear to be Clumbers. The Duke bred them at his estate, Clumber Park, hence their name. The dogs were the preserve of the aristocracy due to their excellent noses and quiet temperament, and were not found among the "commoners." They first arrived in the United States in the late 1800s. Although they were once very popular and make good companions, they are rare today.

SLIGHT FURROW BETWEEN THE EYES

MASSIVE HEAD WITH HEAVY BROW

TRIANGULAR EARS WITH THICK LEATHER AND ROUNDED LOWER EDGE

BROAD, DEEP MUZZLE

WHITE WITH LEMON OR ORANGE MARKINGS, USUALLY ON THE EARS AND FACE

LONG, LOW, RECTANGULAR, AND SUBSTANTIAL IN APPEARANCE

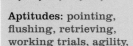
DRENTSCHE PATRIJSHOND : NETHERLANDS

This versatile breed takes its name from the province of Drenthe in the Netherlands, and is also known as the Dutch Partridge Dog. They are of ancient origin developed from Spanish and French pointing dogs and also share some spaniel-like characteristics. In their home area of Drenthe, the dogs were used by gentry and commoners alike for hunting all types of game and vermin, for guarding the farms, and even pulling small carts. Today, they make excellent companions and working dogs.

SLIGHTLY LONGER THAN TALL

HIGH-SET EARS END IN ROUNDED POINT

WEDGE-SHAPED MUZZLE

WHITE WITH PATCHES IN SHADES OF BROWN

HIGH-SET TAIL REACHES ALMOST TO HOCKS

ROUND OR OVAL FEET

ENGLISH COCKER SPANIEL : ENGLAND

The English Cocker, which is slightly larger than the American Cocker, is a lively, cheerful, busy, compact dog that makes a superb family companion and working dog. These are intelligent and inquisitive dogs, always being industrious in some manner, with their tails generally beating out a good rhythm! There is some difference between Cockers bred for showing and working, as in many breeds, but their temperament is typically universally endearing as long as they are well socialized from an early age.

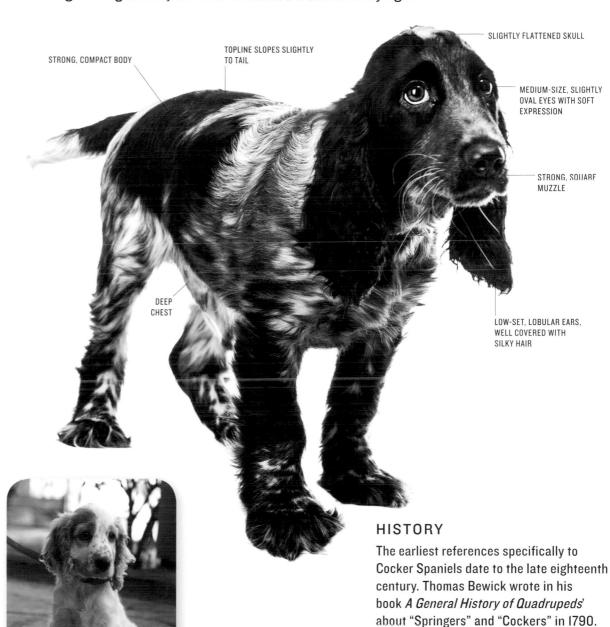

STRONG, COMPACT BODY

TOPLINE SLOPES SLIGHTLY TO TAIL

SLIGHTLY FLATTENED SKULL

MEDIUM-SIZE, SLIGHTLY OVAL EYES WITH SOFT EXPRESSION

STRONG, SQUARE MUZZLE

DEEP CHEST

LOW-SET, LOBULAR EARS, WELL COVERED WITH SILKY HAIR

AT A GLANCE

Size: medium–small

Exercise needed:

Grooming needed:

Aptitudes: hunting, flushing, retrieving, working trials, agility, companion

Height: 15–17 in.

Weight: 26–35 lb.

Average life expectancy: 10–14 yrs

AKC: sporting

CHARACTER

Affection
🐾 🐾 🐾 🐾 🐾

Playfulness
🐾 🐾 🐾 🐾 🐾

Friendliness to dogs
🐾 🐾 🐾 🐾 🐾

Friendliness to strangers
🐾 🐾 🐾 🐾 🐾

Ease of training
🐾 🐾 🐾 🐾 🐾

✚ HEALTH ✚

Generally healthy, but some hereditary problems can include progressive retinal atrophy, familial nethropathy, and hip dysplasia.

COAT CLOSE-UP

SMOOTH & SILKY

Smooth, flat, and silky.

Cocker Spaniels do not like to be left alone for long periods, and puppies in particular need plenty of diversion.

HISTORY

The earliest references specifically to Cocker Spaniels date to the late eighteenth century. Thomas Bewick wrote in his book *A General History of Quadrupeds* about "Springers" and "Cockers" in 1790. This and other early writings reveal that Cockers were originally used in pairs and only for flushing birds. As the range on guns increased, the dogs were also trained to retrieve. The Spaniel Club was founded in England in 1885 to promote the breeding of different types of spaniels for different sporting events, and to create breed standards. The American Spaniel Club was formed in 1881, with one of its first objectives to differentiate between Cocker and Field Spaniels and to prevent crossbreeding. Today, English Cockers remains a favorite in the show ring, as companions, and as noted working dogs.

COMMON COAT COLORS

BLUE ROAN

RED

RED & WHITE

BLACK

Colors include black, liver, red, parti-colors, ticked, or roan with white in combination with black, liver, or red, and tan markings.

ENGLISH SETTER : ENGLAND

The English Setter is one of the true "gentlemen" of the dog world. These lovely dogs combine a gentle, kind, affectionate nature with tremendous working skills and make excellent family companions. Sadly, breed numbers are now low, especially in England, but they are bred in larger numbers in the United States. Four setter breeds are recognized: the English, Irish, Irish Red and White, and the Gordon.

LONG, LEAN HEAD

LOW-SET, PENDULOUS EARS WITH ROUNDED ENDS

SQUARE MUZZLE

MUSCULAR NECK

DEEP CHEST, BUT NOT TOO WIDE

LARGE, NEARLY ROUND EYES

AT A GLANCE

Size: large

Exercise needed:

Grooming needed:

Aptitudes: pointing, flushing, retrieving, working trials, agility, companion

Height: 24–25 in.

Weight: 44–79 lb.

Average life expectancy: 10–14 yrs

AKC: sporting

CHARACTER

Affection

Playfulness

Friendliness to dogs

Friendliness to strangers

Ease of training

ÉPAGNEUL BLEU DE PICARDIE : FRANCE

This unusual breed is also known as the Blue Picardy and was developed at the beginning of the twentieth century in France. These dogs are still relatively unknown outside their homeland, but are gathering interest in the United States and Canada. They are the product of English Setters and local French spaniels that were bred in the hunting areas around the mouth of the River Somme. This is a versatile hunting dog with an excellent temperament, making it increasingly popular as a family companion.

LONG, BROAD MUZZLE

BACK AND LOINS NOT TOO LONG

TAIL DOES NOT REACH BELOW HOCK

PENDULOUS LIPS

LOW TO GROUND AND ROBUST IN APPEARANCE

GRAY-BLACK SPECKLED COAT THAT APPEARS BLUISH, WITH BLACK PATCHES

AT A GLANCE

Size: medium-large

Exercise needed:

Grooming needed:

Aptitudes: hunting, pointing, retrieving, working trials, agility, companion

Height: 22–24 in.

Weight: 43–45 lb.

Average life expectancy: 13 yrs

AKC: not recognized

CHARACTER

Affection

Playfulness

Friendliness to dogs

Friendliness to strangers

Ease of training

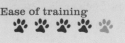

Size: medium

Exercise needed:

Grooming needed:

Aptitudes: hunting, flushing, retrieving, working trials, agility, drug and bomb detection, companion

Height: 19–20 in.

Weight: 40–50 lb.

Average life expectancy: 10–14 yrs

AKC: sporting

CHARACTER

Affection
🐾🐾🐾🐾🐾

Playfulness
🐾🐾🐾🐾🐾

Friendliness to dogs
🐾🐾🐾🐾🐾

Friendliness to strangers
🐾🐾🐾🐾🐾

Ease of training
🐾🐾🐾🐾🐾

✚ HEALTH ✚

Generally healthy, but some hereditary ailments can include eye disorders, hip dysplasia, and ear problems.

ENGLISH SPRINGER SPANIEL : ENGLAND

The English Springer Spaniel is a delightful breed, full of enthusiasm for life, activity, and fun. These are extremely active dogs that have superb temperaments and make excellent companions for the right home. They are popular working gun dogs, but given their intelligence and trainability are also used as drug and bomb-detection animals. They excel at agility and field trials and like nothing better than having an activity or a job to do.

BROAD SKULL, FLAT ON TOP, ROUNDED TO BACK AND SIDES

MEDIUM-SIZE, OVAL EYES WITH A KIND EXPRESSION

FULL LIPS

LONG, WIDE EARS HANG CLOSE TO CHEEKS

STRONG, COMPACT BODY

DEEP CHEST

Hugely popular in their native England, Springer Spaniels respond well to training from an early age.

HISTORY

The Springer derives its name from its original working method when flushing out birds: the dogs work patches of dense undergrowth and startle the birds so they "spring" into the air. The term "spaniel" itself is believed to come from the Roman name for Spain, where the dogs are thought to have developed. The Romans were keen hunters who favored these Spanish dogs and took them across continental Europe and into Britain with them on their conquests. As early as 17 BCE, there were written mentions of "land Spaniels" and "water Spaniels," indicating two types at an early date. Among the earliest true English Springer Spaniels to arrive in the United States were those imported by Ernest Wells in 1907. In 1910 the first Springer, Denne Lucy, was registered with the American Kennel Club.

COMMON COAT COLORS

LIVER & WHITE

BLACK & WHITE

The most common colors are liver and white or black and white, either with tan markings; or blue or liver roan.

COAT CLOSE-UP

FLAT

WAVY

Medium-length flat or wavy coat with a dense undercoat and feathering on ears, chest, legs, and belly.

FIELD SPANIEL : ENGLAND

Size: medium-small

Exercise needed:

Grooming needed:

Aptitudes: hunting, pointing, retrieving, working trials, agility, companion

Height: 17–18 in.

Weight: 40–55 lb.

Average life expectancy: 10–12 yrs

AKC: sporting

CHARACTER

Affection

Playfulness

Friendliness to dogs

Friendliness to strangers

Ease of training

This breed developed approximately 150 years ago and went through a number of changes before arriving at the modern type. Both the English Cocker and Sussex Spaniel, along with other spaniel types, have influenced the Field Spaniel, which is noted today for its working abilities. Field Spaniels have good temperaments with the right socialization and can make good family companions for country life. They are active dogs that are still very much bred for work; they are actually described in the British Kennel Club standard as "not suitable for city living."

KIND, NOBLE, INTELLIGENT EXPRESSION

STRONG, LONG , LEAN MUZZLE

WELL BALANCED, SOLIDLY BUILT, AND SLIGHTLY LONGER THAN TALL

SHORT CROUP

BLACK, LIVER, GOLDEN LIVER; OR BI-COLORED WITH ROAN OR TICKING IN WHITE AREAS

LARGE, ROUND, WEBBED FEET

FRENCH SPANIEL : FRANCE

Size: medium

Exercise needed:

Grooming needed:

Aptitudes: hunting, pointing, retrieving, working trials, agility, companion

Height: 21–24 in.

Weight: 40-60 lb.

Average life expectancy: 10–14 yrs

AKC: ? group

CHARACTER

Affection

Playfulness

Friendliness to dogs

Friendliness to strangers

Ease of training

The elegant and charismatic French Spaniel was first described by Gaston Phebus, Count of Foix, in his famous book on hunting, *Livre de Chasse*, although the breed undoubtedly traces back much further. During the Middle Ages, these dogs were popular among the aristocracy and were invariably found in the French royal kennels. The breed was almost unheard of outside France until the 1970s, but they are now found in England, the United States, and Canada. French Spaniels are affectionate dogs suitable for an active home.

SLIGHTLY CONVEX MUZZLE

STRAIGHT TOPLINE

SLIGHTLY LONGER THAN TALL

WHITE AND BROWN WITH SOME SPOTTING, TICKING, OR FLECKING

BROAD, POWERFUL LOINS

FLAT-COATED RETRIEVER : ENGLAND

The Flat-Coated Retriever developed in the early nineteenth century as a retrieving dog capable of working on land and in water, and they retain both skills, making them versatile hunting dogs. Newfoundland blood along with various setters, spaniels, and sheepdogs contributed toward their development, and they were widely used by fishermen and gamekeepers throughout England. They are noted for their excellent, affable temperaments and easygoing natures, making them highly suitable as companion dogs for active homes.

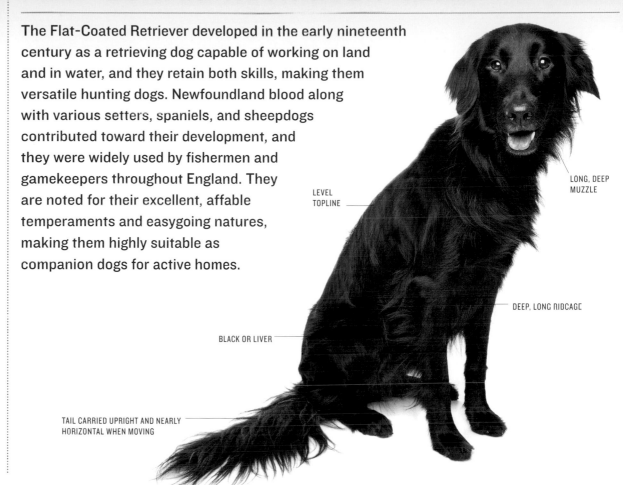

LEVEL TOPLINE

LONG, DEEP MUZZLE

DEEP, LONG RIBCAGE

BLACK OR LIVER

TAIL CARRIED UPRIGHT AND NEARLY HORIZONTAL WHEN MOVING

CURLY-COATED RETRIEVER : ENGLAND

The Curly-Coated Retriever is considered one of the oldest retrieving breeds and was popular with gamekeepers on large country estates by the 1800s. These dogs were renowned for their stamina and ability to work all day with enthusiasm, often in severe weather or freezing water. Their tightly curled, water-resistant coat is a distinctive feature of the breed. They are loyal and highly intelligent dogs that thrive when working, but are also suited to an active family environment.

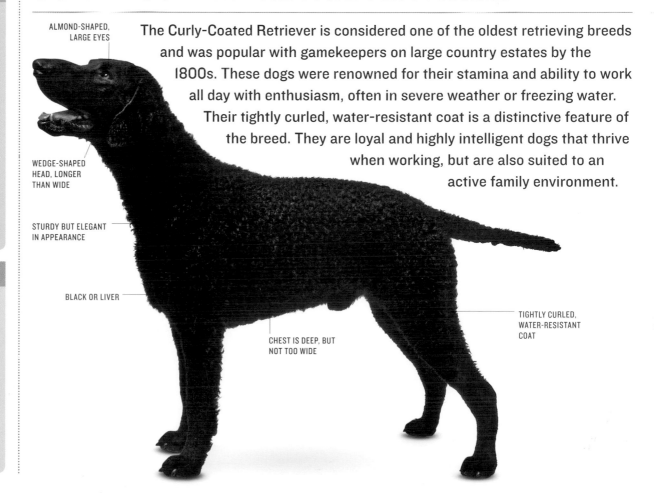

ALMOND-SHAPED, LARGE EYES

WEDGE-SHAPED HEAD, LONGER THAN WIDE

STURDY BUT ELEGANT IN APPEARANCE

BLACK OR LIVER

CHEST IS DEEP, BUT NOT TOO WIDE

TIGHTLY CURLED, WATER-RESISTANT COAT

FRENCH GASCONY POINTER : FRANCE

This ancient French pointing breed is also known as the Braque Français, type Gascogne, or the Braque Français de Grande Taille, and is thought to have developed from the old Spanish Pointer in southwestern France and the central Pyrenees. Although called a pointer, the Gascony is a versatile hunting dog that will flush, retrieve, and trail game. It is not known for its speed, but is a steady and methodical worker. Although it is not widely known outside France, the breed was accepted by the United Kennel Club in the United States in 2006.

CHESTNUT-BROWN OR DARK YELLOW EYES

PENDULOUS LIPS

ROBUST, POWERFUL FRAME

LONG, STRAIGHT FORELEGS

NEARLY ROUND FEET

CHESTNUT BROWN WITH OR WITHOUT WHITE, TICKING, ROANING, AND TAN MARKINGS

FRENCH PYRENEAN POINTER : FRANCE

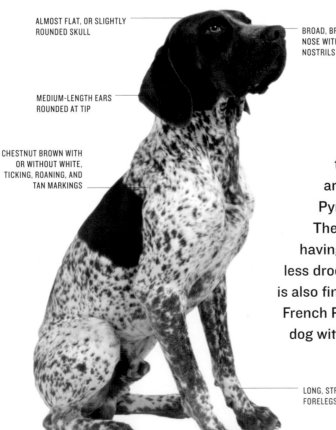

ALMOST FLAT, OR SLIGHTLY ROUNDED SKULL

BROAD, BROWN NOSE WITH WIDE NOSTRILS

MEDIUM-LENGTH EARS ROUNDED AT TIP

CHESTNUT BROWN WITH OR WITHOUT WHITE, TICKING, ROANING, AND TAN MARKINGS

LONG, STRAIGHT FORELEGS

NEARLY ROUND FEET

This breed is also known as the Braque Français, type Pyrénées, or the Braque Français de Petite Taille, and it is similar to the French Gascony Pointer though slightly smaller in size and not quite as robust. Both types of pointer developed in the same area of southwest France and the central Pyrenees and share a similar heritage. The French Pyrenean Pointer is noted as having slightly tighter skin than the Gascony, less droopy lips, and a lighter frame; their coat is also finer and shorter than the Gascony. The French Pyrenean is a versatile and fast hunting dog with a calm temperament.

Size: medium-small

Exercise needed:

Grooming needed:
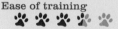

Aptitudes: hunting, flushing, pointing, retrieving, working trials, companion

Height: 17–21 in.

Weight: 44–66 lb.

Average life expectancy: 12–14 yrs

AKC: FSS

CHARACTER

Affection

Playfulness

Friendliness to dogs

Friendliness to strangers

Ease of training

＋ HEALTH ＋

Generally healthy with few hereditary problems.

DEUTSCHER WACHTELHUND : GERMANY

This German hunting dog is often referred to as a German Spaniel, although in Germany they are not classed as spaniels. The breed was developed around 300 years ago to hunt in extreme weather over difficult terrain, and are very tough and tenacious. They are excellent trackers and flushers, and will work on land or in water hunting birds and fur game. They are renowned for going in for the kill and returning with the game to the hunter. Active and intelligent, they can make loyal family companions in a lively environment. In Germany they are normally sold only to hunting homes.

SLIGHTLY OVAL-SHAPED, BROWN TO HAZEL EYES

MUZZLE SAME LENGTH AS SKULL

COMPACT, STRONG BODY

HIGH-SET, ACTIVE TAIL

EARS LIE CLOSE TO HEAD AND COVERED IN LONG, SILKY HAIR

HISTORY

During the Middle Ages, only the wealthiest German families could afford kennels of hunting dogs, and they also controlled all the game. By the 1700s, though, the working classes were able to hunt, and versatile hunting dogs developed from the Stoberhund, including the Deutscher Wachtelhund, which hunted all types of game over any terrain. The breed was given official recognition in 1903 when the German Wachtelhund Club was established; the breed standard was written in 1910.

This breed was bred specifically to bark loudly while trailing game so the dogs could be located in Germany's dense forests.

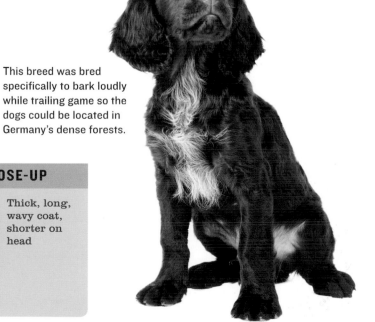

COMMON COAT COLORS

The color is solid brown or brown ticked with white

BROWN   BROWN TICKED

COAT CLOSE-UP

Thick, long, wavy coat, shorter on head

THICK & WAVY

GERMAN SHORTHAIRED POINTER : GERMANY

The German Shorthaired Pointer developed from ancient German hunting dogs, or bird dogs, that had been influenced by Spanish pointers and native scent hounds. The scent hound heritage gave rise to the German Shorthaired Pointer's highly tuned scenting abilities, which, with the addition of some English Foxhound and later English Pointers, led to a versatile hunting dog. It is an all-purpose working breed that is noted for its intelligence and loyalty. It can also make an excellent family companion for an active home.

ALMOND-SHAPED, DARK BROWN EYES

POWERFUL JAWS

SHORT, STRONG, STRAIGHT BACK

HIGH-SET TAIL

UNDERLINE SHOWS TUCK-UP

ROUND OR SPOON-SHAPED FEET

German Shorthaired Pointers are lively, intelligent puppies that exhibit their hunt, point, and retrieve instincts from a young age.

HISTORY

The initial gene pool for the German Shorthaired Pointer was varied, and a number of early dogs were registered with unknown parentage. The pedigree register was established in 1872, with Hecktor I being the first dog entered into the German Kennel Club stud book. Hecktor was liver and white and described as hound-like in appearance. Nero and Treff were two other important early foundation dogs for the breed.

COMMON COAT COLORS

The most common colors are solid liver or liver and white.

LIVER

LIVER & WHITE

COAT CLOSE-UP

Short, thick, tough coat

SHORT & THICK

GERMAN WIREHAIRED POINTER : GERMANY

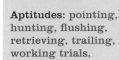

HEAVY EYEBROWS

DISTINCT BEARD

DENSE UNDERCOAT WITH OUTER COAT BEING WIRY, HARSH, STRAIGHT, AND FLAT

DEEP CHEST

SOLID LIVER OR LIVER AND WHITE

ROUND, WEBBED FEET

This charismatic breed was developed in the 1800s by hunters who wanted an all-purpose hunting dog able to work in mountains, forests, and water. Single hunters or small hunting parties used these dogs for tracking, locating, and pointing all manner of game. In addition, German Wirehaired Pointers proved to be a useful watchdogs and affectionate companions. Their distinctive wirehaired coat provides valuable protection against dense undergrowth and is relatively easy to maintain. The modern German Wirehaired Pointer is every bit as versatile and charming as its ancestors and, although extremely energetic, can make a superb companion for an active home.

GERMAN LONGHAIRED POINTER : GERMANY

In the mid-nineteenth century, English Setter and English Pointer blood was introduced to the German pointing dogs, resulting in a faster, lighter animal. In 1879 the best German Longhaired Pointers were exhibited at Hanover, and a breed standard, which remains today, was drawn up. The German Longhaired Pointer is an ideal, tenacious shooting dog and works for any game on land or in water. They are hardy and enduring, with superb hunting skills and a loyal nature, but thrive in a working home and are not ideally suited to city life.

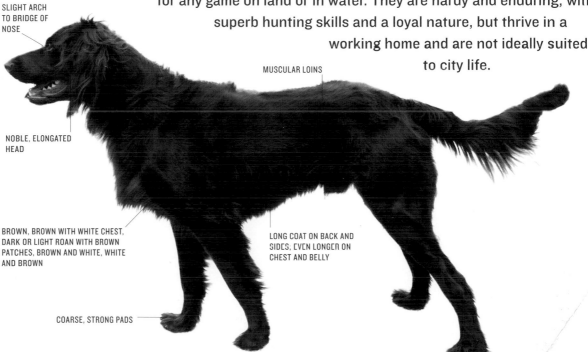

SLIGHT ARCH TO BRIDGE OF NOSE

MUSCULAR LOINS

NOBLE, ELONGATED HEAD

BROWN, BROWN WITH WHITE CHEST, DARK OR LIGHT ROAN WITH BROWN PATCHES, BROWN AND WHITE, WHITE AND BROWN

LONG COAT ON BACK AND SIDES, EVEN LONGER ON CHEST AND BELLY

COARSE, STRONG PADS

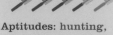

GOLDEN RETRIEVER : SCOTLAND

Goldies, as they are often called, are known for their exceptional temperaments, and although they were bred originally as working dogs, they make the transition to family companions with ease. They are still valued as gun dogs, but are also used in a range of other capacities including search and rescue, drug and bomb detection, and assistance dogs for the deaf and blind. Golden Retrievers are generally easy to train, obedient, and intelligent, which combined with their gentle nature, has led to their immense popularity.

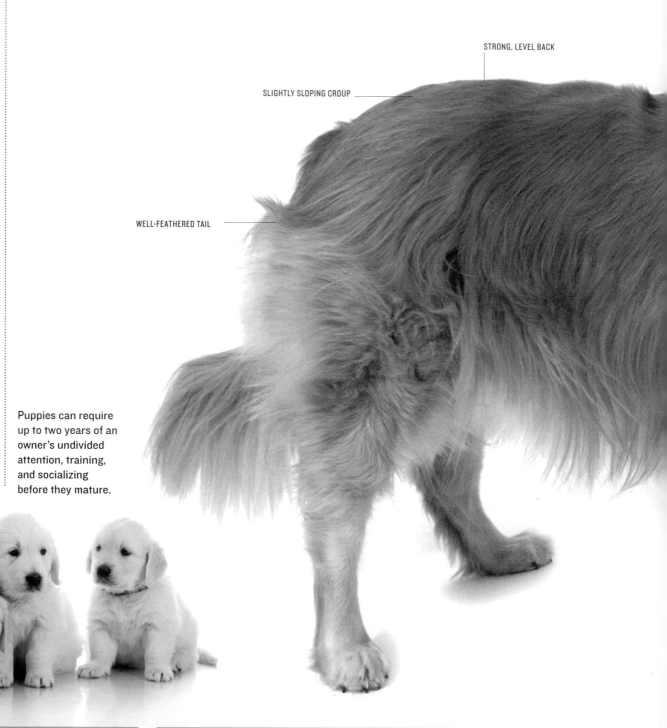

STRONG, LEVEL BACK

SLIGHTLY SLOPING CROUP

WELL-FEATHERED TAIL

Puppies can require up to two years of an owner's undivided attention, training, and socializing before they mature.

COMMON COAT COLORS

These dogs can be any shade of golden.

DARK GOLDEN

COAT CLOSE-UP

Double coated: straight or wavy topcoat, flat to body with a dense, water-resistant undercoat.

WAVY   STRAIGHT

BROAD SKULL

SHORT EARS
CARRIED CLOSE
TO CHEEK

MEDIUM-SIZE, DARK
BROWN EYES WITH
FRIENDLY EXPRESSION

MUZZLE HAS
STRAIGHT PROFILE

MEDIUM-LONG,
MUSCULAR NECK

HISTORY

Originally called the Yellow Retriever, the breed was developed in the nineteenth century in Scotland by Sir Dudley Coutts Marjoribanks, who kept large kennels on his estate and bred hunting dogs. One dog that helped to estabish the breed was Nous, bred to a Tweed Water Spaniel named Belle who produced four yellow puppies. These dogs were crossbred to Red Setters, Wavy Coated Retrievers, Bloodhounds, and Tweed Water Spaniels, eventually giving rise to a specific type. The first Goldie was seen at Crufts Dog Show in 1908, and in 1913, the British Kennel Club recognized the breed. The breed had arrived in the United States by the 1930s with Colonel S. Magoffin. He established the Gilnockie Kennels in Colorado, which account for many of the pedigree lines today.

GRAND GRIFFON VENDÉEN : FRANCE

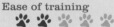
There are several breeds of Griffon (French hunting dogs) from the Vendée region on the west coast of France, with this, the Grand, being the largest and oldest. The breed is believed to trace back to at least the sixteenth century, when hunting was developing on a grand scale in France becoming the sport of the royals. Accordingly, great emphasis was placed on breeding the best hunting dogs. The Grande Griffon is a brave, determined scent hound used for hunting large game, including wild boar. These are amenable, friendly dogs that can be very independent and have a reputation for escaping! They are suitable only for working environments or active homes.

DOMED SKULL

PRONOUNCED EYEBROW

LOW-SET EARS, ENDING IN AN ELONGATED OVAL

LONG, SOMETIMES BUSHY, AND HARSH COAT

BLACK WITH WHITE SPOTTING, BLACK AND TAN, FAWN WITH WHITE SPOTTING, TRICOLOR, FAWN WITH BLACK OVERLAY

KOOIKERHONDJE : NETHERLANDS

The Kooikerhondje is a delightful breed with spaniel-like qualities that is little heard of outside its homeland. Dating back to at least the fifteenth century, these small, orange-white dogs appear in many Dutch paintings. Developed for duck hunting, Kooikerhondje were trained to weave in and out of foliage along river banks to lure ducks into a trap. It is thought the ducks were attracted by the white feathery tail. The breed came close to extinction in the nineteenth century, but was saved largely by the work of Baroness van Hardenbroek. Kooikerhondje make superb companions and still excel in duck hunting.

ALMOND-SHAPED, DARK-BROWN EYES WITH A FRIENDLY, ALERT EXPRESSION

LARGE EARS

WHITE WITH ORANGE-RED PATCHES

STRONG, STRAIGHT, SHORT BACK

WELL-FEATHERED TAIL WITH A WHITE PLUME, USUALLY CARRIED LEVEL OR ERECT

SMALL, SLIGHTLY OVAL FEET

LAGOTTO ROMAGNOLO : ITALY

The Lagotto Romagnolo is an ancient breed of water-retrieving dog that has a distinctive curly coat and was bred to hunt ducks in the marshes of Romagna in northern Italy. As the marshes were gradually drained between 1840 and 1890, the breed began to be used for truffle hunting instead, and today it is the only specialized truffle-hunting breed in the world. These dogs have retained their water-retrieving and gun-dog skills and also make good agility dogs and companions.

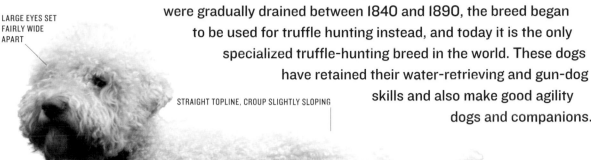

LARGE EYES SET FAIRLY WIDE APART

STRAIGHT TOPLINE, CROUP SLIGHTLY SLOPING

POWERFULLY BUILT

WOOLLY COAT WITH TIGHT, RING-SHAPED CURLS

SOLID OFF WHITE, WHITE WITH BROWN OR ORANGE PATCHES, BROWN ROAN, BROWN WITH OR WITHOUT WHITE, ORANGE WITH OR WITHOUT WHITE

MONTENEGRIN MOUNTAIN HOUND : MONTENEGRO

This rare hound breed was formerly known as the Yugoslavian Mountain Hound and is one of several closely related Balkan hound breeds. The breed developed in the Republic of Montenegro and may be originally descended from ancient hound types introduced to the area by the Phoenicians. The first standard for the breed was drawn up in 1924 and was accepted by the United Kennel Club in the United States in 2008. These are determined, enduring, brave hunting dogs, most often used in packs and capable of hunting wild boar, deer, fox, hare, and small game. They generally have pleasant temperaments, are sociable, and thrive in a working environment.

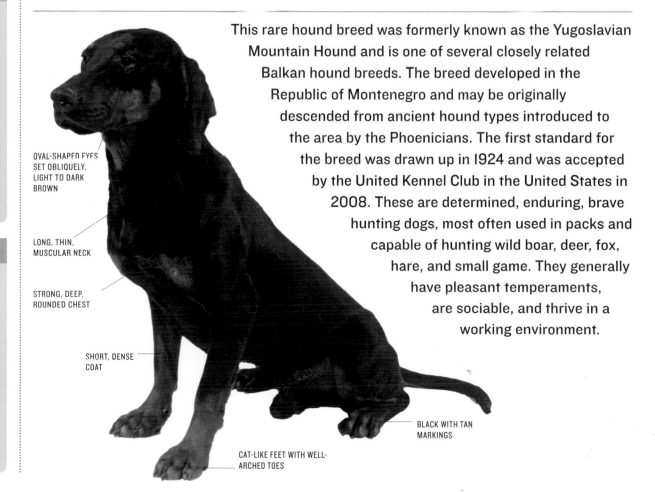

OVAL-SHAPED EYES SET OBLIQUELY, LIGHT TO DARK BROWN

LONG, THIN, MUSCULAR NECK

STRONG, DEEP, ROUNDED CHEST

SHORT, DENSE COAT

BLACK WITH TAN MARKINGS

CAT-LIKE FEET WITH WELL-ARCHED TOES

AT A GLANCE

Size: large

Amount of exercise:

🐕 🐕 🐕 🐕 🐕

Amount of grooming:

🖌 🖌 🖌 🖌 🖌

Aptitudes: hunting, flushing, retrieving, field trials, companion

Height: 25–27 in.

Weight: 60–70 lb.

Average life expectancy: 12–14 yrs

AKC: sporting

CHARACTER

Affection

🐾 🐾 🐾 🐾 🐾

Playfulness

🐾 🐾 🐾 🐾 🐾

Friendliness to dogs

🐾 🐾 🐾 🐾 🐾

Friendliness to strangers

🐾 🐾 🐾 🐾 🐾

Ease of training

🐾 🐾 🐾 🐾 🐾

✚ HEALTH ✚

Generally healthy, but some problems can include canine leukocyte adhesion deficiency, hip dysplasia, epilepsy, hypertrophic osteodystrophy, bloat, hypothyroidism, and progressive retinal atrophy.

IRISH SETTER : IRELAND

The Irish Setter is one of the most popular of the setter breeds and is a particularly fun-loving, enthusiastic, and lively companion. Early in their history, they became associated with the aristocracy, and the dogs themselves have a noble air about them, which belies their outgoing and often "clownish" personalities. The breed has excelled in a variety of hunting activities and is used to hunt many different birds. They are also popular in field trials and also in the show ring with slightly different types emerging to fill both roles. This lovely, boisterous breed is suitable for an active or working home.

LONG, LEAN HEAD

ALMOND-SHAPED, DARK EYES WITH A SOFT EXPRESSION

LOW-SET EARS HANG IN A NEAT FOLD CLOSE TO HEAD

MODERATELY LONG, SLIGHTLY ARCHED NECK

WELL-FEATHERED TAIL NEARLY REACHES HOCKS

RATHER SMALL FEET

HISTORY

The Irish Setter probably developed in the eighteenth century through crosses of Irish Water Spaniels, Irish Terriers, Gordon Setters, English Setters, spaniels, and pointers. Originally bred to be red and white, the characteristic solid red color appeared in Ireland in the late 1800s and became a mark of quality. The Irish Setter was first used to "set" game, sniffing out birds hidden in undergrowth and crouching low to indicate the bird's presence. The hunter could then throw a net to catch the hidden quarry. A breed club for the Irish Setter was formed in 1882.
A breed club for the American Kennel Club in 1878.

COMMON COAT COLORS

The coat is mahogany or rich chestnut.

MAHOGANY   RICH CHESTNUT

COAT CLOSE-UP

Straight, fine, glossy coat, longer on the ears and chest, with feathered tail and legs.

FINE & GLOSSY

Author Dodie Smith described the Irish Setter as "feather brained as well as feathered tailed," but they are actually intelligent and trainable dogs.

IRISH RED AND WHITE SETTER : IRELAND

The Irish Red and White Setter is not as well-known as the Irish (Red) Setter, but is thought to be the older breed. In 1570 English physician John Caius described the breed in his book *De Canibus Britannicis*: "The most part of their skins are white, and if they are marked with any spots they are commonly red and somewhat great." By the end of the nineteenth century, however, the Irish Setter had overtaken the Red and White, and the older breed almost became extinct. Concerted efforts have re-established the breed, though their numbers remain low. Generally this breed is loyal, affectionate, and obedient; they also make very good gun dogs.

BROAD, DOMED SKULL

CLEAN, SQUARE MUZZLE

LONG, SILKY FEATHERING ON LEGS, CHEST, EARS, AND TAIL

WHITE WITH RED PATCHES

ROUNDED CROUP

MODERATE-LENGTH TAIL USUALLY CARRIED LEVEL OR SLIGHTLY LOWER

IRISH WATER SPANIEL : IRELAND

The Irish Water Spaniel has a distinctive tightly curled, water-resistant coat and an unusual tail, called a "rat tail" or "whip tail." There is no mistaking this breed! They are the largest of the spaniels, and the only surviving water spaniel. Bred as working dogs, they excel over difficult marshy or boggy terrain and are renowned for their stamina and tenacity. They are affectionate and loyal dogs that display an innate sense of humor; despite their positive qualities, though, the breed numbers are low.

DARK AMBER OR BROWN, ALMOND-SHAPED EYES

SMOOTH, SHORT FACIAL HAIR

POWERFUL, ARCHED NECK

RICH TO DARK LIVER WITH PURPLISH TINGE

WATER-RESISTANT, DENSE, CURLY COAT

"RAT TAIL," THICK AT BASE AND TAPERING; EITHER BARE OR COVERED IN SHORT HAIR

AT A GLANCE

Size: medium-large

Amount of exercise:

Amount of grooming:

Aptitudes: hunting, retrieving, assistance, service, agility, companion

Height: 21–24 in.

Weight: 55–80 lb.

Average life expectancy: 10–12 yrs

AKC: sporting

CHARACTER

Affection

Playfulness

Friendliness to dogs

Friendliness to strangers

Ease of training

✚ HEALTH ✚

Generally healthy, but some hereditary problems can include hip dysplasia, cancer, obesity, progressive retinol atrophy, and heart problems.

LABRADOR RETRIEVER : CANADA/ENGLAND

Ranked as one of the most popular dog breeds in the world, the Labrador Retriever has worked its way into the hearts of dog lovers everywhere. This breed is versatility at its best; "Labs" make excellent working gun dogs and superb family pets, in addition to being used as service dogs, by the military, as assistance dogs, and for all manner of activities including agility and obedience. Typically Labradors are intelligent, trainable dogs that have a soft, kind nature.

EXPRESSIVE, INTELLIGENT, BROWN OR HAZEL EYES

WIDE NOSE WITH WELL-DEVELOPED NOSTRILS

BROAD HEAD

EARS SET FAR BACK ON HEAD AND HANG CLOSE

DEEP AND REASONABLY WIDE CHEST

STRONG, STRAIGHT FORELEGS

Labradors keep a puppy mentality for a long time after they have matured physically!

COMMON COAT COLORS

Coat can be black, shades of yellow, light to dark fox red, or chocolate.

BLACK

YELLOW

DARK FOX RED

CHOCOLATE

HISTORY

Labrador Retrievers trace back to the St. John's Dog found on the Canadian island of Newfoundland. Labs emerged from a mix of working stock taken to the island by Portuguese, British, and Irish fishermen who settled and traded there in the sixteenth century. The dogs were used in the fishing industry and developed into a water-loving breed with a water-resistant coat. From the early 1800s, fishermen began taking their dogs with them when traveling to Poole Harbor, England, and started to trade the dogs as well as fish. The emergence of the modern Labrador is largely attributed to the fifth-century Duke of Buccleuch and his brother, the Earl of Malmesbury, who bought a number of the dogs in the early nineteenth century and began developing the breed.

"OTTER" TAIL, WITH DISTINCTIVE, ROUNDED APPEARANCE

UNDERLINE ALMOST STRAIGHT

Labs are notoriously fond of food and can be prone to obesity if allowed to overindulge.

COAT CLOSE-UP

Double-coated, water-resistant coat with short, straight, dense hairs.

SHORT & DENSE

AT A GLANCE

Size: large

Amount of exercise:

Amount of grooming:

Aptitudes: hunting, flushing, retrieving, field trials, companion

Height: 23–27 in.

Weight: 45–80 lb.

Average life expectancy: 10–12 yrs

AKC: sporting

CHARACTER

Affection

Playfulness

Friendliness to dogs

Friendliness to strangers

Ease of training

✚ HEALTH ✚

Although generally healthy, some hereditary problems might include gastric torsion, neonatal fatalities, hip dysplasia, and cancer.

GORDON SETTER : SCOTLAND

The Gordon Setter is the largest and most solidly built of the four Setter breeds and works at a slower pace; however, it will continue working all day long. These dogs are highly valued for this great stamina and are intelligent, enthusiastic, and loyal. Gordons can be "one-person" dogs, forming strong bonds with their owners, and are best suited to a working environment as opposed to family life as a companion dog.

LONG MUZZLE

DARK BROWN EYES WITH A WISE EXPRESSION

LONG, ARCHED NECK

TOPLINE SLOPES SLIGHTLY FROM WITHERS TO LOINS

MODERATELY LONG TAIL WITH FEATHERING TO UNDERSIDE

DEEP CHEST, NOT TOO BROAD

HISTORY

Gordon Setter heritage traces back to the fourteenth century to the spaniel group of hunting dogs, and there are many historic references to black-and-tan dogs of setter type. Their modern development began in the early nineteenth century on the Scottish estate of the 4th Duke of Gordon who bred dogs at Gordon Castle in the Scottish Highlands. Other kennels, including the Earl of Leicester's in northern England, also bred black-and-tan working dogs. These dogs are thought to have been crossbred with Bloodhounds to establish the Gordon Setter type. Some of the earliest Gordons in the United States were imported directly from the Gordon Castle Kennels in 1842, and the breed was recognized by the American Kennel Club in 1884.

Gordon puppies are high spirited and playful!

COMMON COAT COLORS

The coat is black with tan markings, either of rich chestnut or mahogany.

BLACK & TAN

COAT CLOSE-UP

Soft, medium-length, shiny coat with feathering on ears, chest, legs, and tail.

SOFT & SHINY

AT A GLANCE

Size: medium-large

Amount of exercise:

Amount of grooming:

Aptitudes: hunting, retrieving, pointing, tracking, agility, companion

Height: 23–25 in.

Weight: 66 lb.

Average life expectancy: 12–13 yrs

AKC: not recognized

CHARACTER

Affection

Playfulness

Friendliness to dogs

Friendliness to strangers

Ease of training

LARGE MÜNSTERLÄNDER : GERMANY

BLACK HEAD; BODY IS WHITE MOTTLED WITH BLACK

ELONGATED HEAD WITH STRONG JAW MUSCLES

BROAD, HIGH-SET, WELL-FEATHERED EARS

BACK SLOPES SLIGHTLY FROM WITHERS TO REAR

LONG, DENSE HAIR

WELL-KNUCKLED FEET WITH DENSE HAIR BETWEEN TOES

This German gun-dog breed is a multipurpose working animal with an excellent nose and a kind, willing temperament. These are active dogs that are happiest when working, but they also make suitable companions for the right busy home environment. The breed developed from ancient long-haired hawking dogs that were found across Europe, with their modern development influenced by German and, to a small degree, English pointers. They were once known as German Longhaired Pointers and have distinctive black, or black-and-white, coats.

SMALL MÜNSTERLÄNDER : GERMANY

The Small Münsterländer dates back to the Middle Ages in Europe and is a popular and versatile hunting dog. They are used to hunt a variety of different furred and feathered game and, despite their size, have historically hunted deer and wild boar. They are loyal, affectionate, and typically non-aggressive dogs that need plenty of exercise, including swimming, and particularly thrive when hunting. They are suitable as companions, but only for an active and, preferably, hunting home.

LEAN, FLAT TO SLIGHTLY ARCHED SKULL

POWERFUL, LONG, STRAIGHT MUZZLE

GLOSSY, DENSE, STRAIGHT, OR SLIGHTLY WAVY, MEDIUM-LENGTH COAT

WELL-FEATHERED FORELEGS

FIRM, WELL-MUSCLED BACK

BROWN AND WHITE, OR BROWN ROAN

AT A GLANCE

Size: medium

Amount of exercise:

Amount of grooming:

Aptitudes: hunting, retrieving, pointing, tracking, agility, companion

Height: 19–22 in.

Weight: 38–58 lb.

Average life expectancy: 12–14 yrs

AKC: FSS

CHARACTER

Affection

Playfulness

Friendliness to dogs

Friendliness to strangers

Ease of training

AT A GLANCE

Size: medium-small

Amount of exercise:
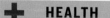

Amount of grooming:

Aptitudes: hunting, retrieving, pointing, tracking, agility, companion

Height: 17–21 in.

Weight: 35–52 lb.

Average life expectancy: 11–13 yrs

AKC: sporting

CHARACTER

Affection
🐾 🐾 🐾 🐾 🐾

Playfulness
🐾 🐾 🐾 🐾 🐾

Friendliness to dogs
🐾 🐾 🐾 🐾 🐾

Friendliness to strangers
🐾 🐾 🐾 🐾 🐾

Ease of training
🐾 🐾 🐾 🐾 🐾

✛ HEALTH ✛

Generally healthy, but hereditary problems can include hip dysplasia and progressive retinol atrophy.

NOVA SCOTIA DUCK TOLLING RETRIEVER : CANADA

The cheerful and busy Nova Scotia Duck Tolling Retrievers are animated and versatile working gun dogs. They were originally bred to work in water, but are also good upland retrievers, and are happiest when working. They have excellent temperaments and, despite their relatively small size, are tenacious and brave dogs that happily retrieve geese or wounded birds. They can make good companions, but are only suitable for an active homelife.

SLIGHTLY WEDGE-SHAPED HEAD

ALMOND-SHAPED EYES

TAPERING MUZZLE WITH STRONG JAWS

HIGH-SET, TRIANGULAR EARS

LEVEL BACK

COMPACT AND POWERFUL IN APPEARANCE

WELL-FEATHERED TAIL REACHES TO AT LEAST THE HOCKS

SLIGHTLY OVAL, WEBBED FEET

HISTORY

"Tolling" is a Middle English word that means "to lure or decoy game." Tolling dogs play along the shoreline attracting the attention of water fowl, which, with curiosity getting the better of them, are lured closer to shore and within netting or gunshot range. It is thought that the Nova Scotia Duck Tolling Retriever was developed in Yarmouth Country, Nova Scotia, from red decoy dogs brought to Canada and crossed with European working collies. The breed has bred true for many generations now and was recognized by the Canadian Kennel Club in 1945. Today they are found in the United States, Europe, Australia, and New Zealand.

Tollers have an unusual, high-pitched "scream" when excited, which can be unnerving the first time it is heard.

COMMON COAT COLORS

RED

DARK RED

The coat can be any shade of red, usually with white on the tail tip, feet, chest, and head.

COAT CLOSE-UP

SILKY

WAVY

The Toller's water-resistant coat is medium length and straight, but can have slight wave on the back. Feathering is soft, and moderate in length.

OLD DANISH POINTER : DENMARK

The Old Danish Pointer is one of just a few Danish breeds and is sadly low in numbers. The breed is believed to have developed from scent hounds, including the St. Hubert's Hound, which gave rise to the Bloodhound. Breeder Morten Bak, who lived in northern Denmark during the eighteenth century, is credited with developing the breed by crossing local farm dogs and gypsy dogs over many generations to produce a consistent white-and-brown type. Spanish Pointers are also thought to have influenced the breed, which is noted for its excellent temperament and working abilities. They can make superb family companions for an active home.

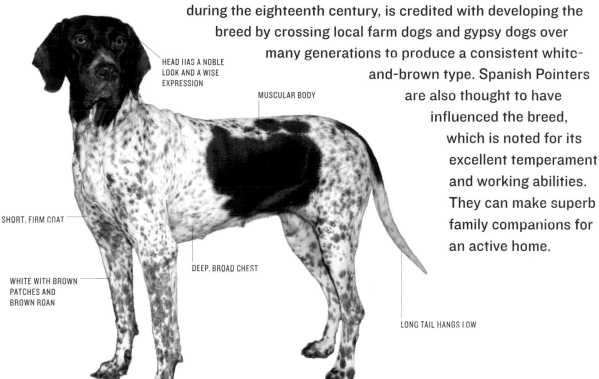

HEAD HAS A NOBLE LOOK AND A WISE EXPRESSION

MUSCULAR BODY

SHORT, FIRM COAT

DEEP, BROAD CHEST

WHITE WITH BROWN PATCHES AND BROWN ROAN

LONG TAIL HANGS LOW

PICARDY SPANIEL : FRANCE

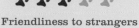
The Picardy Spaniel is rarely seen outside France and is closely related to the French Spaniel, with both breeds sharing several characteristics. The Picardy is an ancient breed thought to have developed by the fourteenth century when similar dogs were described by Gaston Phebus in his work, *Le Livre de Chasse*. Picardys are gentle and playful dogs, good in a family environment, and excellent hunters that work in water and on land and hunt a variety of fur and feathered game.

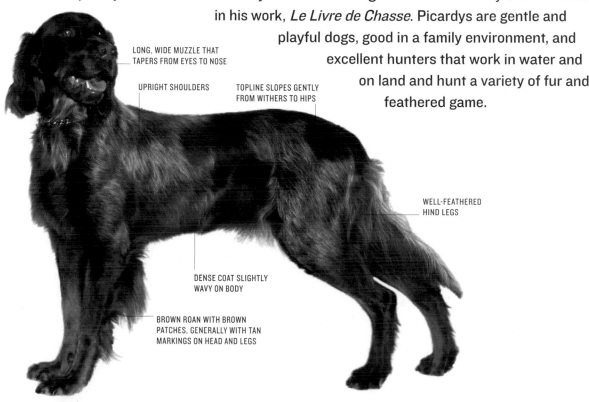

LONG, WIDE MUZZLE THAT TAPERS FROM EYES TO NOSE

UPRIGHT SHOULDERS

TOPLINE SLOPES GENTLY FROM WITHERS TO HIPS

WELL-FEATHERED HIND LEGS

DENSE COAT SLIGHTLY WAVY ON BODY

BROWN ROAN WITH BROWN PATCHES, GENERALLY WITH TAN MARKINGS ON HEAD AND LEGS

POINTER : ENGLAND

Pointers are large, elite working dogs that, like most gun dog breeds, are hardwired to hunt. They were recorded in England in the 1650s, and were the first dogs known to be bred specifically to "stand" game: typically, they will locate game and then remain motionless to indicate its position to the hunter. Pointers have good, loyal, affectionate temperaments and can be suitable as companion dogs but only for extremely active homes.

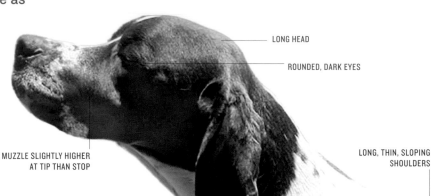

LONG HEAD

ROUNDED, DARK EYES

LONG, THIN, SLOPING SHOULDERS

MUZZLE SLIGHTLY HIGHER AT TIP THAN STOP

EARS SET AT EYE LEVEL AND HANG CLOSE TO HEAD

OVAL FEET

AT A GLANCE

Size: large

Amount of exercise:

Amount of grooming:
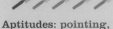

Aptitudes: pointing, hunting, retrieving, tracking, companion

Height: 45–75 in.

Weight: 26–33 lb.

Average life expectancy: 12–15 yrs

AKC: sporting

CHARACTER

Affection

Playfulness

Friendliness to dogs

Friendliness to strangers

Ease of training
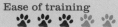

✚ HEALTH ✚

Generally healthy, but some hereditary problems can include hip dysplasia and entropion.

Pointer puppies are particularly mischievous and fun loving! Pointers need a lot of pysical and mental exercise and can be destructive if left alone for long periods.

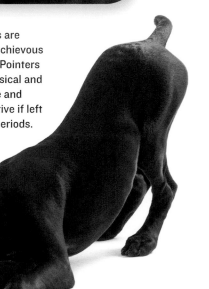

COMMON COAT COLORS

SOLID LIVER

ORANGE

BLACK & WHITE

Solid liver, lemon, black, or orange; or any of these colors in combination with white.

COAT CLOSE-UP

The Pointer's coat is short, dense, and smooth with a glossy sheen.

SHORT

HISTORY

Originally, Pointers in England were used for hunting hare in conjunction with Greyhounds. They were also used by falconers. Their heritage is not clear, but they probably developed from a mix of Fox Hound, Greyhound, Bloodhound, setter-types, and the Spanish Pointer. They became popular in the nineteenth century as working dogs when they were often used in pairs, and have changed very little in appearance since then. The breed is thought to have arrived in the United States during the Civil War. Sensation, a lemon-and-white Pointer, was imported from England in 1876, and became the Westminster Kennel Club emblem. The American Kennel Club recognized the breed in 1879.

BACK SLOPES SLIGHTLY FROM WITHERS TO CROUP

TAIL TAPERS TO TIP AND IS CARRIED IN LINE, OR JUST ABOVE BACK LINE

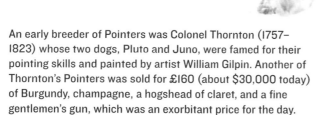

An early breeder of Pointers was Colonel Thornton (1757–1823) whose two dogs, Pluto and Juno, were famed for their pointing skills and painted by artist William Gilpin. Another of Thornton's Pointers was sold for £160 (about $30,000 today) of Burgundy, champagne, a hogshead of claret, and a fine gentlemen's gun, which was an exorbitant price for the day.

PONT-AUDEMER SPANIEL : FRANCE

The rare Pont-Audemer Spaniel is thought to have developed during the nineteenth century through a mixture of water-spaniel types and setters. After World War II, breed numbers were so low that other working breeds were introduced, but numbers remain low today and the Pont-Audemer breed club has now merged with the Picardy Spaniel breed club. Known in France as "the little clown of the marshes," the Pont-Audemer is an affectionate, vivacious, and fun-loving breed that excels when hunting in wet terrain.

LONG, SHINY COAT, SLIGHTLY WAXY, AND SMOOTH ON THE FACE

ROUNDED SKULL WITH CURLY TOPKNOT

SMALL, DARK-AMBER OR HAZEL EYES

LIVER OR LIVER AND WHITE, WITH OR WITHOUT TICKING

DEEP, BROAD CHEST

RELATIVELY SHORT FORELEGS

PORTUGUESE POINTER : PORTUGAL

Portuguese Pointers trace back to at least the twelfth century when they were initially bred by aristocrats. Over time, they were adopted by the working classes and became highly prized for their versatile hunting skills. The Portuguese pedigree book was established in 1932, and the standard in 1938, but the breed remains in relatively low numbers, certainly outside its homeland.

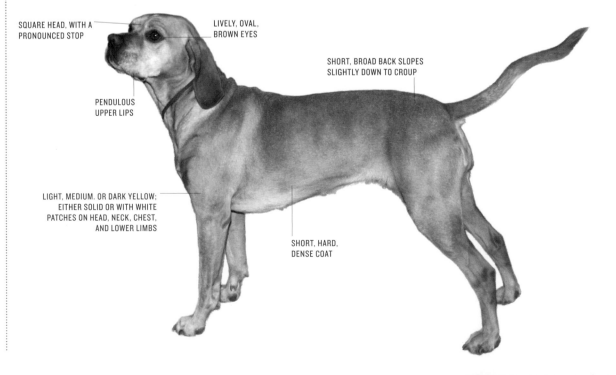

SQUARE HEAD, WITH A PRONOUNCED STOP

LIVELY, OVAL, BROWN EYES

SHORT, BROAD BACK SLOPES SLIGHTLY DOWN TO CROUP

PENDULOUS UPPER LIPS

LIGHT, MEDIUM, OR DARK YELLOW; EITHER SOLID OR WITH WHITE PATCHES ON HEAD, NECK, CHEST, AND LOWER LIMBS

SHORT, HARD, DENSE COAT

PORTUGUESE WATER DOG : PORTUGAL

The Portuguese Water Dog, also known as the Lion Dog, is an intelligent and energetic breed that—with its webbed feet, muscular frame, and water-resistant coat—is a superb water dog. Typically their coats are kept in a lion clip (the coat on hindquarters and muzzle is clipped to the skin) or a retriever clip (the entire coat is clipped to one inch) and requires a lot of attention. These are sociable, lively, friendly dogs that excel in many activities including hunting, obedience, service, assistance, and agility, and thrive when given a job to do.

BLACK OR BROWN EYES SET WIDE APART

LARGE HEAD

LEVEL, FIRM TOPLINE

POWERFUL HINDQUARTERS

SUBSTANTIAL MUZZLE

ROUND, FLAT, WEBBED FEET

AT A GLANCE

Size: small

Amount of exercise:

Amount of grooming:

Aptitudes: retrieving, assistance, service, agility, companion, watchdog

Height: 17–23 in.

Weight: 35–60 lb.

Average life expectancy: 12–15 yrs

AKC: working

CHARACTER

Affection

Playfulness

Friendliness to dogs

Friendliness to strangers

Ease of training
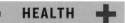

✚ HEALTH ✚

Generally healthy, some hereditary problems can include Addison's disease, progressive retinal atrophy, cancer, and hip dysplasia.

HISTORY

This ancient breed dates to pre-Christian times and is thought to have developed on the Central Asian steppes before spreading westward into Europe with the migrations of nomadic tribes. It is surmised that they share a heritage similar to the German Poodle and gave rise to the Irish Water Spaniel. In Portugal these dogs were widespread among fishing communities and an essential part of fishermen's lives. The dogs accompanied fishermen on their boats, helped to retrieve nets, carried tackle and messages between boats, guarded boats and homes, and even allegedly "herded" fish into nets. They are superbly water adapted and will dive to retrieve and swim with ease. With advancing technology, their role became less important, and the breed began to disappear. They were saved in the 1930s by Vasco Bensaude, a wealthy businessman who began breeding them in Portugal, and they first arrived in the United States in the late 1960s.

COMMON COAT COLORS

BLACK WITH WHITE   BROWN

Colors are black, white, tones of brown, or combinations of black or brown with white.

COAT CLOSE-UP

CURLY   WAVY

Profuse coat with no undercoat and two coat varieties: curly (compact, cylindrical, matt curls) and wavy (falling in gentle waves with a slight sheen).

Portuguese Water Dog puppies can be independent, lively, and like to "voice their opinion"!

AT A GLANCE

Size: medium, small, very small

Amount of exercise:

Amount of grooming:

Aptitudes: companion, retrieving, agility, service dog

Height: toy under 10 in. miniature 10–15 in. standard over 15 in.

Weight: toy 4–8 lb. miniature 12–18 lb. standard over 20 lb.

Average life expectancy: 12–15 yrs

AKC: non-sporting; toy

CHARACTER

Affection

Playfulness

Friendliness to dogs

Friendliness to strangers

Ease of training

✚ HEALTH ✚

Generally healthy, but hereditary problems can include hip dysplasia, cancer, Addison's disease, gastric torsion, thyroid issues, progressive retinol atrophy, and eyelid problems.

POODLE : GERMANY

Poodles are found in three sizes—Standard, Miniature, and Toy—but all share similar traits and can make excellent family pets. The breed is noted for its loyalty and intelligence. They are delightful with their loved ones, but can be standoffish with strangers, and are typically charismatic and full of character. Although the breed requirement for the Standard Poodle is over 15 inches in height, most Standard Poodles range from 20–26 inches and weigh up to 55 pounds. This breed is commonly thought of as French and rarely as a gun dog. However, with their great intelligence, Poodles make excellent gun dogs and their origins trace back to Germany, where they were originally bred as water-retrieving dogs—a role at which they still excel.

LONG, WIDE, AND THICKLY FEATHERED EARS HANG CLOSE TO THE HEAD

LEVEL TOPLINE

HIGH-SET, STRAIGHT TAIL

SQUARELY BUILT AND WELL-PROPORTIONED IN APPEARANCE

DEEP, WIDE CHEST

FEET ARE SMALL AND OVAL WITH WELL-ARCHED TOES

STANDARD

COMMON COAT COLORS

BLUE

GRAY

BROWN

CAFÉ-AU-LAIT

APRICOT

CREAM

WHITE

Can be any solid color, including blue, gray, brown, café-au-lait, apricot, cream, and white.

Poodle puppies under one year old can be shown in a "puppy clip": the coat is long except for the face, throat, feet, and the base of the tail, which are shaved. The classic poodle tail has a distinctive "pompom" on the end.

TOY   **MINIATURE**   **STANDARD**

VERY DARK, OVAL-SHAPED EYES WITH AN INTELLIGENT EXPRESSION

CORDED

HISTORY

Poodles derive their name from the German word *pudel*, meaning to "splash in water," and are believed to share a similar heritage to other water-retrieving breeds, such as the Portuguese Water Dog, Irish Water Spaniel, Hungarian Water Hound, and French Barbet. The Poodle became popular in France during the eighteenth century, where it was known as the *Chien Canard*, meaning "duck dog." France became the breed's surrogate home, and the French Fédération Cynologique Internationale recognizes France as the breed's country of origin.

COAT CLOSE-UP

A curly coat is curly, harsh, and dense; a corded coat hangs in tight even cords of different lengths.

CURLY   **CORDED**

PUDELPOINTER : GERMANY

The versatile Pudelpointer was developed in Germany in the late nineteenth century by crossing working German Poodles with English Pointers. This combination produced a dog with great intelligence, trainability, and a range of hunting skills. Pudelpointers work superbly both on land and in water on a variety of game. They also make wonderful companions for active homes. The breed was introduced to the United States in 1956 by Bobo Winterhelt.

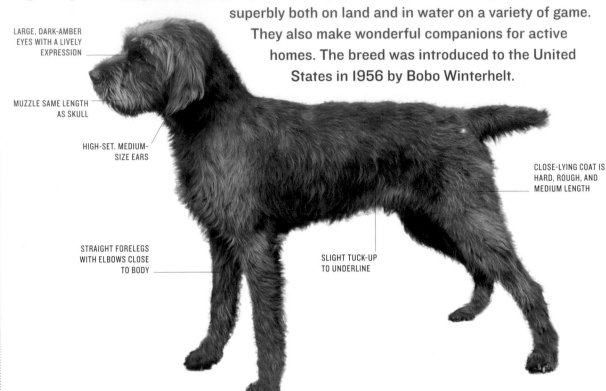

LARGE, DARK-AMBER EYES WITH A LIVELY EXPRESSION

MUZZLE SAME LENGTH AS SKULL

HIGH-SET, MEDIUM-SIZE EARS

CLOSE-LYING COAT IS HARD, ROUGH, AND MEDIUM LENGTH

STRAIGHT FORELEGS WITH ELBOWS CLOSE TO BODY

SLIGHT TUCK-UP TO UNDERLINE

RUSSIAN SPANIEL : RUSSIA

The Russian Spaniel was developed in the twentieth century based on crossbreeding a variety of spaniels, including the English Cocker and English Springer Spaniel. They are popular in Russia where they are used as all-around gun dogs, working on marshy terrain, woodland, and uplands, and will hunt and retrieve all types of small game. True to Spaniel nature, these dogs are affectionate, cheerful, and lively companions who thrive leading busy, preferably working lives.

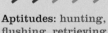

BROAD HEAD, FLAT ON TOP

FLAT, SILKY, SOFT COAT

COMPACT BODY

VARIES FROM SOLIDS TO TRICOLORS

DEEP CHEST, NOT TOO WIDE

LEVEL TOPLINE

AT A GLANCE

Size: medium-small

Amount of exercise:
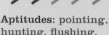

Amount of grooming:

Aptitudes: pointing, hunting, flushing, retrieving, agility, companion

Height: 16–21 in.

Weight: not specified

Average life expectancy: 13–15 yrs

AKC: not recognized

CHARACTER

Affection

Playfulness

Friendliness to dogs

Friendliness to strangers
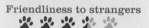

Ease of training
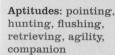

SAINT-USUGE SPANIEL : FRANCE

This small French pointing breed is thought to date back to the sixteenth century, although it had almost disappeared by the end of World War II. The breed was restored through the efforts of Robert Billiard, who found some of the remaining dogs and started a breeding initiative. The Saint-Usuge Spaniel is an intelligent, affectionate, and obedient breed that can work over a variety of terrains including forests, uplands, swamps, and in water. They are best suited to waterfowl and woodcock hunting, although they retrieve any small furred or feathered game.

STRAIGHT TOPLINE

FLAT, TRIANGULAR EARS

BROWN, OR BROWN WITH WHITE MARKINGS

BROAD, WELL-DEVELOPED CHEST

MEDIUM-LONG, SILKY COAT

AT A GLANCE

Size: large

Amount of exercise:

Amount of grooming:

Aptitudes: pointing, hunting, flushing, retrieving, agility, companion

Height: 25–27 in.

Weight: 55–75 lb.

Average life expectancy: over 12–14 yrs

AKC: not recognized

CHARACTER

Affection

Playfulness

Friendliness to dogs

Friendliness to strangers

Ease of training

SLOVAKIAN ROUGH-HAIRED POINTER : SLOVAKIA

This relatively new breed was developed during the second half of the twentieth century in Slovakia by combining Weimaraners, German Wirehaired Pointers, and Cesky Fouseks. More recently there has been the addition of Pudelpointer and more Weimaraner to the breed to increase the gene pool. The combined qualities from all these breeds has made the Slovakian Rough Haired Pointer a tenacious gun dog with great stamina that works on land and in water, hunting a variety of game, including deer. Typically these dogs have excellent temperaments but require very active home lives.

DISTINGUISHED HEAD WITH BEARD AND PROMINENT EYEBROWS

INTELLIGENT EYES RANGE FROM LIGHT TO DEEP AMBER

LONGER IN BODY THAN TALL

MODERATE LENGTH, HARSH, WIRY COAT

ANY SHADE BETWEEN GRAY-BROWN AND PEWTER-SILVER

STABYHOUN : NETHERLANDS

The Stabyhoun, which is thought to have developed in the 1800s in Friesland, in the northwestern Netherlands, was highly regarded as a multipurpose dog by farmers and the working classes. Small enough to keep easily, yet large enough to be useful guard dogs, they were used for hunting on land and in water, for watching over homes, and as affectionate companions. They are highly intelligent as a breed and excel in many different types of sport and activities, such as hunting, agility, endurance, and obedience tests.

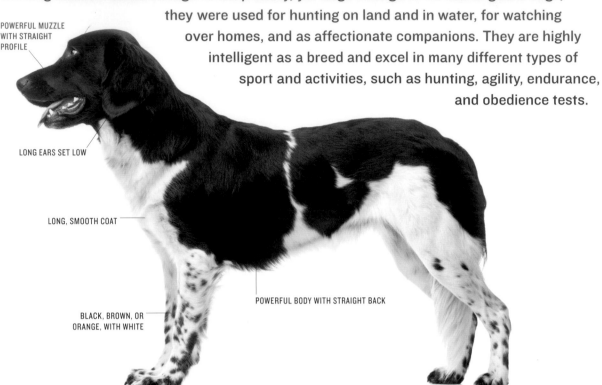

POWERFUL MUZZLE WITH STRAIGHT PROFILE

LONG EARS SET LOW

LONG, SMOOTH COAT

BLACK, BROWN, OR ORANGE, WITH WHITE

POWERFUL BODY WITH STRAIGHT BACK

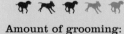
WELSH SPRINGER SPANIEL : WALES

The ancestors to the Welsh Springer Spaniel trace far back in history to some of the earliest hunting breeds, and developed in the relative isolation of their homeland. Red and white dogs with a similar appearance can be seen in paintings from Renaissance times. By the 1700s, the Welsh was popular with the aristocracy, but gradually, the English Springer began to take over. There are fewer Welsh Springers than English now, but they are a similarly versatile breed that can make a wonderful working gun dog or an affectionate family pet in a active home.

STRAIGHT, FLAT, AND SOFT COAT   RICH RED AND WHITE   TAIL CARRIED HORIZONTALLY OR SLIGHTLY ELEVATED

LONG, SLIGHTLY ARCHED NECK   MEDIUM-LENGTH FOREARMS   ROUND FEET

AT A GLANCE

Size: medium-small

Amount of exercise:

Amount of grooming:

Aptitudes: flushing, hunting, retrieving, companion

Height: 13–15 in.

Weight: 35–45 lb.

Average life expectancy: 11–13 yrs

AKC: sporting

CHARACTER

Affection

Playfulness

Friendliness to dogs

Friendliness to strangers
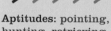

Ease of training

SUSSEX SPANIEL : ENGLAND

The Sussex Spaniel is named after the county in England where the breed was developed and traces back to the eighteenth century. An influential figure in the breed's history was Augustus Fuller who bred them for fifty years at his kennels in Sussex, using the dogs for hunting on foot on his large estate. The Sussex was one of the original nine breeds recognized by the American Kennel Club in 1884. Nowadays, it is one of the less commonly seen Spaniel breeds, but it is a good, slow, methodical working dog with a great nose that is also suitable as a companion.

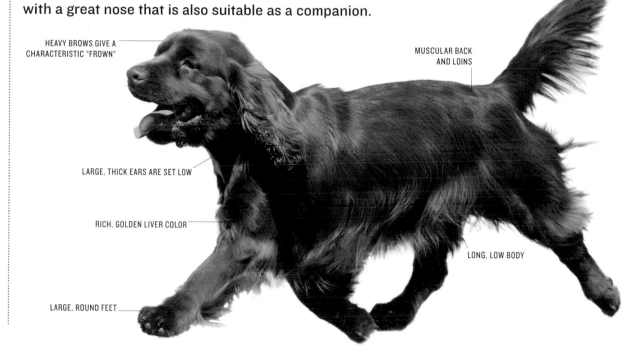

HEAVY BROWS GIVE A CHARACTERISTIC "FROWN"

MUSCULAR BACK AND LOINS

LARGE, THICK EARS ARE SET LOW

RICH, GOLDEN LIVER COLOR

LONG, LOW BODY

LARGE, ROUND FEET

AT A GLANCE

Size: large

Amount of exercise:

Amount of grooming:

Aptitudes: pointing, hunting, retrieving, companion

Height: 22–27 in.

Weight: 62–82 lb.

Average life expectancy: 12–14 yrs

AKC: sporting

CHARACTER

Affection

Playfulness

Friendliness to dogs

Friendliness to strangers

Ease of training

SPINONE ITALIANO : ITALY

This all-purpose hunting dog is highly regarded for its exceptional sense of smell. The Spinone Italiano works in a steady, methodical manner and is one of the slower, but no less effective, gun-dog breeds. They are believed to trace back to Roman times, and have clear pointing blood in their heritage. They are charismatic and endearing, with excellent temperaments that match their very versatile hunting skills, which include working in water and on a variety of terrains. They also make very good family companions.

BULBOUS AND SPONGY NOSE

SLIGHTLY ROMAN MUZZLE

STRONG, THICK, AND MUSCULAR NECK

TOPLINE SLOPES DOWN FROM WITHERS THEN GRADUALLY BACK UP TO AN ARCHED LOIN

TAIL CARRIED HORIZONTALLY OR DOWNWARD

THICK PROTECTIVE SKIN

AT A GLANCE

Size: large

Amount of exercise:

Amount of grooming:

Aptitudes: hunting, pointing, retrieving, agility, companion

Height: 23–27 in.

Weight: 55–90 lb.

Average life expectancy: 10–13 yrs

AKC: sporting

CHARACTER

Affection

Playfulness

Friendliness to dogs

Friendliness to strangers

Ease of training

✚ HEALTH ✚

Generally healthy, but some hereditary problems can include hip dysplasia and gastric torsion.

WEIMARANER : GERMANY

Weimaraners developed as a result of careful and selective breeding, leading to one of the most perfect combinations of working-dog ability, companion-dog temperament, and irresistible good looks. The breed is distinctive as a result of its unusual coat coloring, which ranges from silver-gray to mouse-gray with a beautiful metallic sheen, and has led to the breed being referred to as "gray ghosts." Weimaraners can also be long haired, with that variety recognized in all countries except the United States. Weimaraners excel as working gun dogs and are an intelligent and obedient breed with good stamina. Equally, they have lovely temperaments and are loyal, affectionate, and playful companions.

AMBER, GRAY, OR BLUE-GRAY EYES SET WIDE APART

LONG, NOBLE HEAD

LONG, LOBULAR EARS, SLIGHTLY FOLDED AND SET HIGH

DEEP CHEST

SHORTHAIRED WEIMARANER

Weimaraner puppies form exceptionally strong bonds with their owners, usually more so than with other dogs.

COMMON COAT COLORS

Coat colors are solid and range from mouse-gray to silver-gray.

MOUSE-GRAY   **SILVER**

POWERFUL BODY SLOPES SLIGHTLY
FROM WITHERS TO LOINS

LONGHAIRED WEIMARANER

UNDERLINE SHOWS
TUCK-UP

WELL-ANGULATED STIFLES

HOCKS WELL
LET DOWN

HISTORY

Little is known about the Weimaraners' early history, but they are said to have developed in the seventeenth century from early hunting dogs and bear a close resemblance to dogs in paintings from this period. The St. Hubert Hound from Belgium, which gave rise to the Bloodhound, along with old German and French hounds are often cited as the breed's ancestors. Their traceable history begins with Karl August, Grand Duke of Saxe-Weimar-Eisenach (1757–1828), who kept large kennels where he bred elite hunting dogs. These dogs were called "gray hunting dogs" and were the foundation for the modern Weimaraner. Originally, they were used for hunting big game such as bears, wolves, and wildcats. The breed was controlled and bred only by German aristocrats with the breed standard drawn up in 1896. American hunter Howard Knight was the first to import the breed to the United States, with the earliest breeding stock arriving in 1938. The Weimaraner was recognized by the American Kennel Club in 1943.

COAT CLOSE-UP

The short coat is sleek and smooth with a metallic sheen. The long-haired coat is soft and smooth, or slightly wavy.

SLEEK

WAVY

CHARACTER

Affection

Playfulness

Friendliness to dogs

Friendliness to strangers

Ease of training

✚ HEALTH ✚

Generally healthy, but hereditary problems can include hip dysplasia, epilepsy, and polymyositis.

Vizsla puppies need at least two hours of interactive, lively play with their owners every day.

VIZSLA : HUNGARY

The Vizsla has had a history of highs and lows, facing near-extinction in the twentieth century, but has since been re-established through careful breeding and is now the national dog of Hungary. These are affectionate and lively dogs that thrive on learning and working, and are best suited to an active lifestyle. The Vizsla is a versatile gun dog that works in water as well as on land and exhibits excellent pointing and retrieving skills on a range of furred and feathered game. Vizlas can make very good family dogs but do require extensive exercise.

MEDIUM-SIZE EYES BLEND WITH COAT COLOR

THIN, SILKY EARS, PROPORTIONATELY LONG

STRONG, ARCHED NECK

BODY SLIGHTLY LONGER THAN HEIGHT AT WITHERS

TAIL CARRIED HORIZONTALLY WHEN MOVING

SQUARE, DEEP MUZZLE TAPERS SLIGHTLY TO BROWN NOSE

UNDERLINE HAS SLIGHT TUCK-UP

BROAD, DEEP CHEST

HISTORY

Vizslas are an ancient breed that probably traces back to the Magyar people from western and central Asia. The breed's heritage is likely of mastiff and hound-dog crosses. By 895 CE the Magyar had arrived in the Carpathian Basin where they settled, farmed, and hunted, breeding their dogs to fulfill a range of roles. The earliest reference to a Vizsla dates to 1350 in a village of the same name on the Danube River. By the eighteenth century, the "golden" dogs had become the preserve of the aristocracy. All modern Vizslas in Hungary trace to three males and nine females that were selectively bred in the early twentieth century. The first of the breed arrived in the United States in the 1950s, and they were recognized by the American Kennel Club in 1960.

COMMON COAT COLORS

Varying shades of golden rust.

LIGHT RUST

RED RUST

COAT CLOSE-UP

The coat is short, dense, and smooth.

DENSE & SMOOTH

AT A GLANCE

Size: medium

Amount of exercise:

Amount of grooming:

Aptitudes: hunting,
pointing, retrieving,
companion

Height: 21–25 in.

Weight: 40–55 lb.

Average life expectancy:
12–15 yrs

AKC: FSS

CHARACTER

Affection

Playfulness

Friendliness to dogs

Friendliness to strangers

Ease of training

WIREHAIRED VIZSLA : HUNGARY

This charismatic breed traces to the 1930s when it was developed to combine all the excellent qualities of the Vizsla with a more robust frame and weather-resistant coat. As such, the Wirehaired Vizsla is similar to the smooth-coated variety, but better suited for water retrieving, and working in dense undergrowth, harsh terrain, or frigid winter conditions. The breed's foundation traces to two female Vizslas that were bred to a solid-colored wirehaired German Pointer. The Wirehaired Vizsla is not seen as often as the smooth-coated breed, but is a superb working dog that makes a wonderful companion.

EARS HANG CLOSE TO CHEEKS

DISTINCTIVE BEARD AND EYEBROWS

DENSE, WIRY COAT

GOLDEN RUST IN VARIOUS SHADES

UPPER ARM IS WELL MUSCLED

CAT-LIKE FEET

AT A GLANCE

Size: medium

Amount of exercise:

Amount of grooming:

Aptitudes: hunting,
pointing, retrieving,
companion

Height: 20–24 in.

Weight: 50–60 lb.

Average life expectancy:
12–14 yrs

AKC: sporting

CHARACTER

Affection

Playfulness

Friendliness to dogs

Friendliness to strangers

Ease of training

WIREHAIRED POINTING GRIFFON : NETHERLANDS/FRANCE

LARGE, FRIENDLY EYES

SQUARE-SHAPED HEAD WITH MOUSTACHE AND EYEBROWS

STEEL GRAY WITH BROWN MARKINGS, CHESTNUT BROWN, ROAN, WHITE AND BROWN, WHITE AND ORANGE, BROWN, WHITE

TOPLINE SLOPES DOWN GENTLY FROM WITHERS TO TAIL BASE

LONG, STRAIGHT FORELEGS SET WELL UNDER SHOULDERS

ROUND FEET WITH WEBBED TOES

This breed's ancestors are mentioned as early as 500 BCE, but the modern development of the breed traces only to the nineteenth century and Eduard Korthals, an avid hunter. Korthals wanted to produce a hunting dog with a protective coat and plenty of stamina that could work on all terrains, including in water, in marshes, and on uplands. He bred griffons, spaniels, setters and German and French pointers to achieve his desired result, and then marketed the new dog across Europe. Today the breed is not widely known but is none-the-less a superb gun dog and an excellent companion.

HERDING AND GUARDING DOGS

AIDI : MOROCCO

Also known as the Atlas Mountain Dog, Aidis are rarely heard of beyond their homeland of Morocco, but they share similar characteristics with other mountain dog breeds. The breed is of ancient origin and has been used for guarding livestock and hunting, often in conjunction with sight hounds such as Sloughis. The Aidi is noted for its acute sense of smell and for its bravery—it will protect its family, homestead, and livestock against a range of predators, including wild cats. Aidis can make good companion dogs for an active family.

"BEAR" HEAD WITH A BROAD, FLAT SKULL

MUZZLE IS SHORTER THAN SKULL WITH THIN PIGMENTED LIPS

EYES VARY IN COLOR FROM AMBER THROUGH BROWN

POWERFUL JAWS

VERY DENSE, HARSH AND MODERATELY LONG COAT

NOTICEABLY ROUND FEET

AKBASH : TURKEY

The Akbash is an ancient breed that has been used for many centuries to guard livestock across the rugged interior of Turkey. The dogs live among the livestock, often unsupervised for long periods of time, and are renowned for their bravery in warding off predators. It is believed that the breed has both sight hound and Mastiff in its heritage and exhibits some characteristics from each. These dogs are large and independent and are not suitable for first-time dog owners, although they can make companions with consistent training and socialization.

WEDGE-SHAPED HEAD

ALMOND-SHAPED, BROWN EYES

V-SHAPED, PENDENT EARS

BROAD, WEDGE-SHAPED MUZZLE

TALL, LONG LEGGED, AND MUSCULAR IN APPEARANCE

DOUBLE COAT WITH A DENSE, SOFT UNDERCOAT AND LONGER, COARSER GUARD HAIRS

AMERICAN MASTIFF : UNITED STATES

Although the Mastiff is an ancient breed, the American Mastiff is a relatively recent addition that is now recognized by the Continental Kennel Club. The breed owes its origins to Fredericka Wagner of Flying W Farms in Piketon, Ohio, who used English Mastiffs and Anatolian Mastiffs as the new breed's foundation. Her goal was to create a Mastiff breed of sound health and temperament that produced less slobber than other Mastiff breeds. The American Mastiff is a quiet and dignified breed with a calm, affectionate temperament and protective instincts. These dogs make good companions for people who can provide them with enough space.

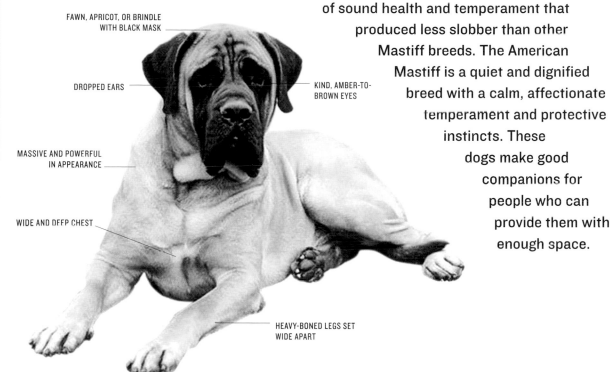

FAWN, APRICOT, OR BRINDLE WITH BLACK MASK

DROPPED EARS

KIND, AMBER-TO-BROWN EYES

MASSIVE AND POWERFUL IN APPEARANCE

WIDE AND DEEP CHEST

HEAVY-BONED LEGS SET WIDE APART

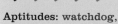
ALAPAHA BLUE BLOOD BULLDOG : UNITED STATES

The early history of this American breed is unclear, but it is most associated with the South. It is believed that its roots trace back to old bulldog types that were introduced to the United States in the 1800s. These bulldog types were continuously bred for working ability, stamina, and bravery until a distinct type began to emerge. They are versatile working dogs with a particularly high guarding instinct that makes them excellent hunters. They can also be good companions for active homes.

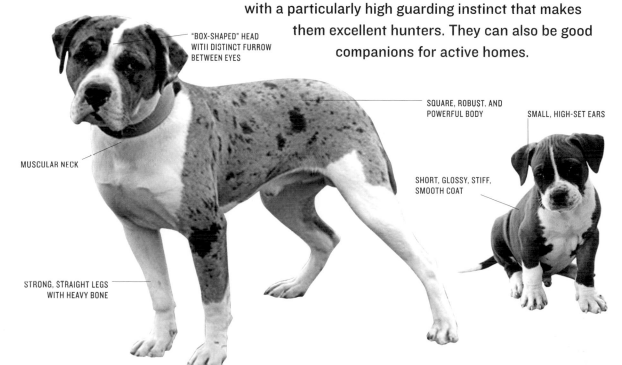

"BOX-SHAPED" HEAD WITH DISTINCT FURROW BETWEEN EYES

SQUARE, ROBUST, AND POWERFUL BODY

SMALL, HIGH-SET EARS

MUSCULAR NECK

SHORT, GLOSSY, STIFF, SMOOTH COAT

STRONG, STRAIGHT LEGS WITH HEAVY BONE

CHARACTER

Affection

Playfulness

Friendliness to dogs

Friendliness to strangers

Ease of training

✚ HEALTH ✚

Generally healthy, but
hereditary problems can
include hip and elbow
dysplasia, entropion, and
cancer.

AMERICAN BULLDOG : UNITED STATES

The American Bulldog is a powerful and athletic breed that benefits from mental as well as physical challenges. This breed is relatively quiet when at rest and in the home, but requires a fairly high amount of daily exercise and plenty of diversions. These are powerful dogs that can make excellent companions as long as they are properly socialized, supervised, and exercised. They have a strong pack instinct and will protect their families and property with vigor. There are two types of American Bulldog, the Standard and the Bully. The Bully is larger, heavier, and has a shorter muzzle.

MEDIUM-SIZE EARS SET HIGH ON HEAD

BROAD MUZZLE WITH WIDE OPEN NOSTRILS

"PUMP-HANDLE" TAIL

BROWN, ALMOND-SHAPED TO ROUND EYES

BROAD HEAD WITH PRONOUNCED MUSCULAR CHEEKS

DEEP, MODERATELY WIDE CHEST

COMPACT BODY

BROAD, WELL-MUSCLED HINDQUARTERS

American Bulldogs can have large litters, producing an average of eleven puppies.

HISTORY

The breed traces back to the early bulldog types brought over to the United States during colonization. The dogs were required to be versatile working farm dogs and were used for protecting homes and livestock, herding cattle, hunting large game, and serving as companions. Sadly, they have also been used for illicit fighting. One man, John D. Johnston, was particularly influential in the development of the modern breed through his breeding initiative shortly after World War II. This helped to stabilize the dwindling population of American Bulldogs, and they now have a dedicated following.

COMMON COAT COLORS

Any color, including brindle, fawn, brown, black, and parti-colored.

PARTI-COLORED   FAWN

COAT CLOSE-UP

The coat is short and smooth.

SMOOTH

ANATOLIAN SHEPHERD DOG : TURKEY

Size: very large

Exercise needed:

Grooming needed:

Aptitudes: guarding livestock, watchdog, companion

Height: 27–29 in.

Weight: 80–150 lb.

Average life expectancy: 10–13 yrs

AKC: working

CHARACTER

Affection

Playfulness

Friendliness to dogs

Friendliness to strangers

Ease of training

This is an ancient breed that originated in Turkey and is perfectly adapted to the harsh climate and difficult terrain of its home. The Anatolian Shepherd has been bred to guard livestock, living unsupervised among the herd, and is incredibly tough with great endurance. They can make good companion animals but thrive when given a job to do. They are very loyal and protective toward their families, but are also intelligent, independent thinkers and do not always respond to commands!

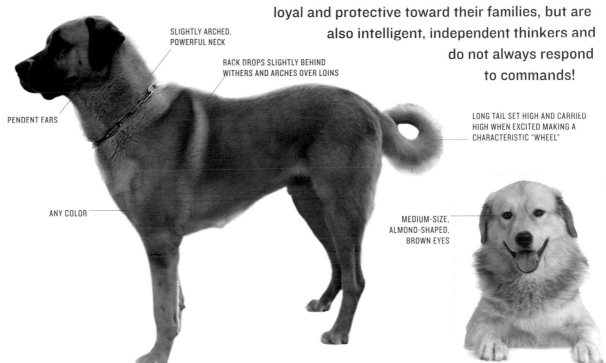

SLIGHTLY ARCHED, POWERFUL NECK

BACK DROPS SLIGHTLY BEHIND WITHERS AND ARCHES OVER LOINS

PENDENT EARS

LONG TAIL SET HIGH AND CARRIED HIGH WHEN EXCITED MAKING A CHARACTERISTIC "WHEEL"

ANY COLOR

MEDIUM-SIZE, ALMOND-SHAPED, BROWN EYES

APPENZELLER SENNENHUND : SWITZERLAND

Size: medium

Exercise needed:

Grooming needed:

Aptitudes: herding, guarding livestock, watchdog, companion

Height: 20–22 in.

Weight: 48–70 lb.

Average life expectancy: 12–14 yrs

AKC: FSS

CHARACTER

Affection

Playfulness

Friendliness to dogs

Friendliness to strangers

Ease of training

The Appenzeller Sennenhund is one of four Swiss mountain-dog breeds that all trace back to the ancient Molossers and are multipurpose working farm dogs. They have been used for centuries to guard and herd livestock, to watch over homes, and farms, and to undertake a range of farm work. They are intelligent and enduring dogs that are incredibly loyal to their families. Playful and lively, they are suitable as companions for active, experienced homes.

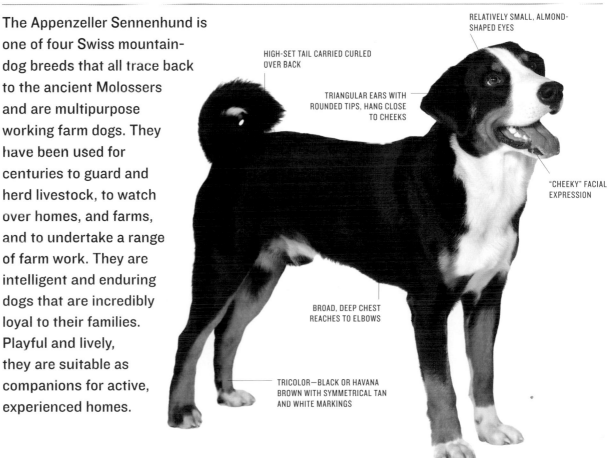

HIGH-SET TAIL CARRIED CURLED OVER BACK

RELATIVELY SMALL, ALMOND-SHAPED EYES

TRIANGULAR EARS WITH ROUNDED TIPS, HANG CLOSE TO CHEEKS

"CHEEKY" FACIAL EXPRESSION

BROAD, DEEP CHEST REACHES TO ELBOWS

TRICOLOR—BLACK OR HAVANA BROWN WITH SYMMETRICAL TAN AND WHITE MARKINGS

AUSTRALIAN WORKING KELPIE : AUSTRALIA

PRICKED EARS WITH THE INSIDE OF THE EAR COVERED WITH HAIR

MUSCULAR FOREQUARTERS WITH SLOPING SHOULDERS

SHORT, FLAT, AND STRAIGHT COAT

FORELEGS ARE MUSCULAR AND STRONG WITH REFINED BONE

BLACK, SHADES OF BLUE (GRAY), SHADES OF RED, SHADES OF FAWN, MAY HAVE TAN MARKINGS

This breed traces back to three pairs of working Collies imported to Australia by early settlers. From their descendants, and from the introduction of other working Scottish dogs, there developed a breed suited to working large numbers of sheep with great efficiency. The Australian Working Kelpie will work all day without flagging, often in extreme heat, and can move enormous flocks with intelligence and dexterity. These are very quick-witted dogs that require a lot of exercise and mental stimulation to thrive.

AUSTRALIAN STUMPY TAIL CATTLE DOG : AUSTRALIA

These dogs were bred specifically with working ability and not appearance in mind. Some of the naturally occurring stumpy-tailed dogs were excellent cattle dogs, which led to ranchers continuing the lines. Eventually two clear breeds began to develop and to exhibit their own characteristics in addition to the tail length. Today, Stumpies are relatively rare, particularly overseas, but they are supported by dedicated breed clubs. They can make wonderful companion animals, as long as they have active home lives.

MODERATELY SMALL, PRICKED EARS

BLUNT, STRONG MUZZLE

POWERFUL JAWS

WELL-BONED, MUSCULAR FORELEGS

POWERFUL, MUSCULAR HINDQUARTERS

BLUE, RED, OR TAN

AUSTRALIAN CATTLE DOG : AUSTRALIA

The Australian Cattle Dog is also called a Blue Heeler, Australian Heeler, or Queensland Heeler, and is one of the most efficient stock dog breeds in the world. They were developed during the nineteenth century through careful selective breeding, specifically to work cattle. In addition to their superb working skills, Australian Cattle Dogs are also efficient watchdogs and protective of their homes and vehicles. They can make excellent family companions, but require substantial exercise and diversions. They can also make very good agility dogs.

AT A GLANCE

AT A GLANCE

Size: medium

Exercise needed:

Grooming needed:

Aptitudes: herding, watchdog, agility, companion

Height: 17–20 in.

Weight: 35–45 lb.

Average life expectancy: 11–13 yrs

AKC: herding

CHARACTER

Affection

Playfulness

Friendliness to dogs

Friendliness to strangers

Ease of training

✚ HEALTH ✚

Generally healthy, but hereditary problems can include hip and elbow dysplasia, progressive retinol atrophy, and deafness.

DARK, OVAL EYES WITH AN INTELLIGENT EXPRESSION

PRICKED EARS, BROAD AT BASE, SET WIDE APART

SLOPING SHOULDERS

BROAD MUSCULAR HINDQUARTERS

MEDIUM LENGTH MUZZLE

VERY STRONG NECK

DENSE, STRONG LEG BONES

DEEP CHEST

COMPACT AND ATHLETIC IN APPEARANCE

Puppies are born white but develop their color within a few weeks of birth.

HISTORY

The Australian Cattle Dog traces to the working breeds brought to Australia with early settlers, particularly a type of Collie known as a Smithfield, which took its name from Smithfield market in London, England. Smithfields were crossed with Australian Dingos, and Rough and Smooth Collies from Scotland, to produce good, non-barking working dogs that became known as Hall's Heelers and were increasingly popular among cattlemen. This basic stock was influenced by Dalmatians and, most significantly, black-and-tan Kelpies. The result was a unique looking working dog with a Dingo-type appearance and unusual coloring. A breed standard was drawn up in 1902, and in the 1960s the Australian Cattle Dog Club of America was established.

COMMON COAT COLORS

BLUE

BLUE MOTTLED

RED SPECKLED

Australian Cattle Dogs can be blue or blue mottled, or red speckled, with or without other markings.

COAT CLOSE-UP

DENSE

Short and coarse double coat, with dense undercoat. Coat is short and hard.

AT A GLANCE

Size: medium

Exercise needed:

Grooming needed:
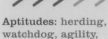

Aptitudes: herding, watchdog, agility, assistance, service, companion

Height: 18–23 in.

Weight: 40–65 lb.

Average life expectancy: 12–15 yrs

AKC: herding

CHARACTER

Affection

Playfulness

Friendliness to dogs

Friendliness to strangers

Ease of training

✚ HEALTH ✚

Generally healthy, but hereditary problems can include hip dysplasia, cataracts, epilepsy, thyroid disease, cancer, and drug sensitivity.

AUSTRALIAN SHEPHERD : UNITED STATES

Despite its name, the Australian Shepherd was developed in the United States and is a particularly versatile working breed. These dogs excel at herding sheep, although they can be used with cattle, and are extremely intelligent and easily trained. The "Aussie" is an active breed that is suited to family life as long as they are given enough exercise and distractions; they also tend to be very good with children and other animals. They excel at activities such as agility and obedience and have been used as assistance dogs and service dogs. The Aussie does best when it is being challenged mentally and physically.

STRAIGHT, STRONG, AND LEVEL BACK

WIDTH OF HINDQUARTERS IS EQUAL TO WIDTH OF FOREQUARTERS AT SHOULDER

Australian shepherds can be particularly attractive with their thick, colorful, coats and striking brown, blue, or amber eyes, but they are working dogs at heart and will thrive as companions only with the most active families.

OVAL FEET WITH WELL-ARCHED TOES

COMMON COAT COLORS

BLUE MERLE & TAN

BLACK TRI-COLORED

RED & WHITE

RED MERLE

Coat can be blue merle, black, red, or red merle, with or without white markings and tan points.

COAT CLOSE-UP

STRAIGHT   **WAVY**

Medium-length, straight to wavy topcoat, with dense undercoat.

TRIANGULAR EARS SET HIGH

HISTORY

The Aussie has a roundabout history that truly began in Europe with the sheep-herding Basque people of the Pyrenees. In the 1800s large numbers of Basque people settled in Australia, taking their sheep and sheepdogs with them. During the same period, many moved from Australia to the western United States, again taking their dogs with them. The working qualities and endurance of their dogs caught the attention of American ranchers who began to breed and use them. With the popularization of Western horse riding and culture following World War II, the breed came into the public eye and has just gotten stronger in the years since. They are an extremely docile and trainable breed, which has greatly contributed to their popularity.

ALMOND-SHAPED EYES CAN BE BROWN, BLUE, OR AMBER IN ANY COMBINATION WITH FLECKS AND MARBLING

MUZZLE IS EQUAL IN LENGTH OR SLIGHTLY SHORTER THAN HEAD

DEEP, BUT NOT BROAD CHEST

Aussies are very smart and lively. They are adept at outsmarting their owners, so it is essential that Aussie puppies go through obedience training.

AT A GLANCE

Size: large

Exercise needed:

Grooming needed:

Aptitudes: herding, guarding livestock, watchdog, service, companion

Height: 24–28 in.

Weight: 65–85 lb.

Average life expectancy: 10–12 yrs

AKC: herding

CHARACTER

Affection

Playfulness

Friendliness to dogs

Friendliness to strangers

Ease of training

BEAUCERON : FRANCE

The intelligent and brave Beauceron is the largest of the French sheepdog breeds and dates back to at least 1578, when it was first mentioned in a French manuscript. The breed has developed with no influence from other foreign breeds and is thought to have originated in La Beauce, the plains region surrounding Paris. By the nineteenth century there were two types of French working breeds, the short-coated Beauceron and the long-coated Briard, each sharing similar histories. The Beauceron was an all-purpose farm dog used for herding, for guarding livestock and property, and as a companion. They are obedient dogs and have been used by the French military in the past. They can make good companions but must be properly socialized and require a lot of exercise.

HIGH-SET EARS

DARK, OVAL-SHAPED EYES

LONG, WELL-CHISELED HEAD

STRAIGHT, STRONG BACK

MUSCULAR FOREARMS

LARGE, ROUND FEET

AT A GLANCE

Size: medium-large

Exercise needed:

Grooming needed:
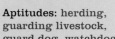

Aptitudes: herding, guarding livestock, guard dog, watchdog, agility, companion

Height: 22–24 in.

Weight: 57–84 lb.

Average life expectancy: 13–14 yrs

AKC: FSS

CHARACTER

Affection

Playfulness

Friendliness to dogs

Friendliness to strangers

Ease of training

BERGAMASCO SHEPHERD : ITALY

These extremely intelligent sheepdogs have distinctive long, thick, felt-like protective coats that insulate them from the weather and act as protective "armor." This ancient breed traditionally cared for huge flocks of sheep, solving problems independently. As a result, the Bergamasco is a quick-thinking breed that is protective and shows great devotion to its family. These dogs can make good companions for an active home but need to be properly socialized and obedience trained.

STRONG, SLIGHTLY ARCHED NECK

TOPLINE INCLINES SLIGHTLY FROM PROMINENT WITHERS TO A BROAD BACK

SOFT, THIN EARS HANG CLOSE TO FACE

LONG, WIDE, AND WELL-MUSCLED UPPER THIGH

MASSIVE, STRONG SHOULDERS

COAT HAS THREE TYPES OF HAIR: UNDERCOAT, "GOAT HAIR," AND OUTER COAT

AT A GLANCE

Size: medium

Exercise needed:

Grooming needed:

Aptitudes: herding, watchdog, trials, agility, companion

Height: 20–22 in.

Weight: 45–55 lb.

Average life expectancy: 12–14 yrs

AKC: herding

CHARACTER

Affection

Playfulness

Friendliness to dogs

Friendliness to strangers

Ease of training

✚ HEALTH ✚

Generally healthy but hereditary problems can include hip dysplasia, epilepsy, cataracts, and colonic disease.

BEARDED COLLIE : SCOTLAND

The "Beardie" is a versatile breed that primarily works sheep, though also cattle, and makes a wonderful companion animal for the right, dedicated home. These dogs excel in sheepdog trials and agility events and are clever and independent. These characteristics can work in their favor if they are properly obedience trained, but can be disastrous if they are not! Beardies have a charismatic, fun-loving, and enthusiastic nature and thrive when being physically and mentally challenged.

BROAD HEAD

LARGE EYES BLEND WITH COAT COLOR

BODY IS LONGER THAN IT IS TALL

SQUARE NOSE

LEVEL TOPLINE

MUSCULAR HINDQUARTERS

DISTINCTIVE, LONG, FLAT COAT

Puppies are born black, brown, blue, or fawn, but with age, these colors will lighten and fade.

HISTORY

Beardies are believed to have developed from the long-haired sheepdog breeds of continental Europe crossed with native Scottish working stock. One of the earliest indications of this is an account of three Polish Lowland Sheepdogs being traded to a Scottish shepherd in 1514, although no breeding records survive. Dogs of Beardie appearance are found in artworks dating to the eighteenth century, but the breed was not properly documented until the nineteenth century when they were described by Hugh Dalziel, in 1879, in his 1879 book *British Dogs*. Dalziel suggested that Beardies were the result of English Sheepdogs and Collie crosses. Regardless of their origin, the Beardies are known for their long, weather-resistant, and protective coats, which were perfect for the harsh Scottish climate. The breed was recognized by the American Kennel Club in 1977.

COMMON COAT COLORS

BLACK

BLUE

The Beardie's coat can be black, brown, blue, or fawn, with or without white markings.

COAT CLOSE-UP

Harsh, flat, long, shaggy topcoat, with a soft undercoat.

SHAGGY

BELGIAN LAEKENOIS : BELGIUM

The Belgian Laekenois is one of four native Belgian breeds and takes its name from the town of Laeken. It was also reputedly the favorite breed of nineteenth-century Queen Marie Henriette, who kept the dogs to guard the sheep on her estates. She also kept a select few with her in Laeken Castle. They are lively, intelligent, and very loyal dogs that are reserved with strangers, but make excellent family companions for an active home. The four breeds of Belgian Shepherd—Laekenois, Groenendael, Tervuren, and Malinois—are regarded as varieties of the same breed by some registries. Although the Laekenois is similar in build and temperament to the other types, it differs significantly, in coat color, texture, and length.

AT A GLANCE

Size: medium

Exercise needed:

Grooming needed:

Aptitudes: livestock guardian, guard dog, watchdog, companion

Height: 22–26 in.

Weight: 45–65 lb.

Average life expectancy: 12–14 yrs

AKC: FSS

CHARACTER

Affection

Playfulness

Friendliness to dogs

Friendliness to strangers

Ease of training

✚ HEALTH ✚

Generally healthy, but hereditary problems can include epilepsy and cancer.

TRIANGULAR, UPRIGHT EARS

CLEAN-CUT, LEAN HEAD

MODERATELY POINTED MUZZLE

SQUARE, WELL BALANCED, AND ELEGANT IN APPEARANCE

BROAD, HEAVILY MUSCLED THIGHS

WITHERS SLOPE TO LEVEL BACK

TAIL RAISED WITH SLIGHT CURVE WHEN IN ACTION

COMMON COAT COLORS

Coat colors can be all shades of red with traces of black on the tail and muzzle.

RED

COAT CLOSE-UP

The Lakenois' rough, coarse coat has a characteristic tousled look.

TOUSLED

HISTORY

The Laekenois can be traced back to a male dog named Vos I de Laeken who was purchased by Jean Baptiste Janssens, a shepherd and dog breeder. Historically, the dogs were used for guarding linen drying in the fields, and for protecting livestock and properties. During World War I and World War II, they were used as messenger dogs.

AT A GLANCE

Size: medium-large

Exercise needed:

Grooming needed:

Aptitudes: herding, livestock guardian, watchdog, tracking, companion

Height: 22–26 in.

Weight: 55–65 lb.

Average life expectancy: 10–12 yrs

AKC: herding

CHARACTER

Affection

Playfulness

Friendliness to dogs

Friendliness to strangers

Ease of training

✚ HEALTH ✚

Generally healthy, but hereditary problems can include epilepsy and cancer.

BELGIAN MALINOIS : BELGIUM

The Belgian Malinois is one of the four types of Belgian livestock working dogs and takes its name from the city of Malines (or Mechelen). The four types all share the same heritage, and it is only in the United States that they each have their own breed standard; they do, however, all exhibit their own characteristics. The Malinois were bred to excel as working animals and have developed into superb livestock-herding and guarding dogs. They are extremely intelligent and trainable and are affectionate with their families. They also serve as good watchdogs without being overly aggressive. However, they will thrive only in the most active homes. The Malinois is popular for use in herding, sledding, obedience, and tracking competitions.

LONG AND OBLIQUE SHOULDER
UPRIGHT, TRIANGULAR EARS
BLACK FACIAL MASK AND EARS
ALERT EXPRESSION WITH INTELLIGENT GAZE
MODERATELY POINTED MUZZLE
GENERALLY LEVEL TOPLINE
ANGLE OF HOCKS IS RELATIVELY SHARP

Belgian Malinois rank among the most naturally energetic of all dog breeds. A typical Malinois will have puppy-like energy until the age of three or four.

COMMON COAT COLORS

The Malinois's coat colors can be rich fawn to mahogany, with black tips on hairs and black masks.

RICH FAWN **MAHOGANY**

COAT CLOSE-UP

The Malinois's coat is short, straight, and coarse.

SHORT

HISTORY

Early breeders prized the Malinois's working character, and, historically, it has been the favorite type of Belgian Shepherd in its homeland. It is used as a working dog for tasks including detecting explosives, accelerants (for arson investigations), and illegal drugs. It is also used in police work for tracking and makes an excellent search-and-rescue dog. The Belgian Malinois was recognized by the American Kennel Club in 1959.

AT A GLANCE

Size: large

Exercise needed:
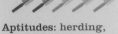

Grooming needed:

Aptitudes: herding, guarding livestock, watchdog, service, assistance, companion

Height: 22–26 in.

Weight: 55–66 lb.

Average life expectancy: 10–14 yrs

AKC: herding

CHARACTER

Affection

Playfulness

Friendliness to dogs

Friendliness to strangers

Ease of training

✚ HEALTH ✚

Generally healthy, but hereditary problems can include epilepsy and cancer.

BELGIAN SHEEPDOG : BELGIUM

In Europe, this breed is more commonly called the Groenendael, and is considered to be one of four types of Belgian Shepherd rather than a breed in its own right. Although bred as a working sheepdog, these dogs quickly proved how versatile they are chiefly due to their excellent temperaments, intelligence, obedience, and trainability. They were widely used by the military for delivering messages, as Red Cross dogs, and defense dogs during both world wars. Today, they are used by the police as search-and-rescue dogs, and they excel as assistance dogs. They can make wonderful, gentle, and devoted family companions for active homes and are vigilant watchdogs, but they are happiest in a working environment where they have plenty of jobs to keep them occupied.

TRIANGULAR, UPRIGHT EARS

ALERT EXPRESSION

MODERATELY POINTED MUZZLE

POWERFUL JAWS

ROUND AND RATHER OUTSTRETCHED NECK

WITHERS SLOPE DOWN INTO LEVEL BACK

TAIL REACHES HOCKS AND CURLS WHEN MOVING

FRONT LEG BONES ARE OVAL RATHER THAN ROUND

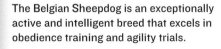
The Belgian Sheepdog is an exceptionally active and intelligent breed that excels in obedience training and agility trials.

COMMON COAT COLORS

The Belgian Sheepdog's coat is traditionally solid black.

BLACK

COAT CLOSE-UP

The coat's guard hairs are long, straight, and abundant.

STRAIGHT

HISTORY

The Belgian Sheepdog traces back to the 1800s when it was called the *Chien de Berger de Races Continentales*, or Continental Shepherd. A versatile breed, it worked as a herder, watchdog, and companion. It was officially given the name Groenendael in 1910 after the village of Groenendael where there was an important breeding kennels. The breed was recognized as the Belgian Sheepdog by the American Kennel Club in 1912.

AT A GLANCE

Size: large

Exercise needed:

Grooming needed:

Aptitudes: herding, livestock guardian, watchdog, agility, companion

Height: 22–26 in.

Weight: 65–75 lb.

Average life expectancy: 12–14 yrs

AKC: herding

CHARACTER

Affection

Playfulness

Friendliness to dogs

Friendliness to strangers

Ease of training

✚ HEALTH ✚

Generally healthy, but hereditary problems can include epilepsy and cancer.

BELGIAN TERVUREN : BELGIUM

The Belgian Tervuren is one of the four Belgian Shepherd dogs that is classified as a separate breed in the United States but is largely considered to be a variant elsewhere. Tervurens are distinguished from the other Belgian Shepherds by their characteristic thick, double coat that is generally mahogany. They were originally used as general farm dogs, but were also highly valued for their affectionate nature and glamorous looks. Tervurens are loyal and form strong bonds with their families, and they may be wary of strangers. The breed was first recognized by the American Kennel Club in 1918 but was registered under Belgian Sheepdogs. Tervurens were separated into their own breed registry in 1959.

MODERATELY POINTED MUZZLE

WELL-CHISELED HEAD WITH INTELLIGENT EXPRESSION

TRIANGULAR EARS, ERECT AND EQUAL IN HEIGHT TO WIDTH AT BASE

LONG AND ELEGANT NECK

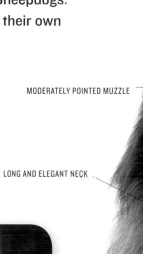

LONG AND WELL-MUSCLED FOREARMS

HISTORY

The Belgian Tervuren, also known as the *Chien de Berger Belge*, takes its name from the Belgian village of Tervuren where dog breeder M. F. Corbeel lived. Corbeel is credited with founding the breed through his two dogs Tom and Poes. The dogs' daughter Miss was bred to a black dog named Duc de Groenendael, giving rise to Milsart, who became the first Tervuren champion in 1907.

The Belgian Tervuren's impressive coat has to be groomed at least twice a week. The breed also needs a substantial amount of daily exercise.

COMMON COAT COLORS

The Tervuren's coat is a rich fawn to russet mahogany, with black overlay and a black face mask.

RICH FAWN

MAHOGANY

BLACK MASK

COAT CLOSE-UP

The Belgian Tervuren has an outercoat of medium harshness and a dense undercoat.

MEDIUM HARSHNESS

BERGER BLANC SUISSE : SWITZERLAND

The Berger Blanc Suisse, also known as the White Swiss Shepherd Dog, is directly related to the better-known German Shepherd. It's defining characteristic is its striking white coat, which is medium length but usually slightly longer and heavier around the neck. These are talented and versatile dogs that excel in many spheres, including stock and military work to assistance and search and rescue. They make excellent companion animals. Most Berger Blanc Suisse dogs are good-natured and very intelligent. They are loyal to their families but may be wary around strangers, which helps to make them highly effective watchdogs. The character of the Berger Blanc Suisse is generally considered to be more gentle and mellow than that of the German Shepherd.

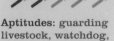

WEDGE-SHAPED HEAD

MODERATELY LONG MUZZLE

MODERATELY LONG NECK

ERECT EARS, SET HIGH AND DIRECTED FORWARD

PRONOUNCED WITHERS

STRONGLY MUSCLED LOINS

BUSHY SABER TAIL

OVAL FEET WITH TIGHT, WELL-ARCHED TOES

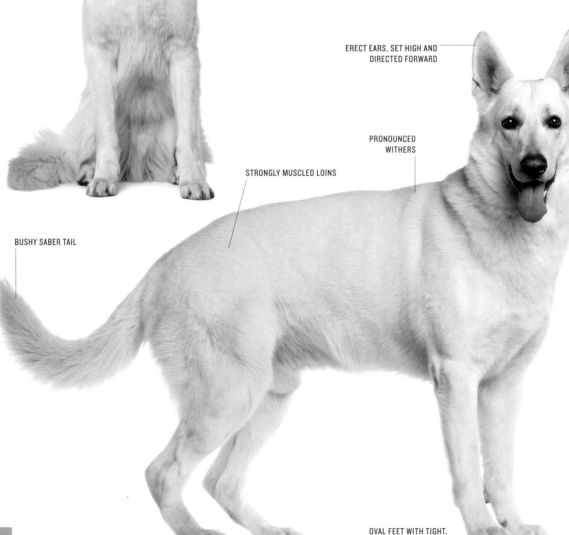

HISTORY

White-coated German Shepherds, although banned from registration in Germany in the 1960s, remained popular in Canada and the United States, where a breed club was formed for them. The first white stud dog to return to Europe was an American-bred dog named Lobo, born in 1966 and registered in Switzerland. From him, the breed was slowly re-established in Europe, with the Fédération Cynologique Internationale recognizing them as the Berger Blanc Suisse in 2003.

BLACK RUSSIAN TERRIER : RUSSIA

The Black Russian Terrier was developed specifically as a military dog by the state-owned Red Star Kennels in Moscow during the 1930s. Over seventeen different breeds were used, with the most significant being the Giant Schnauzer, Rottweiler, Newfoundland, and Airedale. Originally, these dogs were used by military police in prisons and at border crossings and for guarding military areas. The breed is highly intelligent and has a calm and loyal temperament. However, they were bred specifically to guard, and must be obedience trained and well socialized with people and animals. Ideally, they are suited to an experienced dog-owning home.

DARK, OVAL EYES SET RELATIVELY WIDE APART

BROAD MUZZLE TAPERS SLIGHTLY TO NOSE

OBVIOUS MOUSTACHE AND BEARD

STRUCTURE OF BODY GIVES IMPRESSION OF GREAT STRENGTH

FRONT PASTERNS ARE SHORT, THICK, AND ALMOST VERTICAL

LARGE, ROUND, COMPACT FEET

BLUE LACY : UNITED STATES

The Blue Lacy is the state dog of Texas, which is where the breed was developed by the Lacy brothers around the end of the nineteenth century. This is an exceptionally versatile working breed that combines a strong livestock-herding instinct with excellent hunting skills. The Blue Lacy can be used as a stock dog for driving livestock, but is used more often for tracking, treeing game, running trap lines, and hunting wild hogs. Given their athleticism, they also make good agility dogs. The Blue Lacy is a high energy, intense, fun, and tenacious breed that is suitable only for either a working environment or a very active home.

EYES HAVE "WOLF-LIKE" INTENSITY

MUZZLE EQUAL OR SLIGHTLY SHORTER IN LENGTH THAN SKULL

TRIANGULAR EARS WITH ROUNDED TIPS HANG CLOSE TO HEAD

POWERFUL, PROUD HEAD

MUSCULAR, BUT NOT BULKY, FOREQUARTERS

SHADES OF BLUE OR RED, TRICOLOR

CHARACTER

Affection

Playfulness

Friendliness to dogs

Friendliness to strangers

Ease of training

✚ HEALTH ✚

Generally healthy, but hereditary problems can include hip and elbow dysplasia, cancer, cataracts, gastric torsion, and degenerative myelopathy.

BERNESE MOUNTAIN DOG : SWITZERLAND

One of four Swiss working breeds, the gentle Bernese Mountain Dog is most commonly a devoted and loyal family companion. These large dogs were bred as working farm dogs and were often used for pulling small carts—carting has since become a popular sporting activity with the breed. Generally Bernese have exceptional temperaments, calm, affectionate, and forming very strong bonds with their families. The breed has often been used for service, assistance, and mountain search and rescue. They are still also used for herding and guarding livestock and have a naturally protective instinct. Bernese make superb companions for relatively active households. They are generally good with children and other pets as long as they are introduced correctly.

BUSHY TAIL CARRIED LOW

BROAD, MUSCULAR THIGHS

TOPLINE LEVEL FROM WITHERS TO CROUP

BROAD, FLAT SKULL

MEDIUM-SIZE, TRIANGULAR EARS HANG CLOSE TO HEAD

GENTLE, INTELLIGENT EXPRESSION

STRONG, STRAIGHT FORELEGS

HISTORY

The Bernese is generally believed to have developed from dogs introduced to the alpine region of Switzerland by the Romans from 57 BCE. These dogs were likely to have been Molossers (mastiff types), which were then crossed with native Swiss mountain dogs. The Bernese adapted perfectly to its environment with a very thick, weather-resistant coat that also provided protection against predators. The dogs were used in all capacities on farms for centuries and, in some areas, still are. However, little attention was paid to fostering the breed, and by the end of the nineteenth century, they had almost disappeared. Fortunately, Swiss dog fanciers realized the situation and began to implement breeding initiatives and promote the dogs. The breed's popularity spread quickly through Europe, and the first Bernese arrived in the United States in 1926.

COMMON COAT COLORS

The Bernese Mountain Dog's coat is tricolor: black with tan markings and white flashings.

BLACK & TAN   **WHITE FLASHINGS**

COAT CLOSE-UP

The coat is thick, moderately long, and slightly wavy.

LONG AND WAVY

Bernese usually reach their adult height by about fifteen months but continue to mature for another two or three years.

BOERBOEL : SOUTH AFRICA

This large, powerful breed traces to 1652 when Dutch colonist Jan van Riebeeck arrived at the Cape of Good Hope, South Africa, with three ships and his own dog, a bullenbijter. This was a large, heavy mastiff type, which bred with native South African stock. Many other European breeds were introduced to the area as trading grew, and some of these contributed toward the developing South African breed—one of mastiff appearance with great endurance and hardiness. Boerboels were required to be fearless guard dogs in addition to utilitarian, general farm workers. They are not suitable for first-time dog owners.

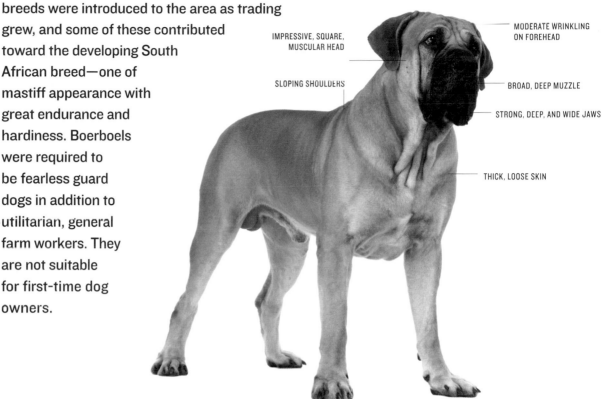

IMPRESSIVE, SQUARE, MUSCULAR HEAD

MODERATE WRINKLING ON FOREHEAD

SLOPING SHOULDERS

BROAD, DEEP MUZZLE

STRONG, DEEP, AND WIDE JAWS

THICK, LOOSE SKIN

BOHEMIAN SHEPHERD : CZECH REPUBLIC

Also known as the Chodský Dog, this is an ancient breed that has been used for centuries as a multipurpose farm dog, herding and guarding livestock and protecting homes. These dogs are widely held to have contributed to the development of the German Shepherd, and the two breeds share some similarities. The Bohemian is lively and intelligent, and it thrives when given a job to do or when mentally or physically challenged. These dogs are people-oriented and make good companions for the right home. They are also excellent watchdogs.

LONG, FLEXIBLE NECK

TAIL COVERED IN A THICK COAT AND GENTLY CURVED

BLACK TO GUNMETAL WITH VIVID YELLOW MARKINGS

GLOSSY, LONG, THICK COAT

SHORT, ERECT, FORWARD-FACING EARS

ALMOND-SHAPED, SLIGHTLY SLANTING EYES

BOUVIER DES ARDENNES : BELGIUM

This rare breed was originally used primarily for cattle drives and herding pigs, sheep, and even horses. They often had to travel long distances and work all day, so they developed into extremely hardy and steadfast dogs. Historically, they were also used by poachers for hunting deer and wild boar, and they have the added characteristic of being an excellent tracking dog, which is a trait not usually associated with herding dogs. Given their working foundation, they are obedient and relatively easy to train. They are tough, engaging, and fun dogs that love to play and can make good family companions for an active home.

FAIRLY SMALL, TRIANGULAR EARS, SET HIGH ON HEAD

STRONG, RELATIVELY SHORT HEAD

POWERFUL, SQUARE BODY

DOUBLE, DENSE, AND WATERPROOF COAT

ANY COLOR EXCEPT WHITE. GENERALLY MIX OF GRAY, BLACK, AND FAWN

STRAIGHT, STRONG FORELEGS

BOUVIER DES FLANDRES : BELGIUM

UPSTANDING EYEBROWS

IMPRESSIVE HEAD WITH OBVIOUS BEARD AND MOUSTACHE

BROAD, STRONG MUZZLE

RELATIVELY LONG SHOULDERS

DOUBLE COAT WITH ROUGH OUTER HAIRS

ROUND, COMPACT FEET

The Bouvier des Flandres developed as a working breed used mainly by butchers, cattle traders, and farmers. These dogs were used for moving and guarding livestock, including cattle, and had to be confident, tireless, brave, and protective. These qualities are still seen in the breed. Little attention was paid to the specifics of the dog, other than its ability to work efficiently, until a standard was drawn up in 1912. They are affectionate and devoted to their families and, in addition, make good watchdogs. Typically they are calm in the house, but still require a great deal of exercise.

BERGER PICARD : FRANCE

The Berger Picard is a rare French breed whose ancestors are thought to have accompanied the Celts when they invaded northern France around 400 BCE. Images of dogs similar in appearance to the Berger Picard, with shaggy coats and tending livestock, can be seen in artwork and tapestries from the Middle Ages. The Berger Picard, with its wiry protective coat, hardiness, and great endurance, has changed little over the years and has always been primarily a working breed—herding, guarding livestock, watching over the home, and providing companionship. They can be wary of strangers and occasionally stubborn, but are loyal and, if properly socialized, can make good companions and watchdogs for an active home.

MEDIUM-SIZE, BROWN EYES WITH LIVELY EXPRESSION

OBVIOUS EYEBROWS, MOUSTACHE, AND BEARD

RUSTIC LOOKING, STURDY, AND MUSCULAR IN APPEARANCE

STRAIGHT, STRONG FORELEGS

ROUND FEET WITH ARCHED TOES

BRIARD : FRANCE

The Briard is an ancient working breed that is said to have been favored by the Frankish King Charlemagne in the eighth century, appearing alongside him in tapestries. Many centuries later Napoléon Bonaparte kept two Briards, possibly as guard dogs. Their original use was for guarding livestock herds and property, and they were valued for their fearlessness. The Briard is loyal and protective with its family, but is an independent thinker and wary of strangers. A good companion for an active and experienced home.

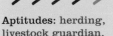
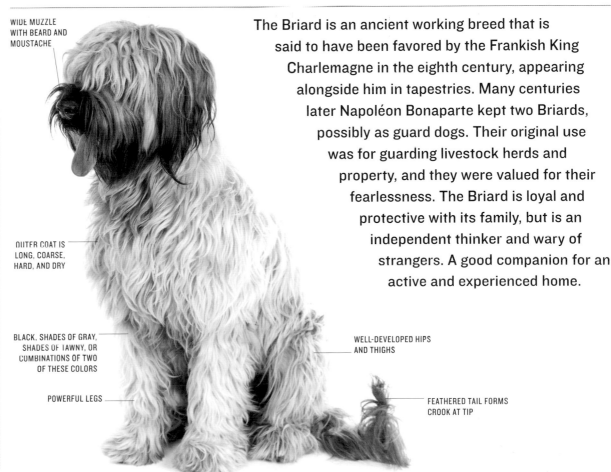

WIDE MUZZLE WITH BEARD AND MOUSTACHE

OUTER COAT IS LONG, COARSE, HARD, AND DRY

BLACK, SHADES OF GRAY, SHADES OF TAWNY, OR CUMBINATIONS OF TWO OF THESE COLORS

POWERFUL LEGS

WELL-DEVELOPED HIPS AND THIGHS

FEATHERED TAIL FORMS CROOK AT TIP

AT A GLANCE

Size: medium-small

Exercise needed:

Grooming needed:

Aptitudes: herding, watchdog, service, assistance, agility, companion

Height: 18–22 in.

Weight: 30–45 lb.

Average life expectancy: 10–14 yrs

AKC: herding

CHARACTER

Affection

Playfulness

Friendliness to dogs

Friendliness to strangers

Ease of training

✚ HEALTH ✚

Generally healthy, but hereditary problems can include hip dysplasia, Collie Eye Anomaly, and epilepsy.

BORDER COLLIE : ENGLAND, SCOTLAND, WALES

The Border Collie is widely considered the leading sheep-herding breed in the world, with few other breeds matching it for speed, agility, working ability, and drive. In addition, they are regularly ranked within the top ten most intelligent dog breeds and are particularly receptive to training. They are sensitive, highly energetic dogs with excellent problem-solving skills. This breed is happiest when working or involved in high-octane activities and requires plenty of exercise. As long as their mental and physical needs are met, Border Collies can be engaging, lively, and rewarding members of the family.

RESPONSIVE, ERECT OR SEMI-ERECT EARS

BROAD, DEEP CHEST

SLIGHTLY ARCHED, MUSCULAR LOINS

COMMON COAT COLORS

LIVER & WHITE

RED MERLE

BLUE & WHITE

RED & WHITE

Coat can be any solid color except pure white; often bi- or tricolor.

RELATIVELY FLAT SKULL WITH
TAPERING MUZZLE

OVAL, WIDE SET, BROWN EYES OF
ANY SHADE, OR BLUE IN MERLES,
WITH INTELLIGENT EXPRESSION

HISTORY

Originally known as the Working Collie, the Border Collie emerged from ancient native British working dogs, developed along the borders of Scotland and England, and was named the Border Collie in 1915. In England, Queen Victoria promoted the breed by owning several, including Sharp, who was frequently photographed with her. Old Hemp, born in 1893; Wilson Cap, born in 1937; and Wiston Cap, born in 1963, were all extremely influential in the breeding of the modern Border Collie, with Wiston Cap's image depicted on the International Sheep Dog Society badge.

Border Collies are still the first choice as sheepdogs across the world and are frequent winners in sheepdog trials; they also excel at agility, fly ball, and most energetic activities.

COAT CLOSE-UP

Two coat types: rough, which is flat or moderately wavy medium-length hair; or smooth, which is short, slightly coarse hair.

ROUGH

Border Collie puppies develop the characteristic "eye" behavior at an early age. This is when the dog fixes something (like sheep) with a steady, hypnotic stare, often adopting a distinctive crouching stance.

AT A GLANCE

Size: medium-large

Exercise needed:

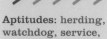

Grooming needed:

Aptitudes: herding, watchdog, service, assistance, agility, companion

Height: 17–21 in.

Weight: 50–80 lb.

Average life expectancy: 8–10 yrs

AKC: working

CHARACTER

Affection

Playfulness

Friendliness to dogs

Friendliness to strangers

Ease of training

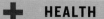

+ HEALTH +

Generally healthy, but hereditary problems can include heart conditions, gastric torsion, cancer, and hip dysplasia.

BOXER : GERMANY

The exuberant and multitalented Boxer is renowned for its playful and enthusiastic outlook on life. These dogs have been used for many purposes over the years and were one of the first breeds to be employed by the German police and military, being used as couriers among other things. They are highly intelligent as a breed and have been successfully trained as service dogs and assistance dogs; they are also very athletic and can excel at agility. Boxers are very people oriented and love to be the center of attention. Although originally bred as working dogs, they are now very popular as companion animals.

DISTINCTIVE HEAD WITH BROAD, BLUNT MUZZLE

SQUARE BODY PROFILE

SHORT, STRAIGHT BACK SLOPES SLIGHTLY TO HINDQUARTERS

VERY MUSCULAR HINDQUARTERS

LOWER JAW PROTRUDES SLIGHTLY BEYOND UPPER JAW

SHALLOW WRINKLES ON FOREHEAD

EARS SET AT HIGHEST POINT OF SKULL

UNDERLINE SHOWS TUCK-UP

HISTORY

Boxers were originally bred from bull-baiting dogs for dog-fighting contests, but in the nineteenth century, they were used by butchers in slaughterhouses to move livestock through the yards, and by cattlemen for driving herds. A Boxer club had formed in Germany by 1895, and the first breed standard was drawn up. Boxers arrived in the United States at the start of the twentieth century, and the breed was recognized by the American Kennel Club in 1904.

COMMON COAT COLORS

FAWN

BRINDLE

BLACK FACE MASK

Boxers can be any shade of fawn or brindle, with a black face mask. They can have limited white markings.

COAT CLOSE-UP

SHORT & SHINY

The boxer's coat is short, shiny, and smooth.

Some Boxer puppies are born white, although this color is not accepted by some of the breed registrations. White in Boxers is not a genetic defect or albino, but simply a color. Some white dogs will be prone to deafness and risk of sunburn.

BULLDOG : ENGLAND

The modern Bulldog bears little physical resemblance to its bull-baiting ancestors and even less similarity in temperament. Following the banning of bull baiting in England in 1835, the breed all but disappeared until breeders started breeding dogs with equable, placid temperaments and exaggerated physical appearance. As such, the Bulldog has become one of the most charming and personable breeds in the modern dog world, still determined and independent, but amiable and even comical in character.

MASSIVE HEAD WITH SHORT FACE

MASSIVE UNDERSHOT JAWS; LOWER JAW PROJECTS

SHORT, BROAD MUZZLE TURNED UPWARD; TIP OF NOSE SET BETWEEN THE EYES

SHORT, THICK POWERFUL NECK

STOUT FORELEGS SET APART

WHEEL BACK, TOPLINE DIPS SLIGHTLY BEHIND SHOULDERS, RISES TO LOINS AND CURVES TO TAIL

MUSCULAR HINDQUARTERS

LOW SLUNG, HEAVY, DEEP BODY

HIND LEGS LONGER THAN FORELEGS

A high percentage of Bulldog puppies have to be delivered by Caesarean section due to the large size of their heads.

HISTORY

The Bulldog takes its name from bull baiting, for which the dogs were specifically bred. The lower jaw that projects beyond the upper jaw allowed it to clamp onto the bull's nose with an unshakeable grip. Bulldogs were noted for their tremendous bravery and ferocity, and for never giving up the fight, despite their inevitable injuries. The original dogs were longer in the legs than the modern breed, lighter in the body, and far more athletic, although they still had a low center of gravity, which aided them when baiting bulls. London dog dealer Bill George is partly responsible for remarketing the Bulldog in the nineteenth century. Having previously supplied dogs for fighting, after the sport was banned he began popularizing the breed as a pet. The Bulldog Club was established in 1875.

COMMON COAT COLORS

WHITE

RED

FAWN

BRINDLE

Bulldogs can be white, red, fawn, or brindle, with white markings.

COAT CLOSE-UP

FINE

The Bulldog's coat is smooth and fine.

BROHOLMER : DENMARK

Also known as the Danish Mastiff, the Broholmer is a rare breed that developed in the 1500s from English Mastiff and other mastiff types. These noble-looking dogs have a long association with the Danish aristocracy and were often given as gifts. Traditionally they were used for guarding properties and livestock, and for hunting. By the 1970s, they had almost disappeared but were saved through the efforts of the Danish Kennel Club. These large, gentle dogs are generally calm around the house and protective of their families.

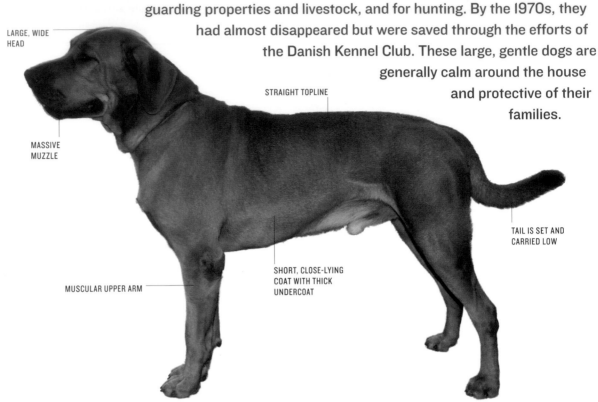

LARGE, WIDE HEAD

MASSIVE MUZZLE

STRAIGHT TOPLINE

TAIL IS SET AND CARRIED LOW

SHORT, CLOSE-LYING COAT WITH THICK UNDERCOAT

MUSCULAR UPPER ARM

BUCOVINA SHEPHERD DOG : ROMANIA

This rustic breed of sheepdog is also known as the Southeastern European Shepherd, and it developed in the Carpathian Mountains of Romania and Serbia, particularly the area of Bucovina. The breed was used by shepherds in rough mountain regions for protecting livestock, herding and moving the livestock, and guarding their farms. The dogs are gentle with their families and are generally held to be good with children and other animals, although wary of strangers. They are good watchdogs and have an intimidating bark. But they need a lot of exercise and consistent socialization and obedience training.

MASSIVE, BUT NOT HEAVY. HEAD

SMALL, ALMOND-SHAPED, BROWN EYES

BLUNT MUZZLE, SAME LENGTH AS SKULL

BROAD, DEEP CHEST REACHES ELBOWS

LONG, FLAT, STRAIGHT, ROUGH HAIR, SHORTER ON HEAD

WHITE OR WHITE BEIGE WITH PATCHES OF GRAY; BLACK OR BLACK WITH RED-FAWN REFLECTIONS

AT A GLANCE

Size: large

Exercise needed:

Grooming needed:

Aptitudes: guarding livestock, guard dog, watchdog, companion

Height: 24–27 in.

Weight: 100–130 lb.

Average life expectancy: 8–10 yrs

AKC: working

CHARACTER

Affection

Playfulness

Friendliness to dogs

Friendliness to strangers
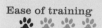

Ease of training

+ HEALTH +

Generally healthy, but hereditary problems can include heart problems, skeletal and joint problems, bloat, kidney failure, hypothyroidism, entropion, cancer, and allergies.

COAT CLOSE-UP

DENSE

The short, dense coat gives good weather protection.

COMMON COAT COLORS

RED

BRINDLE

The coat can be red, brindle, or fawn.

BULLMASTIFF : ENGLAND

Bullmastiffs were developed in the nineteenth century by crossing Bulldogs with Mastiffs to produce a calm but fearless dog to guard large English estates from poachers. The Bullmastiff is an athletic, quiet, and gentle breed unless provoked, and makes an ideal family companion and watchdog for an experienced dog-owning home. They are devoted and exceptionally loyal dogs that must be properly socialized. However, they are not always easy to train.

V-SHAPED EARS CARRIED CLOSE TO CHEEKS

BROAD, DEEP MUZZLE

SLIGHTLY ARCHED NECK

MUSCULAR, BUT NOT LOADED, SHOULDERS

WELL-DEVELOPED SECOND THIGH

HIGH-SET, STRAIGHT OR CURVED TAIL

DEEP, WIDE CHEST

LARGE HEAD WITH A FAIR AMOUNT OF WRINKLES WHEN ALERT

Bullmastiff puppies are undeniably cute, but they grow up into large, powerful dogs, so families must be prepared to offer them the right home environment.

HISTORY

The Bullmastiff, founded on a 60/40 Mastiff to Bulldog cross in the mid-nineteenth century, proved to be the ideal dog for gamekeepers, combining tracking skills with sheer power. They were noted for stealthily tracking down poachers in the dark, knocking them over, and holding them until the gamekeeper arrived. They had to be subtle, extremely brave, and powerful to do so, since poaching was a serious offense in nineteenth-century England (and a capital offense until 1827) and the poachers were desperate to escape.

CANE CORSO : ITALY

This large, powerful breed takes its name from the Latin word *cohors* meaning "guardian and protector," which is exactly what the breed was developed for. They are one of two Italian mastiff breeds that trace back to Roman times and the ancient Molosser Dogs. The breed was used for personal protection as well as for guarding livestock and homesteads, and was also valued as a hunting dog, particularly for large or ferocious game. The Cane Corso is a fearless, athletic breed that is very loyal to its family and has a strong desire to please. They can be wary of strangers and need to be very well socialized. They are not suitable for first-time dog owners.

AT A GLANCE

Size: large

Exercise needed:

Grooming needed:

Aptitudes: guarding, watchdog, companion

Height: 23–28 in.

Weight: 88–110 lb.

Average life expectancy: 10–12 yrs

AKC: working

CHARACTER

Affection

Playfulness

Friendliness to dogs

Friendliness to strangers

Ease of training

✚ HEALTH ✚

Health problems can include bloat, entropion, ectropion, cherry eye, bloat, hip dysplasia, epilepsy, and panosteitis.

COAT CLOSE-UP

SHINY

The Cane Corso's coat is short, stiff, and shiny.

Be warned, these dogs have a tendency to snore loudly and drool profusely!

LARGE BROAD HEAD WITH WELL-DEFINED STOP

EARS HELD TIGHT TO CHEEKS

PENDENT UPPER LIP

VERY BROAD AND DEEP MUZZLE; WIDTH IS ALMOST EQUAL TO LENGTH

WIDE, STRONG, AND MUSCULAR BACK

DEPTH OF RIBCAGE IS EQUAL TO HALF DOG'S TOTAL HEIGHT

COMMON COAT COLORS

  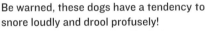

BLACK   **GRAY**   **FAWN**

Common coat colors include black, shades of gray, shades of fawn, and red. Coats can also be brindled. Fawn and red dogs have black or gray masks.

HISTORY

The Cane Corso can probably be traced to the Canis Pugnax, Roman war dogs that were widely used in battle, often wearing heavily spiked metal collars. No actual records exist to prove the Cane Corso's origins, but early surviving images from this time depict dogs that look similar. In addition to being used in battle, they were used in Roman arenas to fight wild animals; as those "sports" declined in popularity, farmers began to favor them for guarding their homes and livestock.

AT A GLANCE

Size: medium-small

Exercise needed:

Grooming needed:

Aptitudes: herding, watchdog, agility, companion

Height: 16–22 in.

Weight: 26–40 lb.

Average life expectancy: 9–12 yrs

AKC: FSS

CHARACTER

Affection

Playfulness

Friendliness to dogs

Friendliness to strangers

Ease of training

PORTUGUESE SHEEPDOG : PORTUGAL

This rare indigenous Portuguese breed is also known as the Cäo da Serra de Aires or the Cäo Macaco, meaning "monkey-faced dog," a reference to the long hair on its face and its cheeky, lively personality. This is an old-fashioned type of sheepdog that has some similarities to Pyrenean Sheepdogs and Briards, and was traditionally used for herding and guarding livestock such as sheep, goats, cattle, and even horses in remote rural areas. They retain strong herding instincts and are an intelligent, trainable breed. They also make good companion animals and are adept at agility and obedience competitions, as well as herding events.

MEDIUM-SIZE EARS, SET HIGH AND HANGING WITHOUT FOLDS

SHORT, STRAIGHT MUZZLE

LONG, LEVEL OR SLIGHTLY HOLLOW BACK

ROUND, DARK EYES WITH A LIVELY EXPRESSION

VERY LONG, SMOOTH OR SLIGHTLY WAVY COAT

AT A GLANCE

Size: medium

Exercise needed:

Grooming needed:

Aptitudes: herding, guarding livestock, guarding, watchdog, companion

Height: 20–24 in.

Weight: 44–88 lb.

Average life expectancy: 11–14 yrs

AKC: not recognized

CHARACTER

Affection

Playfulness

Friendliness to dogs
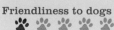

Friendliness to strangers

Ease of training

CÄO DE CASTRO LABOREIRO : PORTUGAL

This rare breed, also known as the Portuguese Cattle Dog, takes its name from the town of Castro Laboreiro in northern Portugal. Although no early records exist, the breed is believed to be ancient. These dogs were typically used by shepherds in remote mountainous regions for herding and guarding livestock, and for guarding homes. The dogs had to be brave enough to tackle predators such as wolves, and needed tremendous stamina and endurance. As farming methods changed, this breed's working role began to disappear. They are now more commonly used as guard dogs and companions.

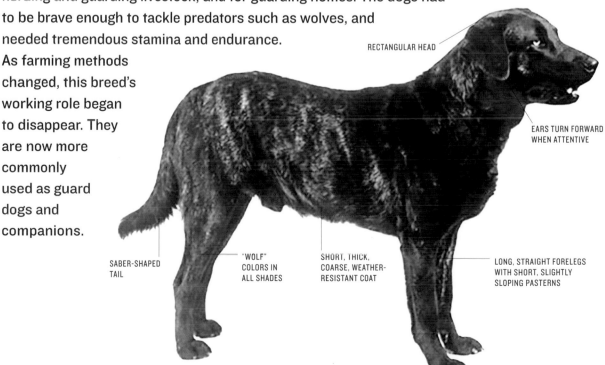

RECTANGULAR HEAD

EARS TURN FORWARD WHEN ATTENTIVE

SABER-SHAPED TAIL

"WOLF" COLORS IN ALL SHADES

SHORT, THICK, COARSE, WEATHER-RESISTANT COAT

LONG, STRAIGHT FORELEGS WITH SHORT, SLIGHTLY SLOPING PASTERNS

CÄO DE FILA DE SAÕ MIGUEL : PORTUGAL

This breed traces to Saõ Miguel Island in the Portuguese archipelago of the Azores, where it was used primarily for working cattle. It is described in the breed standard as "biting low" when moving cattle to prevent injury to the udders. These dogs were also used for guarding livestock and property, and they exhibit the characteristic qualities of fearlessness and tenacity seen in other similar guardian breeds. Today these dogs are primarily used as companions and guard dogs and can be devoted, affectionate, and efficient in both roles. As with any large guardian breed, they must be properly socialized and given plenty of mental and physical diversions.

BROAD, SQUARE SKULL

MEDIUM-LENGTH CROUP THAT IS SLIGHTLY HIGHER THAN WITHERS

SHORT, SMOOTH, DENSE HAIR

FAWN, PALE FAWN WITH BLACK OVERLAY, OR SHADES OF GRAY. ALWAYS BRINDLED

THICK, WELL-MUSCLED FOREARMS

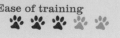
CARPATHIAN SHEPHERD DOG : ROMANIA

This large sheep-herding breed originated in the Carpathian mountains where it has been an invaluable part of shepherds' lives for centuries. Little is known about the breed's history except that it has developed as a perfect adaptation for its environment and role. The breed is noted for its intense loyalty to its family and to the herds it protects, and will tackle predators such as wolves and lynx without hesitation. The first breed standard was drawn up in 1934 and has been updated several times since. The National Club of Carpathian Shepherd Dog Breeders was established in Romania in 1998. This working breed is gentle, calm, and dignified with a natural protective instinct.

WOLF-LIKE HEAD

SLIGHTLY OBLIQUE DARK EYES

POWERFUL MUZZLE

LARGE, WIDE, BLACK NOSE

HARSH, DENSE, AND STRAIGHT COAT WITH THICK UNDERCOAT

CATALAN SHEEPDOG : SPAIN

Also known as the Gos d'Atura Català, the Catalan Sheepdog is a versatile breed originally bred for herding and guarding livestock. Little is known about the breed's origins, but they are most associated with the area around Andorra in Spain and share similarities to the Bergamasco, the Briard, the Bearded Collie, and the Portuguese Sheepdog. They are still used for working livestock in parts of Spain, but are now more commonly bred as companions. These intelligent and loyal dogs make good watchdogs, but need a great deal of exercise.

EXPRESSIVE, ROUND, DARK-AMBER EYES

LONG, LOW-SET TAIL RAISED IN ACTION

UNDERLINE HAS SLIGHT TUCK-UP

TRIANGULAR EARS SET HIGH

LONG, FLAT OR VERY SLIGHTLY WAVY COAT

OVAL FEET WITH HARD, BLACK PADS

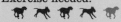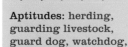
CAUCASIAN OVCHARKA :

GEORGIA, ARMENIA, AZERBAIJAN

The Caucasian Ovcharka, also known as the Caucasian Shepherd, is a large, powerful herding and guarding breed of ancient origin. These dogs are indigenous to a wide area that includes Georgia, Armenia, and Azerbaijani, and developed in harsh areas of geographic isolation.

The dogs exhibit various characteristics depending on their area, but they all share the fundamental herding and guarding skills. Highly prized in their homelands, they are intensely loyal and protective, which can be problematic if they are not properly socialized. They are not suitable for the first-time dog owner.

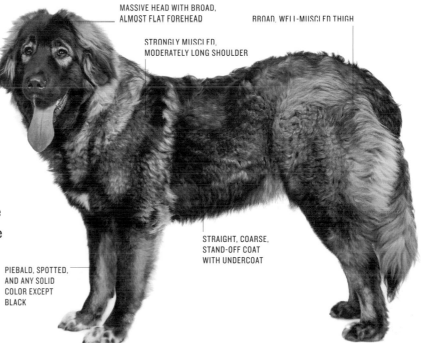

MASSIVE HEAD WITH BROAD, ALMOST FLAT FOREHEAD

BROAD, WELL-MUSCLED THIGH

STRONGLY MUSCLED, MODERATELY LONG SHOULDER

STRAIGHT, COARSE, STAND-OFF COAT WITH UNDERCOAT

PIEBALD, SPOTTED, AND ANY SOLID COLOR EXCEPT BLACK

AT A GLANCE

Size: medium-small

Exercise needed:

Grooming needed:

Aptitudes: companion, watchdog

Height: 10–13 in.

Weight: 25–38 lb.

Average life expectancy: 12–15 yrs

AKC: herding

CHARACTER

Affection

Playfulness

Friendliness to dogs

Friendliness to strangers

Ease of training

+ HEALTH +

Generally healthy, but hereditary problems can include intervertebral disc disease, progressive retinal atrophy, and urolithiasis.

COAT CLOSE-UP

DENSE

The double coat is medium length.

As young puppies, Cardis' ears are dropped, but they start to come upright any time after eight weeks.

CARDIGAN WELSH CORGI : WALES

Today the Cardigan Welsh Corgi, or "Cardi," is primarily kept as a companion, but historically this was a working, farm-dog breed noted for its endurance, tenacity, and boldness. Typically they were used for moving cattle by nipping at their heels, and were short and agile enough to avoid getting kicked. The Cardigan is an exceptionally tough breed that will work all day in any weather. They have huge personalities packed into a low-slung body, and are lively and intelligent dogs that love a physical or mental challenge. Despite being largely companions now, they remain vigilant and effective watchdogs.

ROUNDED MUZZLE, TAPERED NOT POINTED

LARGE, PROMINENT EARS IN PROPORTION TO THE SIZE OF THE DOG

INTELLIGENT AND LIVELY EXPRESSION

LONG, LEVEL BODY

LONG, LOW-SET TAIL

CURVED FOREARMS

LARGE, ROUND FEET POINT SLIGHTLY OUTWARD

LOW-SET HOCKS

HISTORY

The origins of the Cardigan Welsh Corgi are uncertain, but the breed is believed to be ancient, dating back at least 3,000 years. It is widely held that they developed from the Teckel family of dogs, which also gave rise to the Dachshund, and that they were introduced to Wales by Celtic tribes migrating from Central Europe. The breed developed in relative geographic isolation, adapting to the climate and bred specifically to work. Despite their differences, no efforts were made to keep the Cardi separate from the Pembroke Welsh Corgi until 1934, when the British Kennel Club recognized each separately. Cardis arrived in the United States in 1931 when two were imported by Mrs. Robert Bole. The American Kennel Club recognized the breed in 1935.

COMMON COAT COLORS

RED

SABLE

BRINDLE

BLACK

BLUE MERLE

Cardigan Welsh Corgis can be all shades of red, sable, and brindle. Black with or without tan or brindle points. Blue merle with or without tan or brindle points. White flashings are common on the neck, chest, legs, muzzle, underparts, tip of tail, and as a blaze on head.

PEMBROKE WELSH CORGI : WALES

AT A GLANCE

Size: medium-small

Exercise needed:

Grooming needed:

Aptitudes: companion, watchdog

Height: 10–12 in.

Weight: 24–30 lb.

Average life expectancy: 12–15 yrs

AKC: herding

CHARACTER

Affection
🐾 🐾 🐾 🐾 🐾

Playfulness
🐾 🐾 🐾 🐾 🐾

Friendliness to dogs
🐾 🐾 🐾 🐾 🐾

Friendliness to strangers
🐾 🐾 🐾 🐾 🐾

Ease of training
🐾 🐾 🐾 🐾 🐾

✚ HEALTH ✚

Generally healthy, but hereditary problems can include degenerative myelopathy, hip dysplasia, and progressive retinal atrophy.

PEMBROKE WELSH CORGI : WALES

The fox-like Pembroke Welsh Corgi, or "Pem," was, like its relative the Cardigan Welsh Corgi, used for droving cattle and general duties on small farms. These dogs were indispensable in keeping farms free from vermin, in guarding them against intruders, and for watching over the livestock and poultry. Once the day's work was done, however, the Pem loved to head inside and curl up by the fire! These are cheeky, intelligent dogs that are still worked in some areas, but are primarily used as companions now. They make excellent watchdogs and will protect property and vehicles noisily.

MEDIUM-LENGTH BACK   MEDIUM-SIZE, PRICKED EARS   BROWN, OVAL EYES

SLIGHTLY TAPERING MUZZLE

HEAD HAS A FOX-LIKE APPEARANCE

SHORT LEGS WITH GOOD, STRONG BONE   LOW-SLUNG, POWERFUL APPEARANCE   BROAD, DEEP CHEST

HISTORY

The Pem's history is believed to date back to around the ninth or tenth century when Viking raiders began invading Wales, bringing their spitz-type dogs, which bred with native dogs. In particular historians believe that the Swedish Vallhund, Norwegian Buhund, Schipperke, and early Pomeranian could all have influenced the development of the Pem. Pems became extremely popular in the twentieth century when the British Royal Family began to keep them. The first was Dookie, a gift from the Duke of York (later King George VI) to his daughter Margaret. Dookie was followed by Jane, Crackers, and Susan. Queen Elizabeth II still keeps Corgis, with all of them tracing back to Susan. The Pembroke Welsh Corgi Club of America was established in 1936, and the breed ranks among the top thirty most popular breeds in the United States.

COMMON COAT COLORS

BLACK WITH WHITE   **BLACK & TAN**   **RED**

Coats can be black, black and tan, red, sable, or fawn, with or without white markings.

COAT CLOSE-UP

HARD TOPCOAT

The double coat has a medium-length, hard topcoat, and a soft undercoat.

Pems are natural herding dogs that tend to nip at people's heels. This behavior should be discouraged when they are puppies to prevent problems when they grow up.

AT A GLANCE

Size: large

Exercise needed:

Grooming needed:

Aptitudes: guard dog, guarding livestock, companion

Height: 26–28 in.

Weight: 88–110 lb.

Average life expectancy: 10–12 yrs

AKC: FSS

CHARACTER

Affection

Playfulness

Friendliness to dogs

Friendliness to strangers

Ease of training

CENTRAL ASIAN SHEPHERD DOG : RUSSIA

The Central Asian Shepherd is first and foremost a guard dog, and it has been bred for this purpose for many years. The breed is ancient and developed by the process of natural selection by adapting to a range of harsh environments and difficult terrains—from the mountains of Mongolia to the deserts of Kara Kum. These dogs were valued for their ferocity in protecting their families, livestock, and territory. They are typically extremely loyal to their owners and form strong emotional attachments, but are wary of strangers. They are a rewarding breed for an experienced home wanting a guard dog and companion.

HEAD CLOSE TO RECTANGULAR IN SHAPE

STRAIGHT, BROAD, AND MUSCULAR BACK

STRONG, BROAD JAWS

ANY COLOR, EXCEPT BLUE OR BROWN

DEEP, LONG, BROAD CHEST

AT A GLANCE

Size: medium-small

Exercise needed:

Grooming needed:

Aptitudes: guard dog, companion

Height: 14–20 in.

Weight: 33–54 lb.

Average life expectancy: over 12 yrs

AKC: not recognized

CHARACTER

Affection

Playfulness

Friendliness to dogs

Friendliness to strangers

Ease of training

CHINESE CHONGQING DOG : CHINA

The Chinese Chongqing dog is an extremely rare and ancient breed that is little known outside of China and exists only in small numbers in its homeland. The dogs bear a striking resemblance to ancient pottery statuettes from the Han Dynasty (206 BCE–AD 220), and it is assumed they descended from dogs of this period. A number of these statuettes have been recovered near the city of Chongqing, from which the breed takes its name. They were valued as guard dogs, but were also used for hunting. The Chongqing is fearless and devoted to its family. They must be properly socialized, and are not suitable for first-time dog owners.

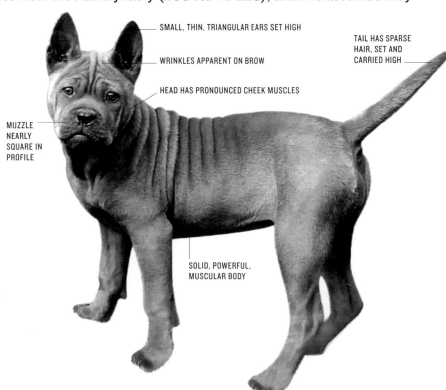

SMALL, THIN, TRIANGULAR EARS SET HIGH

TAIL HAS SPARSE HAIR, SET AND CARRIED HIGH

WRINKLES APPARENT ON BROW

HEAD HAS PRONOUNCED CHEEK MUSCLES

MUZZLE NEARLY SQUARE IN PROFILE

SOLID, POWERFUL, MUSCULAR BODY

CROATIAN SHEEPDOG

AT A GLANCE

Size: medium-small

Exercise needed:

Grooming needed:

Aptitudes: herding, watchdog, agility, companion

Height: 16–21 in.

Weight: 29–44 lb.

Average life expectancy: 13–14 yrs

AKC: not recognized

CHARACTER

Affection

Playfulness

Friendliness to dogs

Friendliness to strangers

Ease of training

CROATIAN SHEEPDOG : CROATIA

This distinctive breed with its curly black coat has a long history that stretches back to at least the fourteenth century when dogs of almost exactly the same appearance were called Canis Pastoralis Croaticus. The dogs were used for herding all kinds of farm livestock in remote regions of Croatia and developed into tough, agile, and enduring dogs. They are an active, intelligent breed and excel at events such as agility and fly ball. They can be prone to excessive barking, which should be discouraged when they are puppies.

TRIANGULAR, ERECT, OR SEMI-ERECT EARS

LIGHT, LEAN, WEDGE-SHAPED HEAD

CAN BE NATURALLY TAIL-LESS

SLIGHTLY PRONOUNCED FORECHEST

SOFT, WAVY, OR CURLY COAT

SMALL, STRONG, RABBIT-LIKE FEET

AT A GLANCE

Size: large

Exercise needed:

Grooming needed:
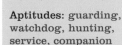

Aptitudes: guarding, watchdog, hunting, service, companion

Height: 24–26 in.

Weight: 44–57 lb.

Average life expectancy: 13–16 yrs

AKC: FSS

CHARACTER

Affection

Playfulness

Friendliness to dogs

Friendliness to strangers

Ease of training

CZECHOSLOVAKIAN VLCAK : CZECHOSLOVAKIA

This is a "new" breed that traces to 1955 when German Shepherds were crossed with Carpathian Wolves in Czechoslovakia to develop dogs with the trainability and temperament of the former combined with the bravery, endurance, and toughness of the latter. The new breed was recognized as the Czechoslovakian Vlcak, "wolfdog," in 1982 and made a national breed. These dogs have been used successfully as service animals such as for the police and search and rescue, and also make good hunting and guard dogs. They need to be carefully introduced to other animals and well socialized to make good companions. This breed is most suitable for an active, experienced home.

SHORT, PRICKED EARS

OVAL, BLACK NOSE

STRONG, SYMMETRICAL JAWS

STRAIGHT, CLOSE COAT WITH THICK UNDERCOAT

LARGE, FRONT FEET TURN SLIGHTLY OUTWARD

YELLOWISH-GRAY TO SILVER-GRAY WITH LIGHT MASKS

AT A GLANCE

Size: medium-small

Exercise needed:

Grooming needed:

Aptitudes: vermin control, hunting, herding, agility, therapy, assistance, companion

Height: 12–15 in.

Weight: 15–15 lb.

Average life expectancy: 10–15 yrs

AKC: FSS

CHARACTER

Affection

Playfulness

Friendliness to dogs

Friendliness to strangers

Ease of training

DANISH–SWEDISH FARMDOG : DENMARK, SWEDEN

A charismatic and versatile small dog that was originally an important part of everyday farm life, the Danish–Swedish Farmdog performed a number of roles including vermin control, hunting, herding, and guarding. It was often used in the circus due to its intelligence and endearing nature. It is thought to trace back to Fox Terrier and Pinscher crosses. As small farms began to close, the breed suffered, but was re-established and given its official name in 1987. These dogs make excellent companions for an active home and are good therapy dogs.

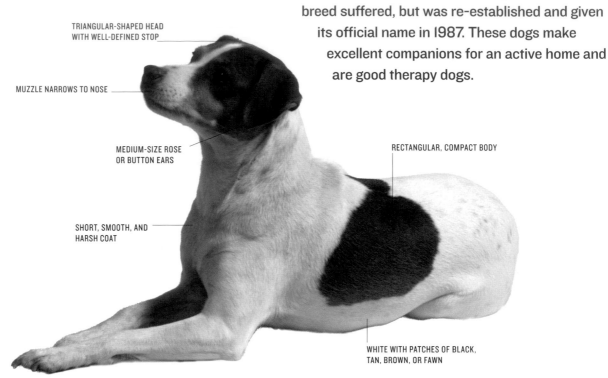

TRIANGULAR-SHAPED HEAD WITH WELL-DEFINED STOP

MUZZLE NARROWS TO NOSE

MEDIUM-SIZE ROSE OR BUTTON EARS

SHORT, SMOOTH, AND HARSH COAT

RECTANGULAR, COMPACT BODY

WHITE WITH PATCHES OF BLACK, TAN, BROWN, OR FAWN

AT A GLANCE

Size: large

Exercise needed:

Grooming needed:
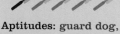

Aptitudes: guard dog, watchdog, hunting, companion

Height: 23–27 in.

Weight: 88–120 lb.

Average life expectancy: 10–12 yrs

AKC: FSS

CHARACTER

Affection

Playfulness

Friendliness to dogs

Friendliness to strangers

Ease of training

DOGO ARGENTINO : ARGENTINA

The distinctive Dogo Argentino, the only Argentinian breed recognized by the Fédération Cynologique Internationale, was developed by Dr. Antonio Nores Martinez in Cordoba in the early twentieth century. The breed was based on the now extinct Cordoba fighting dog, crossed with a variety of others, including the Great Dane, Boxer, Bull Terrier, and Dogue de Bordeaux. Martinez recognized the Dogo Argentino's hunting abilities, and it became a first-class big-game hunting dog. In its homeland, the breed is still used for hunting wild boar, wild cats, and other game, but is also highly regarded as a protective companion. It is banned in some countries under various dangerous-dog acts.

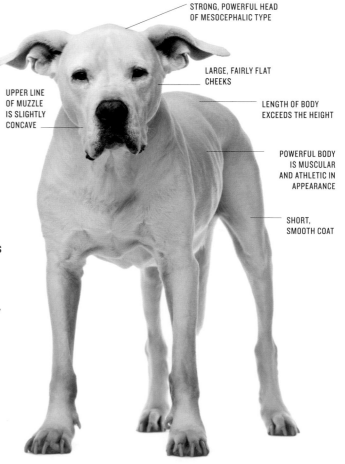

STRONG, POWERFUL HEAD OF MESOCEPHALIC TYPE

LARGE, FAIRLY FLAT CHEEKS

UPPER LINE OF MUZZLE IS SLIGHTLY CONCAVE

LENGTH OF BODY EXCEEDS THE HEIGHT

POWERFUL BODY IS MUSCULAR AND ATHLETIC IN APPEARANCE

SHORT, SMOOTH COAT

DOGUE DE BORDEAUX : FRANCE

Also known as the French Mastiff, these are extremely powerful dogs whose heritage includes English Mastiff, Bulldog, and Bullmastiff. Historically these brave dogs were used in war and were valued for their ferocity in fighting conditions. They have also been used for dog fighting, for animal baiting, and as livestock guardians, the latter being a role they still perform in some areas. In addition, the Dogue de Bordeaux makes an excellent big-game hunter. Despite their violent history, these dogs are gentle and protective with their families. They can make good companion dogs but are not always the easiest to train!

AT A GLANCE

Size: large

Exercise needed:

Grooming needed:

Aptitudes: guard dog, watchdog, hunting, companion

Height: 23–27 in.

Weight: 95–140 lb.

Average life expectancy: 5–7 yrs

AKC: working

CHARACTER

Affection

Playfulness

Friendliness to dogs

Friendliness to strangers

Ease of training

✚ HEALTH ✚

Generally healthy, but hereditary problems can include bloat, heart problems, skin disease, eye problems, eosinophilic panosteitis, and hypothyroidism.

SKULL WIDER THAN HIGH

SMALL, HIGH-SET, PENDENT EARS

HEAVILY WRINKLED FACE

SHORT, BROAD, THICK, POWERFUL MUZZLE

DEEP, LONG, BROAD CHEST

POWERFUL HIND LEGS WITH STRONG BONE

HISTORY

Unusually, the Dogue was greatly valued in France across all social classes. This association helped save the breed from disappearing, particularly during the French Revolution (1789–99) when many of the aristocracy's dogs were slaughtered. The breed suffered during both world wars when it was drafted into active service, often used for hauling carts and stretchers. The French Resistance used the dogs for protection—they were so good at protecting the French that Hitler ordered their destruction in the hundreds. Today the Dogue makes a lovely companion and guardian.

Dogues will continue to grow and mature until they are at least two years old.

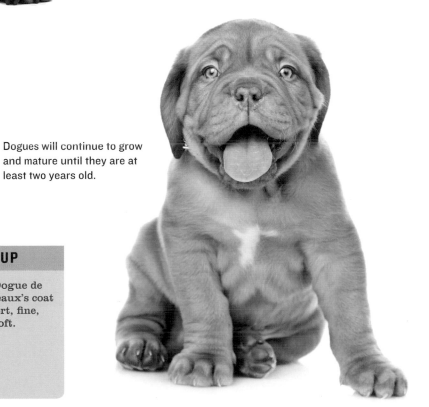

COMMON COAT COLORS

The coat can be any shade of fawn, with or without a dark mask.

FAWN

COAT CLOSE-UP

The Dogue de Bordeaux's coat is short, fine, and soft.

FINE

DOBERMAN PINSCHER : GERMANY

The multitalented Doberman is renowned for its intelligence, loyalty, protectiveness, and agility and, in light of these traits, has been used in a wide range of services. Originally they were valued as guard dogs, at which they still excel, but they have also been used by the military (for everything from message carrying to tracking) and police. Dobermans are generally quick to learn and very easy to train. They are gentle and affectionate with their families, and are a highly effective deterrent to intruders!

LONG, WEDGE-SHAPED HEAD

ALMOND-SHAPED BROWN EYES WITH A LIVELY EXPRESSION

HIGH-SET EARS

Doberman puppies are notoriously rambunctious!

COMMON COAT COLORS

BLACK

RED

Coat colors are black, red, blue, and fawn— all with tan markings.

COAT CLOSE-UP

SMOOTH

The coat is smooth and short.

Superbly athletic, Dobermans excel at agility contests.

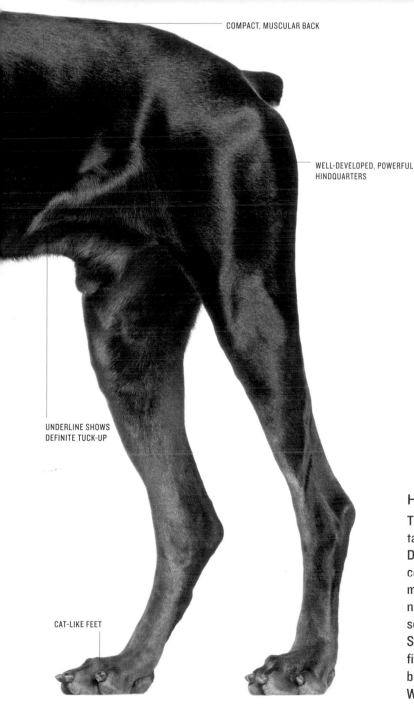

COMPACT, MUSCULAR BACK

WELL-DEVELOPED, POWERFUL HINDQUARTERS

UNDERLINE SHOWS DEFINITE TUCK-UP

CAT-LIKE FEET

HISTORY

The history of the Doberman is well recorded and traces to one man, a German tax collector named Friedrich Louis Dobermann. In the nineteenth century Dobermann set about developing a breed that would protect him when he was collecting taxes, and would be helpful in persuading people to part with their money. The two breed founders were a male named Schnupp and a female named Bisart, whose puppies had the characteristic black and tan coloring seen in the modern breed. Other dogs including German Pinschers, German Shepherds, Great Danes, and Black and Tan Terriers, were also influential. The first Doberman was registered with the American Kennel Club in 1908, and the breed was adopted as the official war dog of the U.S. Marine Corps during World War II. The Doberman Club was founded in England in 1948.

DUTCH SHEPHERD DOG : NETHERLANDS

The Dutch Shepherd is a versatile and intelligent breed whose role has changed in line with changing farming practices. Originally the breed's primary function was herding all types of farm livestock. They had to keep the large flocks of sheep away from the crop fields, protect the vegetable patches from the hens, and gather the cows at milking time. On market day, they drove the livestock to town, and when the farmer was away, they patrolled the farm, keeping watch. As farming decreased, the breed found new roles with the police, search and rescue, and as an assistance dog. The Dutch Shepherd has a lovely nature and makes a good companion dog.

EARS CARRIED FORWARD WHEN ALERT

WEDGE-SHAPED, ELONGATED HEAD

BRIDGE OF MUZZLE IS STRAIGHT

COAT CAN BE SHORT, LONG, OR WIRY

LEG BONES ARE SOLID BUT NOT HEAVY

OVAL FEET WITH ARCHED TOES

ENTLEBUCHER MOUNTAIN DOG : SWITZERLAND

This useful and versatile breed originated in the Entlebuch Valley, from where it takes its name, and is the smallest of the four Swiss Mountain Dog breeds. The breed dates back to the end of the nineteenth century, but for many years, the Entlebucher and the Appenzeller were considered the same. They were finally named two distinct breeds in 1927. The Entlebucher is a compact, muscular dog that was traditionally used for moving herds of livestock between pastures and for gathering dairy herds at milking time. Today the breed exists in relatively small numbers, but is valued as a lively, affectionate, and intelligent companion or worker.

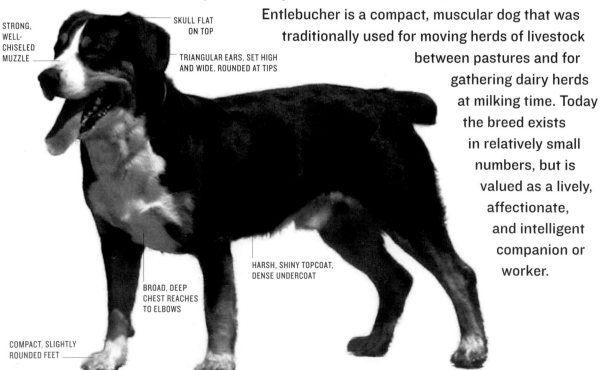

STRONG, WELL-CHISELED MUZZLE

SKULL FLAT ON TOP

TRIANGULAR EARS, SET HIGH AND WIDE, ROUNDED AT TIPS

HARSH, SHINY TOPCOAT, DENSE UNDERCOAT

BROAD, DEEP CHEST REACHES TO ELBOWS

COMPACT, SLIGHTLY ROUNDED FEET

MASTIFF : ENGLAND

Mastiff-type dogs are one of the oldest breed types and, given their size and power, have been used for bloody pursuits throughout history. Nevertheless, the modern Mastiff is a gentle giant far removed from its warring ancestors. The Mastiff was also one of the predominant guard-dog breeds used for guarding livestock and property, and in this respect, they are still excellent deterrents for predators. Mastiffs are relatively low in number in England, but there are greater numbers in the United States. They can make affectionate companions that are good with other dogs.

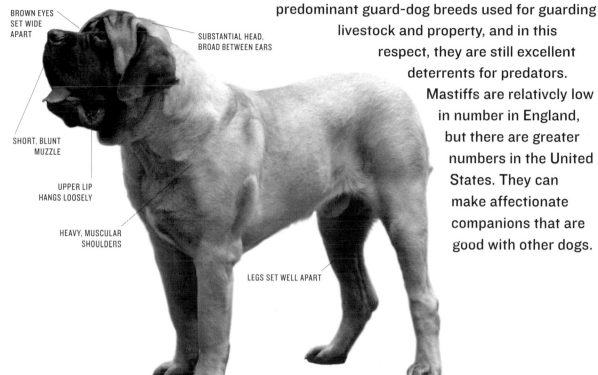

BROWN EYES SET WIDE APART

SUBSTANTIAL HEAD, BROAD BETWEEN EARS

SHORT, BLUNT MUZZLE

UPPER LIP HANGS LOOSELY

HEAVY, MUSCULAR SHOULDERS

LEGS SET WELL APART

ESTRELA MOUNTAIN DOG : PORTUGAL

The Estrela Mountain Dog is an ancient working breed that takes its name from the Portugal's Estrela Mountains. They were, and still are, used primarily for guarding herds and homes, as well as for herding livestock between summer and winter pastures. They were also sometimes used for light-draft purposes. Although relatively unknown outside Portugal, the breed is actively supported in England and in the United States. They are suitable for experienced dog-owning homes.

OVAL, DARK-AMBER EYES WITH A KEEN, INTELLIGENT EXPRESSION

LONG, TAPERING, ALMOST STRAIGHT MUZZLE

EARS SET MODERATELY HIGH

LONG, WIDE SHOULDER BLADES

COMPACT BODY AND A SHORT, STRONG BACK

FAWN, WOLF GRAY, OR YELLOW, ALL WITH DARK MASKS; WITH OR WITHOUT BRINDLING OR WHITE MARKINGS

FILA BRASILEIRO : BRAZIL

HEAVY, MASSIVE HEAD

LARGE, THICK PENDENT EARS

THICK, PENDULOUS UPPER LIPS FORM A PERFECT CURVE

STRONG, WELL-MUSCLED NECK

WHEN VIEWED FROM ABOVE, LOINS ARE NARROWER THAN THORAX

POWERFUL LEGS

The Fila Brasileiro, or Brazilian Mastiff, is an imposing, powerful breed used as a guard dog and renowned for its tracking skills. The breed is descended from English Mastiff, Bloodhound, and Bulldog crossed with native stock and is incredibly loyal to its family. These dogs are valued for protecting property and livestock, herding cattle, and instinctively capturing and holding game during hunts until their master arrives. Extremely wary of strangers, the Fila must be consistently socialized from puppyhood. This breed has been banned in some countries under dangerous-dog legislation.

HOVAWART : GERMANY

The Hovawart is an ancient working breed that takes its name from the old German words: Hova (*hof*), meaning "farm," and wart (*wächter*), meaning "watchman," which describes the breed's chief role. They are thought to have originated in the Harz and Black Forest regions of Germany and were bred by the German aristocracy to guard their estates. The breed was not organized until after World War I when zoologist Dr. Konig began a program to cement their characteristics, introducing German Shepherd, Newfoundland, and Leonberger stock, with the first litter registered in Germany in 1922.

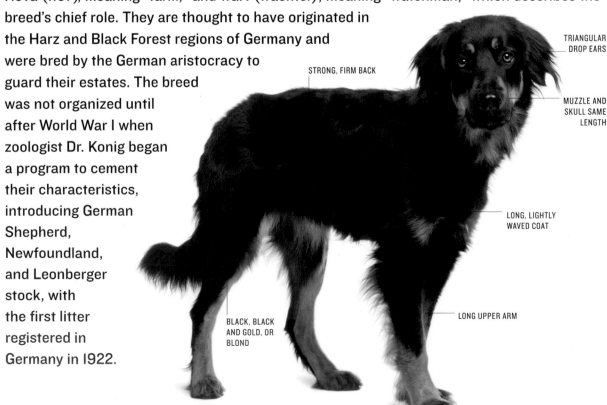

STRONG, FIRM BACK

TRIANGULAR DROP EARS

MUZZLE AND SKULL SAME LENGTH

LONG, LIGHTLY WAVED COAT

LONG UPPER ARM

BLACK, BLACK AND GOLD, OR BLOND

AT A GLANCE

Size: large

Exercise needed:
🐎 🐎 🐎 🐎 🐎

Grooming needed:
🪮 🪮 🪮 🪮 🪮

Aptitudes: herding, guarding livestock, guard dog, watchdog, service, assistance, companion

Height: 22–27 in.

Weight: 80–135 lb.

Average life expectancy: 8–11 yrs

AKC: working

CHARACTER

Affection
🐾 🐾 🐾 🐾 🐾

Playfulness
🐾 🐾 🐾 🐾 🐾

Friendliness to dogs
🐾 🐾 🐾 🐾 🐾

Friendliness to strangers
🐾 🐾 🐾 🐾 🐾

Ease of training
🐾 🐾 🐾 🐾 🐾

✚ HEALTH ✚

Generally healthy but hereditary problems can include hip and elbow dysplasia, bone cancer, gastric torsion, and heart problems.

ROTTWEILER : GERMANY

BROAD BETWEEN THE EARS

TRIANGULAR, PENDENT EARS SET WELL APART

SLIGHTLY ARCHED, THICK, MUSCULAR NECK

BROAD MUZZLE, TAPERS SLIGHTLY TO END

BROAD, DEEP CHEST

The Rottweiler is a big and powerful breed that can make a superb companion animal for an experienced dog-owning home. Due to their size and strength, these dogs must be properly socialized from a young age and must undergo obedience training. When brought up correctly, they are loyal, affectionate, biddable dogs that provide great home protection. Like so many of the herding and guarding breeds, the Rottweiler is multiskilled and exceptionally versatile. Unfortunately, as with many breeds, they have suffered poor press due largely to irresponsible dog ownership.

Puppies of any breed should not be sold under 8 weeks old. It is important that Rottweiler puppies are socialized from a very early age.

HISTORY

The modern Rottweiler probably descended from ancient mastiff-types that were widely used by the Romans. When the Romans settled around the Black Forest in Germany in the first century, they took their dogs with them. Those animals came into contact with the ancestors of mountain breeds such as the Bernese Mountain Dog, Appenzeller, Greater Swiss Mountain Dog, and Entlebucher. By the Middle Ages, this area had become known as *das rote wil* meaning "red roof tiles," and the dogs living there began to be called Rottweils. They were used as butcher's dogs, for driving cattle, in draft work, and for guarding properties. Later they were used by the military and the police. The breed was recognized by the American Kennel Club in 1931, and the first Rottie was imported to England in 1936.

COMMON COAT COLORS

The Rottweiler's coat is black with rust to mahogany markings.

BLACK

COAT CLOSE-UP

The coat is coarse, straight, and dense.

DENSE

GERMAN SHEPHERD : GERMANY

The German Shepherd is one of the most versatile and distinguished breeds and has become a stalwart colleague to humans across many different sectors. German Shepherds were originally bred as livestock dogs to herd, guard, and protect a range of farm animals, which they will still do instinctively. Their great intelligence and trainability was quickly recognized, and they were drafted into police service. They are still recognized as one of the leading police dogs in the world. With the outbreak of World War I, the German Shepherds became a military dogs, delivering messages, working in search and rescue, and acting as sentries and guard dogs. They excel as assistance dogs and have been widely used as guide dogs for the blind; the first German-trained guide dog for the blind sent to the United States was named Lux, and was imported in 1925 as a gift for Minnesota senator Thomas Schall. The breed is still used for these purposes and also makes a wonderful and engaging companion animal.

POINTED, ERECT EARS

STRONG, CHISELED HEAD

POWERFUL, WEDGE-SHAPED MUZZLE

WITHERS SLOPE DOWN TO A LEVEL BACK

AT A GLANCE

Size: large

Exercise needed:

Grooming needed:

Aptitudes: herding, guarding livestock, guard dog, watchdog, service, tracking, assistance, agility, companion

Height: 22–26 in.

Weight: 75–95 lb.

Average life expectancy: 10–12 yrs

AKC: herding

CHARACTER

Affection

Playfulness

Friendliness to dogs

Friendliness to strangers

Ease of training

✚ HEALTH ✚

Generally healthy but hereditary problems can include hip dysplasia, degenerative myelopathy, exocrine pancreatic insufficiency, hemophilia, renal cystadenocarcinoma, pannus, panosteitis, and perianal fistula.

COMMON COAT COLORS

The German Shepherd can be most colors except white. Most are black and tan.

BLACK & TAN

BLACK

COAT CLOSE-UP

The coat is straight and harsh with a relatively short undercoat.

HARSH

HISTORY

Captain Max von Stephanitz is credited with developing the German Shepherd breed based on native working German stock. He purchased a dog named Horand von Grafrath, which had a "wolfish" appearance, from a dog show in Karlsruhe, western Germany, in 1899, and used him as the foundation of his breeding program. Stephanitz established the Society for the German Shepherd Dog, and Horand was the first dog registered. Horand's brother Kuchs was also added to the program. The motto "utility and intelligence" was adopted for the fledgling breed. In 1907 the first German Shepherd was exhibited in the United States, and the following year the American Kennel Club recognized the breed. During World War I, "German" was dropped from the breed name in the United States, and in England the breed name was changed to Alsatian, remaining as such until 1977. The full name was reinstated in the United States some years later, and by 1926 the breed accounted for 36 percent of all registered American dogs. The German Shepherd continues to be extremely popular.

SLIGHTLY SLOPING CROUP

BUSHY TAIL HANGS LOW WITH
A SLIGHT CURVE AT REST

German Shepherds can have very large litters of puppies, sometimes up to fifteen, but on average they have eight.

HUNTAWAY : NEW ZEALAND

The Huntaway was developed in New Zealand approximately 100 years ago specifically to meet the demanding requirements of sheep farming in that country. Farmers needed dogs of great endurance to work the difficult climate and terrain, and also dogs that barked so the farmer could find them when working at long distances. The Huntaway, which developed from the Border Collie and other herding-breed crosses, is noted for its regular and sustained bark, as well as for its agility and stamina. This breed has a good temperament, but the dogs are naturally inclined to bark and are best suited to a working, rural life.

EARS SET WIDE APART AND PENDENT OR HALF FOLDED

EYES CAN BE ORANGE-BROWN, BLUE, OR BROWN

INTENSE, INTELLIGENT EXPRESSION

DENSE COAT CAN BE SHORT OR LONG

BLACK AND TAN, TRICOLOR, OR BRINDLE

LONG LEGS WITH SUBSTANTIAL BONE

AT A GLANCE

Size: medium

Exercise needed:

Grooming needed:

Aptitudes: herding, watchdog, agility, companion

Height: 20–24 in.

Weight: 40–65 lb.

Average life expectancy: 12–14 yrs

AKC: not recognized

CHARACTER

Affection

Playfulness

Friendliness to dogs

Friendliness to strangers

Ease of training

KARAKACHAN DOG : BULGARIA

This ancient breed is named after the Karakachan people—nomadic shepherds descended from Central Europe's Thracian livestock-breeding communities. The Karakachan are noted for preserving historic breeds of sheep and horses in addition to the Karakachan Dog. The dogs are renowned for their bravery and have long been used for protecting livestock herds from wolves and other large predators. They are strongly territorial and will guard homes, vehicles, livestock, and their families with great loyalty. Small numbers of the breed are used in the United States on ranches and farms in guardian-type roles. These are working dogs bred for many years to do a specific job, and they are best suited to that lifestyle.

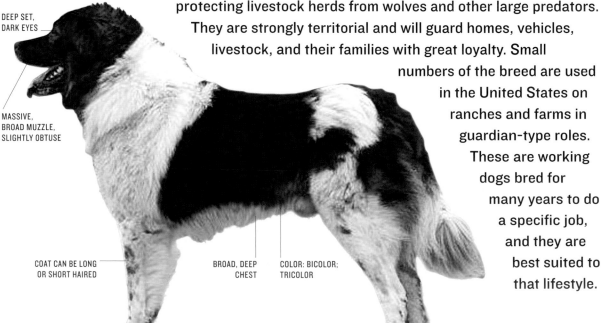

DEEP SET, DARK EYES

MASSIVE, BROAD MUZZLE, SLIGHTLY OBTUSE

COAT CAN BE LONG OR SHORT HAIRED

BROAD, DEEP CHEST

COLOR: BICOLOR; TRICOLOR

AT A GLANCE

Size: large

Exercise needed:

Grooming needed:

Aptitudes: guarding livestock, guard dog, watchdog

Height: 25–30 in.

Weight: 88–125 lb.

Average life expectancy: 12–14 yrs

AKC: not recognized

CHARACTER

Affection

Playfulness

Friendliness to dogs

Friendliness to strangers

Ease of training

GREATPYRENEES 135

AT A GLANCE

Size: very large

Exercise needed:

Grooming needed:

Aptitudes: guarding livestock, watchdog, companion

Height: 25–32 in.

Weight: 85–115 lb.

Average life expectancy: 10–12 yrs

AKC: working

CHARACTER

Affection

Playfulness

Friendliness to dogs

Friendliness to strangers

Ease of training

✚ HEALTH ✚

Generally healthy but hereditary problems can include hip dysplasia, bone cancer, and patellar luxation.

GREAT PYRENEES : FRANCE, SPAIN

This beautiful breed is known as the Pyrenean Mountain Dog in some countries and is distinctive due to its thick, white coat and impressive size. These dogs are valued as livestock guardians and watchdogs, and will live among huge flocks of sheep unsupervised, patrolling for predators. They are formidable and brave against intruders, but gentle and sweet-natured toward their families. Given their primary role, these dogs are independent thinkers and decision makers, which means they can be harder to train than some other breeds.

MODERATELY LONG, BROAD, MUSCULAR BACK

WEDGE-SHAPED HEAD WITH ROUNDED CROWN

FAIRLY SMALL, TRIANGULAR EARS LIE FLAT WHEN RESTING

MEDIUM-LENGTH MUZZLE WITH BLACK NOSE

DOUBLE DEWCLAWS ON HIND LEGS

HIND FEET MAY TURN OUT SLIGHTLY

HISTORY

The ancestors of the Great Pyrenees probably arrived in the Pyrenees Mountains region from Central Asia by 3000 BCE. Once there the breed began to develop in geographic isolation and adapted perfectly to the harsh climate and difficult mountainous terrain. They were first mentioned in 1407 by a French historian from Lourdes, who described them as the "great dogs of the mountain." In the seventeenth century, King Louis XIV of France declared them the royal dog of France, and they became prized by the aristocracy for guarding estates and livestock. During the same period, they accompanied Basque fishermen on their journeys to Newfoundland, and were influential in the development of the Newfoundland dog breed. General Lafayette introduced the breed to the United States in 1824, and in 1844 King Louis Philippe I of France gave one to Queen Victoria. When bears were reintroduced to the Pyrenees at the end of the twentieth century, local shepherds brought in extra Great Pyrenees to protect their flocks.

COMMON COAT COLORS

The coat is white, but can have patches of gray, badger, reddish brown, or tan.

WHITE   **PATCHES OF GRAY**

COAT CLOSE-UP

The topcoat is long, flat, and coarse. The undercoat is woolly.

COARSE

Great Pyrenees puppies are cute little balls of fluff, but they grow up to be exceptionally large dogs!

AT A GLANCE

Size: large

Exercise needed:

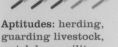

Grooming needed:

Aptitudes: herding, guarding livestock, watchdog, agility, draft, tracking, service, companion

Height: 23–29 in.

Weight: 130–140 lb.

Average life expectancy: 10–12 yrs

AKC: working

CHARACTER

Affection

Playfulness

Friendliness to dogs

Friendliness to strangers

Ease of training

✚ HEALTH ✚

Generally healthy but hereditary problems can include gastric torsion, cancer, distichiasis, entropion, elbow dysplasia, epilepsy, hip dysplasia, osteochondrosis dissecans, splenic torsion, and licking fits.

Swissies take at least two years, and often more, to reach physical and mental maturity.

GREATER SWISS MOUNTAIN DOG : SWITZERLAND

The Greater Swiss Mountain Dog is the largest and oldest of the four Swiss mountain-dog breeds and has been influential in the development of other breeds, such as the St. Bernard and Rottweiler. Given their size, strength, and gentle nature, the Greater Swiss Mountain Dog was frequently used for draft purposes on small holdings and farms, as well as for herding and guarding livestock and for guarding the homestead. Today, "Swissies" compete in a number of sporting events that reflect their history, including draft and weight pulling, as well as rally, herding, tracking, and agility. These are lovely dogs that thrive in a lively home.

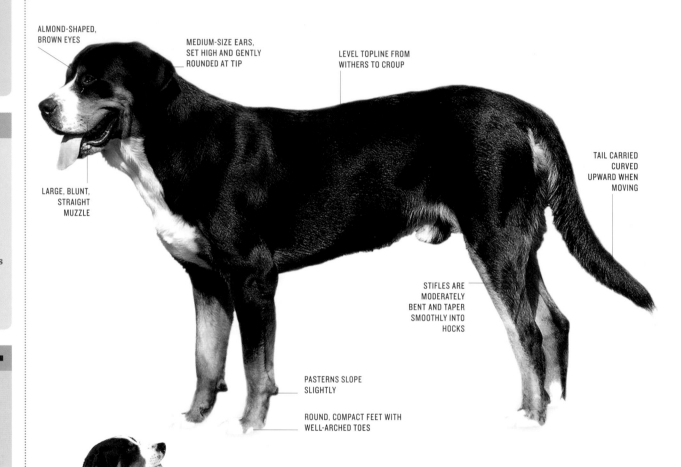

ALMOND-SHAPED, BROWN EYES

MEDIUM-SIZE EARS, SET HIGH AND GENTLY ROUNDED AT TIP

LEVEL TOPLINE FROM WITHERS TO CROUP

TAIL CARRIED CURVED UPWARD WHEN MOVING

LARGE, BLUNT, STRAIGHT MUZZLE

STIFLES ARE MODERATELY BENT AND TAPER SMOOTHLY INTO HOCKS

PASTERNS SLOPE SLIGHTLY

ROUND, COMPACT FEET WITH WELL-ARCHED TOES

HISTORY

Two theories, equally plausible, account for the origins of this ancient breed. The first attributed to mastiff-types introduced by the Romans when they began invading the Alps from 57 BCE. Alternatively, some historians believe that the seafaring Phoenicians took large mastiff-types with them when they settled the Iberian Peninsula from roughly 1100 BCE, and that these dogs migrated eastward influencing many of the large Continental European breeds. In the harsh Alpine region, the mountain breeds developed specific traits, and were in turn bred for their working functionality. Due to their size, Swissies were often used for driving cattle and smaller livestock, and were used to do many other jobs on small farms. As farming methods changed and machinery took over, the dogs began to decrease in number. In 1908 Swiss Professor Albert Heim, a breed expert, pushed for the breed to be recognized as distinct from other mountain dogs, and they were accepted as the Greater Swiss Mountain Dog in the Swiss Stud Book. Although they are rare both in their homeland and abroad, they are supported by dedicated enthusiasts.

COMMON COAT COLORS

The tricolor coat is black with white and tan markings.

TRICOLOR

COAT CLOSE-UP

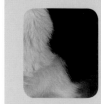

The double coat comprises a dense topcoat and thick undercoat.

DENSE

KARST SHEPHERD : SLOVENIA

The Karst Shepherd developed from ancient Molossian types and has been used for guarding and herding livestock for centuries. Dogs of a similar type are mentioned in Baron Vajkart Valvasor's 1689 book, *The Glory of the Duchy of Carniole*. The breed was originally known as the Illyrian Shepherd and was grouped with other shepherd dogs from former Yugoslavia, but in 1968, the Karst Shepherd was recognized as a separate breed. The dogs are still used to guard people and livestock or as companions.

EYES HAVE A CALM, MELANCHOLIC EXPRESSION

LARGE HEAD IN RELATION TO BODY

LONG, SLOPING SHOULDER BLADES

LONG, BROAD THIGHS

THICK, TIGHT LIPS WITH BLACK PIGMENTATION

LONG, FLAT COAT WITH ABUNDANT UNDERCOAT

KOMONDOR : HUNGARY

This distinctive breed is considered a national treasure in its homeland where, revered for its guarding instincts, it is known as the "king" of livestock-guardian breeds. It is so skilled and fearless that it has been attributed with clearing Hungary of its wolf population. Komondors are independent thinkers and decision makers, which combined with their natural protectiveness makes it essential that they live in an experienced dog-owning home. They are happiest when working outside and need consistent obedience training and socialization. For the right family, they are rewarding and dedicated workers and companions.

WHITE COAT

EARS HANG LOW AND ARE SHAPED LIKE ELONGATED TRIANGLES WITH ROUNDED TIPS

MUZZLE IS WIDE, COARSE, AND TRUNCATED

MUSCULAR NECK WITH NO DEWLAP

COAT HANGS IN TASSEL-LIKE CORDS WITH A WOOLLY UNDERCOAT

STRONG, LARGE FEET

AT A GLANCE

Size: very large

Exercise needed:

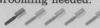

Grooming needed:

Aptitudes: watchdog, companion

Height: 28–30 in.

Weight: 110–180 lb.

Average life expectancy: 7–10 yrs

AKC: working

CHARACTER

Affection

Playfulness

Friendliness to dogs

Friendliness to strangers

Ease of training

✚ HEALTH ✚

Generally healthy but hereditary problems can include gastric torsion, hip and elbow dysplasia, bone cancer, and cardiomyopathy.

GREAT DANE : GERMANY

This majestic breed is one of the largest in the world and yet also one of the most elegant, lacking the bulky frame typical of most mastiff-types. Instead, the lovely Great Dane combines all the best parts of the mastiff with those of the hound. Historically the breed was renowned for its ferocity and used for hunting large game and for guarding the aristocracies' castles and estates. Today the breed is noted as a true gentle giant, loyal to its family, good with children, generally good with other animals, and protective of its home.

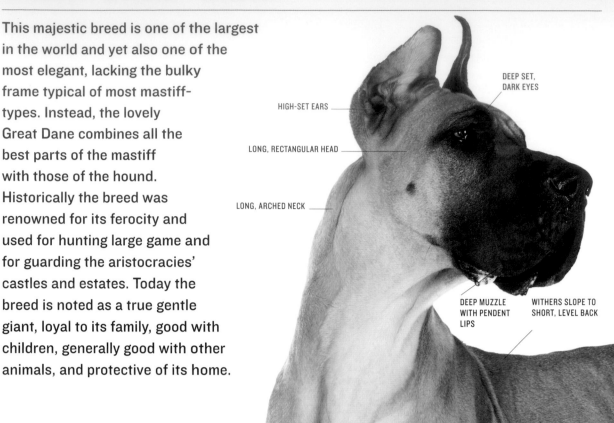

HIGH-SET EARS

LONG, RECTANGULAR HEAD

LONG, ARCHED NECK

DEEP SET, DARK EYES

DEEP MUZZLE WITH PENDENT LIPS

WITHERS SLOPE TO SHORT, LEVEL BACK

SLOPING SHOULDERS

Great Dane puppies go through rapid growth spurts and should not be overexercised.

COMMON COAT COLORS

Great Danes are often black, fawn, harlequin, brindle, or blue.

BLACK   FAWN   HARLEQUIN

HISTORY

Great Danes got their misleading name (they are not Danish) in the 1700s when French naturalist Comte de Buffon saw them in Denmark and assumed they originated there. It is something of a mystery why the name stuck! The breed probably descended from the original mastiff-types of prehistory that migrated from Central Asia westward into Europe, developing different characteristics over time. Greyhounds, Irish Wolfhounds, and Scottish Deerhounds are thought to have contributed to this giant breed. Historically, Great Danes were the preserve of the aristocracy and were greatly valued for their bravery when hunting. Although they often have their ears cropped in the United States, this practice was banned in England in 1894 by Edward, Prince of Wales. The breed became very popular in England, and two important kennels—the Send and Ouborough—were established in the 1920s and 1930s. Great Danes were recognized by the American Kennel Club in 1887, and since that time, the breed has consistently risen in popularity.

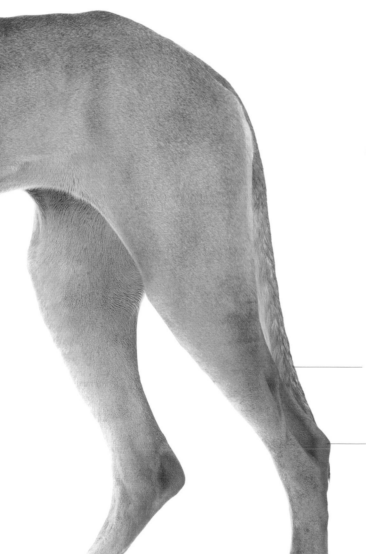

TAIL SET HIGH, CARRIED LEVEL WITH BACK WHEN ACTIVE

HOCKS SET LOW

COAT CLOSE-UP

The coat is short and smooth.

SMOOTH

KUVASZ : HUNGARY

AT A GLANCE

Size: large

Exercise needed:

Grooming needed:

Aptitudes: guarding livestock, guard dog, watchdog, companion

Height: 26–30 in.

Weight: 70–115 lb.

Average life expectancy: 10–12 yrs

AKC: working

CHARACTER

Affection

Playfulness

Friendliness to dogs

Friendliness to strangers

Ease of training

ALMOND-SHAPED, SOMEWHAT SLANTED EYES

WELL-DEVELOPED LOWER JAW

DEEP CHEST WITH LONG, WELL-SPRUNG RIBS

CAT-LIKE FEET

THICK DOUBLE COAT, COARSE IN TEXTURE AND RANGING FROM WAVY TO STRAIGHT

These noble-looking dogs were historically associated with the aristocracy in Hungary; the fifteenth-century king Mathias I reputedly always had at least one Kuvasz with him at all times. The origin of their name is believed to be Turkish, roughly translating as "armed guard of the nobility." The breed's guarding skills became legendary, and they eventually began to be used by farmers for protecting their livestock and farms. Kuvasz are spirited, devoted, and protective dogs that can make good companions for the right home. However, they require lots of space and consistent obedience training and socialization.

LANCASHIRE HEELER : ENGLAND

AT A GLANCE

Size: small

Exercise needed:

Grooming needed:

Aptitudes: herding, watchdog, agility, companion

Height: 10–12 in.

Weight: 12–14 lb.

Average life expectancy: 12–16 yrs

AKC: FSS

CHARACTER

Affection

Playfulness

Friendliness to dogs

Friendliness to strangers

Ease of training

The origins of this small, charismatic breed are not known, but it may have developed through Welsh Corgi and Manchester Terrier crosses, possibly when Corgis were being used to drive cattle to markets from Wales into northwest England. Some historians, however, insist that the Lancashire Heeler is the older breed and that it gave rise to the Corgi! Either way, the breed was valued for driving cattle and other livestock. These are bright, cheerful dogs that enjoy family life, keep homes free of vermin, and sound a vigorous alarm in response to intruders.

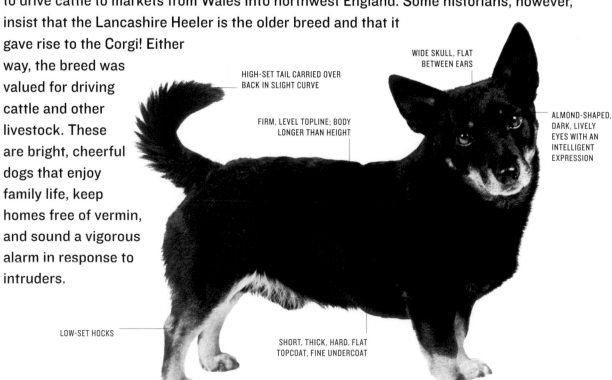

HIGH-SET TAIL CARRIED OVER BACK IN SLIGHT CURVE

WIDE SKULL, FLAT BETWEEN EARS

FIRM, LEVEL TOPLINE; BODY LONGER THAN HEIGHT

ALMOND-SHAPED, DARK, LIVELY EYES WITH AN INTELLIGENT EXPRESSION

LOW-SET HOCKS

SHORT, THICK, HARD, FLAT TOPCOAT, FINE UNDERCOAT

LANDSEER EUROPEAN CONTINENTAL : EUROPE

There are two types of Landseer: the European Continental, which is registered as a breed by the Fédération Cynologique Internationale; and a color variation of the Newfoundland, simply known as Landseer. The two were originally from the same stock, but specific breeding in Europe has seen the Landseer European Continental diverge away from the Newfoundland in type. The name Landseer was derived from the British painter, Sir Edwin Landseer, and his famous 1838 painting, *A Distinguished Member of the Humane Society*, depicting a black-and-white Newfoundland. The Continental is taller than Newfoundlands and has a shorter coat.

STRIKINGLY MODELED HEAD WITH NOBLE EXPRESSION AND FREE OF WRINKLES

MEDIUM-SIZE EARS, SET HIGH AND CARRIED CLOSE TO SIDES OF HEAD

LENGTH OF MUZZLE IS EQUAL TO ITS DEPTH

LONG, STRAIGHT, DENSE TOPCOAT, UNDERCOAT IS LESS DENSE THAN NEWFOUNDLAND'S

BODY IS WIDE AND STRONG FROM WITHERS TO CROUP

LEGS ARE SLIGHTLY FRINGED DOWN TO PASTERN

McNAB : UNITED STATES

The McNab is a herding breed that traces back to about 1885 to Alexander McNab, a Scottish farmer who emigrated to Mendocino County, California. Dissatisfied with the working ability of local dogs, he returned to Scotland and brought two Scotch Collies, Peter and Fred, back to the United States. Those were bred to Spanish dogs belonging to local Basque sheep-herders as well as to other imported Scotch Collies. The McNab is a versatile livestock dog that will "head" and "heel" and is also used for hunting. They are obedient, intelligent, enduring, and friendly and, as such, are popular with ranchers and farmers. They have no formal breed standard.

ALMOND-SHAPED EYES; BROWN, HAZEL, OR COPPER

MOSTLY PRICKED EARS, THOUGH SOME MAY FLOP OVER

COAT IS SHORT TO MEDIUM

BLACK WITH WHITE; RED WITH WHITE

AT A GLANCE

Size: very large

Exercise needed:

Grooming needed:

Aptitudes: watchdog, therapy, companion

Height: 25–32 in.

Weight: 100–170 lb.

Average life expectancy: 8–9 yrs

AKC: working

CHARACTER

Affection

Playfulness

Friendliness to dogs

Friendliness to strangers

Ease of training

LEONBERGER : GERMANY

The Leonberger traces to the nineteenth century and the efforts of Heinrich Essig, from Leonberg, in Germany. He is said to have used Newfoundlands, St. Bernards, and Great Pyrenees to establish the breed, and he exported them in large numbers. The first breed standard was written in 1895. Imposing, powerful dogs, they were used as farm dogs and for light draft. They also make wonderful family companions provided they are obedience trained and socialized. They have a naturally gentle and sweet temperament and are generally good with children and other dogs. Leonbergers have also been widely used as therapy dogs.

HEAD DEEPER THAN BROAD

DARK BROWN, MEDIUM-SIZE EYES

RELATIVELY LONG MUZZLE

NECK BLENDS SMOOTHLY INTO WITHERS

MEDIUM-TO-LONG, WATER-RESISTANT DOUBLE COAT

UNDERLINE SLIGHTLY TUCKED UP

AT A GLANCE

Size: very large

Exercise needed:

Grooming needed:

Aptitudes: guarding, watchdog, companion

Height: 27–32 in.

Weight: 100–150 lb.

Average life expectancy: over 10 yrs

AKC: not recognized

CHARACTER

Affection

Playfulness

Friendliness to dogs

Friendliness to strangers

ining

MOSCOW WATCHDOG : RUSSIA

The Moscow Watchdog was developed after World War II by the Soviet army specifically as a guard dog that could live in frigid sub-zero temperatures. The breeding program was led by General Medvedev at the Central School of Military Kynology and involved the use of three main breeds: St. Bernards, Caucasian Ovcharkas, and Russian Spotted Hounds. In 1986 a number of Moscow Watchdogs were taken to Hungary where they are now bred by a group of dedicated breeders. These dogs are instinctively protective and need to be consistently obedience trained. They also require quite a lot of exercise and regular grooming. However, they also have a sweet, calm nature and can be good family companions.

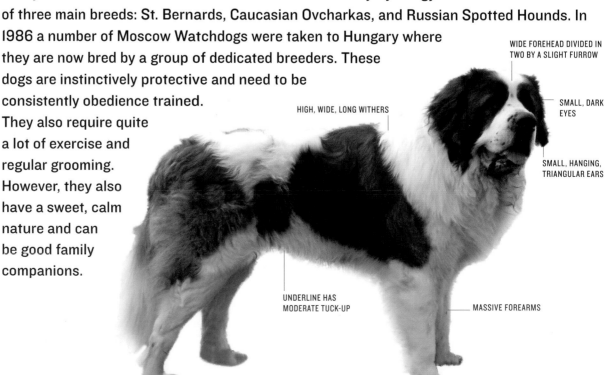
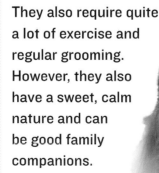

WIDE FOREHEAD DIVIDED IN TWO BY A SLIGHT FURROW

SMALL, DARK EYES

HIGH, WIDE, LONG WITHERS

SMALL, HANGING, TRIANGULAR EARS

UNDERLINE HAS MODERATE TUCK-UP

MASSIVE FOREARMS

MAREMMA SHEEPDOG : ITALY

The imposing Maremma Sheepdog developed in Italy's Abruzzi region in ancient times and has been the mainstay of shepherds' lives there for centuries. The dogs are natural livestock guardians and are instinctively territorial. Typically, they would be left to protect large flocks completely unattended and are independent thinkers. Fearless and loyal, Maremmas can make good companions for an experienced home, but are wary of strangers. They need to have consistent obedience training and socialization.

ALMOND-SHAPED, DARK EYES

SLIGHT ARCH OVER LOINS

GENTLY TAPERING MUZZLE

LOW SET TAIL WITH GENTLE CURVE AT TIP

FORELEGS ARE WELL BONED AND MUSCLED, WITHOUT HEAVINESS

LONG, HARSH COAT CAN HAVE A SLIGHT WAVE, UNDERCOAT IS THICK

MIORITIC : ROMANIA

The Mioritic is a large working breed that originated in the relative isolation of the Carpathian Mountains in Romania. The dogs were bred to protect livestock from wolves, bears, lynx, and other large predators, and are fearless guardians. They have extremely strong protective instincts and are wary of strangers, but balance this with a gentle and affectionate nature. They are also notably good with children. They are generally calm and level headed with a degree of independent thinking, and can make excellent family companions as long as they are properly obedience trained and socialized.

SLIGHTLY DOMED SKULL

LEVEL, STRONG, MUSCULAR BACK

ABUNDANT, HARSH TOPCOAT, WITH DENSE UNDERCOAT

LONG, POWERFUL FORELEGS

OVAL, COMPACT, AND MASSIVE FEET

WHITE, GRAY, OR PIEBALD COLOR

MUDI : HUNGARY

This breed is known as the "driver dog of Hungary" and is a source of great pride among local shepherds. The Mudi's heritage is closely entwined with that of the Pumi and Puli. Although not well known outside Hungary, in their homeland, these dogs are highly valued for their no-nonsense working skills and versatility. In addition to herding and guarding livestock, they can hunt small game, and have been used successfully as detection dogs. Less popular than the Pumi and the Puli, they are nevertheless playful, intense, and friendly dogs. They can be prone to shyness, which must be addressed through consistent socialization.

PRICKED EARS COVERED IN ABUNDANT HAIR

STRIKING WEDGE-SHAPED HEAD

NARROW, SLIGHTLY OBLIQUE EYES

STRONG MUZZLE WITH STRAIGHT BRIDGE

WAVY OR SLIGHTLY CURLED, DENSE, SHINY COAT

FAWN, BLACK, BLUE MERLE, ASH, BROWN, OR WHITE

AT A GLANCE

Size: medium-small

Exercise needed:
🐎 🐎 🐎 🐎 🐎

Grooming needed:

Aptitudes: herding, guarding livestock, watchdog, agility, drug detection, companion

Height: 15–18 in.

Weight: 18–29 lb.

Average life expectancy: 13–14 yrs

AKC: FSS

CHARACTER

Affection
🐾 🐾 🐾 🐾 🐾

Playfulness
🐾 🐾 🐾 🐾 🐾

Friendliness to dogs
🐾 🐾 🐾 🐾 🐾

Friendliness to strangers
🐾 🐾 🐾 🐾 🐾

Ease of training
🐾 🐾 🐾 🐾 🐾

NEW ZEALAND HEADING DOG : NEW ZEALAND

KEEN, ALERT, AND INTELLIGENT EXPRESSION

SLIGHTLY LONGER IN THE BODY THAN TALL IN HEIGHT

GENTLY TAPERING MUZZLE

UNDERLINE SHOWS SOME TUCK-UP

BLACK AND WHITE; BROWN AND WHITE; OR BLACK, WHITE, AND TAN

LONG LEGS WITH STRONG, FINE BONE

The New Zealand Heading Dog, or Eye Dog, is an excellent working breed of Border Collie origin. These dogs work in a similar manner to Border Collies, circling the flocks of sheep to move them, and establishing an intense eye contact to direct them. These are extremely quick, agile, and athletic dogs that are highly intelligent and respond well to training. They generally have very good temperaments but require a high-energy or working environment to thrive. There is no breed standard currently in place.

AT A GLANCE

Size: medium

Exercise needed:
🐎 🐎 🐎 🐎 🐎

Grooming needed:
🪮 🪮 🪮 🪮 🪮

Aptitudes: herding, watchdog, agility, companion

Height: 80–22 in.

Weight: 30–45 lb.

Average life expectancy: 10–14 yrs

AKC: not recognized

CHARACTER

Affection
🐾 🐾 🐾 🐾 🐾

Playfulness
🐾 🐾 🐾 🐾 🐾

Friendliness to dogs
🐾 🐾 🐾 🐾 🐾

Friendliness to strangers
🐾 🐾 🐾 🐾 🐾

Ease of training
🐾 🐾 🐾 🐾 🐾

AT A GLANCE

Size: very large

Exercise needed:

Grooming needed:

Aptitudes: guarding, watchdog, companion

Height: 24–31 in.

Weight: 150–110lb.

Average life expectancy: 8–10 yrs

AKC: working group

CHARACTER

Affection

Playfulness

Friendliness to dogs
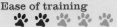

Friendliness to strangers

Ease of training

NEAPOLITAN MASTIFF : ITALY

The Neapolitan Mastiff traces its history back to ancient times and the war dogs used by the Roman army. Artwork from this period, and even earlier, depicts dogs with a similar appearance. These ancient war dogs gave rise to a number of the modern mastiff breeds, of which the Neapolitan is one. Over time, Italians focused their breeding on developing dogs for protecting large estates and castles. The breed began to be actively promoted after World War I, when six were exhibited and a breed standard drawn up in 1949. The standard was rewritten in 1971. The breed is distinctive due to its thick, loose skin; extensive wrinkles; voluminous dewlap; massive frame; and slow, lumbering gait. They are not suitable for first-time dog owners.

HEAD LARGE IN PROPORTION TO BODY AND COVERED WITH EXTENSIVE WRINKLES

DEEP-SET EYES ALMOST HIDDEN BY DROOPING EYELIDS

MUZZLE AS BROAD AS IT IS LONG

HEAVY, THICK, LONG, AND PENDULOUS LIPS

VOLUMINOUS AND WELL-DIVIDED DEWLAP

SHORT, DENSE COAT

AT A GLANCE

Size: medium-small

Exercise needed:

Grooming needed:

Aptitudes: guard dog, watchdog, companion

Height: 16–20 in.

Weight: 50–80 lb.

Average life expectancy: 9–14 yrs

AKC: not recognized

CHARACTER

Affection

Playfulness

Friendliness to dogs

Friendliness to strangers

Ease of training

OLDE ENGLISH BULLDOGGE : UNITED STATES

This recent breed was developed in the 1970s by David Leavitt in Pennsylvania using English Bulldogs, Bullmastiffs, American Bulldogs, and American Pit Bull Terriers. His objective was to re-create "the Regency period bull baiter," returning to the renowned athleticism of the historic English Bulldog type, while maintaining the excellent temperament of the modern breed. The United Kennel Club recognized the Olde English Bulldogge standard on January 1, 2014. These are friendly, confident, and alert dogs that can make suitable companions and are good watchdogs.

LARGE SKULL WITH DEFINED FURROW FROM STOP TO BACK OF HEAD

ROSE EARS PREFERRED BUT CAN BE BUTTON OR TULIP, SET HIGH, WIDE AND TO THE BACK OF SKULL

BODY IS STURDY, POWERFUL, AND SLIGHTLY RECTANGULAR

SQUARE, WIDE, AND DEEP MUZZLE

WIDE, SLIGHTLY ARCHED NECK WITH DOUBLE DEWLAP

FORELEGS HAVE MEDIUM BONE AND SET STRAIGHT

OLD ENGLISH SHEEPDOG : ENGLAND

This lovely breed is most distinctive for its long, shaggy coat and appealing appearance, so much so that the Old English Sheepdog has often been used in advertising. Despite their rather glamorous appearance when groomed, however, these are agile, enduring, and powerful working dogs that were favored by shepherds for their herding, droving, and protective instincts. Their tremendous coat insulates them against the worst weather and provides protection against predators. Old English Sheepdogs are affectionate, intelligent, and lively dogs that make wonderful family companions.

AT A GLANCE

Size: medium

Exercise needed:

Grooming needed:

Aptitudes: herding, watchdog, agility, companion

Height: 21–22 in.

Weight: 60–90 lb.

Average life expectancy: 10–12 yrs

AKC: herding

CHARACTER

Affection
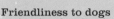

Playfulness

Friendliness to dogs

Friendliness to strangers

Ease of training

✚ HEALTH ✚

Generally healthy but hereditary problems can include hip dysplasia, gastric torsion, cerebellar ataxia, eye problems, and ear infections.

LONG HAIR COVERS FACE

SMALL EARS CARRIED FLAT TO HEAD

SQUARE MUZZLE

SMALL, ROUND FEET

SQUARISH HEAD WITH A BROAD SKULL

LARGE, BLACK NOSE

SHORT, COMPACT BODY

SLOPING SHOULDERS

HISTORY

This breed traces back to Russian Ovcharka and Bearded Collie ancestry, with the possible addition of Briard, although no early records exist. In the eighteenth century, a dog tax was introduced on pet dogs, but working dogs, differentiated by having "bobbed" tails, were exempt. So Old English Sheepdogs had their tails docked and were often known as Bobtails. By the nineteenth century, they had developed a specific type and were common in the South Downs region of Sussex, where they were used for driving cattle, sheep, and sometimes ponies to market. The first UK standard was written in 1888 and the first American one in 1904. In the United States, the breed became fashionable among the wealthiest families including the Guggenheims and Vanderbilts who did much to promote the dogs. They are now popular on both sides of the Atlantic.

COMMON COAT COLORS

GRAY

GRIZZLE

BLUE

The coat can be shades of gray, grizzle, blue, or blue merle; with or without white markings.

COAT CLOSE-UP

SHAGGY

Long, shaggy and harsh coat.

Old English Sheepdogs are particularly cute as puppies, but as they come into their full coat, it will take a serious time commitment to keep them properly groomed. Puppies' coats will invariably darken with age.

AT A GLANCE

Size: large

Exercise needed:
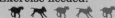

Grooming needed:

Aptitudes: search and rescue, draft, companion

Height: 26–28 in.

Weight: 100–150 lb.

Average life expectancy: 8–10 yrs

AKC: working

CHARACTER

Affection

Playfulness

Friendliness to dogs

Friendliness to strangers

Ease of training

✚ HEALTH ✚

Generally healthy, some hereditary problems can include hip dysplasia, elbow dysplasia, gastric torsion, subvalvular aortic stenosis, and arthritis.

NEWFOUNDLAND : CANADA

This remarkable breed has been an incredible servant to humankind and is known for its inherent instinct to protect and save people from danger, in particular water rescues. Tales of the breed's heroism are legion. Their gentle, calm, and devoted temperament makes them wonderful companions. Newfoundlands are large dogs that require moderate exercise and grooming, and relish the opportunity to swim.

BROAD, LARGE HEAD

SMALL, WIDE-SET, DARK EYES

LARGE, MUSCULAR HINDQUARTERS

SMALL EARS LIE CLOSE TO HEAD

SHORT, SQUARE MUZZLE

STRONG NECK OF MODERATE LENGTH

DEEP, BROAD CHEST

LONG TAIL CARRIED SLIGHTLY ELEVATED WHEN MOVING

STRONG WEBBING BETWEEN PADS

HISTORY

The breed traces back to the Canadian island of Newfoundland and to crosses between European breeds, taken there by fisherman, and native stock. It is thought that British and Portuguese Mastiff-types and mountain-dog breeds like the Great Pyrenees contributed to a type known as the St. Johns Dog. The St. Johns Dog developed into two types, one leading to the Labrador and the other to the Newfoundland. The Newfoundland was widely used in the fishing industry in all manner of roles, including hauling nets and boats, swimming out to retrieve boats, and search and rescue. Breed numbers were decimated during both world wars, but they have been re-established in the United States and beyond, and are still valued for their search and rescue skills.

COMMON COAT COLORS

BLACK

BLACK & WHITE

Black, black and white, brown, or gray.

COAT CLOSE-UP

Water-resistant, medium-length, coarse, straight or wavy topcoat, with soft, dense undercoat.

STRAIGHT OR WAVY

Newfoundland puppies grow very quic[k...] reach around two thirds of their adult [...] time they are eight months old.

POLISH TATRA SHEEPDOG : POLAND

SLIGHTLY ROUNDED SKULL

THICK, TRIANGULAR EARS, WELL FURNISHED WITH HAIR

WITHERS DISTINCTLY MARKED AND BROAD

LONG AND MASSIVE BODY

WHITE COAT

LONG, THICK, STRAIGHT, OR SLIGHTLY WAVY COAT WITH PROFUSE UNDERCOAT

This rare breed originated in the Podhale region of southern Poland in the Carpathian Mountains and has been bred over many years specifically as for guarding livestock and for herding. These dogs particularly excel as livestock guardians, and they will remain among their flock unattended for long periods. The breed deters predators instead of attacking, although it will attack if it is left no option. Tatras are large, beautiful, and gentle dogs with a massive build and great strength; they are vigilant guard and watchdogs and have a tendency to bark. They are best suited to an experienced home that will provide them with consistent socialization.

POLISH LOWLAND SHEEPDOG : POLAND

Also known as the Polish Owczarek Nizinny, this breed is popular in its homeland and is increasingly popular overseas. It is related to the Puli and is believed to have influenced the development of the Bearded Collie, to which it bears a close similarity. They are superb working dogs and will herd sheep and cattle as well as act as a livestock guardian. More recently, they have become popular companion animals and thrive in a busy, active home. They will provide a good measure of home security and are generally sweet natured and loyal with their families.

PROFUSE HAIR ON FOREHEAD, CHEEKS, AND CHIN MAKE HEAD APPEAR LARGER THAN IT IS

HEART-SHAPED, PENDENT EARS

MEDIUM-LENGTH, MUSCULAR, AND STRONG NECK

HEAVILY MUSCLED SHOULDERS

LONG, DENSE, SHAGGY DOUBLE COAT

ANY COLOR, MOST COMMONLY WHITE WITH BLACK, GRAY, OR SANDY PATCHES

PULI : HUNGARY

The origin of the Puli is a mystery. There is speculation that they developed either from herding dogs of the Magyar people who settled in the Danube region in the ninth century, or that they arrived with the Cumans in the thirteenth century. Both peoples had herding and guarding dogs, and the Hungarian Komondor, Puli, Pumi, and Mudi are believed to share a similar heritage. Pulis are intensely tough working dogs whose enormous corded coats provides them with great protection against the elements and predators. They are inclined to bark excessively and are active, agile, comical, curious, and headstrong. They are fiercely protective of their families and can be wary of other dogs.

OUTERCOAT IS WAVY OR CURLY, UNDERCOAT IS SOFT AND WOOLLY. COAT CLUMPS TOGETHER TO FORM CORDS

LARGE, DEEP-SET, DARK EYES

STRONG, STRAIGHT MUZZLE

STRONG, MUSCULAR NECK

RUSTY BLACK, BLACK, SHADES OF GRAY, WHITE

STRAIGHT, STRONG, MEDIUM-BONED FORELEGS

AT A GLANCE

Size: medium-small

Exercise needed:

Grooming needed:

Aptitudes: herding, guarding livestock, watchdog, companion

Height: 16–17 in.

Weight: 25–35 lb.

Average life expectancy: 10–15 yrs

AKC: herding

CHARACTER

Affection

Playfulness

Friendliness to dogs

Friendliness to strangers

Ease of training

PUMI : HUNGARY

The delightful Pumi is a lively herding breed of similar heritage to the Puli. The Pumi is thought also to have some influence from terrier types, Briards, and possibly Keeshonds. The term Pumi was first used in 1801, but this was probably a generic term for Hungarian herding dogs. They were divided into separate breeds in 1921 by Dr. Emil Raitsis. Pumis are brave, bright, and engaging dogs that are still used for herding cattle, sheep, and pigs in addition to being used to hunt wild boar. They can have a tendency to bark but make great family companions for an active home.

LONG HEAD; MUZZLE 40 TO 50 PERCENT OF LENGTH OF HEAD

HARSH TOPCOAT AND SOFT UNDERCOAT

LONG, STRAIGHT FORELEGS WITH MEDIUM BONE

CAT-LIKE FEET WITH TIGHT-KNIT TOES

BLACK. WHITE, SHADES OF GRAY, OR SHADES OF FAWN

AT A GLANCE

Size: medium-small

Exercise needed:

Grooming needed:

Aptitudes: herding, guarding livestock, watchdog, companion

Height: 15–19 in.

Weight: 22–29 lb.

Average life expectancy: 12–13 yrs

AKC: FSS

CHARACTER

Affection

Playfulness

Friendliness to dogs

Friendliness to strangers

Ease of training

PERRO DE PASTOR MALLORQUIN : SPAIN

Little is known about the origin of these black livestock dogs that are used across the Balearic Islands, but they are valued by local farmers for their guarding skills and general farm work. It is unusual for a dark-coated breed to have adapted so well to a hot climate The dogs have been bred for working skills not appearance and have a slightly rugged look. They are instinctively protective and can be aggressive to intruders. The breed is best suited to a working environment or an experienced dog-owning home.

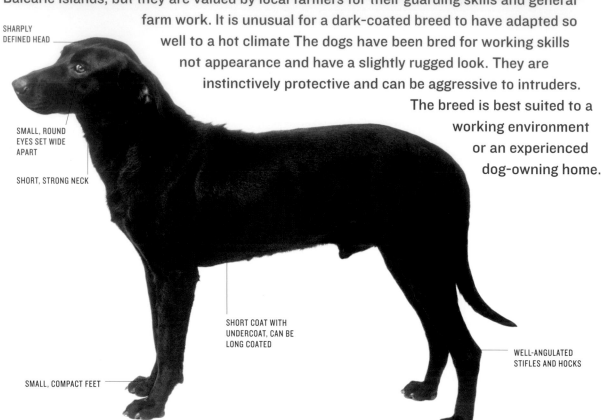

SHARPLY DEFINED HEAD

SMALL, ROUND EYES SET WIDE APART

SHORT, STRONG NECK

SHORT COAT WITH UNDERCOAT, CAN BE LONG COATED

WELL-ANGULATED STIFLES AND HOCKS

SMALL, COMPACT FEET

PERRO DE PRESA MALLORQUIN : SPAIN

The history of the Perro de Presa Mallorquin, also known as the Ca de Bou, is undocumented but it is believed to have developed from mastiff-types. Dog fighting and bull baiting were popular sports on Majorca until the late 19th century, with dogs on the island bred specifically for these purposes. By 1923 the Perro de Presa had an established type and was entered into the Spanish Stud Book. The breed was almost extinct following World War II but has been on the increase. These dogs are not suitable for first-time dog owners.

LARGE, OVAL DARK EYES

SHORT SHOULDERS

BROAD, CONICAL MUZZLE

STRONG, PROTRUDING JAW MUSCLES

STRONG, THICK NECK WITH SLIGHT DEWLAP

BRINDLE, FAWN, OR BLACK

PERRO DE PRESA CANARIO : SPAIN

MASSIVE HEAD COVERED WITH THICK SKIN

WIDE-SET EYES

WIDE MUZZLE NARROWS SLIGHTLY TO NOSE

NECK SHORTER IN LENGTH THAN HEAD, WITH SLIGHT DEWLAP

LONG, BROAD, DEEP BODY

SHADES OF BRINDLE OR FAWN

These imposing dogs have a history that is documented to the fifteenth century. They are likely descended from mastiff-type war dogs taken to the Canary Islands by the Spanish conquistadors. The dogs developed their specific characteristics on the islands and became noted for their guarding skills and for driving and holding cattle. They also became popular for dog fighting before that gruesome blood sport was banned. In the 1940s, the breed almost disappeared, but has been re-established and was recognized by the Real Canine Society Central of Spain in 1983. They are not suitable for first-time dog owners.

PYRENEAN MASTIFF : SPAIN

The Pyrenean Mastiff is an ancient breed descended from prehistoric Molosser dogs that lived in the Pyrenean region between Aragon and Navarra. These imposing dogs were used for herding and guarding the shepherds' flocks from bears and wolves. They wore spiked, metal collars to protect their necks. Predator populations diminished by the 1930s, and the Pyrenean Mastiff almost disappeared too, but was saved by the efforts of enthusiasts. They make loyal companions and are excellent guard and watchdogs.

LARGE, STRONG, FAIRLY LONG HEAD

MEDIUM-SIZE, V-SHAPED EARS

DOUBLE DEWLAPS

HEAVILY BONED HINDQUARTERS

RECTANGULAR BODY SHOWS GREAT POWER

SLIGHTLY OVAL, CAT-LIKE FEET

PYRENEAN SHEPHERD : FRANCE

The lively and charismatic Pyrenean Shepherd is known locally as Le Berger des Pyrenees. These dogs have been used for hundreds of years in the Pyrenees Mountains of southern France as the shepherd's helper, chiefly herding livestock but also providing good guardianship. The breed was virtually unknown outside its home until World War I, when thousands of them were drafted into active service and used as "communications dogs"— ferrying messages at high speed. They were described by an officer as being "the most intelligent, cunning … and the fastest" of all the breeds used. Pyreneans are charming, agile dogs, slightly wary of strangers but devoted family companions for an active home.

EARS ARE FAIRLY SHORT AND WIDE AT BASE

LONG NECK FLOWS SMOOTHLY INTO SHOULDERS

LONG BODY, WITH SHORT LOINS

INTELLIGENT AND SLIGHTLY CHEEKY EXPRESSION

SHADES OF FAWN WITH OR WITHOUT MIXTURE OF BLACK HAIRS; GRAY; MERLES; BRINDLE; BLACK WITH WHITE MARKINGS

FORELEGS ARE LIGHT BONED AND SINEWY

SCHAPENDOES : NETHERLANDS

The Schapendoes, or Dutch Sheepdog, developed in the Drenthe province of the Netherlands where it has been a working livestock breed for many centuries. The dogs were used for a variety of roles on farms, but excelled at herding, and are still used for this today. Although they were once widespread in the Netherlands, the breed was close to extinction by the end of World War II. It was re-established by enthusiasts, notably the Dutch author and martial-arts pioneer Pieter Toepoel. They are related to the Bearded Collie, Puli, Briard, and Owczarek Nizinny. Schapendoes are engaging, intelligent dogs that make wonderful family companions for an active home, and excel at events such as agility.

HEAD IS COVERED IN HAIR WITH CHARACTERISTIC "TOPKNOT" AND BEARD

LARGE EYES, PLACED MORE TO FRONT THAN SIDES OF HEAD

EARS ARE SET HIGH AND ARE AMPLY FEATHERED

THICK, LONG, LIGHTLY WAVY COAT WITH UNDERCOAT;

LARGE FEET

SAARLOOSWOLFHOUND : NETHERLANDS, GERMANY

HEAD AND NECK FORM HORIZONTAL WHEN DOG IS TROTTING

WEDGE-SHAPED HEAD THAT RESEMBLES A WOLF

MUSCULAR NECK MERGES INTO BACK WITH FLOWING LINE

WOLF GRAY, BROWN, OR WHITE

DOUBLE COAT; IN WINTER UNDERCOAT PREDOMINATES, AND IN SUMMER GUARD HAIRS OF TOPCOAT PREDOMINATE

This relatively new breed was developed by Leendert Saarloos in the twentieth century based on a male German Shepherd named Gerard van der Fransenum and a female wolf named Fleuri. Further German Shepherd and wolf blood was later introduced. Saarlooswolfhounds were originally bred to be service or guide dogs, but proved unsuitable because they retain the independence of the wolf. They are only suitable for experienced dog-owning homes that can provide them with extensive space and exercise.

ŠARPLANINAC : SERBIA, REPUBLIC OF MACEDONIA

The Šarplaninac is an ancient breed that developed in the southeastern mountainous regions of former Yugoslavia. The breed is a preeminent livestock guardian and has had little influence from outside breeds. They are calm, dignified dogs that are defensive rather than aggressive, although if provoked they will protect their herds with vigor. Their protectiveness transfers to their families and they are intensely loyal. They are best suited to a working, experienced home.

SLIGHTLY DOMED SKULL, BROAD BETWEEN THE EARS

EARS COVERED IN SHORT, DENSE HAIR

BROAD, DEEP MUZZLE TAPERS SLIGHTLY TO NOSE

ANY SOLID COLOR FROM WHITE TO DARK BROWN

MUSCULAR HINDQUARTERS SET SLIGHTLY WIDER APART THAN FORELEGS

AT A GLANCE

Size: medium-small

Exercise needed:

Grooming needed:

Aptitudes: herding, watchdog, agility, companion

Height: 22–26 in.

Weight: 50–75 lb.

Average life expectancy: 8–12 yrs

AKC: herding

CHARACTER

Affection

Playfulness

Friendliness to dogs

Friendliness to strangers

Ease of training

✚ HEALTH ✚

Generally healthy, but hereditary problems can include Collie eye anomaly, gastric torsion, and progressive retinal atrophy.

COLLIE : SCOTLAND

The beautiful Collie goes by a number of names: Rough Collie, English Collie, Scottish Collie, and also, simply, Collie. As if this were not confusing enough, there is also the Smooth Collie, which in some countries is considered a separate breed, and in others, such as the United States, is considered a coat variety of the rough-coated Collie. The Collie was developed as a working breed chiefly to herd livestock, but it also has some protective and guardian instincts. Today this lovely breed is an active, intelligent, and highly trainable companion animal that is good with children and other animals.

Collies have a tendency to bark a lot. It is worth trying to dissuade them from this habit when they are puppies.

LONG, HEAVILY FEATHERED TAIL CARRIED LOW

HISTORY

The Collie developed in the Scottish Highlands and the upland and moorland areas of the British Isles through a combination of local working stock. Borzoi was also introduced to the breed, as were Deerhounds and Greyhounds. The "Colley Club" was established in 1881 in England and set a breed standard that has not changed much since. Collies were promoted by the British Royal family; Queen Victoria became an enthusiastic owner. The breed arrived in the United States in 1879, President Calvin Coolidge and his wife had several Collies, which helped to popularize them. The Collie regularly ranks among the top forty most popular breeds in the United States and is staunchly supported in England.

COMMON COAT COLORS

The Collie's coat is often sable and white, blue merle, or tricolor.

SABLE & WHITE   **BLUE MERLE**   **TRICOLOR**

COAT CLOSE-UP

The topcoat is straight, harsh, and long; the undercoat is thick and soft.

STRAIGHT

SMALL, VELVETY EARS CARRIED
SEMI-ERECT WHEN ALERT, WITH
TIPS TIPPING FORWARD

HEAD RESEMBLES
BLUNT, LEAN WEDGE

KIND, DARK EYES

LONG, MUSCULAR,
ARCHED NECK

LONG BODY

DEEP CHEST

STRAIGHT FORELEGS
WITH FEATHERING

The Collie's sable coloring traces to
Old Cockie who was born in 1867.
Another important early Collie was
Trefoil, born in 1873. Trefoil had a
verifiable pedigree and was owned
by British politician Sewallis Shirley
who established the Kennel Club in
England. Every Collie today can trace
its heritage back to Trefoil.

SMOOTH COLLIE : SCOTLAND

Like its relative the Collie, the Smooth Collie was originally bred for herding livestock and watching over the homestead, and the breed still exhibits both of these skills. Although Smooth Collies are still worked in some areas, they are mostly companion animals now and make wonderful additions to active homes. Smooth Collies are energetic, athletic dogs that excel in agility classes as well as herding classes, fly ball, and all manner of fast-paced pursuits. They are affectionate with their families and like to be actively involved in everything that is going on. They will vigorously sound the alarm if strangers approach their property.

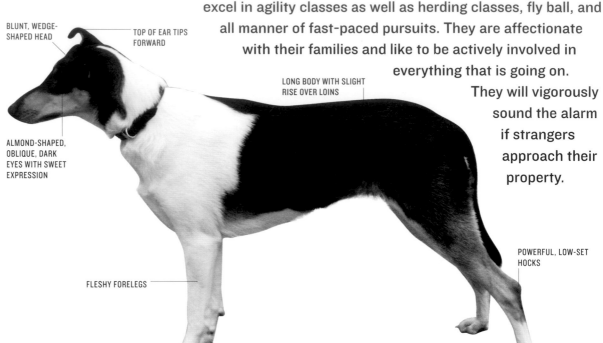

BLUNT, WEDGE-SHAPED HEAD

TOP OF EAR TIPS FORWARD

LONG BODY WITH SLIGHT RISE OVER LOINS

ALMOND-SHAPED, OBLIQUE, DARK EYES WITH SWEET EXPRESSION

POWERFUL, LOW-SET HOCKS

FLESHY FORELEGS

SPANISH WATER DOG : SPAIN

This ancient breed goes back at least 800 years, and developed on the Iberian Peninsula. A written account of "woolly-coated" dogs in this area dates to 1100, and historians assume that these were the Spanish Water Dogs' ancestors. These dogs were primarily used for herding livestock in central and southern Spain, and in the northern coastal areas, they were valued for helping fishermen by retrieving nets and guarding boats. They are loyal and personable, but require lots of exercise and diversions.

DROOPING, TRIANGULAR EARS

MUZZLE IS WIDE AT BASE AND TAPERS SLIGHTLY TO TIP

BROAD CHEST REACHES AT LEAST TO THE ELBOWS

CHARACTERISTIC CURLY, WOOLLY COAT

CHARACTER

Affection

Playfulness

Friendliness to dogs

Friendliness to strangers

Ease of training

✚ HEALTH ✚

Generally healthy, but hereditary problems can include hemophilia, cancer, Collie eye anomaly, cataracts, hip and elbow dysplasia, and dental problems.

SHETLAND SHEEPDOG : SCOTLAND

The Shetland Sheepdog is more commonly known as the "Sheltie" and is a delightful small working breed, that is full of character. These are effectively working Collies on a small scale and exhibit Collie characteristics. They are exceptionally obedient dogs, are easy to train, and adapt to a variety of living conditions. The Sheltie is highly intelligent and agile, and when it is not working, excels at agility and obedience classes. These dogs are affectionate and loyal with their families, occasionally wary of strangers, and have a tendency to bark. When they are herding (sheep, poultry, children, or anything else!) they often bark. Shelties make excellent companion dogs for active homes.

SMALL, FLEXIBLE EARS, SET HIGH; ERECT WITH TIP FOLDING FORWARD

LONG, BLUNT, WEDGE-SHAPED HEAD

TAIL CARRIED STRAIGHT DOWN OR SLIGHTLY CURVED UPWARD, HIGHER WHEN ALERT BUT NOT ABOVE BACK

MUSCULAR, ARCHED NECK

BRISKET REACHES TO THE ELBOW

CLEAN CUT, ANGULAR, SINEWY HOCK JOINTS

OVAL, COMPACT FEET WITH WELL-ARCHED TOES

HISTORY

The Sheltie developed in the nineteenth century in the remote and rugged location of the Shetland Islands situated off the northeast coast of Scotland. Historians speculate that spitz-type dogs from Scandinavia might have played a part in the Sheltie's development, in addition to small breeds like the King Charles Spaniel and, of course, the original Collie. Visitors to the Shetland Islands were enamored with the small, beautiful dogs, and locals began to sell them. One of the main early breeders was James Loggie at his Lerwick Kennels. The breed was first registered in Lerwick in 1908, the same year Shelties arrived in the United States. The American Kennel Club recognized the breed in 1911.

COMMON COAT COLORS

SABLE

TRICOLOR

The coat can be sable, black, or blue merle; with white and/or tan markings.

COAT CLOSE-UP

STRAIGHT

The Sheltie's topcoat is straight, harsh, and long; the undercoat is thick and soft.

Sheltie puppies should be brushed and groomed as early as possible and encouraged to enjoy the experience—it will make life much easier when they are older!

SOUTH RUSSIAN OVCHARKA : UKRAINE, RUSSIA

The South Russian Ovcharka is a large guardian breed, and its instinct to protect is extremely strong. These dogs will identify who their families are (including other family pets) and will defend them rigorously against any perceived threat. They are extremely independent thinkers, as are most livestock guardians, and will make their own decisions. They need excellent obedience training and consistent socialization to fit into family life. The South Russian Ovcharka makes a wonderful guard dog and family companion, but is not suitable for first-time dog owners

SHORT, BROAD, AND ROUNDED LOIN

SMALL, TRIANGULAR, HANGING EARS

MODERATE TUCK-UP

OVAL FEET COVERED WITH LONG HAIR

MODERATELY BROAD FOREHEAD

AT A GLANCE

Size: large

Exercise needed:

Grooming needed:

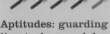

Aptitudes: guarding livestock, guard dog, watchdog, companion

Height: 24–26 in.

Weight: 100–110 lb.

Average life expectancy: 9–11 yrs

AKC: not recognized

CHARACTER

Affection

Playfulness

Friendliness to dogs

Friendliness to strangers

Ease of training

✚ HEALTH ✚

Generally healthy, but hereditary problems can include hip dysplasia, entropion, heart failure, and epilepsy.

Puppies should be placed in their new homes when they are between eight and ten weeks old and socialization should start immediately. These puppies need consistent training and socialization, but they should not be overexercised.

COMMON COAT COLORS

The coat is usually white, gray, or beige.

WHITE

COAT CLOSE-UP

The Ovcharka has a long, coarse, dense topcoat, with thick undercoat.

DENSE

HISTORY

One of three Russian Ovcharka breeds—*ovcharka* means "sheepdog"—South Russian Ovcharkas are most associated with the Crimea in the Ukraine and specifically with the Askania Nova sheep-farming area. Historically these dogs accompanied vast flocks that traveled from Spain to the Ukraine. The sheep were driven on foot over land, protected along the way by shaggy European sheepdog breeds. Once they arrived in Askania Nova, sometimes two years later, the dogs crossed with local stock like the Komondor, Caucasian Ovcharka, and Crimean Greyhound, giving rise eventually to the modern South Russian Ovcharka. Four or five of the dogs were used to protect 1,000 sheep, and by the nineteenth century, they were widespread in the area. The South Russian Ovcharka has been bred for its guarding skills and on occasion aggression, although this is now a disqualification on the breed standard. It takes its duties very seriously and is a superb guard dog.

AT A GLANCE

Size: medium-small

Exercise needed:

Grooming needed:

Aptitudes: watchdog, agility, companion

Height: 18–20 in.

Weight: 45–60 lb.

Average life expectancy: 8–10 yrs

AKC: non-sporting

CHARACTER

Affection
🐾 🐾 🐾 🐾 🐾

Playfulness
🐾 🐾 🐾 🐾 🐾

Friendliness to dogs
🐾 🐾 🐾 🐾 🐾

Friendliness to strangers
🐾 🐾 🐾 🐾 🐾

Ease of training
🐾 🐾 🐾 🐾 🐾

✚ HEALTH ✚

Generally healthy, but hereditary problems can include hip dysplasia, patellar luxation, eyelid problems, ear problems, and allergies.

CHINESE SHAR-PEI : CHINA

There is no mistaking the distinctive furrowed brow of the lovely Shar-Pei, whose frown, according to folklore, was enough to ward off evil spirits. These calm and dignified dogs were originally bred as all-purpose farm dogs to herd and guard livestock, to hunt, track, and protect the home. Today they are mostly found as companion animals and make a wonderful addition to the family. Shar-Peis are often aloof with strangers but fiercely loyal and protective of their families, and they will get along with other pets and children if correctly introduced. They are affectionate in nature, plucky in spirit, and love a good game, a romp, or an agility circuit.

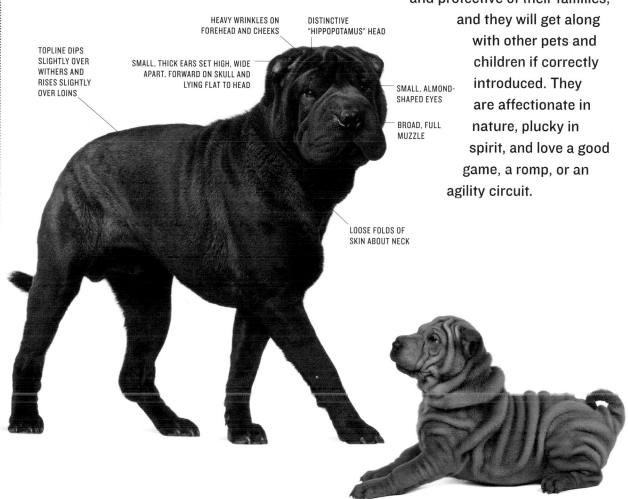

HEAVY WRINKLES ON FOREHEAD AND CHEEKS

DISTINCTIVE "HIPPOPOTAMUS" HEAD

TOPLINE DIPS SLIGHTLY OVER WITHERS AND RISES SLIGHTLY OVER LOINS

SMALL, THICK EARS SET HIGH, WIDE APART, FORWARD ON SKULL AND LYING FLAT TO HEAD

SMALL, ALMOND-SHAPED EYES

BROAD, FULL MUZZLE

LOOSE FOLDS OF SKIN ABOUT NECK

Shar-Pei puppies grow into their wrinkles as they mature.

HISTORY

The Shar-Pei is an ancient breed tracing back to at least the Chinese Han period, 206 BCE–220 CE, and they are depicted on pottery from this period. They may be related to the Chow Chow and share many similarities with the Tibetan Mastiff. Historically, they were used for farming and fighting, with the village of Tai Leh in southern China famous for its dog fights; the Shar-Pei is often said to have developed there. The breed was almost destroyed in 1911 during the Communist Revolution and again in 1949 when the People's Republic of China was established and dogs were deemed an unnecessary luxury, leading to their mass extermination. Some were smuggled out of the country to Hong Kong, Macao, and Taiwan in the 1960s, and during the same period, a few Shar-Pei were imported to the United States. In 1978 *Guinness World Records* recorded the breed as the rarest dog breed in the world. Breed numbers have since increased, and the Shar-Pei is now enthusiastically supported in the United States, England, and across much of the world.

COMMON COAT COLORS

BROWN

TAN

CREAM

SABLE

The Shar-Pei's coat can be any solid color including brown, tan, cream, and sable.

COAT CLOSE-UP

HARSH

The short coat is harsh and "off standing"—with a distinctive bristly texture.

SWEDISH VALLHUND : SWEDEN

The Swedish Vallhund, or Viking Dog, is a big dog in a small package, much like the Corgi to which it is related. Swedish Vallhunds are believed to trace back more than 1,000 years in Sweden, to the time of the Vikings, and were probably taken to Wales in the eighth or ninth century, giving rise to the Corgi. The Swedish Vallhund is a multipurpose farm dog with a no-nonsense attitude. These animals were used for herding, hunting, tracking, and watching over livestock and property. The breed is noted for its lively temperament and loyalty, and makes a wonderful companion for an active home.

MEDIUM-SIZE, PRICKED, EXPRESSIVE EARS

OVAL, DARK EYES

LONG, CLEAN, WEDGE-SHAPED HEAD

BROAD AND SLIGHTLY SLOPING CROUP

LEVEL TOPLINE

BODY LONGER THAN IT IS HIGH

SPANISH MASTIFF : SPAIN

This breed is generally considered to be ancient, its ancestors being taken to the Iberian Peninsula by the Phoenicians before the Roman invasions of the first century. Mastiffs are mentioned a number of times by Roman historians who remarked on their size, their ability to tend herds, and their skill at fighting predators such as wolves. Over time, these giant dogs were used as war dogs and were taken to the Americas by the conquistadors for use against the native people. More often, however, they were used for herding, primarily guarding huge herds of cattle and sheep. The Spanish Mastiff is brave, protective, independent, calm, kind, and dignified. However, these dogs are suitable companions only for an experienced, rural home.

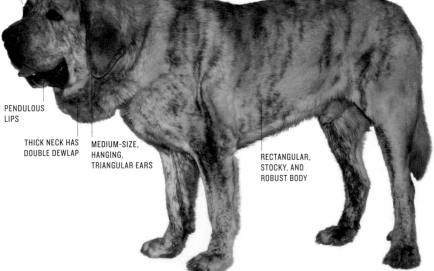

SMALL, ALMOND-SHAPED EYES

BIG, STRONG, BROAD HEAD

PENDULOUS LIPS

THICK NECK HAS DOUBLE DEWLAP

MEDIUM-SIZE, HANGING, TRIANGULAR EARS

RECTANGULAR, STOCKY, AND ROBUST BODY

ST. BERNARD : ITALY, SWITZERLAND

This lovely breed is most famous for its search-and-rescue history, helping to locate people lost in the mountains, and it is still used for this purpose in some areas. More typically though, St. Bernards are mostly companion dogs. These are intelligent, kind, protective dogs that excel in obedience competitions, as well as draft and weight pulling. They make a superb addition to a family home (one that is not averse to slobber) but need to be provided with plenty of space.

AT A GLANCE

Size: very large

Exercise needed:

Grooming needed:

Aptitudes: search and rescue, watchdog, draft, weight pulling, companion

Height: 25–28 in.

Weight: 120–200lb.

Average life expectancy: 8–10 yrs

AKC: working

CHARACTER

Affection

Playfulness

Friendliness to dogs

Friendliness to strangers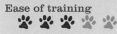

Ease of training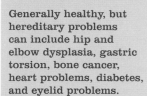

✚ HEALTH ✚

Generally healthy, but hereditary problems can include hip and elbow dysplasia, gastric torsion, bone cancer, heart problems, diabetes, and eyelid problems.

LOWER EYELIDS FORM AN ANGULAR WRINKLE
MEDIUM-SIZE EARS LIE CLOSE TO HEAD
SLOPING SHOULDERS
LEVEL, BROAD BACK
LONG, MUSCULAR NECK
DEEP, WIDE CHEST
HIGH-SET TAIL, CARRIED LOW, SHOULD NEVER CURL OVER BACK
BROAD FEET

HISTORY

The St. Bernard traces back to the Great St. Bernard Hospice established around 1050 by Saint Bernard de Menthon on the oldest known pass through the western Alps. The hospice kept mastiff-type dogs crossed with local farm dogs, originally valuing the dogs as watchdogs and livestock guardians. The earliest accounts of the hospice dogs finding lost travelers date to the eighteenth century when they accompanied monks searching for survivors after storms. Sometimes the dogs were sent out in pairs unsupervised to locate people; one dog would remain with the victim while the other returned to the hospice to raise the alarm. The monks continued to breed their dogs for these traits, introducing Great Danes and English Mastiffs. The Swiss Kennel Club recognized the breed in 1884. It was recognized by the American Kennel Club in 1885.

St. Bernard puppies weigh approximately 1½ pounds when they are born and grow rapidly in their first year.

COMMON COAT COLORS

The St. Bernard's coat can be red and white, or brindle with white. Its muzzle, chest, feet, tail tip, and collar must all be white. It can have a dark mask and ears.

RED & WHITE

COAT CLOSE-UP

The coat can be short haired—smooth, short and dense. Or it can be long haired—straight or slightly wavy.

SHORT & DENSE

STANDARD SCHNAUZER : GERMANY

The Schnauzer gets its name from the German word for "moustache," in reference to their distinctive facial hair, which also includes prominent eyebrows. These hairy additions to their faces lend them a particularly appealing and expressive look. The Standard Schnauzer is an intelligent, fun-loving breed that although originally a working dog, is now largely a companion breed. These are versatile and adaptable dogs that make superb family pets and are good with children and other pets as long as they are introduced correctly. They can be wary of other dogs and strangers, however.

AT A GLANCE

Size: medium

Exercise needed:

Grooming needed:

Aptitudes: guarding livestock, watchdog, vermin control, service, agility, companion

Height: 17–20 in.

Weight: 35–45 lb.

Average life expectancy: 12–14 yrs

AKC: working

CHARACTER

Affection

Playfulness

Friendliness to dogs
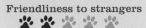

Friendliness to strangers
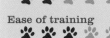

Ease of training

✚ HEALTH ✚

Generally healthy, but hereditary problems can include hip dysplasia, and cancer.

OVAL-SHAPED EYES WITH LONG EYEBROWS THAT SHOULD NOT IMPAIR VISION

STRONG, RECTANGULAR, LONG HEAD

V-SHAPED EARS SET HIGH, DROPPING FORWARD

LONG, SLIGHTLY ARCHED NECK

BLUNT-ENDING MUZZLE WITH CHARACTERISTIC BEARD

SMALL, COMPACT FEET

HISTORY

The Standard Schnauzer is the oldest of the three Schnauzer breeds and is thought to trace to at least the fourteenth century in Germany. They are believed to have originated in Württemberg and Bavaria in the southwest and southeast of Germany, probably based on terrier, hunting, and general farm-dog types. Early Schnauzers were multi-skilled farm dogs used for vermin control, watching over the property and livestock, and for driving livestock to market. It was not until the mid-nineteenth century that there was a move to make these dogs more uniform in appearance, and to do this, breeders introduced black German Poodles and gray Wolfspitz. Schnauzers were originally called Wire Haired Pinschers; the name Schnauzer was adopted in 1879. Standard Schnauzers were recognized by the American Kennel Club in 1904 and became very popular in the United States during the 1940s due to actor Errol Flynn's fondness for the breed.

When a Schnauzer puppy is about five months old, its permanent teeth start to erupt. They will end up with 42 teeth.

COMMON COAT COLORS

Coat can be black or salt and pepper.

BLACK   SALT & PEPPER

COAT CLOSE-UP

Dense, harsh, wiry, medium-length coat with a weather-resistant undercoat and distinctive moustache, beard, and eyebrows.

WIRY

GIANT SCHNAUZER : GERMANY

Despite its name, the Giant Schnauzer is not a "giant" breed; it is simply a larger and more powerful version of the Standard Schnauzer, which was the breed originator. The Giant is an intelligent breed that has a degree of problem-solving ability, which can translate into stubbornness during training. However, once this has been overcome, this breed is thoroughly rewarding and a great addition to an active family. These dogs love to be involved in everything that is going on, and do not like to be left out. They thrive when doing a job or an activity, such as agility, which will challenge them mentally and physically. The Giant is naturally protective of its family and makes a good watchdog.

AT A GLANCE

Size: large

Exercise needed:

Grooming needed:

Aptitudes: guarding livestock, watchdog, vermin control, service, agility, companion

Height: 23–28 in.

Weight: 65–90 lb.

Average life expectancy: 10–12 yrs

AKC: working

CHARACTER

Affection
🐾🐾🐾🐾🐾

Playfulness
🐾🐾🐾🐾🐾

Friendliness to dogs
🐾🐾🐾🐾🐾

Friendliness to strangers
🐾🐾🐾🐾🐾

Ease of training
🐾🐾🐾🐾🐾

✚ HEALTH ✚

Generally healthy, but hereditary problems can include hip and elbow dysplasia, progressive retinal atrophy, skin complaints, cancer, and heart conditions.

V-SHAPED BUTTON EARS

RECTANGULAR, ELONGATED HEAD

DEEP-SET, DARK BROWN OVAL EYES

FLAT, SLIGHTLY SLOPING SHOULDERS AND HIGH WITHERS

TAIL SET AND CARRIED HIGH

COMPACT, SUBSTANTIAL BODY SHOWING GREAT POWER AND AGILITY

WELL-ARCHED, COMPACT, CAT-LIKE FEET

HISTORY

Like the Standard, the Giant developed in Württemberg and Bavaria and was bred by local cattlemen and farmers who wanted the qualities of the Standard, but in a bigger package. The Giant was used to drive cattle to market and became popular with butchers, who used them for moving cattle around the livestock pens. The Giants were also used for guarding properties, including many German breweries. During World War I, the dogs were drafted into military service and were also used by the police. The first Giant Schnauzers arrived in the United States during the 1930s, but the breed did not become well known until the 1960s. They are popular in obedience competitions, as well as agility and carting.

COMMON COAT COLORS

Pepper and salt, or pure black.

BLACK   **SALT & PEPPER**

COAT CLOSE-UP

Dense, harsh, wiry, medium-length coat with weather-resistant undercoat and prominent moustache, beard, and eyebrows.

WIRY

On average, Schnauzers have three to six puppies in a litter, although occasionally they will have eight to nine.

TAMASKAN DOG : FINLAND

The beautiful Tamaskan Dog has a wolfish appearance. These animals were developed in Finland, the United States, and England with foundation stock based on primarily Siberian Huskies, Alaskan Malamutes, and German Shepherds. The Tamaskan is first and foremost a sled dog and excels at working in arctic conditions. They are highly intelligent and trainable and thrive when given a job to do, whether it is obedience, agility, service, or therapy. They are generally sweet-natured and affectionate and make good companions for an extremely active, experienced home.

TRIANGULAR EARS, SMALL IN PROPORTION TO HEAD

YELLOW, AMBER, OR BROWN EYES

IMMENSE UNDERCOAT IN WINTER, STRAIGHT, CLOSE TOPCOAT

CLOSE-FITTING ELBOWS

WOLF GRAY; RED GRAY; BLACK GRAY

TAIL REACHES HOCK JOINT, CARRIED SLIGHTLY ELEVATED WHEN EXCITED

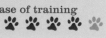
TORNJAK : BOSNIA, HERZEGOVINA, CROATIA

Little is known about the origins of the large and powerful Tornjak, although it is believed to be related to the Tibetan Mastiff. Tornjaks have existed in parts of Bosnia, Herzegovina, and Croatia for hundreds of years primarily as livestock guardians, watchdogs, and herding dogs. They are first mentioned in documents that date back to 1067. By 1972 the breed was virtually extinct and has been salvaged only through the dedicated efforts of enthusiasts. These are primarily working dogs, which can become companions but require lots of space, exercise, and interaction. They are best suited to an experienced home in a rural location.

TRIANGULAR, FOLDED, PENDENT EARS

RECTANGULAR MUZZLE WITH STRAIGHT BRIDGE OF NOSE

POWERFUL NECK

SHORT, BROAD BACK

LONG COATED, WITH SHORT COAT ON FACE AND LEGS. TOPCOAT IS LONG, THICK, AND COARSE

ELBOWS ARE CLOSE TO THE BODY

TIBETAN MASTIFF : TIBET

The Tibetan Mastiff is one of the most ancient breeds and many dog experts believe it gave rise to the modern mastiff breeds, mountain dogs, and many of the large working breeds. Isolated in the remote Himalayas, Tibet, Nepal, and Bhutan, the Tibetan developed uninfluenced by other breeds. Here it was a preeminent guard dog, traditionally kept tied up during the day in entrances and gateways and let loose at night to fend off predators and intruders. These animals are still renowned for their deep bark and protectiveness. The Tibetan is a calm, independent, and intelligent dog that is inherently protective. They are not suitable for first-time dog owners.

BROAD, STRONG HEAD WITH HEAVY BROW RIDGES

NOBLE, INTELLIGENT AND ALOOF EXPRESSION

DEEP-SET EYES, WELL APART

V-SHAPED, HIGH-SET, PENDENT EARS DROP FORWARD AND HANG CLOSE TO HEAD

BROAD, SQUARE MUZZLE

DOUBLE COATED WITH FAIRLY LONG, THICK, COARSE GUARD HAIR AND HEAVY UNDERCOAT

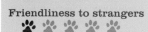
TOSA : JAPAN

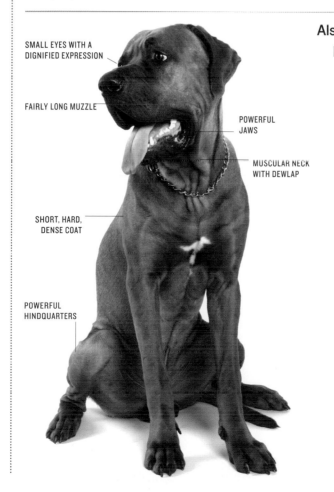

SMALL EYES WITH A DIGNIFIED EXPRESSION

FAIRLY LONG MUZZLE

POWERFUL JAWS

MUSCULAR NECK WITH DEWLAP

SHORT, HARD, DENSE COAT

POWERFUL HINDQUARTERS

Also known as the Tosa Inu or Tosa Token, this breed originated on Shikoku, the smallest of the four Japanese islands, in the old Tosa (now Kochi) Prefecture. These dogs were bred for dog fighting, and with their power, strength, and agility, they excelled in that capacity. European mastiff-type breeds were introduced, increasing the size and bulk of the Tosa, and the breed gained great notoriety across Japan. The Tosa nearly disappeared during World War II, but has since been re-established and is source of pride for Japan. Tosas are calm, dignified dogs that will react aggressively when provoked, and the breed has been banned in a number of countries. Although Tosas can make companion dogs with consistent socialization and training, they are only suitable for very experienced homes.

SCENT HOUNDS

AT A GLANCE

Size: medium-large

Exercise needed:

Grooming needed:

Aptitudes: trailing fox

Height: 21–25 in.

Weight: 40–65 lb.

Average life expectancy:
11–13 yrs

AKC: hounds

CHARACTER

Affection

Playfulness

Friendliness to dogs

Friendliness to strangers

Ease of training

✚ HEALTH ✚

Generally very healthy,
but hereditary problems
can include hip dysplasia,
deafness, and platelet
abnormalities.

COAT CLOSE-UP

SHORT

The coat is short and
smooth, but should not
be too thin or soft.

AMERICAN FOXHOUND : UNITED STATES

The American Foxhound traces to the seventeenth century and the efforts of Robert Brooke, a wealthy landowner who moved from England to Maryland, taking his foxhounds with him. He established a huge estate and bred his hounds to have speed and endurance to cope with all the wide open space in his new home. Fox hunting was becoming increasingly popular in the United States, and many new hunt clubs were established. The racy American Foxhounds were used for field trials, fox hunting with a single huntsman, following a trail, and hunting in packs. Today they are known as chiefly pack animals and do best living in this type of environment. American Foxhounds are gentle and pleasant in nature and generally get along well with other dogs.

HISTORY

President George Washington was a keen hunter and bred hounds that were significant in the development of the American Foxhound. He wrote in his diaries that he wanted to create a "perfect pack of hounds" by mixing English Foxhounds with Irish, French, and German hounds to produce a stronger, faster type suitable for the Virginia countryside.

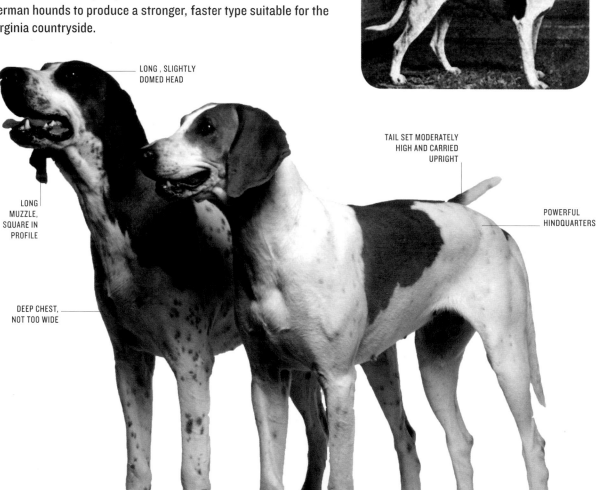

LONG , SLIGHTLY DOMED HEAD

LONG MUZZLE, SQUARE IN PROFILE

TAIL SET MODERATELY HIGH AND CARRIED UPRIGHT

POWERFUL HINDQUARTERS

DEEP CHEST, NOT TOO WIDE

ROUNDED FEET

The American Foxhound is one of the United States' rarest breeds.

COMMON COAT COLORS

TAN & WHITE

TRICOLOR

The American Foxhound can be any solid color from cream to red. It can also be particolored, ticked, or roan.

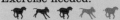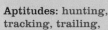
ALPINE DACHSBRACKE : AUSTRIA

The Alpine Dachsbracke is a small but powerful scent hound that is believed to have been developed in the mid-nineteenth century and is linked to the kennels of Austria's Crown Prince Rudolf. The crown prince's gamekeepers kept Alpine Dachsbrackes (or their ancestors) and used the low-slung dogs for tracking wounded deer and scenting out hare and foxes. Crown Prince Rudolf is said to have taken some of his Dachsbrackes with him when hunting in Egypt and Turkey. These cheerful, bold dogs are primarily used for hunting, but they can make good companions and are noted for getting along with children and other dogs if properly introduced.

LIGHTLY ARCHED SKULL WITH WELL-DEFINED FURROW IN FOREHEAD

TAIL SET HIGH AND CARRIED SLIGHTLY DOWNWARD

BROAD, SMOOTH, HIGH-SET EARS, HANGING WITHOUT FOLDS

FORELEGS APPEAR SHORT IN RELATION TO BODY

STRONG, WELL-MUSCLED, AND ELONGATED TRUNK

BASSET ARTÉSIEN NORMAND : FRANCE

The Basset Artésien Normand was developed by Leon Verrier from the Artois Hound in the early twentieth century, and its breed standard is based on Verrier's female Belette. The word *basset* means "low set," which is an apt description of these keen scent hounds that can hunt singly or in packs. They are cheerful dogs, full of character, with a superb temperament that makes them good companions. They can be independent in nature and are known for their deep, loud voices.

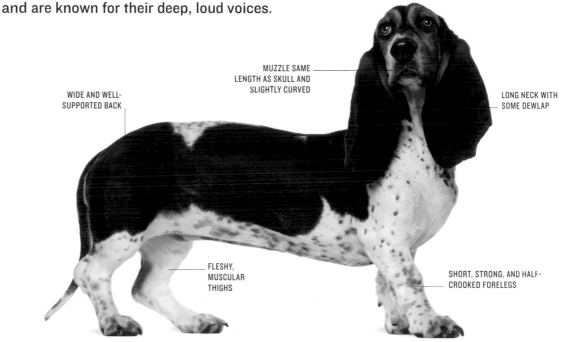

MUZZLE SAME LENGTH AS SKULL AND SLIGHTLY CURVED

LONG NECK WITH SOME DEWLAP

WIDE AND WELL-SUPPORTED BACK

FLESHY, MUSCULAR THIGHS

SHORT, STRONG, AND HALF-CROOKED FORELEGS

GRIFFON FAUVE DE BRETAGNE : FRANCE

The Griffon Fauve de Bretagne is widely considered to be one of the oldest of the French hound breeds and dates back to the early Middle Ages. They were widespread in northern France and were typically used for hunting wolves in packs—a testament to their great bravery and tenacity. As the wolf population began to decline, breed numbers dropped, although they were still used to hunt deer, fox, hare, and wild boar. Following World War II, breeding initiatives have led to an increase in the numbers of this exceptionally gentle and charismatic hound.

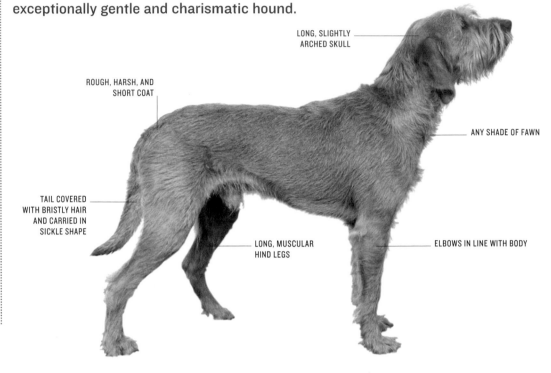

LONG, SLIGHTLY ARCHED SKULL

ROUGH, HARSH, AND SHORT COAT

ANY SHADE OF FAWN

TAIL COVERED WITH BRISTLY HAIR AND CARRIED IN SICKLE SHAPE

LONG, MUSCULAR HIND LEGS

ELBOWS IN LINE WITH BODY

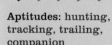
BASSET FAUVE DE BRETAGNE : FRANCE

The Basset Fauve de Bretagne is believed to have developed from the old French Fauve hounds, of which there were four types, divided by coat color and texture. Today only one survives, the Griffon Fauve de Bretagne. The Basset Fauve de Bretagne was probably created by breeding the smallest Griffons together, although no records exist. By the nineteenth century, however, there were packs of the small, courageous hounds living throughout France. In the twentieth century, the Basset Fauve de Bretagne was influenced by Basset Griffon Vendéen to improve its hunting skills, and Red Standard Wire Haired Dachshund improved the color. These are brave, tenacious hounds with superb temperaments that can make wonderful family companions.

HEAD IS LONG AND BROAD BETWEEN THE EARS

DARK-BROWN EYES WITH LIVELY EXPRESSION

MUZZLE SAME LENGTH AS SKULL

DEEP, BROAD BODY WITH ROUNDED RIBCAGE

FORELEGS PREFERABLY STRAIGHT, BUT SLIGHT CURVE ALLOWED

BRIQUET GRIFFON VENDÉEN : FRANCE

The word *briquet* translates as "medium-size dog," which is appropriate for this breed that was bred down in size from the larger Grande Griffon Vendéen. There are four Vendéen hounds: the two aforementioned, the Petit Basset Griffon Vendéen (the smallest), and the Grand Basset Griffon Vendéen. The Briquet was developed prior to World War I, but by World War II had almost disappeared, although they have since been re-established. The Briquet will pick up a cold or a hot trail and is a determined and tough hunting dog. They also make good family companions as long as they get plenty of exercise, but can be difficult to obedience train and often have their own strong opinions!

MUZZLE SAME LENGTH AS SKULL, NOT TOO BROAD AT TIP

DARK EYES WITH LIVELY EXPRESSION

HARSH OUTER COAT, SOMETIMES BUSHY, AND DENSE UNDERCOAT

STRONG FOREQUARTERS, BUT NOT HEAVY

WELL-ARCHED, TIGHT TOES

CHIEN D'ARTOIS : FRANCE

This is an ancient breed of scent hound whose history traces back to the fifteenth century and the larger Grand Chien d'Artois from which it developed. The dogs were used for hunting in small packs, both on foot and to accompany hunters on horseback. They are mostly used on small game, but these brave hounds will also hunt wild boar, deer, and other large game. The breed was influenced by crossbreeding to gun-dog types in the nineteenth century and will occasionally point.

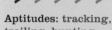
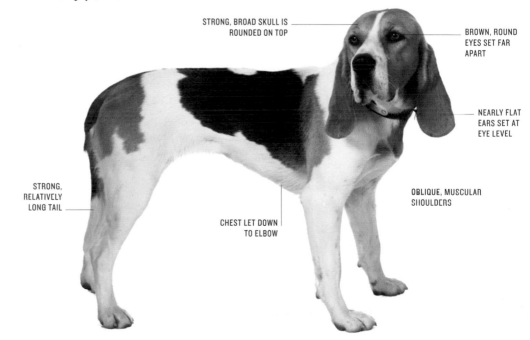

STRONG, BROAD SKULL IS ROUNDED ON TOP

BROWN, ROUND EYES SET FAR APART

NEARLY FLAT EARS SET AT EYE LEVEL

STRONG, RELATIVELY LONG TAIL

OBLIQUE, MUSCULAR SHOULDERS

CHEST LET DOWN TO ELBOW

BASSET HOUND : FRANCE

The charismatic Basset Hound, among the most recognizable of all breeds, originated in France during the Middle Ages. These low-slung dogs, along with their taller relative the Bloodhound, are used for the slow trail of game and for driving small game from dense undergrowth into open country where a hunter can access them. They are typically used in packs, although they can work alone, and are also a much-loved companion breed.

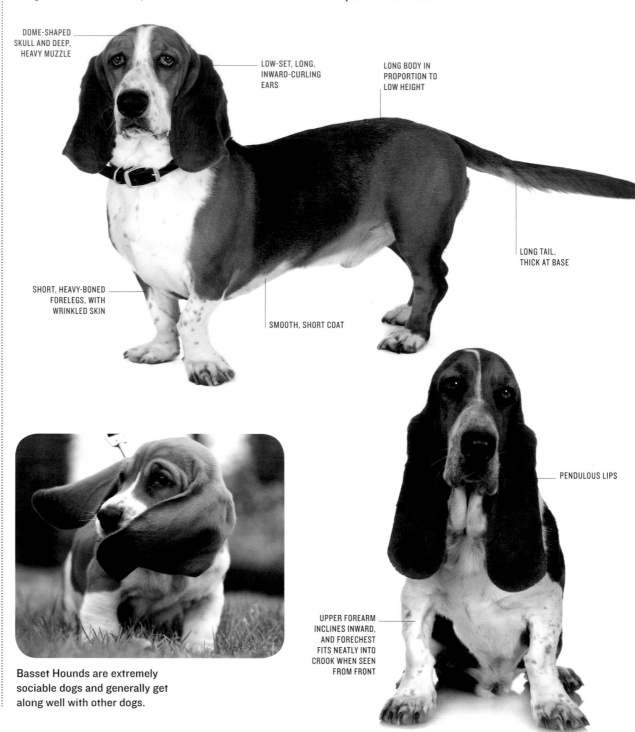

DOME-SHAPED SKULL AND DEEP, HEAVY MUZZLE

LOW-SET, LONG, INWARD-CURLING EARS

LONG BODY IN PROPORTION TO LOW HEIGHT

LONG TAIL, THICK AT BASE

SHORT, HEAVY-BONED FORELEGS, WITH WRINKLED SKIN

SMOOTH, SHORT COAT

PENDULOUS LIPS

UPPER FOREARM INCLINES INWARD, AND FORECHEST FITS NEATLY INTO CROOK WHEN SEEN FROM FRONT

Basset Hounds are extremely sociable dogs and generally get along well with other dogs.

AT A GLANCE

Size: small

Exercise needed:
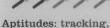

Grooming needed:

Aptitudes: tracking, trailing, companion

Height: less than 14 in.

Weight: 40–60 lb.

Average life expectancy: 8–12 yrs

AKC: hounds

CHARACTER

Affection

Playfulness

Friendliness to dogs

Friendliness to strangers

Ease of training

+ HEALTH +

Conditions that might be found in the Basset Hound include bleeding disorders, bloat, elbow and hip dysplasia, glaucoma, and luxating patella.

COAT CLOSE-UP

SILKY

The medium-length double coat is silky and flat or slightly wavy.

COMMON COAT COLORS

TRICOLOR

BROWN & WHITE

Basset Hounds can be any color from cream to red, including brown, and are usually parti-colored. Can be ticked or roan.

HISTORY

Basset Hounds are believed to have developed from the St. Hubert Hounds that were bred by monks at the Monastery of St. Hubert in Belgium. In the late seventh and early eighth centuries, Hubert supplied the aristocracy with hounds from his monastery. It is possible that the Basset arrived through genetic mutations of these large hounds resulting in short-legged dogs that were bred together.

BAVARIAN MOUNTAIN HOUND : GERMANY

The Bavarian Mountain Hound is one of Germany's preeminent hunting dogs and has outstanding tracking and trailing abilities. These are one of the German "bloodhound" breeds in that they instinctively follow a blood trail, making them valuable for tracking wounded game. Their scenting ability is acute, and they can track a "cold" trail that is several days old. They have great stamina and endurance and are well suited to hunting in the mountains. These dogs form strong bonds with their owners but may be reserved with strangers.

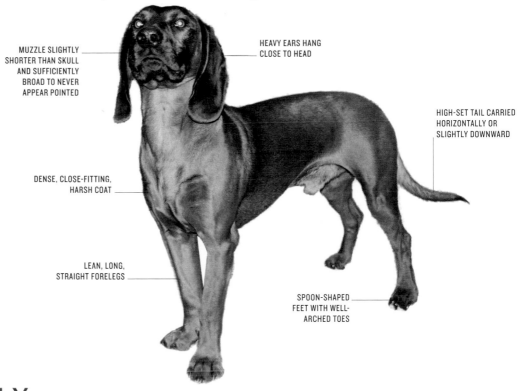

MUZZLE SLIGHTLY SHORTER THAN SKULL AND SUFFICIENTLY BROAD TO NEVER APPEAR POINTED

HEAVY EARS HANG CLOSE TO HEAD

HIGH-SET TAIL CARRIED HORIZONTALLY OR SLIGHTLY DOWNWARD

DENSE, CLOSE-FITTING, HARSH COAT

LEAN, LONG, STRAIGHT FORELEGS

SPOON-SHAPED FEET WITH WELL-ARCHED TOES

BILLY : FRANCE

This rare breed of French hound was developed during the nineteenth century primarily by Monsieur Gaston Hublot du Rivault at his Chateau de Billy in Poitou, a province in west central France. The Billy was based on several old French hound breeds such as the Montaimboeuf, Ceris, and Larye, which no longer exist, and has had a more recent introduction of Foxhound blood. The Billy is an elegant-looking hound with a great turn of speed. They have exceptional scenting abilities and a deep, sonorous bay.

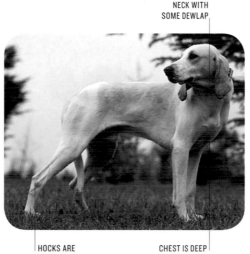

STRONG, ROUND NECK WITH SOME DEWLAP

EARS ARE MEDIUM SIZE, FLAT, AND THE ENDS TURN IN SLIGHTLY

SLIGHTLY DOMED FOREHEAD WITH A WELL-DEFINED STOP

HOCKS ARE SLIGHTLY BENT, WIDE, AND STRONG

CHEST IS DEEP AND NARROW

AT A GLANCE

Size: small

Exercise needed:

Grooming needed:

Aptitudes: trailing, tracking, hunting, therapy, companion

Height: under 13 in./ 13–15 in.

Weight: 18–30 lb.

Average life expectancy: 12–15 yrs

AKC: hound

CHARACTER

Affection

Playfulness

Friendliness to dogs

Friendliness to strangers

Ease of training

✚ HEALTH ✚

Generally healthy, but hereditary problems can include hip dysplasia and intervertebral disk disease.

COAT CLOSE-UP

SHORT

The Beagle's coat is smooth and short, but should not be too thin or soft.

BEAGLE : ENGLAND

The Beagle is a superb small hunting hound that has also become popular as a companion animal, particularly in the United States. Beagles have an engaging, lively, and often comical nature; they are highly entertaining, interactive, and affectionate. On the downside, and as is the case with most hound breeds, Beagles can be very noisy. They are suitable for urban living as long as their barking is managed and they are given plenty of exercise and diversions. Due to their pleasing temperament and compact size, Beagles are often used as therapy dogs, and also for bomb and drug detection.

TAIL SET HIGH AND CARRIED UPRIGHT

SHORT, MUSCULAR BACK

ROUND FEET

COMMON COAT COLORS

The beagle can be any true hound color, but is commonly tricolored or white and tan.

TRICOLOR

WHITE & TAN

LONG, SLIGHTLY
DOMED SKULL

STRONG, SQUARE-
CUT MUZZLE

LONG EARS WITH
ROUNDED TIP, SET
MEDIUM LOW

LARGE BROWN OR HAZEL
EYES WITH APPEALING
EXPRESSION

Beagles are gregarious,
pack-oriented dogs
that are generally not
happy to be alone.

HISTORY

Accounts of small hounds used for tracking hare date back to Xenophon (c. 430–354 BC) in Ancient Greece and his treatise *On Hunting*. The Romans probably took these small hounds on their conquest of Europe, including into England, where the Beagle developed. Many written accounts of small hounds of Beagle type indicate that various monarchs such as Edward II and Henry VII kept packs at the Royal kennels. The term "beagle" was introduced in the fifteenth century by Edward, Second Duke of York, in his treatise *The Master of the Game*. Early in their history, Beagles were bred in different sizes including the Glove or Pocket Beagle, so called because it could fit into a gauntlet cuff or a saddle bag. Elizabeth I kept a pack of Pocket Beagles and had her portrait painted with one of them. In the United States, Beagles are divided into two height divisions: 13 inches and 15 inches. The American Kennel Club registered the first Beagle in 1885, and the National Beagle Club of America was established in 1888.

BLACK AND TAN COONHOUND : UNITED STATES

The American Black and Tan Coonhound is a stylish-looking hound that traces back to the nineteenth century to the southern United States. They were developed primarily from American Foxhounds with the addition of Bloodhound, which gave rise to the Black and Tan's color; its long, pendent ears; and heavy frame. Black and Tans have superb scenting abilities and can follow a "cold" trail—one that is several days old. They are excellent tracking and treeing dogs and, as their name suggests, are particularly suited to hunting raccoons.

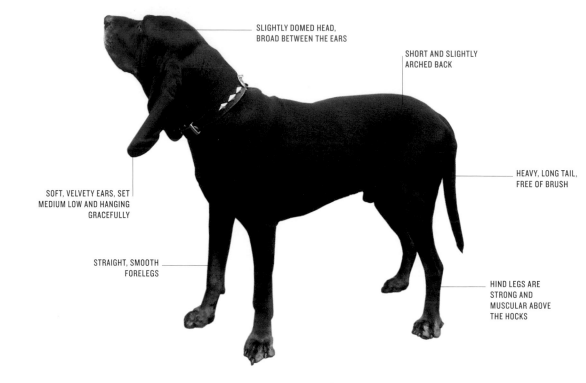

SLIGHTLY DOMED HEAD, BROAD BETWEEN THE EARS

SHORT AND SLIGHTLY ARCHED BACK

HEAVY, LONG TAIL, FREE OF BRUSH

SOFT, VELVETY EARS, SET MEDIUM LOW AND HANGING GRACEFULLY

STRAIGHT, SMOOTH FORELEGS

HIND LEGS ARE STRONG AND MUSCULAR ABOVE THE HOCKS

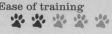
BLUETICK COONHOUND : UNITED STATES

The Bluetick Coonhound was developed in the southern United States based on English Foxhounds bred to other hound types; the breed's distinctive coloring is attributed to the influence of French breeds like the Grand Bleu de Gascogne. Blueticks are noted for their loud, drawn-out bay that reaches different pitches depending on the stage of the hunt. They are bred for tracking and treeing game and will hunt a wide variety, including bobcats, mountain lions, bears, and, most commonly, raccoons.

BROAD, SLIGHTLY DOMED HEAD

LARGE, WIDE-SET, BROWN EYES WITH "PLEADING" EXPRESSION

TAIL CARRIED HIGH WITH SLIGHT CURVE, BUT NOT OVER BACK

SMOOTH, GLOSSY COAT

DEEP CHEST, NOT TOO WIDE

AT A GLANCE

Size: large

Exercise needed:

Grooming needed:

Aptitudes: tracking, trailing, hunting

Height: 24–28 in.

Weight: 55–65 lb.

Average life expectancy: 10–12 yrs

AKC: not recognized

CHARACTER

Affection

Playfulness

Friendliness to dogs

Friendliness to strangers

Ease of training

CHIEN FRANÇAIS BLANC ET NOIR : FRANCE

This upstanding breed exhibits all the classic hound features and, although originally developed for use on small game, is highly regarded for hunting large game such as deer. These dogs hunt in packs and retain strong pack instincts. They give good voice when hunting and are noted for their superb sense of smell and great staying power. The breed is believed to have been developed during the early 1900s by Henri de Falandre, a keen huntsman. He used a foundation of Gascon Saintongeois and Bleu de Gascogne with some English Foxhound to create the desired qualities of scenting ability, stamina, and temperament.

EARS ARE SLIGHTLY CURLED AND REACH TO THE NOSE

BACK IS LONG BUT FIRM

LONG, IMPOSING HEAD

LIPS COVER LOWER JAW AND ARE WELL PIGMENTED

HIPS ARE LONG AND SLANTED

CHEST IS DEEPER THAN IT IS BROAD

ELONGATED FEET

AT A GLANCE

Size: large

Exercise needed:

Grooming needed:

Aptitudes: tracking, trailing, hunting

Height: 23–28 in.

Weight: 55–65 lb.

Average life expectancy: 10–12 yrs

AKC: not recognized

CHARACTER

Affection

Playfulness

Friendliness to dogs

Friendliness to strangers

Ease of training

CHIEN FRANÇAIS TRICOLORE : FRANCE

This breed of medium to large French hound was, like the related Chien Français Blanc et Orange and the Chien Français Blanc et Noir, bred specifically to hunt large game. The hounds are always worked in packs and have a strong pack mentality, so they are not suited to living alone. They have a loud, deep bay, which is useful for the huntsman, and they can alter the tone and pitch of their bay depending on the stage of the hunt. They generally have kind natures but do not make good companion animals unless they are kept with other dogs in a rural location—they are happiest when doing what they were bred to do.

EARS ARE SET AT EYE LEVEL AND SLIGHTLY CURLED

LONG, MUSCULAR THIGHS

LONG HEAD

BIG BROWN EYES WITH AN INTELLIGENT EXPRESSION

FORELEGS ARE STRAIGHT AND WELL APART

LONG TAIL

CHARACTER

Affection

Playfulness

Friendliness to dogs

Friendliness to strangers

Ease of training
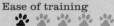

HEALTH

Generally healthy, but hereditary problems can include gastric torsion, ear problems, skin-fold dermatitis, hip and elbow dysplasia, and eyelid problems.

COAT CLOSE-UP

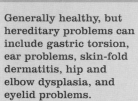

SHORT

The coat is smooth and short.

BLOODHOUND : BELGIUM/ENGLAND

The Bloodhound is one of the foremost trailing and tracking dogs in the world, with superlative scenting skills and the ability to track old trails over virtually any terrain—even occasionally across water. These dogs are used extensively by the police for tracking, as well as by search-and-rescue organizations. The breed name is based on the dog's ability to follow a blood trail. Bloodhounds have exceptional temperaments: they are kind, gentle, and mostly good with children and other animals. However, they require lots of space, like to be with other dogs, have a tendency to bay loudly when excited, and can be difficult to obedience train. They are not, therefore, ideal for first-time dog owners.

A Bloodhound puppy will usually grow by four to seven pounds (and one inch) each week.

LONG NECK

LONG TAIL, CARRIED HIGH WHEN MOVING

MUSCULAR SHOULDERS

COMMON COAT COLORS

Black and tan, liver and tan, or red.

BLACK & TAN　　　**RED**

HISTORY

Known as the Chien de Saint Hubert in most of continental Europe, the modern Bloodhound is generally believed to have developed from the ancient St. Hubert's Hound, which was bred by monks at the Monastery of St. Hubert in Belgium from the eighth century. These hounds were often sent to kings and aristocrats as gifts to curry favor for the monastery, and accordingly, word of their fine hunting skills spread throughout Europe. The dogs were taken to England early in their history, possibly by William the Conqueror, and were described in detail in 1570 by John Caius in his book *Of Englishe Dogges*. Bloodhounds were first specifically mentioned in the United States in 1619 at the Virginia Assembly when it was made illegal to sell them to Native Americans. Bloodhounds were accepted by the American Kennel Club in 1885, but numbers remained low until the twentieth century. The breed is now relatively well supported in the United States and England.

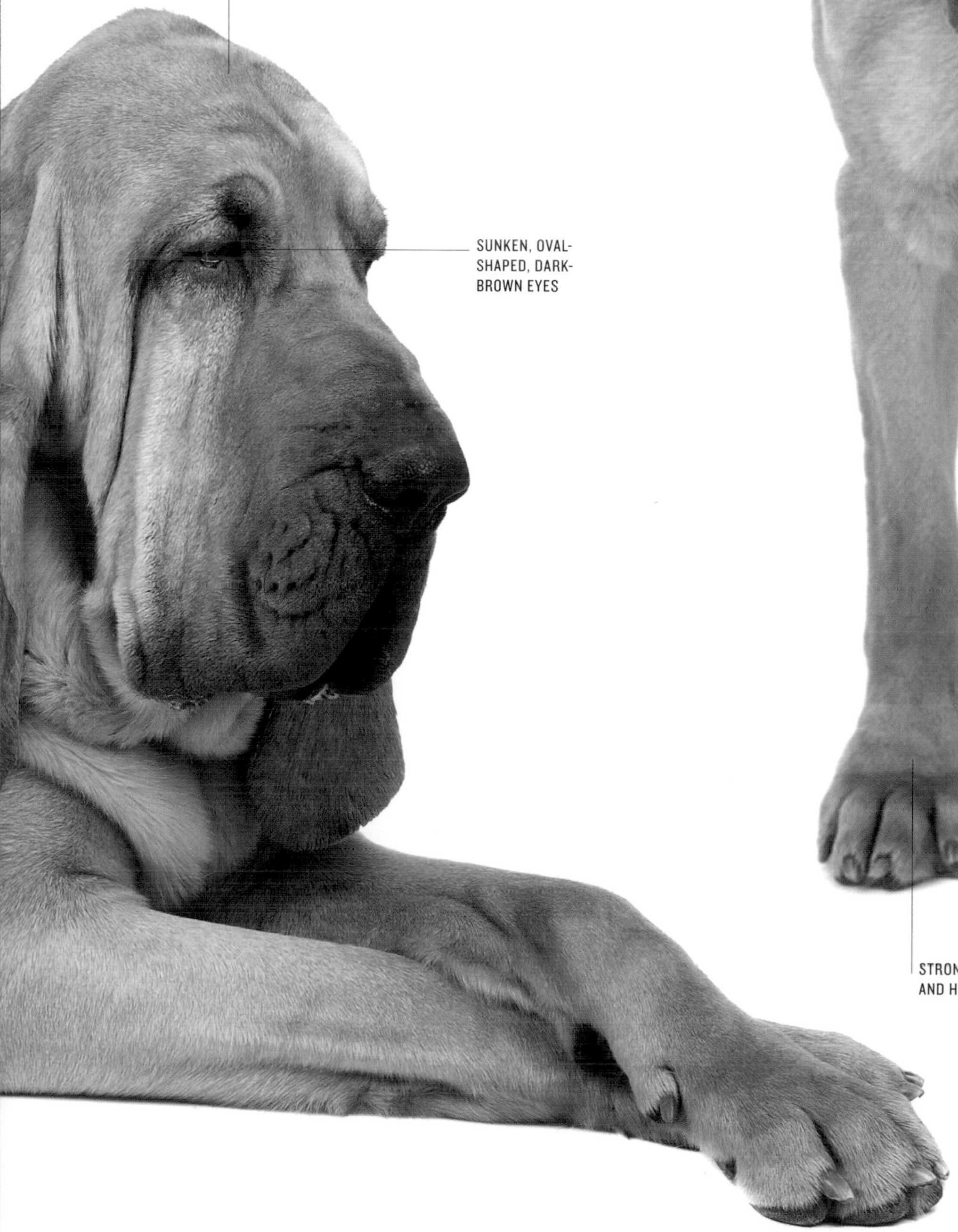

PROPORTIONATELY LONG, NARROW HEAD WITH PENDENT FOLDS OF LOOSE SKIN AROUND THE JOWLS AND NECK

LONG, THIN, LOW-SET EARS

SUNKEN, OVAL-SHAPED, DARK-BROWN EYES

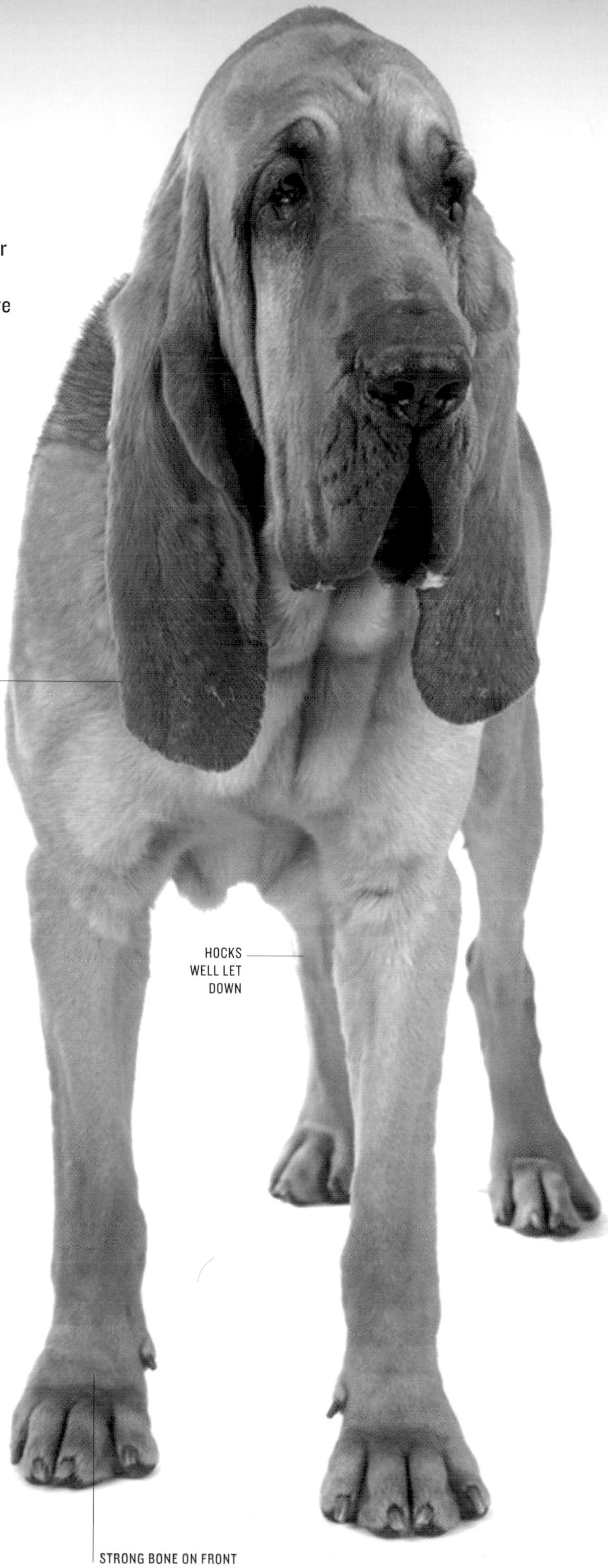

HOCKS WELL LET DOWN

STRONG BONE ON FRONT AND HIND LEGS

DREVER : SWEDEN

The Drever is a low-slung, versatile hound primarily used for hunting deer at slow speeds, but can also hunt smaller game such as hare. The breed developed in the 1850s in Southern Germany, Austria, and Switzerland from the Westphalian Dachsbracke, and was imported to Sweden in the early twentieth century. In 1947 their name was changed to Drever—from the Swedish word *drev*, meaning "drive," reflecting the breed's ability to drive game to the hunter. Although good-natured, the Drever is not suited to a non-working lifestyle.

LARGE HEAD IN PROPORTION TO BODY

BRIGHT, BROWN EYES FULL OF EXPRESSION

HARSH, STRAIGHT, CLOSE-LYING COAT

BROAD, MEDIUM-LONG, LOW-SET EARS

STIFLES AND HOCKS ARE WELL ANGULATED

LONG, BROAD, MUSCULAR, SLOPING SHOULDERS

THE DISTANCE FROM THE STERNUM TO THE GROUND IS 40 PERCENT OF THE TOTAL HEIGHT AT THE WITHERS

DUNKER : NORWAY

The Dunker is a specialized hare-hunting hound developed in the nineteenth century by Captain Wilhelm Dunker by crossbreeding several different hound types. In 1902 Norwegian hare hounds were divided into two groups, the Dunker and the Hygen Hound. The Dunker has a characteristically blue-marbled coat, although other colors are allowed. It is a determined hunter with a very pleasant nature, being affable and easy to train. Sadly, breed numbers are extremely low.

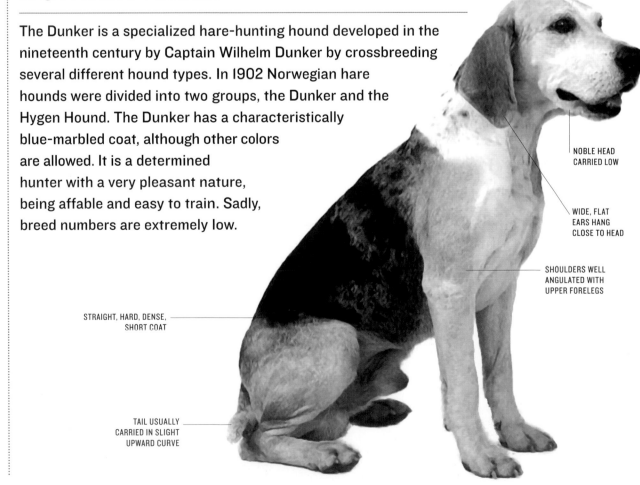

NOBLE HEAD CARRIED LOW

WIDE, FLAT EARS HANG CLOSE TO HEAD

SHOULDERS WELL ANGULATED WITH UPPER FORELEGS

STRAIGHT, HARD, DENSE, SHORT COAT

TAIL USUALLY CARRIED IN SLIGHT UPWARD CURVE

CHARACTER

Affection

Playfulness

Friendliness to dogs

Friendliness to strangers

Ease of training
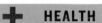

✚ HEALTH ✚

This is a very healthy and robust breed that suffers from few hereditary conditions.

COAT CLOSE-UP

SILKY

The double coat is medium length, silky, and flat or slightly wavy.

COMMON COAT COLORS

Estonian Hounds can be any color from cream to red, including brown, and are usually parti-colored. Can be ticked or roan.

TRICOLOR

ESTONIAN HOUND : ESTONIA

Rarely seen outside their native country in Eastern Europe, these scent hounds were developed in the mid-twentieth century from Dachshunds, Foxhounds, Beagles, Swiss Bernese Hounds, Swiss Lucerne Hounds, and Russian-Polish Hounds. The Estonian Hound is a highly efficient hunter of rabbits and foxes. They are personable dogs that can make good companions for an active home, and they excel at events like agility. However, like many pack hounds, they do not like to be left on their own, even for short periods.

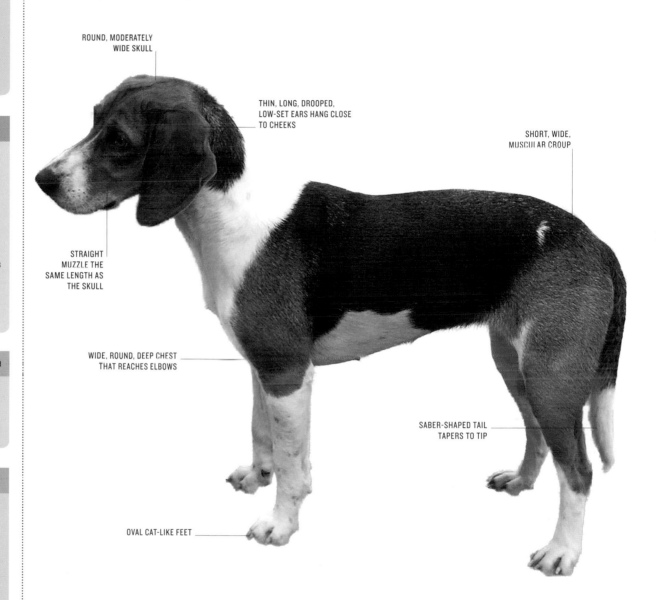

ROUND, MODERATELY WIDE SKULL

THIN, LONG, DROOPED, LOW-SET EARS HANG CLOSE TO CHEEKS

SHORT, WIDE, MUSCULAR CROUP

STRAIGHT MUZZLE THE SAME LENGTH AS THE SKULL

WIDE, ROUND, DEEP CHEST THAT REACHES ELBOWS

SABER-SHAPED TAIL TAPERS TO TIP

OVAL CAT-LIKE FEET

HISTORY

The Estonian Hound is a relatively new breed and the only one to originate in Estonia. These scent hounds were developed in 1947 when the Ministry of Economy in the former USSR decided each Soviet Republic should have its own dog breed. It is now the national dog of Estonia.

The Estonian was specially developed as a hunting dog and can withstand the extreme cold of its native home.

REDBONE COONHOUND : UNITED STATES

The stylish Redbone Coonhound was developed from red foxhound types from Scotland and Ireland and was brought into the country by immigrants in the eighteenth century. The foundation of the modern Redbone is attributed to George Birdsong of Georgia—a renowned breeder and hunter. Redbones are fast and agile over a variety of terrains and are excellent swimmers. In addition to hunting raccoons, the fearless Redbones hunt larger animals, including bobcats, bears, and cougars.

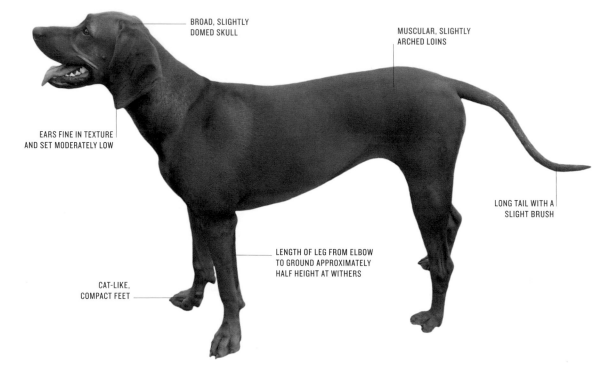

BROAD, SLIGHTLY DOMED SKULL

MUSCULAR, SLIGHTLY ARCHED LOINS

EARS FINE IN TEXTURE AND SET MODERATELY LOW

LONG TAIL WITH A SLIGHT BRUSH

LENGTH OF LEG FROM ELBOW TO GROUND APPROXIMATELY HALF HEIGHT AT WITHERS

CAT-LIKE, COMPACT FEET

TREEING WALKER COONHOUND : UNITED STATES

In the 1850s, Appalachian hunter George Washington Maupin acquired a hound of unknown heritage named Tennessee Lead and bred him extensively to Walker Hounds. The result was what eventually came to be known as the Treeing Walker Coonhound. These dogs are fast, hot-nosed hunters with an excellent voice and superb treeing ability. They are often used in competitions. They also have wonderful temperaments and can make excellent family dogs for an active home.

LONG, MUSCULAR, LEVEL BACK

BROAD SKULL, FULL AND SLIGHTLY ROUND

LONG MUZZLE, TAPERS SLIGHTLY, WITH FLEWS SUFFICIENT TO GIVE SQUARED-OFF APPEARANCE

SMOOTH, GLOSSY, FINE, HARD, AND PROTECTIVE COAT

STRAIGHT, STRONG FORELEGS

STRONG, FIRM STIFLE AND HOCK JOINTS, WITH MODERATE ANGULATION

AMERICAN ENGLISH COONHOUND : UNITED STATES

Also known as the English Coonhound or the Redtick Coonhound, this breed traces back to the earliest English Foxhounds brought to the southern United States in the mid-seventeenth century and crossed with local types adapted to the harsher climate and terrain. Today these are particularly agile, fast, and enduring hounds. They have an excellent voice, which they put to good use! The breed is known for its kind temperament and can fit into family life if given a lot of exercise, but they are happiest when hunting.

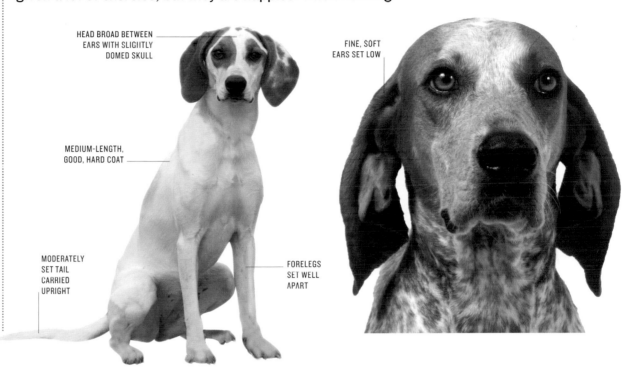

HEAD BROAD BETWEEN EARS WITH SLIGHTLY DOMED SKULL

FINE, SOFT EARS SET LOW

MEDIUM-LENGTH, GOOD, HARD COAT

MODERATELY SET TAIL CARRIED UPRIGHT

FORELEGS SET WELL APART

PLOTT : UNITED STATES

This elegant all-American hound is a spirited and tenacious hunter that is fearless and will hunt all day. They are independent thinkers and can be headstrong and difficult to obedience train, although once they have been trained they are thoroughly rewarding dogs. They have a high activity requirement and are best suited to a hunting home. Plotts have a distinctive "chop"—a loud, ringing bark that they use when hunting. They may also be noisy if they become bored and are not ideal for an urban environment.

HIGH-SET, BROAD, PENDENT EARS

TAIL IS QUITE LONG AND CARRIED HIGH WITH GENTLE CRESCENT MOON CURVE

MEDIUM-LENGTH, STRONG MUZZLE

MODERATELY WIDE, DEEP CHEST

BODY IS HIGHER AT WITHERS THAN HIPS

AT A GLANCE

Size: small

Exercise needed:
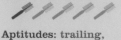

Grooming needed:

Aptitudes: trailing, tracking, hunting above and below ground, companion

Height: Standard 8–9 in. Miniature 5–6 in.

Weight: Standard over 11 lb./Miniature under 11 lb.

Average life expectancy: 12–14 yrs

AKC: hound

CHARACTER

Affection

Playfulness

Friendliness to dogs

Friendliness to strangers

Ease of training

✚ HEALTH ✚

Generally healthy, but hereditary problems can include intervertebral-disc disease and eye problems.

DACHSHUND : GERMANY

In Germany the Dachshund, which translates as "badger hound," is more commonly referred to as a Teckel. These low-slung, tenacious hunters are valued for their use on small game such as rabbit, hare, badger, and fox. They are unusual in that they can locate and track prey above ground and also dig down, kill, and retrieve prey that has gone underground. There are two recognized sizes of the Dachshund now—miniature and standard—but in Germany they are measured according to the circumferences of their chests, which determines into what size hole they can follow their prey. Dachshunds are perhaps more commonly known as companion animals today, but they are also still widely used for hunting, particularly in Germany. As companions, they are full of personality, loyal to their families, and love to have fun. They can, however, be wary of strangers and have a tendency to bark.

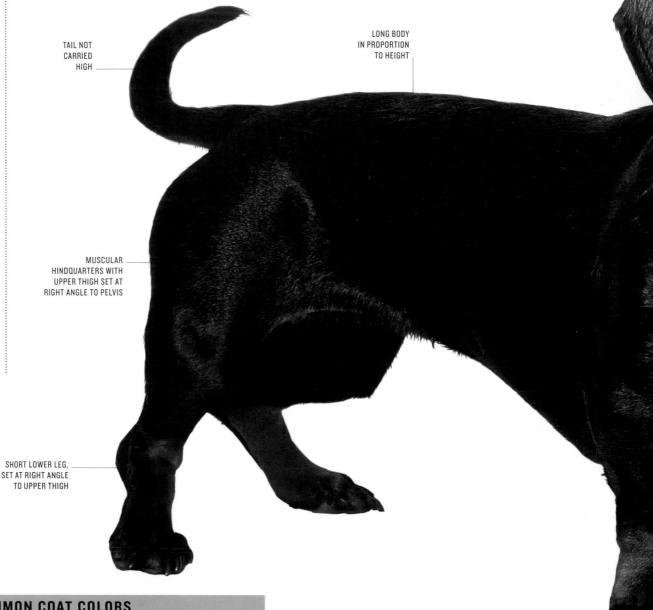

TAIL NOT CARRIED HIGH

LONG BODY IN PROPORTION TO HEIGHT

MUSCULAR HINDQUARTERS WITH UPPER THIGH SET AT RIGHT ANGLE TO PELVIS

SHORT LOWER LEG, SET AT RIGHT ANGLE TO UPPER THIGH

COMMON COAT COLORS

BLACK & TAN

CHOCOLATE

RED

Dachshund colors include black and tan, chocolate, red, and cream.

HISTORY

Long-bodied dogs low to the ground have been recorded since the Middle Ages. Accounts from the 1500s indicate that short-legged, powerful dogs were used in Germany for hunting badgers, and in 1685, author Christian Paullini refers to Dachshunds in his book on dogs. There are no records about how these dogs developed, but historians speculate that German Pinschers, bassetts, French hounds, and terriers might all have had some influence. Certainly the breed is designed for digging and hunting underground; they are extremely powerful but slender, and the structure of their front legs, which may incline outward slightly, allows for a free digging movement. Dachshunds became popular in England during the nineteenth century when Queen Victoria developed a fondness for them, and they made their way to the United States at around the same time. The American Kennel Club registered its first Dachshund in 1885, and the Dachshund Club of America was established in 1895.

ALMOND-SHAPED, DARK EYES

HEAD TAPERS TO END OF NOSE

BROAD, HIGH-SET, WELL-ROUNDED EARS OF MODERATE LENGTH

FINE, SLIGHTLY ARCHED MUZZLE

POWERFUL FRONT END WITH PROMINENT BREASTBONE

Dachshund puppies are very bright, so it is essential to keep them interested, alert, and happy, particularly when puppy training starts.

SHORT FRONT LEGS, MAY INCLINE SLIGHTLY OUTWARD

COAT CLOSE-UP

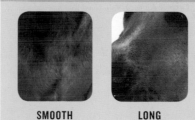

Dachshunds have three coat types: smooth, long, and wirehaired. The smooth is dense and short; the long haired is straight or slightly wavy; the wirehaired has a rough, harsh topcoat, and a dense undercoat.

SMOOTH   **LONG**

AT A GLANCE

Size: large

Exercise needed:

Grooming needed:

Aptitudes: trailing, tracking, hunting

Height: 23–25 in.

Weight: 55–75 lb.

Average life expectancy: 10–11 yrs

AKC: hound

CHARACTER

Affection

Playfulness

Friendliness to dogs

Friendliness to strangers

Ease of training

✚ HEALTH ✚

Generally healthy, but hereditary problems can include hip dysplasia and renal disease.

COAT CLOSE-UP

SHORT

The English Foxhound's coat is smooth, short, and dense.

ENGLISH FOXHOUND : ENGLAND

English Foxhounds are fast, agile, and extremely enduring hounds that hunt in packs and accompany horsemen. They hunt at a quick pace and are "hot-nosed" hunters, meaning they pick up and follow very fresh trails. The English Foxhound is very much a pack animal and is happiest when living and working in this type of environment. They are extremely sociable and get along well with other dogs. Foxhounds are not typically kept as purely pets, despite having lovely temperaments. They are kind-natured animals and generally good with children, but their greatest joy in life is to hunt.

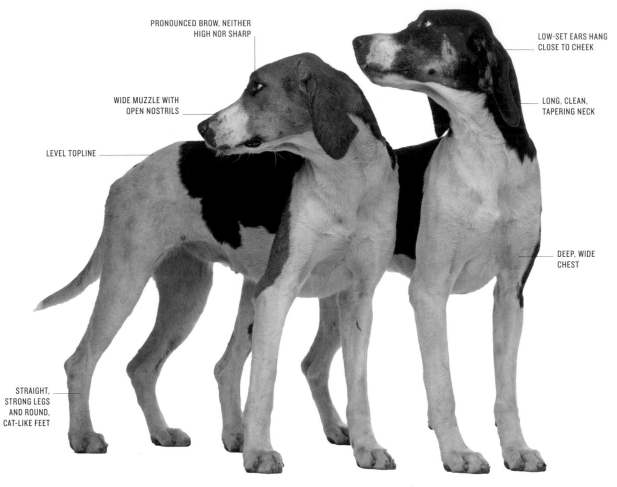

PRONOUNCED BROW, NEITHER HIGH NOR SHARP

LOW-SET EARS HANG CLOSE TO CHEEK

WIDE MUZZLE WITH OPEN NOSTRILS

LONG, CLEAN, TAPERING NECK

LEVEL TOPLINE

DEEP, WIDE CHEST

STRAIGHT, STRONG LEGS AND ROUND, CAT-LIKE FEET

HISTORY

English hounds were originally bred to hunt hare and stag. The English Foxhound developed gradually from the sixteenth century as fox hunting gained popularity. Fox hunting was formalized when George Villiers established the oldest fox hunt, the Bilsdale Hunt in Yorkshire, in 1668. Hounds were bred specifically to hunt fox and had to be very fast, agile enough to clear hedges and fences, and tough enough to keep going until they caught the prey. The Masters of Fox Hounds Association has registered Foxhound puppies since 1841 and currently represents 186 Foxhound packs in England, Wales, and Scotland. Some hunts maintain their own pedigree records that stretch back more than 300 years.

COMMON COAT COLORS

LEMON & WHITE

TRICOLOR

BLACK & WHITE

The coat can be any solid color from cream to red, including brown. Commonly parti-colored; can also be ticked or roan.

GRAND ANGLO-FRANÇAIS BLANC ET NOIR : FRANCE

The Grand Anglo-Français Blanc et Noir is one of three Grand Anglo-Français breeds that are all historic breeds derived through crossing English Foxhounds with French scent hounds. In many cases this resulted in hounds with both "hot-nose" and "cold-nose" qualities: they were able to follow a fresh, or "hot," trail at great speed, but could also follow an old, or "cold," trail with greater deliberation. The Grand Anglo-Français Blanc et Noir is hunted in large packs and used for hunting large game such as deer and wild boar, though it may also be used on smaller animals, such as fox. These dogs are not ideal companion animals; they are happiest living in a pack environment and hunting for a living.

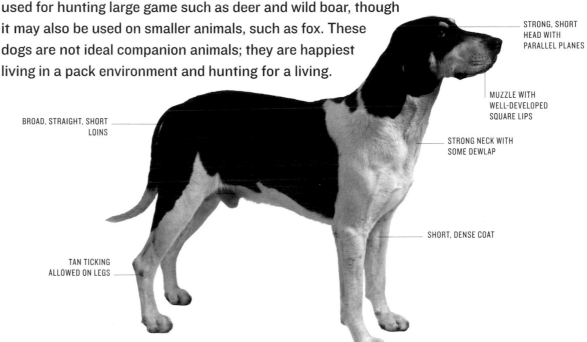

STRONG, SHORT HEAD WITH PARALLEL PLANES

MUZZLE WITH WELL-DEVELOPED SQUARE LIPS

STRONG NECK WITH SOME DEWLAP

BROAD, STRAIGHT, SHORT LOINS

SHORT, DENSE COAT

TAN TICKING ALLOWED ON LEGS

GRAND ANGLO-FRANÇAIS TRICOLORE : FRANCE

This breed was developed in the 1800s by crossing French scent hounds with English Foxhounds. The three Grand Anglo-Francais hounds were not divided into separate breeds until the twentieth century when they were categorized primarily by coat color. The Grand Anglo-Français Tricolore largely derived through Poitevin (tricolored) and English Foxhound crosses and exhibits the characteristic robustness of the Poitevin with the scenting skills of the Foxhound. They are a tough and rugged breed that hunts on any terrain with vigor.

EARS SET AT EYE LEVEL, FLAT AT BASE AND THEN SLIGHTLY CURLED

WELL-CHISELED MUZZLE WITH STRAIGHT NASAL BONE

LONG, STRONG NECK WITH NO DEWLAP

LOIN IS SHORT AND MUSCULAR

DEEP, BROAD CHEST

GRAND BASSET GRIFFON VENDÉEN : FRANCE

The Grand Basset Griffon Vendéen is the fastest of all the basset scent hounds and is skilled in hunting hare, and all small game. These are lovely, charming dogs that can make wonderful companions for the right home. They also have enormous personalities, and are affectionate, kind, and loyal. First and foremost, however, they are hunters, and they will give chase if the opportunity arises. They also have a reputation for being escape artists, and so must have a very well-fenced yard.

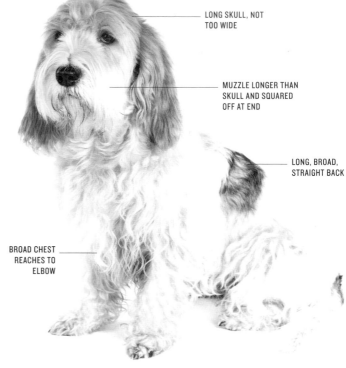

LONG SKULL, NOT TOO WIDE

MUZZLE LONGER THAN SKULL AND SQUARED OFF AT END

LONG, BROAD, STRAIGHT BACK

BROAD CHEST REACHES TO ELBOW

LIPS ARE PENDULOUS WITH MOUSTACHE

PETIT BASSET GRIFFON VENDÉEN : FRANCE

The Petit Basset Griffon Vendéen, the smallest of the four Vendéen breeds, traces to the La Vendee region on the western coast of France. They were developed to hunt small game over difficult terrain; they are also skilled rabbit and hare hunters, and have been used on birds. The Petit Basset and the Grand Basset were not given their own standards until the 1950s. The Petit is a wonderful addition to an active home and thrives on diversions and exercise. These are intelligent dogs with big personalities and a propensity to bark when bored.

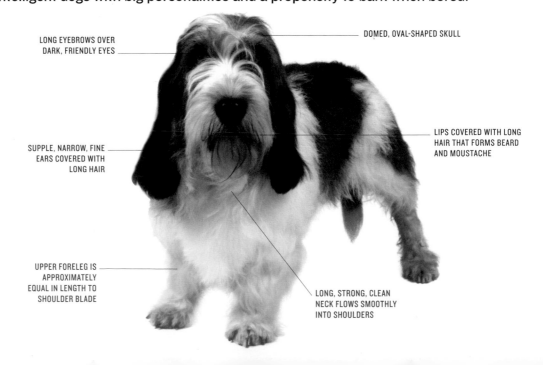

LONG EYEBROWS OVER DARK, FRIENDLY EYES

DOMED, OVAL-SHAPED SKULL

LIPS COVERED WITH LONG HAIR THAT FORMS BEARD AND MOUSTACHE

SUPPLE, NARROW, FINE EARS COVERED WITH LONG HAIR

UPPER FORELEG IS APPROXIMATELY EQUAL IN LENGTH TO SHOULDER BLADE

LONG, STRONG, CLEAN NECK FLOWS SMOOTHLY INTO SHOULDERS

GRAND BLEU DE GASCOGNE : FRANCE

One of the oldest and finest hound breeds, the Grand Bleu is thought to have developed from hounds brought into France by the seafaring Phoenicians, and the now extinct Chien de Courant. These are one of the largest hound breeds and are extremely powerful. They hunt at a slow but persistent pace and have an exceptional voice. They are used on large game, such as deer and boar, and are hunted in packs. Their pack instinct is very strong, and although they have lovely temperaments they are happiest in a hunting environment.

THIN, LOW-SET EARS TWIST INWARD AND TAPER TO POINT

STRONG, ELONGATED HEAD COVERED WITH LOOSE SKIN TO FORM ONE OR TWO WRINKLES ON THE CHEEKS

LONG, SLIGHTLY AQUILINE MUZZLE WITH PENDULOUS LIPS

SHORT, DENSE COAT

FORELEGS STRONGLY BONED, WITH PROMINENT TENDONS

GRIFFON BLEU DE GASCOGNE : FRANCE

One of the four Bleu de Gascogne breeds, the Griffon is distinctive from the other three through its wiry coat. All three share similar roots and developed in the Pyrenean region of Gascony in southwestern France. The Griffon Bleu de Gascogne is believed to have developed through crossing the Grand Bleu de Gascogne with the the Griffon Nervais and possibly the Grand Griffon Vendéen. They are an excellent hunting dog and used on a variety of game in a pack or singly. They are noted for their calm, affable temperaments and easygoing nature.

LARGE, BLACK NOSE WITH WELL-OPENED NOSTRILS

MUZZLE SAME LENGTH AS SKULL, WITH STRAIGHT OR SLIGHTLY ARCHED NASAL BRIDGE

WELL-DEVELOPED CHEST

HARD, ROUGH, AND SHAGGY COAT

TAIL IS WELL-COVERED WITH HAIR AND CARRIED HAPPILY

LOW-SET HOCKS

PETIT BLEU DE GASCOGNE : FRANCE

This ancient breed of scent hound is descended from the Grand Bleu de Gascogne and was developed in Gascony Province, on the southwest coast of France. The Petit Bleu de Gascogne was originally developed to hunt small game, whereas the Grand was used on large game. The Petit is noted for hunting hare, and hunts methodically at a relatively moderate speed. They are pack animals and are happiest in a pack environment.

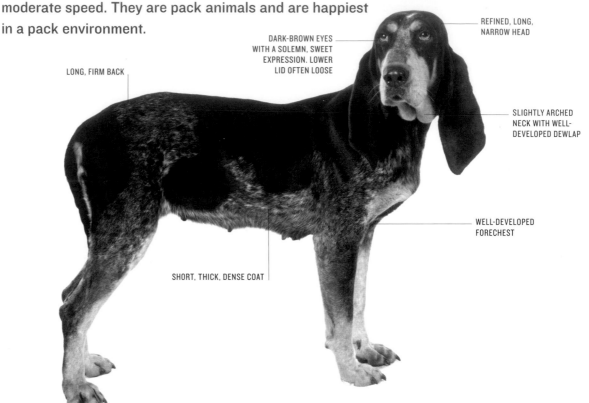

REFINED, LONG, NARROW HEAD

DARK-BROWN EYES WITH A SOLEMN, SWEET EXPRESSION. LOWER LID OFTEN LOOSE

LONG, FIRM BACK

SLIGHTLY ARCHED NECK WITH WELL-DEVELOPED DEWLAP

WELL-DEVELOPED FORECHEST

SHORT, THICK, DENSE COAT

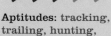
GRIFFON NIVERNAIS : FRANCE

The Griffon Nivernais is most associated with the mountains of central France where they were bred to hunt wolves and wild boar. This is an exceptionally brave breed that will hunt all day in any weather, and never backs down from its prey. Like many hound breeds, these dogs also have wonderful temperaments, and although they are generally pack dogs, they can adapt to being companions as long as they have lots of activity and are not left on their own.

TOPLINE LEVEL FROM WITHERS TO LOINS

MUZZLE SAME LENGTH AS SKULL, TAPERS SLIGHTLY TO NOSE

HIGH-SET TAIL CARRIED LIKE A SABER OR A LITTLE BENT OVER BACK

STRONG FORELEGS

DEEP RIBCAGE

FINNISH HOUND : FINLAND

The Finnish Hound was developed from the eighteenth century by breeders who wanted to create a hound that was suited to the difficult, snowy, mountainous terrain and harsh climate of Finland. Foxhounds, Harriers, German, Swiss, and Polish hounds were used in the breed foundation, along with Russian hounds and local Finnish dogs. The first breed standard was written in 1893, but the modern standard was adopted in 1932. The breed is very popular in Finland for hunting hare and fox and is noted for its excellent voice. They are not commonly found outside Finland.

LOIN IS SHORT AND POWERFUL

SLIGHT ARCH AT CREST OF NECK

SLIGHTLY CONVEX FOREHEAD WITH A SLIGHT BUT DEFINED STOP

OVAL, DARK-BROWN EYES

ELBOWS SET WELL BACK UNDER AND CLOSE TO BODY

HAMILTONSTÖVARE : SWEDEN

The Hamiltonstövare traces to the 1800s, when it was developed by Count Adolf Patrick Hamilton, the founder of the Swedish Kennel Club. He wanted to establish a hound that could hunt hare and fox across difficult terrain in harsh weather. He used English Foxhounds, Harriers, and three German hounds that are now extinct; the foundation dogs were named Pang and Stella. The Hamiltonstövare is always hunted on its own or in a pair, never a pack. They are versatile, friendly, outgoing dogs that can make companions for an active home.

MUZZLE AS LONG AS SKULL AND FAIRLY SQUARE

SOFT, FLAT EARS SET FAIRLY HIGH

RECTANGULAR SHAPED BODY

THE LIPS ARE THIN AND ROUNDED, MALES SHOULD HAVE MORE LIP THAN FEMALES

LONG, POWERFUL NECK SET WELL INTO THE SHOULDERS

OVAL FEET WITH WELL-KNUCKLED, TIGHT TOES

HARRIER : ENGLAND

The Harrier is an ancient English breed that sits halfway between the English Foxhound and the Beagle. The first recorded pack of Harriers in England was established by Sir Elias de Midhope in 1260. Their popularity quickly spread throughout western England and into Wales. The dogs are used to hunt fox and hare. They hunt in packs, generally with hunters on horseback, but they can also hunt with men on foot. They are pleasant-natured hounds, sociable and friendly, but can also be very noisy and independent.

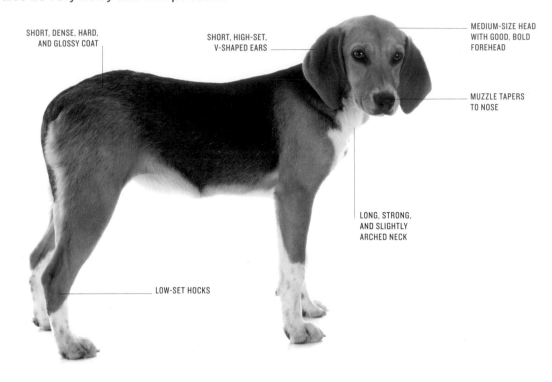

SHORT, DENSE, HARD, AND GLOSSY COAT

SHORT, HIGH-SET, V-SHAPED EARS

MEDIUM-SIZE HEAD WITH GOOD, BOLD FOREHEAD

MUZZLE TAPERS TO NOSE

LONG, STRONG, AND SLIGHTLY ARCHED NECK

LOW-SET HOCKS

HANOVER HOUND : FRANCE

The Hanover Hound traces back to the liam hounds of the Middle Ages; these were "leash hounds" that hunted on a leash, held by a hunter on foot. As hunting methods changed with the invention of firearms, it became necessary to develop hounds that could search for wounded game. The old leash hound proved the most adapted to this, so they were bred specifically for these qualities. The Hanover Hound was established on the large hunting estates in the Kingdom of Hanover, where its breeding was carefully monitored. A breed club was founded in 1894 to oversee their continued success. The Hanover Hound is used solely for large game and is a specialist in tracking cloven-hoof game.

HIGH-SET EARS HANG CLOSE TO HEAD

FOREHEAD SLIGHTLY WRINKLED

LOINS ARE BROAD WITH A SLIGHT ARCH

LOOSE SKIN ON THROAT

STRONG, DEEP, BROAD MUZZLE

HYGENHUND : NORWAY

This rare breed was developed by Hans Fredrik Hygen in the 1830s. Hygen's son continued his breeding program and was a founding member of the Special Club for Norwegian Hare Hounds, founded in 1902. It was also Hygen Junior who wrote the first breed standard for the Hygenhund in the same year. These dogs are easy to train and have an easygoing, affectionate nature.

STRAIGHT, STRONG BACK

WEDGE-SHAPED HEAD WITH SLIGHTLY DOMED SKULL

THIN, SOFT, HIGH-SET EARS, ROUNDED AT TIP

RIBCAGE APPEARS LONG

LONG, DEEP CHEST

STRAIGHT, DENSE, AND SHINY COAT

ISTRIAN SHORTHAIRED HOUND : CROATIA

Hounds of similar appearance to the Istrian Shorthaired Hound appear in art as far back as the fifteenth century, so historians believe that this is a very ancient breed, although no actual records exist. The Istrian is considered to be the oldest hound breed in the Balkan region, and gave rise to the slightly larger, wire-coated Istrian Coarse-haired Hound. Both types were prized for their hunting skills on hare, fox, and rabbit, and both are still used for hunting today. They have a good, solid, calm temperament, but they can be prone to barking.

DARK, OVAL EYES WITH BRIGHT EXPRESSION

LONG MUZZLE, BROAD AT BASE, TAPERING TO TIP

WELL-DEVELOPED, DEEP, BROAD CHEST

FORELEGS PERFECTLY STRAIGHT

AT A GLANCE

AT A GLANCE

Size: medium

Exercise needed:

Grooming needed:

Aptitudes: trailing, tracking, hunting, companion

Height: 22–24 in.

Weight: 40–60 lb.

Average life expectancy: 12–14 yrs

AKC: not recognized

CHARACTER

Affection

Playfulness

Friendliness to dogs

Friendliness to strangers

Ease of training

KERRY BEAGLE : IRELAND

Although the Kerry Beagle is one of Ireland's oldest hounds, the breed is not recognized by any of the major kennel clubs and is rarely heard of beyond its homeland. They were originally bred for tracking large game, but are now mostly used for small game such as hare, which they hunt in packs with hunters on foot. The Kerry Beagle is an outgoing, sociable dog that requires a lot of exercise and is not suited to urban living. They are generally good with children and other dogs, but are prone to barking when left unattended.

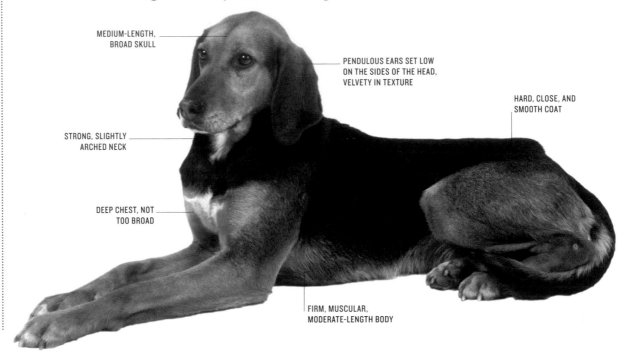

MEDIUM-LENGTH, BROAD SKULL

PENDULOUS EARS SET LOW ON THE SIDES OF THE HEAD, VELVETY IN TEXTURE

HARD, CLOSE, AND SMOOTH COAT

STRONG, SLIGHTLY ARCHED NECK

DEEP CHEST, NOT TOO BROAD

FIRM, MUSCULAR, MODERATE-LENGTH BODY

AT A GLANCE

Size: large

Exercise needed:

Grooming needed:

Aptitudes: hunting, companion

Height: 24–27 in.

Weight: 80–115 lb.

Average life expectancy: 10–13 yrs

AKC: hound

CHARACTER

Affection

Playfulness

Friendliness to dogs

Friendliness to strangers

Ease of training

OTTERHOUND : ENGLAND

The Otterhound is a delightful, though rare, breed that, as its name suggests, was originally bred to hunt otters. When otter hunting was banned in England in 1978, there was a huge decline in breed numbers. These dogs are of ancient origin and are believed to have been smooth coated before the seventeenth century. The earliest mention of a pack of Otterhounds dates to 1653. Their tremendous, shaggy, protective coat is possibly the result of rough-coated French Hounds introduced to the breed in the 1800s. Otterhounds have wonderful personalities and are very affectionate; they make excellent companion animals.

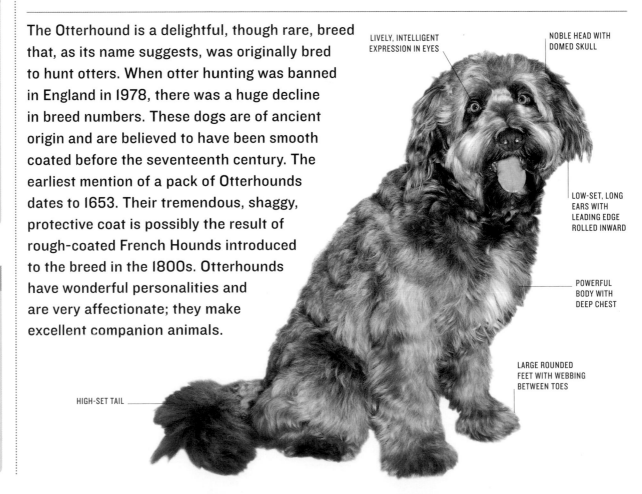

LIVELY, INTELLIGENT EXPRESSION IN EYES

NOBLE HEAD WITH DOMED SKULL

LOW-SET, LONG EARS WITH LEADING EDGE ROLLED INWARD

POWERFUL BODY WITH DEEP CHEST

LARGE ROUNDED FEET WITH WEBBING BETWEEN TOES

HIGH-SET TAIL

PHU QUOC RIDGEBACK DOG : VIETNAM

The rare Phu Quoc Ridgeback is one of only three ridgeback breeds in the world. It is found on Phu Quoc Island off Vietnam's southern Kien Giang province, and is an exceptional athlete. These dogs have keen scenting abilities on hot and cold trails, are capable of great speed, and are also excellent swimmers. They generally have good temperaments but can be inclined to bark, and because they are exceptional jumpers, they need a well-fenced, secure yard. The breed is not recognized by any major registry, and no official standard exists.

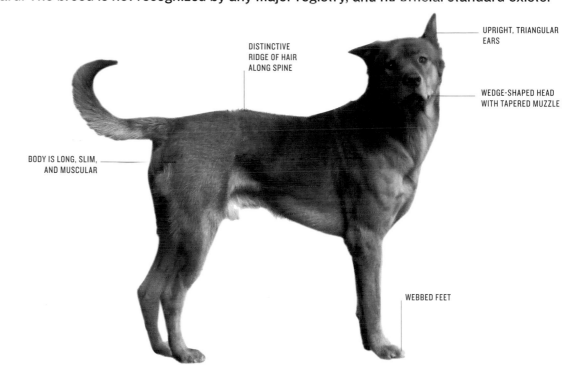

DISTINCTIVE RIDGE OF HAIR ALONG SPINE

UPRIGHT, TRIANGULAR EARS

WEDGE-SHAPED HEAD WITH TAPERED MUZZLE

BODY IS LONG, SLIM, AND MUSCULAR

WEBBED FEET

POLISH HOUND : POLAND

Hounds are first mentioned in Poland in the fourteenth century. They were used by the aristocracy to hunt large and small game. Polish Hounds are described as being mostly black and tan and having a deep, rich bark when on the hunt. In the 1600s, Poland began several centuries of political turmoil, which affected the dogs' bloodline: many kennels were lost, and the breed was not kept pure. By the twentieth century, the original Polish Hound had almost disappeared. The breed was re-established in 1959 by hunt enthusiast Colonel Peter Kartawik based largely on three dogs: Storm, Zorka, and Chita. Polish Hounds have wonderful temperaments, but are inclined to be independent and noisy.

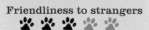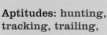
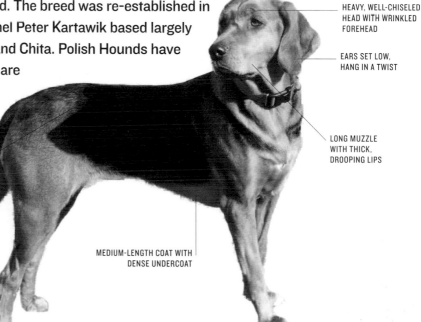

HEAVY, WELL-CHISELED HEAD WITH WRINKLED FOREHEAD

EARS SET LOW, HANG IN A TWIST

LONG MUZZLE WITH THICK, DROOPING LIPS

LONG, BROAD, AND MUSCULAR BACK

MEDIUM-LENGTH COAT WITH DENSE UNDERCOAT

LOW-SET TAIL, SLIGHTLY RAISED IN ACTION

POLISH HUNTING DOG : POLAND

There is a long history of scent hounds in Poland that is entwined with the fortunes of the aristocracy. The Polish Hunting Dog was largely developed during the mid-twentieth century in the Podkarpacie region of Poland by the famous cynologist, Jozef Pawuslewicz. He wrote the first breed standard for Polish Hunting Dogs, and through his efforts, the Polish Cynological Association accepted the breed. These are energetic dogs that thrive in high-octane pursuits and agility trials.

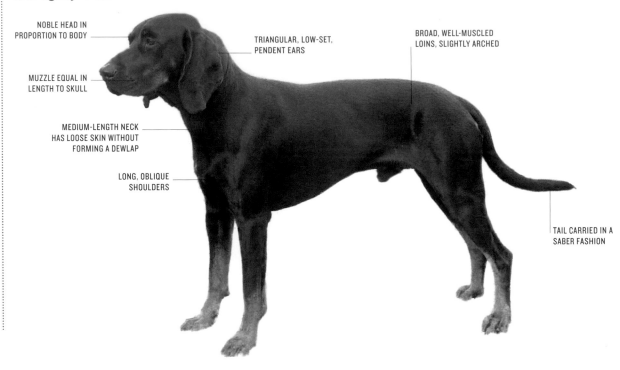

NOBLE HEAD IN PROPORTION TO BODY

MUZZLE EQUAL IN LENGTH TO SKULL

MEDIUM-LENGTH NECK HAS LOOSE SKIN WITHOUT FORMING A DEWLAP

LONG, OBLIQUE SHOULDERS

TRIANGULAR, LOW-SET, PENDENT EARS

BROAD, WELL-MUSCLED LOINS, SLIGHTLY ARCHED

TAIL CARRIED IN A SABER FASHION

POSAVAC HOUND : CROATIA

The Posavac Hound is one of Croatia's ancient hound breeds. Its name loosely means "hound from the Sava Valley," since the densely forested Sava Valley in central Croatia is where the breed originated. Frescoes in the Chapel of St. Mary, Beram, near the west coast city of Pazin, date to 1474, and depict hounds of similar appearance to the modern Posavac. Historians speculate that these were its ancestors. Hounds from the Sava Valley were prized throughout Croatia and were originally called Boskini; they were not officially called Posavac until 1969. These are good scent hounds used to hunt hare and fox.

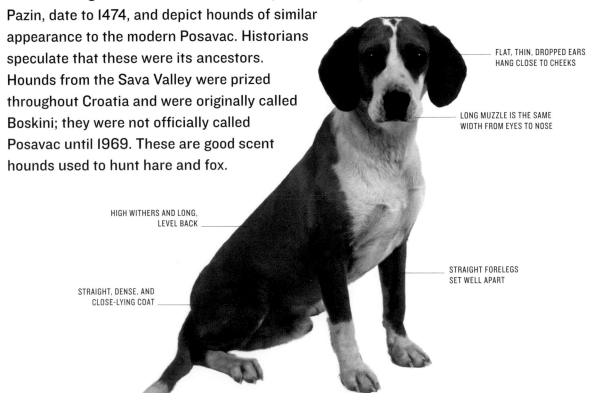

FLAT, THIN, DROPPED EARS HANG CLOSE TO CHEEKS

LONG MUZZLE IS THE SAME WIDTH FROM EYES TO NOSE

HIGH WITHERS AND LONG, LEVEL BACK

STRAIGHT, DENSE, AND CLOSE-LYING COAT

STRAIGHT FORELEGS SET WELL APART

PORCELAINE : FRANCE

This unusual-looking hound is also known as the Chien de Franché-Comté after a region in eastern France that borders Switzerland. The dog's ancestry probably includes Talbot Hounds, Harriers, and Swiss Laufhunds. Porcelaines were kept by the aristocracy on their large estates, and the breed all but disappeared during the French Revolution. They were re-established by enthusiasts in the nineteenth century, but breed numbers remain low. This dog takes its name from its shiny, white coat, which looks like porcelain. The Porcelaine is used on hare, deer, and wild boar, and usually hunts in packs.

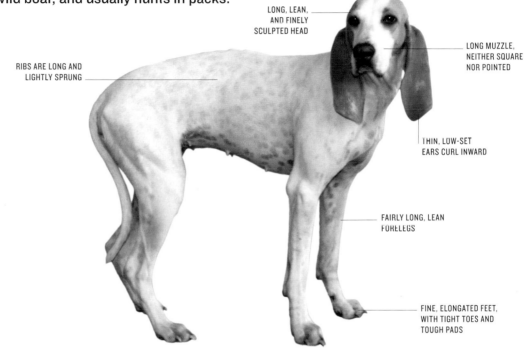

LONG, LEAN, AND FINELY SCULPTED HEAD

LONG MUZZLE, NEITHER SQUARE NOR POINTED

RIBS ARE LONG AND LIGHTLY SPRUNG

THIN, LOW-SET EARS CURL INWARD

FAIRLY LONG, LEAN FORELEGS

FINE, ELONGATED FEET, WITH TIGHT TOES AND TOUGH PADS

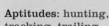
SABUESO ESPAÑOL : SPAIN

The Sabueso Español, or Spanish Scent hound, originated in northern Spain many centuries ago and was used for hunting all types of large game, including bear, wolf, wild boar, and deer, and smaller animals like hare and fox. These are dedicated, driven, and tough hounds that will hunt all day long in harsh environments. By modulating their loud voices they alert the hunters as the hunt develops. They are also used for traditional *caza a trailla*, leashed-hound hunting, on wild boar.

SLIGHTLY DOMED SKULL

RECTANGULAR, STRONG, ROBUST BODY

MUZZLE APPEARS RECTANGULAR WHEN SEEN FROM ABOVE

LARGE, LONG, HANGING EARS WITH SOFT TEXTURE, RECTANGULAR WITH ROUNDED TIPS

POWERFUL, BROAD, HORIZONTAL CROUP

POWERFUL CHEST WITH A PROMINENT STERNUM

SCHILLERSTÖVARE : SWEDEN

Also known as the Schiller Hound, this breed is perfectly adapted to hunting in freezing weather over difficult terrain. The breed traces to southern Germany and was founded on a pack of famous hounds kept at the Kaflas Estate Kennels. Farmer Per Schiller acquired some of these hounds, including Tamburini and Ralla, and exhibited them at a dog show in 1886. The Schiller Hound was named after him and the dogs were further influenced by the introduction of Harriers. The breed was recognized by the Swedish Kennel Club in 1907.

LONG MUZZLE WITH LEAN CHEEKS

BODY IS SLIGHTLY LONGER THAN IT IS TALL

SOFT, HIGH-SET EARS HANG FLAT

OVAL FEET WITH TIGHT WELL-ARCHED TOES

FORELEGS ARE STRAIGHT AND POWERFUL WITH ELBOWS CLOSE TO THE BODY

SLOVENSKÝ KOPOV : SLOVAKIA

The Slovenský Kopov is also known as the Black Forest Hound in North America, but is not widespread outside its homeland of Slovakia. This breed is a preeminent wild-boar hunter despite its relatively small size in comparison to that ferocious prey. These dogs have a formidable reputation for endurance trailing of boar and other large predators, and will continue to work and hunt all day long, giving voice. They are thought to have developed from Chart Polskis, Austrian Black and Tan Hounds, and Hungarian Greyhounds. These are loyal, affectionate, and independent hounds that can be wary of strangers and make good watchdogs.

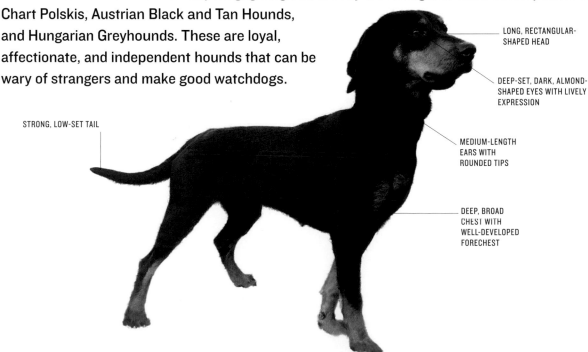

LONG, RECTANGULAR-SHAPED HEAD

DEEP-SET, DARK, ALMOND-SHAPED EYES WITH LIVELY EXPRESSION

MEDIUM-LENGTH EARS WITH ROUNDED TIPS

DEEP, BROAD CHEST WITH WELL-DEVELOPED FORECHEST

STRONG, LOW-SET TAIL

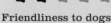
SEGUIGIO ITALIANO : ITALY

This Italian scent hound is extremely popular in its homeland, but little known beyond. The hounds are of ancient origin and are outstanding hunters. They were originally used for flushing boar, but are now used for hunting hare and driving them toward the hunter. The hounds can be used in packs, or singly, and are extremely determined and tenacious hunters. They are intelligent dogs that show great loyalty to their owners but can be wary of strangers. They are not typically kept in non-working or non-hunting homes.

SHORT, MUSCULAR BACK RISES SLIGHTLY OVER LOINS

HIGH-SET TAIL CARRIED HIGH IN A SABER CURVE WHEN MOVING

ELONGATED, NARROW, SLIGHTLY ARCHED SKULL

MEDIUM-LENGTH, SLIGHTLY ARCHED NECK

FINE, LOW-SET, TRIANGULAR EARS

DEEP, STRONG, MUSCULAR CHEST

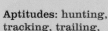
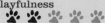
SERBIAN TRICOLOR HOUND : SERBIA

The Serbian Tricolor Hound was originally classed as a variety of the Serbian Hound, but in 1946 it got its own status; the two breeds are similar and share the same ancestry. The Tricolor is most commonly used for hunting large game such as wild boar, or smaller game like hare and fox. It is known for its good nose and stamina, and will hunt all day long. These are loyal and devoted dogs that bond strongly with their owners.

SKULL SLIGHTLY ROUNDED WITH PRONOUNCED FRONTAL FURROW

UPPER LIP OVERHANGS LOWER LIP

WELL-ARCHED NECK

ELBOWS CLOSE TO BODY

MEDIUM-SIZE, OVAL EYES SET SLIGHTLY OBLIQUELY

LONG, STRONG, STRAIGHT BACK

CAT-LIKE FEET

SWISS BERNESE HOUND : SWITZERLAND

By the nineteenth century, there were five varieties of the Swiss Hound, and in 1882 each got its own breed standard, although by 1909 one of the five, the Thurgovie, had disappeared. In 1933 a revised single standard was applied to the four remaining hounds, which are considered different types (based largely on color) of the same breed. These are the Bernese Hound, Lucerne Hound, Schwyz Hound, and Jura Hound. The Bernese is white with black patches and tan facial markings.

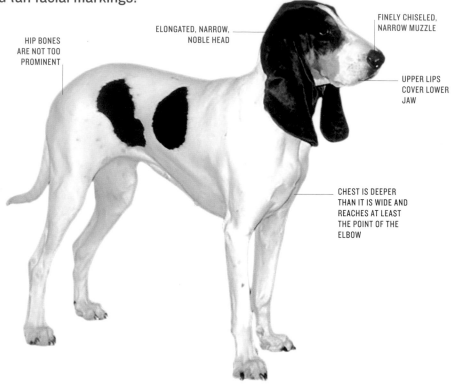

HIP BONES ARE NOT TOO PROMINENT

ELONGATED, NARROW, NOBLE HEAD

FINELY CHISELED, NARROW MUZZLE

UPPER LIPS COVER LOWER JAW

CHEST IS DEEPER THAN IT IS WIDE AND REACHES AT LEAST THE POINT OF THE ELBOW

SWISS JURA HOUND : SWITZERLAND

Also known as the Bruno Jura Hound, these rare dogs have broad heads and heavy wrinkles, which differentiate them from the other Swiss hounds. They are known for hunting fox, hare, and sometimes even small deer. The Jura Hound is a skilled cold-trail follower and is capable of following the slightest trace of a scent over the rough terrain of Switzerland's Jura Mountains. Bloodhound influence is very apparent.

NECK, BACK, CROUP, AND TAIL SHOULD FORM A HARMONIOUS OUTLINE

EXCEPTIONALLY LONG, PENDENT EARS

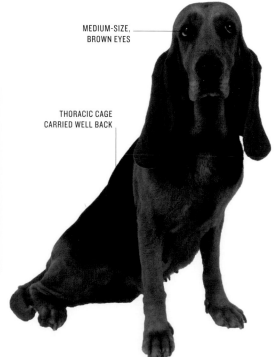

MEDIUM-SIZE, BROWN EYES

THORACIC CAGE CARRIED WELL BACK

SWISS LUCERNE HOUND : SWITZERLAND

French hound breeds have been influential in the bloodlines of the Swiss Hound, but this is perhaps most apparent in the Swiss Lucerne Hound, which is similar in conformation to the French Ariegoise Hound. It is "steel-blue" or blue mottled with extensive dark patches. Some Lucernes have pale-yellow or tan markings, usually on the head, chest, and legs.

CROUP IS LONGISH AND SLIGHTLY INCLINED

FIRM, STRAIGHT BACK

FINELY CHISELED, NARROW MUZZLE

HIP BONES ARE NOT TOO PROMINENT

EARS DROOP AND TWIST, AND ARE SET BELOW EYE LEVEL

UNDERLINE SHOWS SLIGHT TUCK-UP

SWISS SCHWYZ HOUND : SWITZERLAND

The Swiss Schwyz Hound is white with orange-fawn spots or an orange-fawn saddle, sometimes very lightly speckled. An orange-fawn mantle is also allowed. The Schwyz is generally reserved for rabbit and hare, but like all Swiss Hounds, it is a hardy, vigorous, versatile, calm dog with great endurance. These animals are gentle, docile, and very attached to their owners. Swiss Hounds make pleasant companions for an active home.

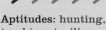
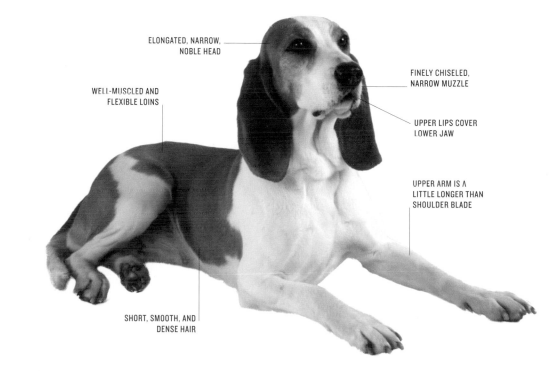

ELONGATED, NARROW, NOBLE HEAD

FINELY CHISELED, NARROW MUZZLE

WELL-MUSCLED AND FLEXIBLE LOINS

UPPER LIPS COVER LOWER JAW

UPPER ARM IS A LITTLE LONGER THAN SHOULDER BLADE

SHORT, SMOOTH, AND DENSE HAIR

AT A GLANCE

Size: medium-large

Exercise needed:

Grooming needed:

Aptitudes: hunting, tracking, trailing, companion

Height: 21–26 in.

Weight: over 55 lb.

Average life expectancy: 10–14 yrs

AKC: not recognized

CHARACTER

Affection

Playfulness

Friendliness to dogs

Friendliness to strangers

Ease of training

TRANSYLVANIAN HOUND : HUNGARY

This rare breed of Hungarian Hound traces back to the Middle Ages when it was widespread and bred across the Carpathian Basin by aristocrats and royalty. The brave hounds were used for hunting big game such as boar, wolf, bear, and lynx in the mountains and on the plains. Due to the different terrains they hunted on, two types of hounds developed: a long-legged variety and a shorter-legged type. As large predators began to disappear, the breed began to diminish. Efforts by breeders have re-established the Transylvanian Hound, but only the long-legged variety exists today.

WITHERS PRONOUNCED WITH STRAIGHT TOPLINE

EARS HANG CLOSE TO CHEEKS WITHOUT BEING FOLDED

DOMED SKULL WITH A SLIGHT STOP

TAIL CURVED BUT NOT CURLED OVER BACK

LIGHT FOLDS OF SKIN UNDER NECK

LARGE FEET

AT A GLANCE

Size: medium

Exercise needed:

Grooming needed:
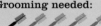

Aptitudes: hunting, tracking, trailing, companion

Height: 16–20 in.

Weight: 42–46 lb.

Average life expectancy: 12–14 yrs

AKC: not recognized

CHARACTER

Affection

Playfulness

Friendliness to dogs

Friendliness to strangers

Ease of training

TYROLEAN HOUND : AUSTRIA

The Tyrolean Hound traces to the mountainous state of Tyrol in western Austria and to the ancient Celtic Hounds, which also gave rise to the Austrian Black and Tan Hound. There are written references to Tyroleans that date back many hundreds of years. Specific breeding for type did not begin in earnest until the 1860s, however. The first breed standards were adopted in 1896, the same year the Tyrolean was first exhibited at a show in Innsbruck. The Tyrolean often hunts singly and excels in wooded areas and mountains. They are mostly used for hunting hare and fox, and for tracking wounded game.

BROAD, HIGH-SET EARS WITH ROUNDED TIPS

MUZZLE IS DEEP AND STRAIGHT

SLOPING SHOULDER BLADES AND UPPER ARMS

RECTANGULAR BODY WITH DEEP, BROAD CHEST

HIGH-SET TAIL, CARRIED HIGH WHEN ALERT

AT A GLANCE

Size: medium-small

Exercise needed:

Grooming needed:

Aptitudes: hunting, tracking, trailing

Height: 18–21 in.

Weight: 33–40 lb.

Average life expectancy: 12–14 yrs

AKC: not recognized

CHARACTER

Affection

Playfulness

Friendliness to dogs
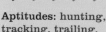

Friendliness to strangers

Ease of training

STYRIAN COARSE-HAIRED HOUND : AUSTRIA

The Styrian Coarse-haired Hound was developed in Austria by industrialist Carl Peintinger in the 1870s, and was originally known as the Peintinger Bracke. Peintinger crossed his female Hanoverian Scent Hound, Hela I, with a Coarse-Haired Istrian Hound, which produced a litter of excellent hunting dogs. The best of these were selectively bred until a type began to emerge. These dogs are tenacious and fearless hunters that give voice throughout the hunt. They are used for tracking wild boar in the Austrian mountains and are tough and enduring. Although they have pleasant temperaments, the breed is most commonly used as a hunting dog.

FLAT-LYING EARS COVERED WITH FINE HAIR

SLIGHTLY ROUNDED SKULL

SLOPING CROUP

STRAIGHT, STRONG MUZZLE WITH FIRM LIPS

MEDIUM LENGTH TAIL CARRIED WITH A SLIGHT UPWARD SICKLE, BRUSH TO UNDERSIDE

COAT IS ROUGH, HARSH, AND COARSE

BROAD, DEEP CHEST

AT A GLANCE

Size: medium

Exercise needed:

Grooming needed:

Aptitudes: hunting, tracking, trailing, companion

Height: 16–20 in.

Weight: 42–46 lb.

Average life expectancy: 12–14 yrs

AKC: not recognized

WESTPHALIAN DACHSBRACKE : GERMANY

This rare breed originated in the Westphalia region of Germany. These dogs are said to have been bred from Deutsche Brackes and Dachshunds to produce a powerful, low-slung animal suited for small game. The Westphalian was fundamental in the development of the Swedish Drever, which has now largely overtaken the Westphalian. These dogs are dedicated and serious hunters that drive their prey toward the hunter giving voice, and can access areas large hounds cannot. They can make suitable companion animals, but are independent-minded and noisy.

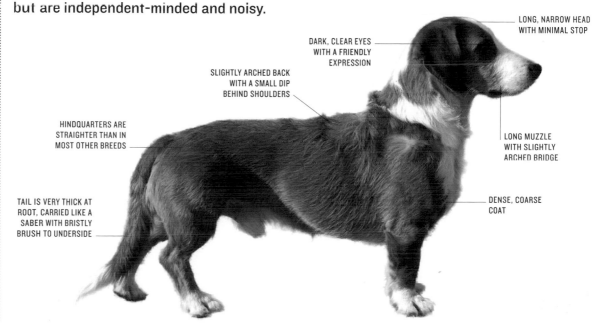

LONG, NARROW HEAD WITH MINIMAL STOP

DARK, CLEAR EYES WITH A FRIENDLY EXPRESSION

SLIGHTLY ARCHED BACK WITH A SMALL DIP BEHIND SHOULDERS

HINDQUARTERS ARE STRAIGHTER THAN IN MOST OTHER BREEDS

LONG MUZZLE WITH SLIGHTLY ARCHED BRIDGE

TAIL IS VERY THICK AT ROOT, CARRIED LIKE A SABER WITH BRISTLY BRUSH TO UNDERSIDE

DENSE, COARSE COAT

CHARACTER

Affection

Playfulness

Friendliness to dogs

Friendliness to strangers

Ease of training

SPITZ-TYPE DOGS

ALASKAN KLEE KAI : UNITED STATES

The Alaskan Klee Kai is a relatively new breed that was developed in the 1970s in Wasilla, Alaska, by Linda Spurlin and her family. Siberian and Alaskan Huskies were used in the breed's foundation, along with smaller Spitz-type dogs such as the Schipperke and American Eskimo Dog to reduce the size. These are lively, charismatic, devoted animals that make superb family companions and worthy watch dogs. This rare breed is divided into three size categories: toy, miniature, and standard.

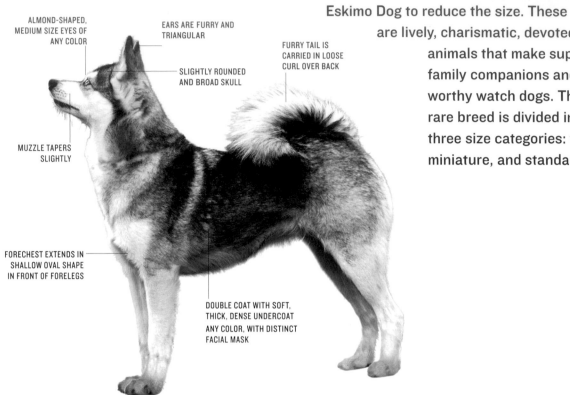

ALMOND-SHAPED, MEDIUM SIZE EYES OF ANY COLOR

EARS ARE FURRY AND TRIANGULAR

SLIGHTLY ROUNDED AND BROAD SKULL

FURRY TAIL IS CARRIED IN LOOSE CURL OVER BACK

MUZZLE TAPERS SLIGHTLY

FORECHEST EXTENDS IN SHALLOW OVAL SHAPE IN FRONT OF FORELEGS

DOUBLE COAT WITH SOFT, THICK, DENSE UNDERCOAT ANY COLOR, WITH DISTINCT FACIAL MASK

NORWEGIAN ELKHOUND : NORWAY

This powerful and ancient breed has developed over time into a superb hunting dog in the most frigid weather conditions. They were and are used to track and hold big game such as elk, moose, bear, and reindeer, holding the prey until the hunter arrives to deal with it. They have seemingly endless stamina and appear impervious to the cold; they have been described as the "Dogs of the Vikings" and were an important part of Viking life. They can make good companions for an active home, but can be strong on a lead, may bark a lot and have a strong prey drive with smaller creatures.

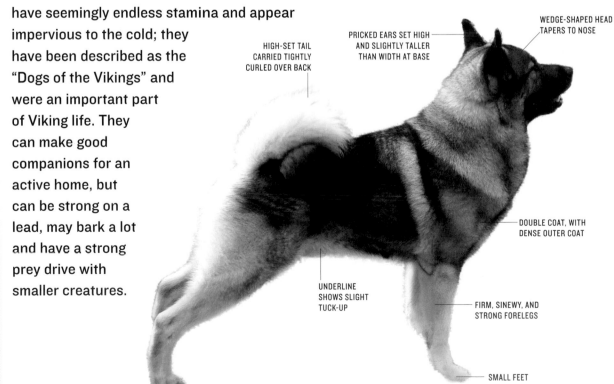

HIGH-SET TAIL CARRIED TIGHTLY CURLED OVER BACK

PRICKED EARS SET HIGH AND SLIGHTLY TALLER THAN WIDTH AT BASE

WEDGE-SHAPED HEAD TAPERS TO NOSE

DOUBLE COAT, WITH DENSE OUTER COAT

UNDERLINE SHOWS SLIGHT TUCK-UP

FIRM, SINEWY, AND STRONG FORELEGS

SMALL FEET

ALASKAN MALAMUTE : UNITED STATES

This no-nonsense working breed has a wonderful temperament and a great spirit. Malamutes are tough, brave dogs that were instrumental in sustaining life for native cultures in Alaska. They have been used by the military, by the U.S. Postal Service in remote Alaska, and by miners during the Klondike Gold Rush. They make good family dogs, but only for those willing to make a substantial time commitment. Malamutes require extensive exercise including speed work, and they are prone to digging and howling if left alone. They can also be strong on a leash and have a strong predatory instinct for smaller animals, so a fenced yard is a must.

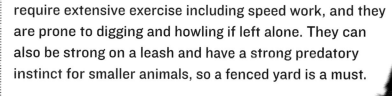

SMALL, TRIANGULAR, PRICKED EARS

ALMOND-SHAPED EYES

LARGE MUZZLE WITH BLACK OR BROWN NOSE

MUSCULAR FRONT END

BUSHY TAIL CARRIED OVER BACK WHEN WORKING

POWERFUL HINDQUARTERS

ANY SHADE OF GRAY WITH WHITE SHADING, WHITE MASK; ANY SHADE OF SABLE OR RED WITH WHITE SHADING; WHITE

STRONG LEGS

DOUBLE COAT WITH COARSE OUTER COAT AND SOFT, DENSE, WOOLLY UNDERCOAT

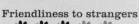
CANADIAN ESKIMO DOG : FRANCE

This French-bred dog with its excellent sense of smell was developed during the nineteenth century in the Ariège area of the Pyrenees Mountains primarily as a pointing dog, although they are also useful retrievers. They are active, powerful animals rarely seen outside their homeland, and are typically used for hunting partridge and hare. They are relatively sociable and thrive when working, but are not generally used solely as companion dogs.

SHORT, THICK, ERECT EARS WITH SLIGHTLY ROUNDED ENDS

SMALL, WIDE-SPACED EYES

MASSIVE, WEDGE-SHAPED HEAD

BROAD SHOULDERS OBLIQUELY SET WITH MODERATE MUSCLING

DOUBLE COAT WITH DENSE UNDERCOAT AND WEATHER-RESISTANT OUTER COAT

LARGE, BUSHY TAIL GENERALLY CARRIED UP OR CURLED OVER BACK

MUSCULAR HIND QUARTERS

WIDE RANGE OF COAT COLORS

AT A GLANCE

Size: large

Exercise needed:

Grooming needed:

Aptitudes: guard dog, watch dog, companion

Height: 22–27 in.

Weight: 70–120 lb.

Average life expectancy: 10–12 yrs

AKC: working

CHARACTER

Affection

Playfulness

Friendliness to dogs

Friendliness to strangers

Ease of training

✚ HEALTH ✚

Although generally healthy, hereditary problems can include auto-immune disease, hip dysplasia, progressive retinal atrophy, Von Willebrands Disease, and hypothyroidism

AKITA : JAPAN / UNITED STATES

The Akita, also known as the Akita Inu or Japanese Akita, is a self-possessed and independent breed that requires consistent, knowledgeable training and socialization. As long as they get this, Akitas can make wonderful family pets. They are good with children and exceptionally loyal and devoted companions. Wary of strangers, they also make excellent watch dogs, but Akitas can be aggressive toward other dogs. Given their powerful physique and complex character, the Akita is not suitable for first-time dog owners.

WITHERS SLIGHTLY HIGHER THAN CROUP

DOUBLE COAT WITH SOFT, THICK, DENSE UNDERCOAT

FURRY TAIL CARRIED IN A LOOSE CURL OVER BACK

FORECHEST EXTENDS IN A SHALLOW OVAL SHAPE IN FRONT OF FORELEGS

POWERFUL CHEST

ANY COLOR, WITH A DISTINCT FACIAL MASK

COMMON COAT COLORS

RED FAWN

FAWN

BRINDLE

WHITE

PINTO

Any color including fawn, brindle, white or pinto with or without a mask or blaze.

SLIGHTLY ROUNDED,
BROAD SKULL

ALMOND-SHAPED, MEDIUM-
SIZE EYES OF ANY COLOR OR
COMBINATION OF COLORS

PRICKED,
TRIANGULAR EARS

MUZZLE TAPERS SLIGHTLY

HISTORY

Akitas are most associated with Odate City (called Dog City) and the surrounding area of the Akita prefecture on the northern end of Honshu Island. This area was home to a number of regional types of large spitz dogs collectively called Matagi-Inu, which were used for hunting large game, as guard dogs, and for dog fighting. During the nineteenth century, European breeds like Mastiffs, German Shepherds, and Great Danes were introduced, and crossbreeding with the local stock gave rise to the Tosa Inu and increased the size of the Matagi-Inu. The original Japanese type was in danger of disappearing, so in 1927, a preservation society was set up and the name Akita was adopted for the Matagi-Inu. After World War II, Akitas had all but disappeared, and the breed was salvaged using two breeding lines: the Ichinoseki and the Dewa. Dogs of the Dewa line were taken to the United States and founded the American Akita, whereas those of the Ichinoseki lines gave rise to the Akita-Inu. Despite the differences between the two types, some Kennel Clubs have only recently acknowledged them as separate.

American Akita

COAT UP-CLOSE

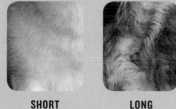

Double coat with thick, short undercoat and a straight, harsh outer coat that stands somewhat off the body

SHORT   LONG

Akita puppies need lots of socialization and obedience training from a young age. They also need to be with their owners as much as possible and do not do well when left on their own for long periods of time.

CHOW CHOW : CHINA

Recent DNA testing has revealed that the Chow Chow is directly descended from the earliest domesticated dogs and is one of the ancestors of the modern Spitz-type breeds. Chow Chows are believed to have developed in the Arctic Circle before moving south into Mongolia, Siberia, and China. The Chow Chow is a quiet, reserved, and dignified breed. These dogs are loyal to their families, but not overly demonstrative. Although they are mostly companions now, historically they were used as versatile farm dogs for draft work, guarding, herding livestock, and hunting; they were even kept for their meat.

SMALL, MODERATELY THICK, TRIANGULAR-SHAPED EARS CARRIED STIFFLY FORWARD

DARK BROWN, DEEP-SET, ALMOND-SHAPED EYES

SCOWLING BUT DIGNIFIED EXPRESSION

CHARACTERISTIC BLUE-BLACK TONGUE

SHORT, COMPACT, CLOSE-COUPLED BODY

RED, BLACK, BLUE, CINNAMON, OR CREAM COAT

HIND LEGS WITH LITTLE APPARENT ANGULATION

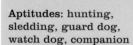
EAST SIBERIAN LAIKA : RUSSIA

The East Siberian Laika is an ancient breed, descended from dogs taken to Eastern Siberia by nomadic tribes—some migrated from the west, and others traveled north from Mongolia and China. The dogs were bred specifically to cope with the frigid climate, hostile environment, and heavy workloads, and are among the toughest of all breeds. They are used for hunting all types of game in deep snow, and make good guard and sled dogs. They are not suitable for urban living, though, or for first-time dog owners, and do best in a working environment with lots of exercise.

SICKLE-SHAPED OR RING-SHAPED TAIL

PRICKED, TRIANGULAR EARS

WELL-DEVELOPED WITHERS RISE OUT OF BACK LINE

WEDGE-SHAPED HEAD

WEDGE-SHAPED MUZZLE WITH TIGHT, DRY LIPS

NEARLY SQUARE IN PROPORTION

ROUND FEET

EURASIER : GERMANY

Also known as the Eurasian, this relatively new breed was developed in Germany in the 1960s as a companion animal. Breeders initially crossed Chow Chows with Keeshonds, trying to produce the best qualities from both breeds. At first, the new breed was called the Wolf-Chow, but after Samoyed was also introduced to the breed, the name was changed to the Eurasier. These dogs have a lovely temperament—calm, affectionate, and obedient. They are very loyal to their families, reserved but unaggressive with strangers, and generally have no hunting instinct.

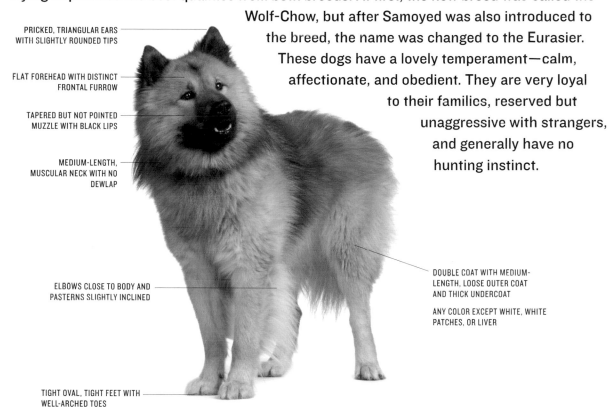

PRICKED, TRIANGULAR EARS WITH SLIGHTLY ROUNDED TIPS

FLAT FOREHEAD WITH DISTINCT FRONTAL FURROW

TAPERED BUT NOT POINTED MUZZLE WITH BLACK LIPS

MEDIUM-LENGTH, MUSCULAR NECK WITH NO DEWLAP

ELBOWS CLOSE TO BODY AND PASTERNS SLIGHTLY INCLINED

DOUBLE COAT WITH MEDIUM-LENGTH, LOOSE OUTER COAT AND THICK UNDERCOAT

ANY COLOR EXCEPT WHITE, WHITE PATCHES, OR LIVER

TIGHT OVAL, TIGHT FEET WITH WELL-ARCHED TOES

GERMAN SPITZ : GERMANY

The German Spitz traces its ancestry to ancient Nordic herding dogs used by nomadic cultures living in the frigid Arctic. These dogs, like the Samoyed, made their way to Germany and Holland, possibly with the Vikings, and were crossed with local, native sheepherding breeds. The earliest record of the German Spitz dates to 1450. In Germany these dogs are recognized in five different sizes: Wolfspitz (also known as the Keeshond), Giant Spitz, Mittel, Klein, and Dwarf (also known as the Pomeranian). The German Spitz is a fairly new arrival to the United States, and is registered in two sizes: the Mittel and the Klein. Both are bright, lively, bold-natured dogs that can be noisy if left alone. They thrive on company and challenges, and require only moderate amounts of exercise, but need regular grooming.

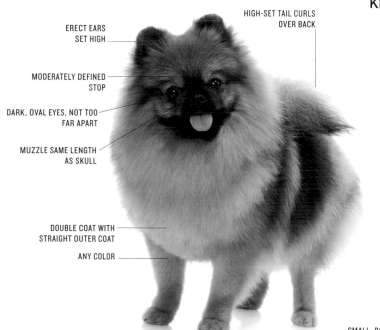

HIGH-SET TAIL CURLS OVER BACK

ERECT EARS SET HIGH

MODERATELY DEFINED STOP

DARK, OVAL EYES, NOT TOO FAR APART

MUZZLE SAME LENGTH AS SKULL

DOUBLE COAT WITH STRAIGHT OUTER COAT

ANY COLOR

SMALL, ROUNDED, CAT-LIKE FEET

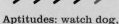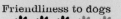

FINNISH LAPPHUND : FINLAND

This is a breed of ancient origin that developed across the large frozen areas of northern Finland, Sweden, Norway, and parts of Russia. These dogs trace back to reindeer farmers who relied on them to herd livestock. Although Finnish Lapphunds are now primarily pets and are among the most popular breeds in Finland, they retain strong herding instincts. They are intelligent, eager to please, and gentle, and generally get along well with children and other dogs. They can also make excellent companions.

MEDIUM-SIZE, TRIANGULAR, PRICKED, AND MOBILE EARS

LARGE, OVAL EYES WITH A KIND EXPRESSION

NECK IS MEDIUM LENGTH AND HAS A THICK RUFF OF HAIR

PROFUSE, DENSE DOUBLE COAT WITH LONG, COARSE OUTER COAT AND THICK UNDERCOAT COLOR: ANY COLOR

FORELEGS ARE WELL BONED

COMPACT OVAL FEET ARE COVERED WITH THICK HAIR

BODY IS COMPACT, DEEP, AND FLEXIBLE

BROAD, WEDGE-SHAPED HEAD WITH A STRONG OUTLINE

FINNISH SPITZ : FINLAND

Also known as Finkies, this ancient Finnish breed was an essential part of early settlers' lives and was used for hunting birds and larger game. They are noted for their vigorous bark and for "giving voice" while hunting, a characteristic so highly valued that there is an annual competition in Finland to crown the dog with the greatest vocal talent as the "King of Barking." Finnish Spitzes are most adapted to hunting the capercaillie, a bird found mostly in Europe and Asia. Finkies are charismatic and make good companions and watch dogs.

FOX-LIKE HEAD WITH LIVELY EXPRESSION

NARROW MUZZLE

MEDIUM-LENGTH, HARSH OUTER COAT AND SHORT, SOFT UNDERCOAT

PLUMED TAIL CURVES OVER BACK AND RESTS AGAINST THIGH

SQUARE, MUSCULAR BODY

SHADES OF RED TO GOLD

ROUNDED, COMPACT FEET

GREENLAND DOG : GREENLAND

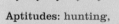
The Greenland Dog is one of the "powerhouse" Spitz breeds, and also one of the oldest. Ancient remains of Spitz-type dogs found on the New Siberian Islands off the northern Russian coast have been dated to around 9,000 years ago, and there is evidence that the dogs reached Greenland with the Sarqaq people by around 5,000 years ago. This is a remarkable sled-dog breed that is widely used in polar expeditions and for hunting seals and polar bears. They are incredibly tough, independent, and strong, and it is essential they have consistent, patient, and firm training in addition to extensive, high-octane exercise. They are good-natured dogs, but are suitable only for an experienced home that can provide them with the exercise and supervision they need.

SLIGHTLY ARCHED SKULL, BROADEST BETWEEN THE EARS

SMALL, TRIANGULAR, PRICKED, EXPRESSIVE EARS

DOUBLE COAT, DENSE, COARSE, STRAIGHT OUTER COAT, SOFT UNDERCOAT

HIGH-SET, THICK, BUSHY TAIL, CARRIED IN A CURVE

STRAIGHT, STRONG UPPER FORELEG

LARGE, POWERFUL, ROUND FEET

JÄMTHUND : SWEDEN

Also known as the Swedish Elkhound, this breed used to be grouped with the Norwegian Elkhound and was only recognized as its own breed in 1946. These dogs are most associated with the province of Jämtland in central Sweden and, despite their recent recognition, are believed to be ancient in origin. They have been used for centuries for big-game hunting, including moose and elk, and are one of the few breeds that will face a bear. They have a calm, level temperament, but can be intolerant of other dogs.

LONG HEAD WITH DEFINED STOP

OVAL EYES WITH A KEEN BUT CALM EXPRESSION

TAIL SET HIGH AND CARRIED IN A CURL

ERECT, MOBILE, HIGH-SET EARS

TAPERED MUZZLE WITH TIGHT LIPS

OUTER COAT IS CLOSE LYING BUT NOT FLAT; UNDERCOAT IS SOFT AND SHORT

LIGHT OR DARK GRAY

OVAL FEET

AT A GLANCE

Size: small

Exercise needed:

Grooming needed:

Aptitudes: watch dog, agility, companion

Height: 9–19 in.

Weight: 6–40 lb.

Average life expectancy: 12–14 yrs

AKC: non-sporting

CHARACTER

Affection

Playfulness

Friendliness to dogs

Friendliness to strangers

Ease of training

HEALTH

Although generally healthy, some hereditary problems include hip dysplasia, cancer, Addison's disease, gastric torsion, progressive retinol atrophy, and eyelid problems.

AMERICAN ESKIMO DOG : UNITED STATES

Despite its name, this delightful breed has nothing to do with the Eskimo, or Inuit, culture and descended from European Spitz breeds. These dogs are divided into Toy, Miniature, and Standard sizes, all prized for their beautiful appearance. Not just a pretty face, "Eskies" are also charismatic, intelligent, and friendly (although independent). They make excellent companion and watch dogs, and are highly protective of their families and homes. They need plenty of exercise though, and their spectacular coats need regular grooming. Alert and active, American Eskimo Dogs also excel in agility and love to learn new tricks. They require substantial amounts of mental stimulation as well as physical exercise, so they are happiest in an active home.

TAIL SET MODERATELY HIGH, CARRIED LOOSELY OVER BACK WHEN MOVING

COMPACT, STRONG BODY WITH LEVEL TOPLINE

ERECT, BLUNT-TIPPED, TRIANGULAR EARS

WEDGE-SHAPED HEAD

LION-LIKE RUFF AROUND NECK

BROAD MUZZLE

THICK, DENSE, AND STRAIGHT STAND-OFF DOUBLE COAT

DEEP, WIDE CHEST

COMMON COAT COLORS

The coat can be white or "biscuit cream."

WHITE   BISCUIT CREAM

COAT UP-CLOSE

The stand-off double coat is thick, dense, and straight.

LONG

HISTORY

The American Eskimo Dog traces back to small German and other European Spitz breeds brought to the United States with European immigrants. By the 1910s, these dogs had become known as American Spitz, reflecting anti-German sentiments during and after War War I. The American Spitz grew in popularity due to its fame as a performing breed in the traveling circuses. The first dogs of the breed were registered in 1913 with the United Kennel Club under the name American Eskimo Spitz. The breed was recognized by the American Kennel Club in 1994.

American Eskimo dogs are rare with only about 1,000 registered in the United States.

KAI KEN : JAPAN

The Kai Ken, also known as the Kai Dog or Tora Inu (Tiger Dog), is a rare Japanese breed that has started to appear outside Japan only recently. The breed is ancient in origin and traces back to the mountainous province of Kai on Honshu island. These dogs developed in geographic isolation and have been influenced little by other breeds. Kai Kens are noted for their hunting abilities and are used on a range of game, including pheasants, deer, wild boar, and even bears. They tend to bond strongly with one person and are intelligent, calm, and friendly dogs that are fairly easy to train. They are very loyal and make good companions for an active, outdoor-orientated home.

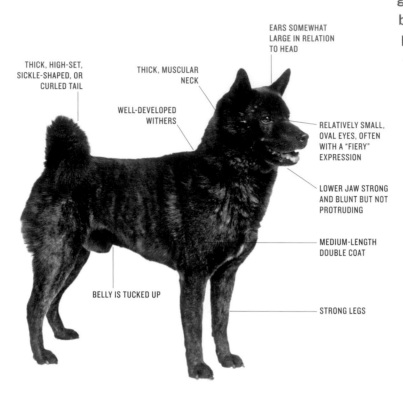

EARS SOMEWHAT LARGE IN RELATION TO HEAD

THICK, MUSCULAR NECK

THICK, HIGH-SET, SICKLE-SHAPED, OR CURLED TAIL

WELL-DEVELOPED WITHERS

RELATIVELY SMALL, OVAL EYES, OFTEN WITH A "FIERY" EXPRESSION

LOWER JAW STRONG AND BLUNT BUT NOT PROTRUDING

MEDIUM-LENGTH DOUBLE COAT

BELLY IS TUCKED UP

STRONG LEGS

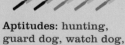
KARELIAN BEAR DOG : FINLAND

Karelian Bear Dogs are ancient and trace to northwestern Europe when Spitz-types were an essential part of life for farmers and peasants: guarding, hunting, and protecting. These outstanding and fearless hunting dogs are used mostly on large game. Typically they hunt silently and give voice only when the game has stopped or been treed. These dogs are most associated with Karelia, an area in Russia and Finland, and are believed to have developed from the Komi dog. The Karelian Bear Dog is an active, intelligent, and independent breed that is best suited to an energetic, experienced home.

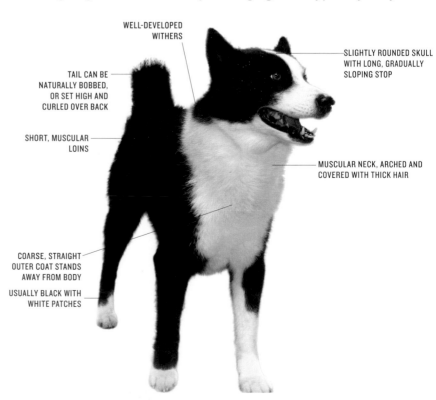

WELL-DEVELOPED WITHERS

SLIGHTLY ROUNDED SKULL WITH LONG, GRADUALLY SLOPING STOP

TAIL CAN BE NATURALLY BOBBED, OR SET HIGH AND CURLED OVER BACK

SHORT, MUSCULAR LOINS

MUSCULAR NECK, ARCHED AND COVERED WITH THICK HAIR

COARSE, STRAIGHT OUTER COAT STANDS AWAY FROM BODY

USUALLY BLACK WITH WHITE PATCHES

AT A GLANCE

Size: medium-small

Exercise needed:

Grooming needed:

Aptitudes: guard dog,
watch dog, livestock
guardian, companion

Height: 16–18 in.

Weight: 25–45 lb.

Average life expectancy:
14–15 yrs

AKC: herding

CHARACTER

Affection

Playfulness

Friendliness to dogs

Friendliness to strangers

Ease of training

ICELANDIC SHEEPDOG : ICELAND

The rugged, tough Icelandic Sheepdog traces its history to ancient times with dog remains of a similar type uncovered in graves dating back to around 8000 BCE. Iceland was colonized in 874 by Norwegian Vikings who arrived with their dogs. These dogs adapted to the climate and terrain of Iceland, and were used for guarding property and livestock, as well as ridding farms of vermin and providing companionship. Few other dog breeds were imported over the centuries, and in 1901, the importation of any other animals onto the island was banned. This means that Icelandic Sheepdogs have been little influenced by other breeds throughout their history. They are often aptly described as big dogs in small bodies and are full of personality. They are playful, fun, and lively in nature.

ALMOND-SHAPED EYES

MOBILE, ERECT, TRIANGULAR EARS

THICK AND WATERPROOF DOUBLE COAT

WHITE, TAN, CHOCOLATE-BROWN, GRAY, OR BLACK

MUZZLE SLIGHTLY SHORTER THAN SKULL AND TAPERS EVENLY TO NOSE

HIGH-SET TAIL CARRIED CURLED OVER BACK

STRONG, RECTANGULAR BODY

SLIGHTLY OVAL FEET WITH WELL-ARCHED TOES

AT A GLANCE

Size: medium-small

Exercise needed:

Grooming needed:

Aptitudes: hunting,
guard dog, watch dog,
companion

Height: 16–19 in.

Weight: 35–45 lb.

Average life expectancy:
12–14 yrs

AKC: non-sporting

CHARACTER

Affection

Playfulness

Friendliness to dogs

Friendliness to strangers

Ease of training

KEESHOND : NETHERLANDS/GERMANY

In Germany the Keeshond is considered a size variety of the German Spitz. In the United States, England, and a number of other countries, the Keeshond is recognized as a separate breed whose history is most closely associated with the Netherlands. The Keeshond became popular there during the seventeenth century and was mostly used for guarding barges. This breed makes an excellent watch dog and has a fierce bark, but it is not aggressive in nature. These are highly intelligent and charismatic dogs that have been used for search and rescue, but are most commonly kept as companions.

SMALL, DARK, ERECT EARS

WEDGE-SHAPED HEAD

DARK MUZZLE AND BLACK NOSE

MODERATELY LONG, ARCHED NECK

COMPACT BODY

THICK RUFF AROUND NECK

THICK DOUBLE COAT WITH PALE UNDERCOAT

MIXTURE OF GRAY AND BLACK

ALMOND-SHAPED EYES WITH "SPECTACLE" MARKINGS

KISHU KEN : JAPAN

The Kishu is a rare breed of Japanese Spitz that is seldom seen outside its homeland. The dogs have ancient roots and developed in the rugged, isolated mountains of Kishu, now the Wakayama Prefecture. They were and are used for hunting deer and wild boar and excel in this role. Originally Kishu Kens exhibited a range of coat colors, but hunters came to prefer pure white dogs because they were easy to spot in the forests. Gradually the dogs were bred with white as the choice color, but other solid colors are also allowed.

AT A GLANCE

Size: medium-small

Exercise needed:

Grooming needed:

Aptitudes: hunting, guard dog, watch dog, companion

Height: 18–21 in.

Weight: 30–50 lb.

Average life expectancy: 12–13 yrs

AKC: FSS

CHARACTER

Affection

Playfulness

Friendliness to dogs

Friendliness to strangers

Ease of training

TAIL IS THICK, SET HIGH, AND CARRIED CURLED OVER BACK

SHORT, STRAIGHT BACK

SMALL, TRIANGULAR EARS SET WELL APART

BROAD FOREHEAD WITH AN ABRUPT STOP

MUZZLE IS WEDGE SHAPED AND THICK

DOUBLE COAT WITH HARSH, STRAIGHT OUTER COAT AND DENSE, SOFT UNDERCOAT COLOR: WHITE; RED; SESAME

TOUGH, STRONG HOCKS

FORELEGS ARE STRAIGHT WITH PASTERNS SLIGHTLY INCLINED

JINDO : KOREA

The Korean Jindo Dog originated on the island of Jindo, located off the western coast of Korea. These dos developed in geographic isolation and with little influence from other breeds. No records exist to reveal their actual origins, but some believe Jindos developed from ancient indigenous dogs. Others think they are descendants of Mongolian dogs that bred with Korean stock during battles in the thirteenth century. What is not disputed is the breed's long history, its purity, and its excellence at hunting and guarding. These dogs are also exceptionally clean and easy to house-train. Jindos were designated as a "National Treasure" by the South Korean government in 1962.

AT A GLANCE

Size: medium-small

Exercise needed:

Grooming needed:

Aptitudes: hunting, guard dog, watch dog, companion

Height: 17–22 in.

Weight: 33–50 lb.

Average life expectancy: 12–14 yrs

AKC: FSS

CHARACTER

Affection
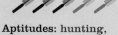

Playfulness

Friendliness to dogs

Friendliness to strangers
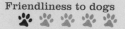

Ease of training

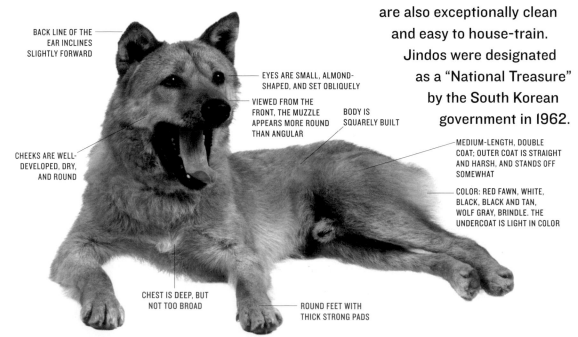

BACK LINE OF THE EAR INCLINES SLIGHTLY FORWARD

EYES ARE SMALL, ALMOND-SHAPED, AND SET OBLIQUELY

VIEWED FROM THE FRONT, THE MUZZLE APPEARS MORE ROUND THAN ANGULAR

BODY IS SQUARELY BUILT

CHEEKS ARE WELL-DEVELOPED, DRY, AND ROUND

MEDIUM-LENGTH, DOUBLE COAT; OUTER COAT IS STRAIGHT AND HARSH, AND STANDS OFF SOMEWHAT

COLOR: RED FAWN, WHITE, BLACK, BLACK AND TAN, WOLF GRAY, BRINDLE. THE UNDERCOAT IS LIGHT IN COLOR

CHEST IS DEEP, BUT NOT TOO BROAD

ROUND FEET WITH THICK STRONG PADS

NORWEGIAN BUHUND : NORWAY

Although they trace back to the Vikings, modern Buhunds developed in western Norway where they were used as general-purpose farm dogs, herding and guarding livestock, hunting, and guarding property. Today they are mostly companion animals, although some are still livestock guardians. They have also been used as assistance dogs. Buhunds have calm, affectionate, and loyal temperaments; are generally good with children and other dogs; and will watch over their homes and property. They do have a tendency to bark excessively and molt profusely at certain times of the year.

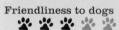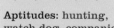
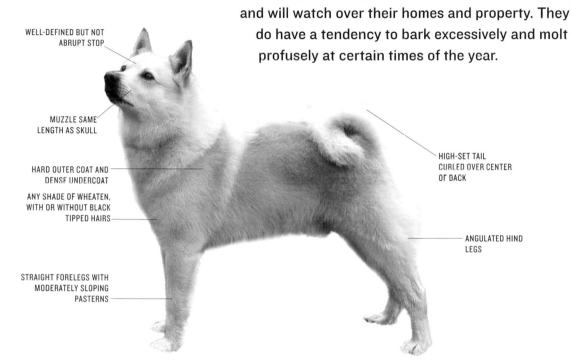

WELL-DEFINED BUT NOT ABRUPT STOP

MUZZLE SAME LENGTH AS SKULL

HARD OUTER COAT AND DENSE UNDERCOAT

ANY SHADE OF WHEATEN, WITH OR WITHOUT BLACK TIPPED HAIRS

STRAIGHT FORELEGS WITH MODERATELY SLOPING PASTERNS

HIGH-SET TAIL CURLED OVER CENTER OF BACK

ANGULATED HIND LEGS

NORWEGIAN LUNDEHUND : NORWAY

The thoroughly unique Lundehund developed in geographic isolation on the Norwegian Lofoten Islands and is a product of natural selection and adaptation, free from the influence of other breeds. The breed takes its name from the Norwegian word, *lunde*, which means "puffin," and was used as a puffin-hunting dog. Lundehunds have five three-jointed toes and at least one two-jointed toe, all fully muscled, which makes them excellent rock climbers. They are also flexible, which enables them to navigate difficult, tight rocks while carrying a heavy bird. Lundehunds require lots of socialization as they can be naturally shy. They are also intelligent and independent, and can be difficult to train. The breed barks a lot and has a natural small-prey drive, but these dogs make wonderful companions for patient, experienced homes.

MOBILE, ERECT EARS

DENSE DOUBLE COAT WITH SOFT, THICK UNDERCOAT

LEVEL BACK

HIGH-SET, BUSHY TAIL, CARRIED OVER BACK

WHITE WITH RED OR DARK MARKINGS; SHADES OF TAN WITH WHITE MARKINGS

FEET TURN SLIGHTLY OUTWARD AND HAVE ADDITIONAL FULLY DEVELOPED TOES

RUSSO-EUROPEAN LAIKA : RUSSIA

AT A GLANCE

Size: medium

Exercise needed:

Grooming needed:

Aptitudes: hunting, watch dog, companion

Height: 19–23 in.

Weight: 44–55 lb.

Average life expectancy: 10–12 yrs

AKC: not recognized

CHARACTER

Affection
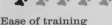

Playfulness

Friendliness to dogs

Friendliness to strangers

Ease of training

The Russo-European Laika developed in the heavily forested and icy regions of northern Europe and Russia, roughly between the Ural Mountains and Finland, and is one of several Spitz-type Russian hunting dogs (Laikas). These dogs are used on large and small game and have great endurance. They are also lively and excitable and need a lot of exercise and activity to thrive. Laikas are affectionate and good with children, and they make good family dogs for an experienced home. They are capable watch dogs, but are prone to barking, can be aggressive to other dogs, and are wary of strangers.

FAIRLY SMALL HEAD

SMALL, OVAL, DARK, SLANTING EYES

SICKLE-SHAPED OR RINGED TAIL

SHORT, SLIGHTLY ARCHED LOINS

HARSH AND STRAIGHT OUTER COAT, AND WELL-DEVELOPED UNDERCOAT

BLACK, GRAY, OR SALT AND PEPPER; WITH WHITE MARKINGS

STRAIGHT FORELEGS WITH MEDIUM-LENGTH, FLEXIBLE PASTERNS

OVAL FEET WITH STRONG, TIGHT TOES

SHIKOKU : JAPAN

AT A GLANCE

Size: medium-small

Exercise needed:

Grooming needed:

Aptitudes: hunting, watch dog, companion

Height: 17–21 in.

Weight: 35–55 lb.

Average life expectancy: 13–15 yrs

AKC: not recognized

CHARACTER

Affection

Playfulness

Friendliness to dogs

Friendliness to strangers

Ease of training

The ancient Shikoku developed in the remote mountains of Kochi, on the Japanese island of Shikoku, with little influence from any other breeds. The dogs developed in two lines: the Eastern Shikoku and the Western Shikoku. In each line, there were various types. During the twentieth century, the Japanese Dog Protective League was established to preserve Japanese breeds and prevent them being influenced by European breeds. Three varieties of the breed are recognized today: the Awa, the Hongawa, and the Hata, each named after the area where it was bred.

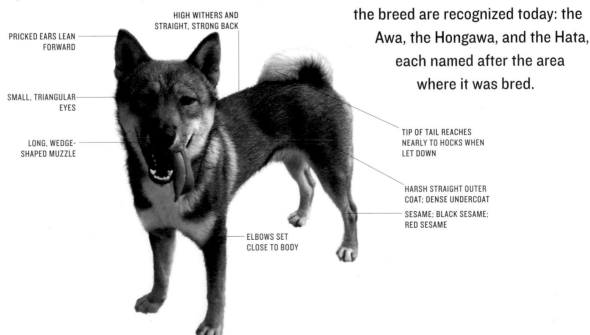

HIGH WITHERS AND STRAIGHT, STRONG BACK

PRICKED EARS LEAN FORWARD

SMALL, TRIANGULAR EYES

LONG, WEDGE-SHAPED MUZZLE

TIP OF TAIL REACHES NEARLY TO HOCKS WHEN LET DOWN

HARSH STRAIGHT OUTER COAT; DENSE UNDERCOAT

SESAME; BLACK SESAME; RED SESAME

ELBOWS SET CLOSE TO BODY

AT A GLANCE

Size: medium-small

Exercise needed:

Grooming needed:

Aptitudes: watch dog, companion

Height: 16–22 in.

Weight: 35–45 lb.

Average life expectancy: 12–16 yrs

AKC: not recognized

CHARACTER

Affection

Playfulness
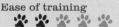

Friendliness to dogs

Friendliness to strangers

Ease of training

THAI BANGKAEW DOG : THAILAND

The Thai Bangkaew Dog traces to Bangkaew, a village in Phitsanulok Province, Thailand, and to the Wat Bangkaew Buddhist monastery near the Yom River. Legend says that the breed's foundation was a pregnant black-and-white dog named Tah Nim who was given to Luang Puh Maak Metharee, the head of the monastery. Tah Nim had been bred by a wild dog or a Jackal, and her puppies were bred to local dogs. The Thai Bangkaew Dog is widely bred in Thailand today, but rarely seen outside its homeland. These are lively, intelligent, loyal dogs that are devoted to their families but wary of strangers. They also love to swim and dig.

SMALL, SLIGHTLY HOODED EARS SET HIGH ON HEAD

BLACK OR DARK BROWN, MEDIUM-SIZE EYES

STRONG, MUSCULAR NECK CARRIED PROUDLY

STRAIGHT, COARSE OUTER COAT; DENSE UNDERCOAT

WHITE WITH PATCHES OF BLACK, RED, FAWN, TAN, OR GRAY; WITH OR WITHOUT BLACKENED HAIR TIPS

AT A GLANCE

Size: medium-small

Exercise needed:

Grooming needed:
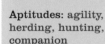

Aptitudes: agility, herding, hunting, companion

Height: 16–20 in.

Weight: 33–53 lb.

Average life expectancy: 10–12 yrs

AKC: FSS

CHARACTER

Affection

Playfulness

Friendliness to dogs

Friendliness to strangers

Ease of training

SWEDISH LAPPHUND : SWEDEN

The Swedish Lapphund is the oldest of the native Swedish breeds and also the rarest. These dogs trace back to the nomadic Sami People of Lapland whose lives revolved around their reindeer. The "Lappic," as the dogs are known, was central to the Sami's lives and used for hunting, guarding, and herding. The Lappie is known for its fearsome bark, which is used to deter predators and intruders, but was also useful when herding the reindeer—the herdsman could locate the dog, and the reindeer came to recognize the noise as that of a friend, not a predator. Lappies today retain their herding instincts. They are generally good with children, interactive, and thrive on mental and physical challenges. But if they get bored, they have a tendency to bark.

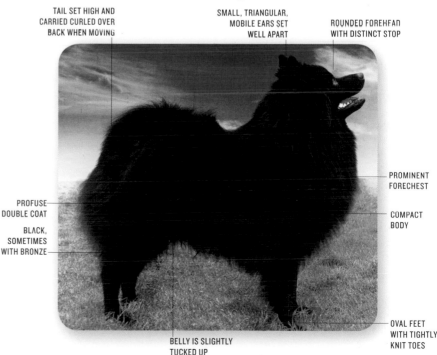

TAIL SET HIGH AND CARRIED CURLED OVER BACK WHEN MOVING

SMALL, TRIANGULAR, MOBILE EARS SET WELL APART

ROUNDED FOREHEAD WITH DISTINCT STOP

PROMINENT FORECHEST

PROFUSE DOUBLE COAT

BLACK, SOMETIMES WITH BRONZE

COMPACT BODY

BELLY IS SLIGHTLY TUCKED UP

OVAL FEET WITH TIGHTLY KNIT TOES

SIBERIAN HUSKY : SIBERIA

The Siberian Husky is the fastest of the Sled Dog breeds and matches its speed with endurance, determination, and a competitive edge. They are a favorite for dog sledding and combine their working abilities with exceptional temperaments. Due to their lovely nature, they have become popular as companion animals, but they require extensive, high-octane exercise and should not be considered unless that requirement can be met. Not surprisingly, they are very powerful dogs on a leash, they have a high small-prey drive, and they are notorious for escaping. They are also excellent diggers and often like to swim.

AT A GLANCE

Size: medium

Exercise needed:

Grooming needed:

Aptitudes: sledding, weight pulling, dry land mushing, skijoring, bikejoring, canicross, dog scootering, companion

Height: 20–24 in.

Weight: 35–60 lb.

Average life expectancy: 11–13 yrs

AKC: working

CHARACTER

Affection

Playfulness

Friendliness to dogs

Friendliness to strangers

Ease of training

✚ HEALTH ✚

Although generally healthy, some health problems can include eye problems such as corneal dystrophy, canine glaucoma, and progressive retinal atrophy.

STRONG, STRAIGHT BACK

FOX-BRUSH TAIL CARRIED TRAILING OR CURVED OVER BACK

COMMON COAT COLORS

BLACK & WHITE

RED & WHITE

WHITE

FAWN & WHITE

Any color from black to white with a variety of markings on the head

COAT UP-CLOSE

STRAIGHT

Dense, soft undercoat with a medium-length, straight outer coat.

SKULL IS SLIGHTLY
ROUNDED ON TOP

ALMOND-SHAPED EYES CAN
BE BLUE, BROWN, ONE OF
EACH, OR PARTI-COLORED

WOLF-LIKE
APPEARANCE

WELL-SLOPED
SHOULDERS

MEDIUM-LENGTH
MUZZLE

DEEP CHEST

OVAL FEET

Siberian Huskies need a lot of grooming, particularly when they are shedding. It is a good idea to get puppies used to being groomed at an early age.

HISTORY

Siberian Huskies are directly descended from the ancient Chukchi Dogs. Originating in Central Asia, the Chukchi people migrated northeast and settled on the remote Chukchi Peninsular of far eastern Siberia, where they built their livelihoods around reindeer. Their dogs were vital components of their lives, pulling sleds, guarding and herding livestock, protecting their homes, and offering companionship. Huskies owe their modern development to Leonard Seppala, Elizabeth Richter, Harry Wheeler, Eva Seeley, and Lorna Demidoff, all early breeders. During World War II, Huskies were used extensively by the American military for search and rescue, and it was around the same time that the breed arrived in England.

CHARACTER

Affection

Playfulness

Friendliness to dogs

Friendliness to strangers

Ease of training

+ HEALTH +

Although generally healthy, some health problems include gastric torsion and hip dysplasia

SAMOYED : RUSSIA

This lovely breed is often called the "smiling dog" on account of its cheerful disposition and characteristic "smile." Samoyeds are one of the most amiable, good-natured, and even-tempered breeds—combined with their beautiful looks that makes them a popular choice for a companion. They are intelligent and independent, which means they need clear, consistent obedience training, but once trained, they are usually exemplary. Samoyeds were used by the American military during World War II—one dog, Soldier Frosty of Rimini, was even awarded the Good Conduct Medal and a Victory Medal.

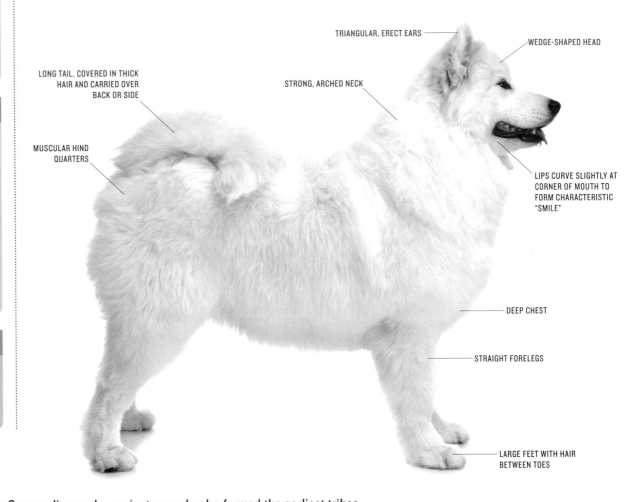

TRIANGULAR, ERECT EARS

WEDGE-SHAPED HEAD

LONG TAIL, COVERED IN THICK HAIR AND CARRIED OVER BACK OR SIDE

STRONG, ARCHED NECK

MUSCULAR HIND QUARTERS

LIPS CURVE SLIGHTLY AT CORNER OF MOUTH TO FORM CHARACTERISTIC "SMILE"

DEEP CHEST

STRAIGHT FORELEGS

LARGE FEET WITH HAIR BETWEEN TOES

HISTORY

The breed is named after the Samoyedic people, ancient nomads who formed the earliest tribes of Central Asia. They migrated northwest into the Arctic Circle, taking their dogs with them, and established their homes on land that was uninhabitable to most people. The dogs were essential to the Samoyedic way of life, accompanying their owners on hunting trips, pulling sleds, guarding homes, herding and guarding reindeer, and even being left to watch over children. The dogs lived in almost complete isolation until the late sixteenth century when the Russians began to explore and colonize Siberia. Recognizing the dogs' many qualities, the Russians began to use them too, chiefly for pulling sleds. Norwegian explorer Fridtjof Nansen relied on Samoyeds when he traveled to the North Pole in 1895. Around the same time, Queen Victoria's granddaughter, who was married to Czar Nicolas II of Russia, sent Samoyeds to England as a gift for the Prince of Wales, later King Edward VII. In 1904, the first of the breed was registered with the American Kennel Club.

COMMON COAT COLORS

The coat can be white, cream, biscuit, or white and biscuit.

WHITE

BISCUIT

COAT UP-CLOSE

The Samoyed has a thick double coat with a harsh, medium-length outer coat, and a soft, woolly undercoat.

Like most breeds with pricked ears, Samoyeds have floppy ears at birth that gradually become erect as the puppies age.

AT A GLANCE

Size: small

Exercise needed:

Grooming needed:
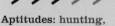

Aptitudes: hunting, watch dog, companion

Height: 13–17 in.

Weight: 17–25 lb.

Average life expectancy: 12–15 yrs

AKC: non-sporting

CHARACTER

Affection

Playfulness

Friendliness to dogs

Friendliness to strangers

Ease of training

+ HEALTH +

The Shiba Inu is a healthy breed but occasional issues include allergies, glaucoma, cataracts, hip dysplasia, and allergies.

COAT UP-CLOSE

 The stiff, straight outer coat is about 2 inches long

Shiba Inu puppies look like teddy bears and are exceptionally cute. They are also spirited and lively—when they are not sleeping!

SHIBA INU : JAPAN

The Shiba Inu is the smallest Japanese breed and the most popular companion dog in its homeland. In Japan, Shiba Inus are sometimes called Little Brushwood Dogs in reference to their skill at hunting small game through dense undergrowth that larger breeds were unable to penetrate. Shiba Inus nearly disappeared after World War II, but were successfully re-established. Today, they are chiefly companions and watch dogs. The Shiba Inu is highly intelligent and independent. These dogs need clear, consistent training and socialization from an early age. They have a lively, slightly aloof nature and prefer life on their own terms. They are an active breed and thrive on mental and physical stimulation.

SMALL, THICK, TRIANGULAR EARS

BROAD, FLAT FOREHEAD WITH WELL-DEFINED STOP

EYES SLANT UPWARD TOWARD THE OUTSIDE BASE OF THE EAR

TOPLINE LEVEL TO TAIL

TAPERING MUZZLE GIVES A FOX-LIKE APPEARANCE

DEEP CHEST IS 45 TO 50 PERCENT OF OVERALL HEIGHT

SHORT, THICK HOCKS JOINT

COMMON COAT COLORS

RED   BLACK

Colors include red, a mix of red and black, black-and-tan. All colors have urajiro—cream markings on the sides of the muzzle, cheeks, inside ears, underjaw, upper throat, inside legs, abdomen, and tail.

HISTORY

The Shiba Inu is the oldest of all Japanese dogs. In 1928 an organization called the Nihon Ken Hozonkai was established to save Japanese dog breeds from extinction, and in 1936 the native Japanese breeds, including the Shiba Inu, were designated as National Treasures to preserve them. A military family brought the first Shiba Inu into the United States in 1954, and in 1979 the first litter of puppies was born there. The breed was recognized by the American Kennel Club in 1993.

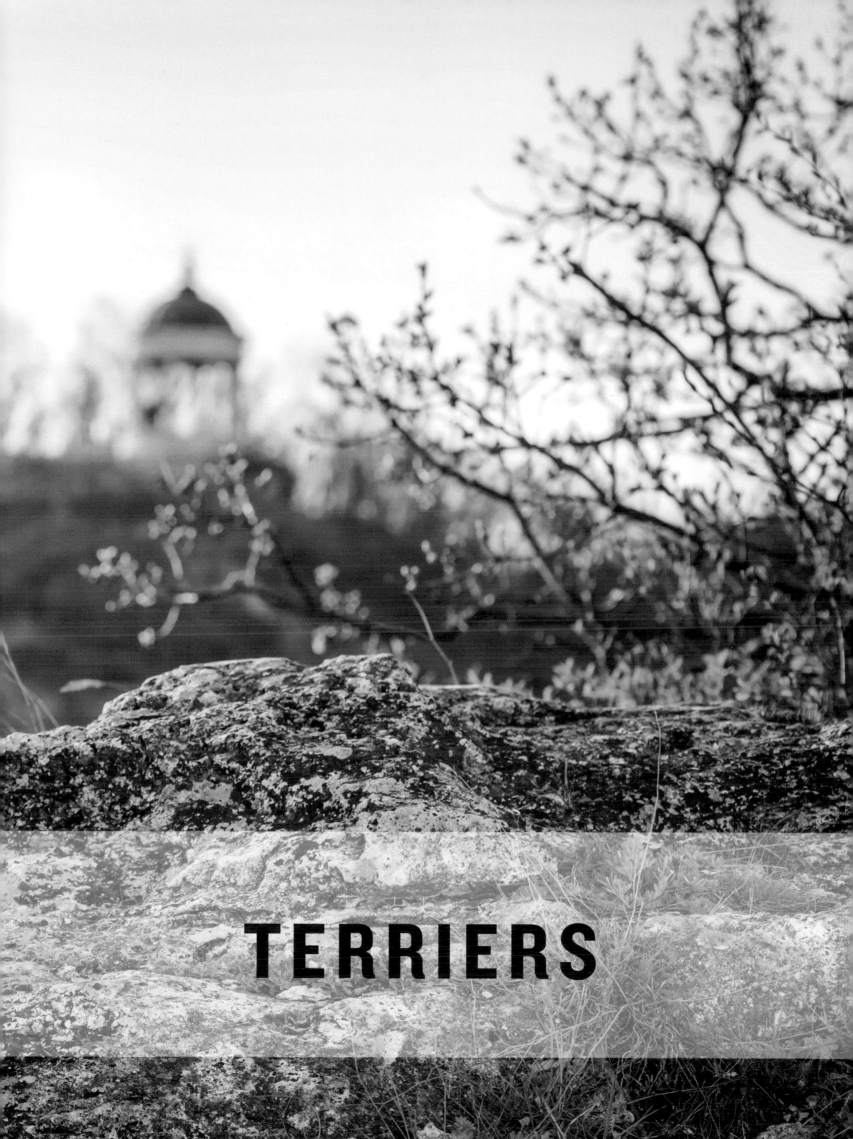

TERRIERS

AFFENPINSCHER : GERMANY

The German word *affenpinscher* translates as "monkey terrier," which is an appropriate description for these small, cheeky dogs. In France they are known as *diablotin moustachu*, meaning "moustached little devil"! The breed's origins are not documented, but small terriers of this type were widespread in Germany by the seventeenth century, and depictions of similar dogs appear in paintings from much earlier. Affenpinschers were kept on farms and used for their rat-killing skills, but were also popular as ladies' pets. They still excel in both these regards and make fun, lively, though occasionally stubborn, companions. The Affenpinscher is bold, athletic, playful, occasionally noisy, and generally good with other pets.

AT A GLANCE

Size: small

Exercise needed:

Grooming needed:

Aptitudes: watchdog, vermin control, companion

Height: 9–12 in.

Weight: 7–9 lb.

Average life expectancy: 12–14 yrs

AKC: toy

CHARACTER

Affection

Playfulness

Friendliness to dogs

Friendliness to strangers

Ease of training

HIGH-SET, V-SHAPED EARS

PROMINENT FOREHEAD WITH CLEARLY DEFINED STOP

LOWER JAW PROTRUDES BEYOND UPPER JAW

DENSE, ROUGH, HARSH COAT WITH EYEBROWS, BEARD, AND CHARACTERISTIC MOUSTACHE

SQUARE, STURDY, AND COMPACT IN APPEARANCE

BLACK, SILVER, GRAY, BLACK AND TAN, OR RED

HIND FEET ARE LONGER THAN FOREFEET

AMERICAN HAIRLESS TERRIER : UNITED STATES

The American Hairless Terrier is a lively, charismatic, and affectionate companion breed. Although they are terriers by heritage, these engaging dogs were specifically designed for companionship. They are playful, intelligent, trainable, and enjoy activities like agility and obedience. They will happily live with cats if they are brought up with them and generally get along well with other dogs. They require regular bathing, but are less prone to skin problems than most hairless breeds.

AT A GLANCE

Size: small

Exercise needed:

Grooming needed:

Aptitudes: vermin control, watchdog, agility companion

Height: 10–18 in.

Weight: 12–16 lb.

Average life expectancy: 12–15 yrs

AKC: FSS

CHARACTER

Affection

Playfulness

Friendliness to dogs

Friendliness to strangers

Ease of training

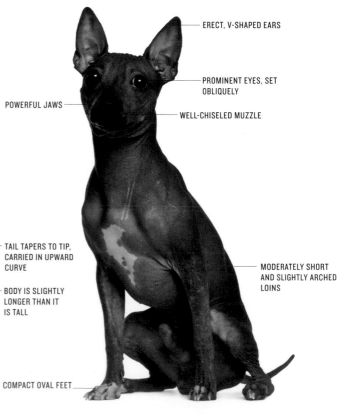

ERECT, V-SHAPED EARS

PROMINENT EYES, SET OBLIQUELY

WELL-CHISELED MUZZLE

POWERFUL JAWS

MODERATELY SHORT AND SLIGHTLY ARCHED LOINS

COMPACT OVAL FEET

TAIL TAPERS TO TIP, CARRIED IN UPWARD CURVE

BODY IS SLIGHTLY LONGER THAN IT IS TALL

AUSTRALIAN TERRIER

AT A GLANCE

Size: small

Exercise needed:

Grooming needed:

Aptitudes: watchdog, vermin control, companion

Height: 10–11 in.

Weight: 12–14 lb.

Average life expectancy: 12–14 yrs

AKC: terrier

CHARACTER

Affection

Playfulness

Friendliness to dogs

Friendliness to strangers
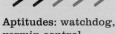

Ease of training

AUSTRALIAN TERRIER : AUSTRALIA

The rugged Australian Terrier traces to Tasmania where breeders wanted to develop a small, tough terrier that was suited to the climate, was able to control rodent populations, and could serve as a watchdog. Some Australian Terriers were also used for herding sheep.

The breed was founded on a mix of mostly British terrier breeds, including the Dandie Dinmont, Skye, Manchester, and Yorkshire Terriers. The Australian Terrier was the first Australian breed be recognized and shown in its home country. These dogs are dedicated ratters and worked in gold mines, around harbor areas, and on farms to control rat populations. They make good watchdogs and are excellent family companions, but can be reserved with other people and dogs.

SMALL, POINTED, ERECT EARS

SKULL IS LONG, FLAT, AND COVERED WITH A SOFT, SILKY TOPKNOT

SMALL, DARK-BROWN, OVAL EYES WITH A KEEN EXPRESSION

BODY IS LONG IN PROPORTION TO HEIGHT

HARSH, STRAIGHT, DENSE TOPCOAT, WITH SOFT UNDERCOAT

BLUE AND TAN, SANDY, OR RED

AT A GLANCE

Size: medium-small

Exercise needed:

Grooming needed:

Aptitudes: watchdog, vermin control, companion

Height: 16–20 in.

Weight: 26–40 lb.

Average life expectancy: 12–14 yrs

AKC: not recognized

CHARACTER

Affection

Playfulness

Friendliness to dogs

Friendliness to strangers

Ease of training

AUSTRIAN PINSCHER : AUSTRIA

The Austrian Pinscher is descended from ancient stock and was a valued and versatile working farm dog by the nineteenth century. The breed had a natural instinct for working cattle and had outstanding rodent-killing abilities. In addition, with their slightly wary nature and loud bark, they made very good watchdogs. Today, the Austrian Pinscher has an improved temperament and is calm, affectionate, and loyal. They are still wary of strangers, but generally get along well with other dogs. Socialization and training are important.

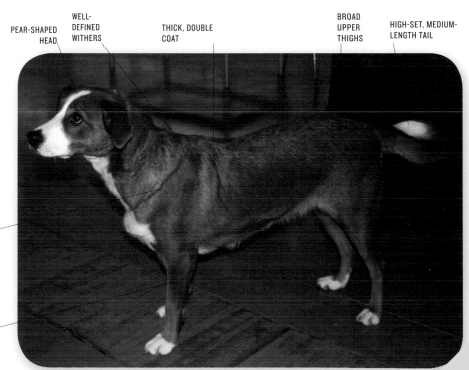

PEAR-SHAPED HEAD

WELL-DEFINED WITHERS

THICK, DOUBLE COAT

BROAD UPPER THIGHS

HIGH-SET, MEDIUM-LENGTH TAIL

RUSSET GOLD, BROWNISH YELLOW, STAG RED, OR BLACK; OFTEN WITH WHITE MARKINGS

FORELEGS ARE STRAIGHT WITH STRONG BONE AND SLIGHTLY SLOPING PASTERNS

AMERICAN PIT BULL TERRIER : UNITED STATES

The American Pit Bull Terrier has a similar ancestry to the American Staffordshire Terrier and traces back to English Bulldogs and terriers. In the nineteenth century, English dog breeders wanted a faster, more athletic bulldog and crossed it with a variety of regional terriers. The result became known as the Bull and Terrier, Half and Half, Pit Dog, or Pit Bullterrier; the term "pit" references dog fighting, which was commonly held in pits to contain the gruesome "entertainment." These crossbred dogs were taken to the United States with immigrants and used by ranchers for rounding up and driving livestock, hunting, guarding, and fighting. The American Pit Bull Terrier has received much bad press and is banned in England under the Dangerous Dog Act. However, if properly socialized, trained, and cared for, they can make a good, loyal companions. They are not suitable for first-time dog owners.

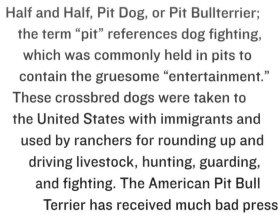

HIGH- SET EARS

ROUND EYES SET WELL APART

BROAD, FLAT SKULL

DEEP, WIDE MUZZLE

DEEP, FAIRLY WIDE CHEST

GLOSSY, SMOOTH COAT

ANY COLOR EXCEPT MERLE

TAIL IS A NATURAL EXTENSION OF TOPLINE

AMERICAN STAFFORDSHIRE TERRIER : UNITED STATES

Like the American Pit Bull Terrier, the American Staffordshire Terrier also developed from English Bulldog and terrier crosses. When immigrants arrived in the United States, they brought their bull and terrier crosses, later known as American Bull Terriers (the name was revised in 1969to American Staffordshire Terrier). Those animals developed into larger more powerful dogs than their relatives in England. Although originally bred for fighting, these dogs also had to be easy to handle and gentle with people, which is characteristic of the breed. Despite their bad press, they are often affectionate, playful, and loyal. They can be aggressive to other dogs, but this can be overcome with proper socialization and training. They are not suitable for first-time dog owners.

BROAD SKULL WITH PRONOUNCED CHEEK MUSCLES

ANY SOLID COLOR; PARTI OR PATCHED ALLOWED

HIGH-SET EARS

MEDIUM-LENGTH MUZZLE WITH WELL-DEFINED JAWS

MUSCULAR, SLOPING SHOULDERS

FRONT LEGS SET WELL APART

SHORT, STIFF, GLOSSY COAT

BEDLINGTON TERRIER : ENGLAND

This distinctive breed is one of the fastest terriers, noted for its great turn of speed. The breed developed in Northumberland and was first mentioned in the eighteenth century. Although their precise origins are not known, Bedlingtons are thought to have Whippet, Rough-Coated Scotch Terrier, and Dandie Dinmont in their foundations. These dogs take their name from the northern mining town of Bedlington, England. They are affectionate, demonstrative, and calm in nature, but can be reserved and occasionally aggressive with other dogs. Their coats require a lot of upkeep.

NARROW, DEEP ROUNDED HEAD WITH TOPKNOT

SMALL, ALMOND-SHAPED EYES

LOW-SET EARS WITH VELVETY HAIR FORMING TASSLE AT TIP

BACK HAS NATURAL ARCH OVER LOINS

LONG, TAPERING NECK

HIND LEGS LOOK SLIGHTLY LONGER THAN FRONT

MIX OF HARD AND SOFT HAIR STANDS OUT FROM SKIN

DOGS ARE USUALLY BORN DARK, AND THEIR COLOR FADES AS THEY AGE, MATURING INTO A PALE BLUISH-GRAY, BLUE, SANDY, OR LIVER, WITH OR WITHOUT TAN MARKINGS

BORDER TERRIER : SCOTLAND / ENGLAND

This charismatic breed has won the hearts of people across the world. These dogs developed along the border areas of Northumberland and Scotland and were used to hunt foxes and other small prey. Borders are noted for being exceptionally tough, rugged, and plucky little dogs. They accompanied Foxhound packs, and when the fox hid in a burrow or hole, the Border would go in after it. Borders also had to be fast enough to keep up with the Foxhounds and people on horseback. They are highly intelligent, obedient, and full of personality. Borders generally get along well with other dogs, but are prone to barking if they get bored. And they like to dig—a lot!

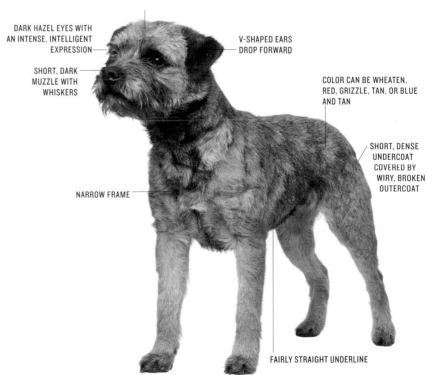

"OTTER-LIKE" HEAD

DARK HAZEL EYES WITH AN INTENSE, INTELLIGENT EXPRESSION

V-SHAPED EARS DROP FORWARD

SHORT, DARK MUZZLE WITH WHISKERS

COLOR CAN BE WHEATEN, RED, GRIZZLE, TAN, OR BLUE AND TAN

NARROW FRAME

SHORT, DENSE UNDERCOAT COVERED BY WIRY, BROKEN OUTERCOAT

FAIRLY STRAIGHT UNDERLINE

AIREDALE TERRIER : UNITED KINGDOM

AT A GLANCE

Size: medium

Exercise needed:
🐎 🐎 🐎 🐎 🐎

Grooming needed:
🖌 🖌 🖌 🖌 🖌

Aptitudes: watchdog, hunting, service, agility, companion

Height: 23 in.

Weight: 55 lb.

Average life expectancy: 10–13 yrs

AKC: terrier

The Airedale is the tallest of the terrier breeds and is often referred to as the "King of Terriers." These are extremely versatile dogs that have been used to perform a variety of functions since their development during the nineteenth century. The Airedale is an intelligent and trainable breed, which has led to its use in the police force and military. In addition, they have superb hunting, tracking, and retrieving skills, and were widely used on farms for vermin control. They also make useful watchdogs and devoted companions. Their heritage is largely unknown, but they are believed to have developed through now-extinct Black and Tan Rough Terrier from the South Yorkshire area, crossed with Bull Terriers and Irish Terriers. They were referred to as Working, Bingley, or Waterside Terriers for some years before being named Airedale Terriers in 1879.

V-SHAPED, SMALL EARS, TOPLINE OF FOLD ABOVE LEVEL OF HEAD

SMALL, DARK INTELLIGENT EYES

TAIL CARRIED UPRIGHT, BUT NOT CURLED OVER BACK

LONG, FLAT SKULL NARROWS SLIGHTLY TO THE EYES

SHORT, STRONG, LEVEL BACK

STRONG, MUSCULAR HINDQUARTERS

CHARACTERISTIC BEARD

LONG, SLOPING SHOULDERS

DENSE, HARD WIRY COAT

TAN WITH BLACK OR GRIZZLE SADDLE

SMALL, ROUND COMPACT FEET

CHARACTER

Affection
🐾 🐾 🐾 🐾 🐾

Playfulness
🐾 🐾 🐾 🐾 🐾

Friendliness to dogs
🐾 🐾 🐾 🐾 🐾

Friendliness to strangers
🐾 🐾 🐾 🐾 🐾

Ease of training
🐾 🐾 🐾 🐾 🐾

BULL TERRIER : ENGLAND

AT A GLANCE

Size: medium

Exercise needed:
🐎 🐎 🐎 🐎 🐎

Grooming needed:
🖌 🖌 🖌 🖌 🖌

Aptitudes: vermin control, watchdog, companion

Height: 21–22 in.

Weight: 40–70 lb.

Average life expectancy: 11–14 yrs

AKC: terrier

During the 1850s, breeder James Hinks set out to create a "Gentleman's Companion" using bulldogs and terriers originally bred for fighting, crossing them with Dalmations and English White Terriers, which are now extinct. He aimed to develop a white dog, which became known as the "White Cavalier." Later introductions of Greyhound, Spanish Pointer, Foxhound, Whippet, Borzoi, and Collie were made to achieve the head's distinctive curved profile, and in the 1900s, Staffordshire Bull Terriers were used to reintroduce color to the breed. Bull Terriers are humorous, assertive, bold, affectionate dogs with enormous personalities and a great sense of fun. They can be stubborn, though, and may be aggressive with other dogs.

SMALL, THIN EARS SET CLOSE TOGETHER

DISTINCTIVE, FULL, OVAL FACE, CURVES FROM TOP OF SKULL TO TIP OF NOSE

SMALL, DARK, SUNKEN EYES

SHORT, FLAT, GLOSSY AND HARSH COAT

LONG, MUSCULAR, ARCHED NECK

ANY COLOR, INCLUDING WHITE, BRINDLE, RED, AND FAWN

BROAD CHEST

STRONG, BUT NOT HEAVY, LEGS

UNDERLINE FORMS GRACEFUL UPWARD CURVE

CHARACTER

Affection
🐾 🐾 🐾 🐾 🐾

Playfulness
🐾 🐾 🐾 🐾 🐾

Friendliness to dogs
🐾 🐾 🐾 🐾 🐾

Friendliness to strangers
🐾 🐾 🐾 🐾 🐾

Ease of training
🐾 🐾 🐾 🐾 🐾

AT A GLANCE

Size: small

Exercise needed:

Grooming needed:

Aptitudes: vermin
control, watchdog,
companion

Height: 10–14 in.

Weight: 25–33 lb.

Average life expectancy:
11–14 yrs

AKC: terrier

CHARACTER

Affection

Playfulness
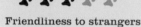

Friendliness to dogs

Friendliness to strangers

Ease of training

MINIATURE BULL TERRIER : ENGLAND

The Miniature Bull Terrier is identical to the Bull Terrier in every way except size. The breeds share the same history and developed from bulldog and terrier types during the nineteenth century. The first class for Miniature Bull Terriers was held in 1863. Some breeders scaled down the breed further producing a Toy size, which was largely unsuccessful and of poor type. The Miniature Bull Terrier Club was established in 1938. "Minis" are devoted, loyal, and great fun. They have an innate sense of humor and like to be the center of attention, although they can be single minded and stubborn.

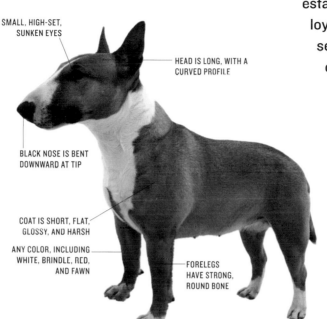

SMALL, HIGH-SET, SUNKEN EYES

HEAD IS LONG, WITH A CURVED PROFILE

BLACK NOSE IS BENT DOWNWARD AT TIP

COAT IS SHORT, FLAT, GLOSSY, AND HARSH

ANY COLOR, INCLUDING WHITE, BRINDLE, RED, AND FAWN

FORELEGS HAVE STRONG, ROUND BONE

HIND LEGS ARE PARALLEL WHEN VIEWED FROM BEHIND

GREAT DEPTH FROM WITHERS TO BRISKET

AT A GLANCE

Size: small

Exercise needed:

Grooming needed:

Aptitudes: vermin
control, watchdog,
companion

Height: 13–16 in.

Weight: 22 lb.

Average life expectancy:
12–15 yrs

AKC: not recognized

CHARACTER

Affection

Playfulness

Friendliness to dogs

Friendliness to strangers

Ease of training

BRAZILIAN TERRIER : BRAZIL

The Brazilian Terrier developed from various terrier breeds that were taken into Brazil by European immigrants, including Jack Russell Terriers, Fox Terriers, and Pinschers. Today, the Brazilian bears a close resemblance to the Jack Russell Terrier, and shares many of that breed's qualities. The Brazilian was, and still is, widely used on farms and in homes to keep vermin populations at bay, but it has also become popular as a companion animal and serves as an efficient watchdog. Brazilians are often used in conjunction with Filo Brasileiros when guarding properties. They have adapted to their climate and environment with ease and are tenacious hunters. These are lively, intelligent dogs that do best in active homes that challenge them physically and mentally.

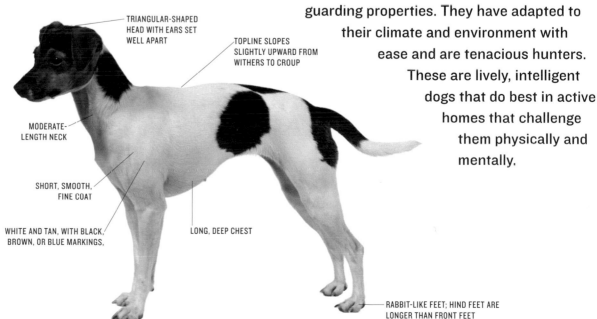

TRIANGULAR-SHAPED HEAD WITH EARS SET WELL APART

TOPLINE SLOPES SLIGHTLY UPWARD FROM WITHERS TO CROUP

MODERATE-LENGTH NECK

SHORT, SMOOTH, FINE COAT

WHITE AND TAN, WITH BLACK, BROWN, OR BLUE MARKINGS,

LONG, DEEP CHEST

RABBIT-LIKE FEET; HIND FEET ARE LONGER THAN FRONT FEET

CAIRN TERRIER : SCOTLAND

The Cairn Terrier traces back to the indigenous working terriers of the Scottish Highlands and islands and developed from the same stock that also gave rise to the Skye, Scottish, and West Highland White Terriers. These small, rugged working dogs were first mentioned in the sixteenth century, when they were most valued for their hunting abilities and described as "earth dogges." By the eighteenth century, they were prized for hunting otters and badgers, and for their ferlessness—they never back down from a fight. During the nineteenth century, there was an effort to distinguish between the different types of terrier, with the Cairn first known as the Short-Coated Skye or Prick-Ear Skye. The Cairn got its official name in 1910. Cairns are plucky, cheeky dogs that love to hunt. They can be stubborn, are prone to barking and digging, and can be aggressive with other dogs.

SMALL, POINTED, ERECT EARS

DEEP EYES WITH SHAGGY EYEBROWS

HEAD WELL FURNISHED WITH HAIR, GIVING A "FOXY" LOOK

SHORT TAIL, CARRIED UPRIGHT

WEATHER-RESISTANT, DOUBLE COAT

CREAM, WHEATEN; RED, GRAY, OR CHARCOAL

STRAIGHT FORELEGS; FEET MAY TURN IN SLIGHTLY

AT A GLANCE

Size: small

Exercise needed:

Grooming needed:

Aptitudes: vermin control, watchdog, companion

Height: 11–12 in.

Weight: 14–16 lb.

Average life expectancy: 12–14 yrs

AKC: terrier

CHARACTER

Affection

Playfulness

Friendliness to dogs

Friendliness to strangers

Ease of training

CESKY TERRIER : CZECH REPUBLIC

The Cesky Terrier, or Czech Terrier as it is also known, was developed in the mid-twentieth century by geneticist and dog breeder Frantisek Horak. He had bred Scottish and Sealyham Terriers, which he used for hunting, but was convinced that a better hunting dog could be achieved by crossbreeding the two. He began breeding for the Cesky in 1949, keeping rigorous notes, and by 1959 the new dog was breeding to standard. Horak developed the Cesky specifically to hunt fox, rabbit, pheasant, duck, and wild boar, wanting a dog that would track game into holes or burrows and also hunt on open terrain. Cesky Terriers are skilled hunters and combine this with a pleasant temperament. They are generally good with children, but can be aggressive with other dogs unless carefully introduced. They are bright, active, and engaging and also serve well as watchdogs. Unlike most other terriers, they are trimmed with clippers instead of being "stripped."

LONG, BLUNT, WEDGE-SHAPED HEAD

TRIANGULAR, DROPPED EARS SET HIGH

SKIN LOOSE AT THROAT, BUT DOES NOT FORM DEWLAP

STRONG BACK WITH SLIGHTLY ARCHED LOINS

PROMINENT CHEEKBONES AND STRONG JAWS

SOFT, FINE, FIRM, SLIGHTLY WAVY COAT

GRAY, COFFEE BROWN, OR BLUE

LARGE FEET WITH ARCHED TOES; HIND FEET SMALLER THAN FRONT

AT A GLANCE

Size: small

Exercise needed:

Grooming needed:

Aptitudes: hunting, vermin control, watchdog, companion

Height: 10–12 in.

Weight: 13–20 lb.

Average life expectancy: 12–15 yrs

AKC: terrier

CHARACTER

Affection
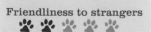

Playfulness

Friendliness to dogs

Friendliness to strangers

Ease of training

DANDIE DINMONT TERRIER : SCOTLAND

The long, low-slung Dandie Dinmont has lived around the border of Scotland and England for centuries, although their precise heritage is unknown. During the eighteenth century, they were kept by farmers for hunting all kinds of prey, including otters and badgers. They were originally known as Pepper and Mustard Terriers due to their coat colors. The dogs became known as Dandie Dinmonts in the early nineteenth century following the publication in 1815 of Sir Walter Scott's novel *Guy Mannering*. A breeder named James Davidson lived near Scott, and Davidson's terriers and others like them were named after a terrier-owning character in Scott's novel. These are playful, loyal, and brave dogs. They can, however, be reserved with strangers and aggressive to other dogs.

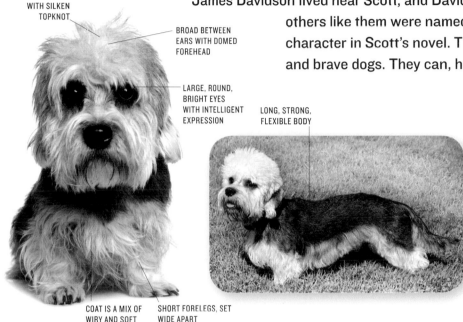

DISTINCTIVE HEAD WITH SILKEN TOPKNOT

BROAD BETWEEN EARS WITH DOMED FOREHEAD

LARGE, ROUND, BRIGHT EYES WITH INTELLIGENT EXPRESSION

LONG, STRONG, FLEXIBLE BODY

COAT IS A MIX OF WIRY AND SOFT HAIR

SHORT FORELEGS, SET WIDE APART

AT A GLANCE

Size: small

Exercise needed:

Grooming needed:

Aptitudes: vermin control, watchdog, companion

Height: 8–11 in.

Weight: 18–24 lb.

Average life expectancy: 11–13 yrs

AKC: terrier

CHARACTER

Affection
🐾🐾🐾🐾🐾

Playfulness
🐾🐾🐾🐾🐾

Friendliness to dogs
🐾🐾🐾🐾🐾

Friendliness to strangers
🐾🐾🐾🐾🐾

Ease of training
🐾🐾🐾🐾🐾

CHILEAN FOX TERRIER : CHILE

Also known as the *Ratonero*, which means "rat hunter," the Chilean Fox Terrier is a superb vermin-killing breed. These dogs trace to the nineteenth century and developed through crossbreeding the European Fox Terrier, to which they bear a resemblance, and native Chilean stock of unknown heritage. Over time, they became perfectly adapted to the climate and terrain of Chile, and became popular with farmers. Chilean Fox Terriers are smart problem solvers, with tremendous tenacity and a loyal, devoted nature. They may be wary of other people and dogs, and can be prone to barking. They are best suited to an active home where they are included in all activities.

HALF UPRIGHT EARS WITH POINTED TIPS

SMALL, DARK, ALMOND-SHAPED EYES

WHITE WITH BLACK-AND-TAN, BROWN-AND-TAN, OR BLUE-AND-TAN MARKINGS ON HEAD

COMPACT, ALMOST SQUARE BODY

ALMOST FLAT FOREHEAD

HIGH, WELL DEFINED WITHERS

SHORT, TIGHT, LUSTROUS COAT

COMPACT HARE FEET

AT A GLANCE

Size: small

Exercise needed:

Grooming needed:

Aptitudes: vermin control, watchdog, companion

Height: 11–15 in.

Weight: 9–17 lb.

Average life expectancy: 12–15 yrs

AKC: not recognized

CHARACTER

Affection
🐾🐾🐾🐾🐾

Playfulness
🐾🐾🐾🐾🐾

Friendliness to dogs
🐾🐾🐾🐾🐾

Friendliness to strangers
🐾🐾🐾🐾🐾

Ease of training
🐾🐾🐾🐾🐾

DUTCH SMOUSHOND : NETHERLANDS

This rare breed of Dutch Terrier almost completely disappeared after World War II and was re-established only through the efforts of a handful of breeders. Historians believe that the Smoushond had its foundation with the Schnauzer, possibly as a color variant (which has always been unaccepted by Schnauzer breeders). In the 1800s, the Smoushond was popular as a gentleman's stable dog or coach dog, and was noted for its ratting skills. When the breed was reconstructed in the 1970s, a mix of terrier breeds was used, including Border Terriers crossed with the few remaining examples of the original breed. The Smoushond is devoted, affectionate, and lively in nature.

ROUNDED FOREHEAD

HIGH-SET PENDENT EARS

MUZZLE IS HALF THE LENGTH OF THE SKULL

SHORT, MUSCULAR NECK

STURDY BODY WITH BROAD CHEST

COARSE, WIRY, HARSH, AND STRAIGHT COAT

ALL SHADES OF YELLOW

ROUND, NEAT, SMALL FEET

SMOOTH FOX TERRIER : ENGLAND

The Smooth Fox Terrier was favored by hunters during the nineteenth century and used in conjunction with a pack of Foxhounds. The Fox Terrier located the fox after it had hidden in a burrow or hole and barked vigorously to alert the hunters. Originally both Smooth and Wire Fox Terriers were classed as one breed and often bred together. It was not until the latter part of the nineteenth century that breeders started to keep the two separate, and in 1876 the Officers of the Fox Terrier Club established separate breed standards. Smooth Fox Terriers are believed to have developed from Old English Terriers, Black and Tan Terriers, Bull Terriers, Beagles, and Greyhounds. They make lively companions for active homes, but can be wary of strangers and other dogs. They also have a tendency to bark and dig.

LONG, NARROW HEAD

SQUARE BODY WITH A SHORT, LEVEL BACK

HIGH-SET TAIL, CARRIED ERECT

DARK EYES HAVE AN INTELLIGENT, SOMETIMES "FIERY," EXPRESSION

HIGH-SET, V-SHAPED EARS FOLD FORWARD

HOCKS SET LOW

STRONG MUZZLE TAPERS SLIGHTLY FROM STOP TO NOSE

SHORT, CLOSE-LYING, PREDOMINANTLY WHITE COAT

AT A GLANCE

Size: small

Exercise needed:

Grooming needed:

Aptitudes: vermin control, watchdog, companion

Height: 10–12 in.

Weight: 6–8 lb.

Average life expectancy: 11–13 yrs

AKC: not recognized

CHARACTER

Affection

Playfulness

Friendliness to dogs

Friendliness to strangers

Ease of training

ENGLISH TOY TERRIER : ENGLAND

In nineteenth-century England, the English Toy Terrier's ancestors were known as the best ratting dogs around, used for the sport of ratting that was popular in public houses and other venues across the country. Dogs were let loose in special "rat pits" and judged on how many rats they could kill, and how quickly. The dogs were also prized for their vermin control on farms, and in towns, factories, dockyards, and homes. A fashion arose for miniaturizing the breed, which almost led to its destruction, but the dogs were salvaged by a handful of breeders who reinstated their excellent qualities. These are charming, lively and gregarious dogs with a high prey drive for small animals. They are intelligent and relatively easy (for a terrier) to train, but may show aggression to strange dogs if not properly socialized.

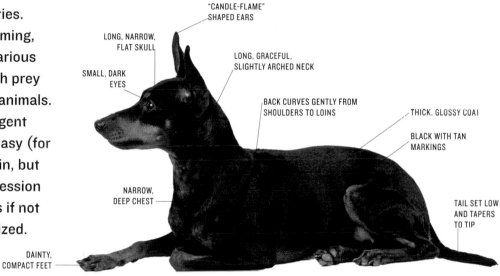

"CANDLE-FLAME" SHAPED EARS

LONG, NARROW, FLAT SKULL

SMALL, DARK EYES

LONG, GRACEFUL, SLIGHTLY ARCHED NECK

BACK CURVES GENTLY FROM SHOULDERS TO LOINS

THICK, GLOSSY COAT

BLACK WITH TAN MARKINGS

NARROW, DEEP CHEST

DAINTY, COMPACT FEET

TAIL SET LOW AND TAPERS TO TIP

AT A GLANCE

Size: small

Exercise needed:

Grooming needed:

Aptitudes: vermin control, hunting, watchdog, companion

Height: 13–16 in.

Weight: 15–18 lb.

Average life expectancy: 10–13 yrs

AKC: terrier

CHARACTER

Affection

Playfulness

Friendliness to dogs

Friendliness to strangers

Ease of training

WIRE FOX TERRIER : ENGLAND

The Wire Fox Terrier shares its history with the Smooth Fox Terrier, although opinion is divided over their heritage; some speculate that the Wire Fox Terrier developed from rough coated Black and Tan Terriers. Regardless, both breeds were used extensively by fox hunters for locating foxes that were hidden in burrows. The earliest recorded Wire Fox Terrier was named Old Tip, bred by the Master of the Sinnington Hounds, Yorkshire, around 1866. Old Tip sired three champions and was a great influence on the breed's development. These are intelligent, energetic dogs that love to play, hunt, dig, and bark. They make excellent companions for active homes.

HIGH-SET TAIL, CARRIED ERECT

CLEAN MUSCULAR NECK OF MODERATE LENGTH

POWERFUL HINDQUARTERS

SMALL, DEEP SET, DARK ROUND EYES

HIGH-SET, V-SHAPED EARS

BARELY PERCEPTIBLE STOP

WIRY, MEDIUM-LENGTH, PREDOMINANTLY WHITE COAT

FRONT PASTERNS ARE SHORT, POWERFUL, AND STRAIGHT

ROUND, COMPACT FEET

IRISH TERRIER : IRELAND

The Irish Terrier is often described as "the poor man's sentinel, the farmer's friend, and the gentleman's favorite," which perfectly sums up the breed. These dogs are eminently versatile and have been recorded in Ireland for several hundred years, working on farms, hunting any prey, and watching over homes. They were even widely used by the military during both world wars. Irish Terriers are noted for their bravery and cheerful personalities, but can be aggressive with other dogs and are often reserved with strangers.

EARS ARE DARKER THAN BODY HAIR

SMALL, DARK-BROWN EYES WITH INTENSE EXPRESSION

SMALL V-SHAPED EARS, NEATLY FOLD FORWARD

TAIL SET AND CARRIED HIGH

SMALL FRILL OF HAIR ON EACH SIDE OF NECK

DENSE, WIRY COAT

FAIRLY LONG BODY

BRIGHT RED, GOLDEN RED, RED WHEATEN, WHEATEN

HOCKS NEAR TO GROUND

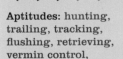
JAGDTERRIER : GERMANY

The Jagdterrier was developed in Germany around 1900 specifically as a hunting dog. Breeders crossed English Fox Terriers with Black and Tan Hunting Terriers and spent many years selectively breeding for hunting skills. These fearless dogs were used on wild boar, badger, fox, weasel, raccoon, and squirrel. They are devoted, loyal, protective, and intolerant of strangers, so they make excellent watch and guard dogs. They have a high exercise requirement and are best suited to a hunting home where they can do what they have been bred to do.

V-SHAPED EARS

SMALL EYES WITH DETERMINED EXPRESSION

STRONG, STRAIGHT BACK

BLACK AND TAN PREFERRED; BUT CAN ALSO BE BLACK AND GRAY, OR DARK BROWN

LONG UPPER THIGH

FRONT FEET ARE LARGER THAN HIND FEET

JAPANESE TERRIER : JAPAN

Japanese Terriers are rare in Japan and seldom heard of beyond their homeland. They developed during the seventeenth century when Smooth Fox Terriers were exported to Nagasaki from the Netherlands and bred to other small dogs. Selective breeding did not start in earnest until the 1920s, however, with a clear type emerging by the 1930s. Unusually for a Terrier breed, the Japanese Terrier was bred primarily to be a lap dog, and not with a working purpose, although they will hunt small vermin. They have lively, cheerful natures, and are intelligent, friendly. and relatively easy to train for a terrier breed.

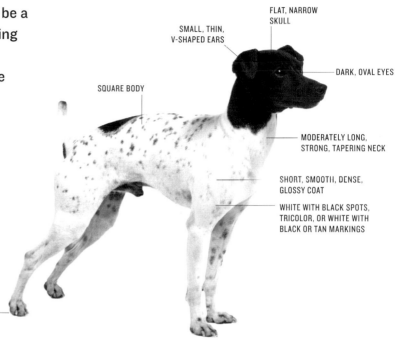

FLAT, NARROW SKULL
SMALL, THIN, V-SHAPED EARS
DARK, OVAL EYES
SQUARE BODY
MODERATELY LONG, STRONG, TAPERING NECK
SHORT, SMOOTH, DENSE, GLOSSY COAT
WHITE WITH BLACK SPOTS, TRICOLOR, OR WHITE WITH BLACK OR TAN MARKINGS
TIGHT FEET WITH ELASTIC PADS

LAKELAND TERRIER : ENGLAND

The Lakeland Terrier developed in the Lake District of northern England where it was used by farmers to catch vermin. These feisty terriers often accompanied Foxhound packs, and alerted the hounds to the location of the fox once it had hidden in a burrow. The terriers gained a reputation for fearlessness and endurance, and became extremely popular. They were given the name Lakeland in 1921. A particularly famous Lakeland is Champion Stingray of Derryabah, aka Skipper, who won Best in Show at Crufts in 1967. The following year he won Best in Show at Westminster in the United States. Lakelands are game, bold, playful, and fun family dogs. They can be determined and single minded, but are also sensitive and require patient, consistent training.

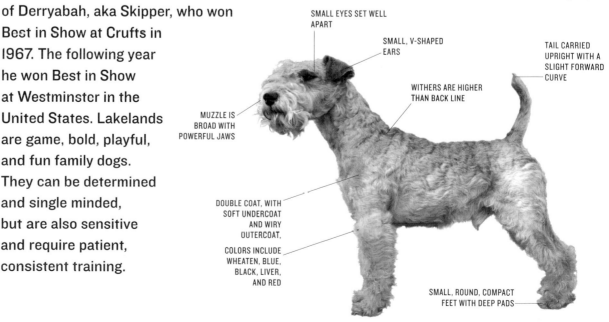

SMALL EYES SET WELL APART
SMALL, V-SHAPED EARS
TAIL CARRIED UPRIGHT WITH A SLIGHT FORWARD CURVE
WITHERS ARE HIGHER THAN BACK LINE
MUZZLE IS BROAD WITH POWERFUL JAWS
DOUBLE COAT, WITH SOFT UNDERCOAT AND WIRY OUTERCOAT,
COLORS INCLUDE WHEATEN, BLUE, BLACK, LIVER, AND RED
SMALL, ROUND, COMPACT FEET WITH DEEP PADS

AT A GLANCE

Size: small

Exercise needed:

Grooming needed:

Aptitudes: hunting, vermin control, agility, watchdog, companion

Height: 10–12 in.

Weight: 11–13 lb.

Average life expectancy: 13–15 yrs

AKC: terrier

CHARACTER

Affection

Playfulness

Friendliness to dogs

Friendliness to strangers

Ease of training

✚ HEALTH ✚

Although generally healthy, some health problems include lens luxation and progressive retinal atrophy.

Jack Russell Terriers have a low boredom threshold and need to be entertained. They do not do well left to their own devices and may become destructive and noisy.

JACK RUSSELL TERRIER : ENGLAND

The Jack Russell Terrier is one of the best-known and most recognized breeds. Nevertheless, there is often confusion surrounding the breed: it is often mistaken for the Parson Russell terrier, and sometimes subdivided into Jack Russells and Russells—the latter being a shorter-legged, stockier variety. "Jacks" are the definition of a big dog in a small body and have tremendous personalities. They are lively, energetic, nosey individuals who want to be at the center of everything. They are devoted to their families, highly intelligent, and independent thinkers. They can be aggressive with other dogs, though, and need thorough socialization.

HIGH-SET TAIL, CARRIED STRAIGHT OR CURVED FORWARD WHEN MOVING

CHEST CAN BE COMPRESSED TO ALLOW DOG TO WORK UNDERGROUND

LOW-SET HOCKS

COMMON COAT COLORS

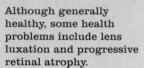

WHITE

Predominately white with any combination of black, brown, or tan markings.

COAT CLOSE-UP

ROUGH   SMOOTH   BROKEN

There are three coat types: rough—double coat with dense undercoat and wiry outercoat; smooth—short, flat coat; and broken—in between rough and smooth.

V-SHAPED EARS

DARK, DEEP-SET, ALMOND-SHAPED EYES

BLACK, FULLY PIGMENTED NOSE

BODY IS SLIGHTLY LONGER THAN IT IS TALL

MUZZLE SLIGHTLY SHORTER THAN SKULL

STRONG, STRAIGHT FORELEGS

HISTORY

The Jack Russell Terrier shares its history with the Parson Russell Terrier and traces back to the nineteenth century and the efforts of the Reverend John Russell, a fox-hunting, dog-breeding enthusiast. Russell developed a pack of Fox Terriers, largely white in color, which he bred for working ability, shunning the show ring. His terriers became known as Parson Jack Russell Terriers. A shorter-legged, longer-bodied terrier began to develop from these and was used for hunting rabbits and other small animals. These smaller terriers were often called "Shorties" or "Puddin' Dogs" before becoming known as Jack Russell Terriers in England, Ireland, and Australia.

AT A GLANCE

Size: small

Exercise needed:

Grooming needed:

Aptitudes: hunting, vermin control, agility, watchdog, companion

Height: 12–14 in.

Weight: 13–17 lb.

Average life expectancy: 13–15 yrs

AKC: terrier

CHARACTER

Affection

Playfulness

Friendliness to dogs

Friendliness to strangers

Ease of training

✚ HEALTH ✚

Although generally healthy, some problems can include lens luxation, progressive retinal atrophy, and late onset ataxia.

Parson Russell Terriers have a high hunting drive and will roam if left unattended. It is essential they have a well-fenced yard!

PARSON RUSSELL TERRIER : ENGLAND

Breeders have worked hard to maintain the working qualities of these dogs, and the standard has changed little over the years. Parson Russell Terriers are perfectly adapted to working underground and are fearless when it comes to hunting. They are known for not backing down and are dedicated and tenacious. Although they are kept as companions and make very good ones, they are a working breed, and hunting is what they thrive on. They are bold, lively, outgoing, and loyal to their families. They can be aggressive with other dogs and are reserved with strangers. They have a relatively low tolerance level, and can be snappy if bothered, so they should not be left unattended with very young children. (No dog should.) They also like to dig and can be noisy.

FLAT, BROAD SKULL TAPERS SLIGHTLY TOWARD MUZZLE

EARS ARE SET TO THE OUTSIDE EDGE OF THE SKULL WITH TIPS CARRIED CLOSE TO THE HEAD

DARK EYES WITH MISCHIEVOUS EXPRESSION

HIGH-SET TAIL CARRIED STRAIGHT OR CURVED FORWARD WHEN ACTIVE

POWERFUL HINDQUARTERS

DEEP CHEST, BUT NOT TOO WIDE

PASTERNS ARE SHORT, POWERFUL AND FLEXIBLE

ROUND, SMALL FEET

HISTORY

The Parson Russell Terrier was developed by Reverend John Russell, a fox hunting enthusiast, during the nineteenth century. Russell had a pack of Fox Terriers that became known as Parson Russell Terriers. Most of his dogs traced to a terrier named Trump, whom he bought in 1819. The Reverend Russell shunned the show world and bred his dogs specifically for their working qualities. Other breeders of Fox Terriers (Smooth and Wire) concentrated on breeding them for the show ring, and there was a gradual change in type between the Parson Russell Terrier and the Fox Terrier, leading to their separate recognition.

COMMON COAT COLORS

Predominately white with any combination of black, brown, or tan markings.

WHITE

COAT CLOSE-UP

There are three coat types: rough—double coat with dense undercoat and wiry outercoat; smooth—short, flat coat; and broken—in between rough and smooth.

ROUGH   **SMOOTH**   **BROKEN**

MANCHESTER TERRIER : ENGLAND

The Manchester Terrier traces back to the original Black-and-Tan Terrier that was widespread by the sixteenth century. These dogs were less refined than the modern Manchester and were used to control huge populations of rats. They became associated with the mining areas of northern England, factories, wharves, and farms, eventually becoming known as the Manchester. During the nineteenth century, Whippet was introduced to the breed, making it faster and sleeker in appearance.

They were popular for "ratting" in pits, but due to their elegant appearance, were also kept as pets by the middle and upper classes. Manchesters are devoted, loyal, and intelligent. They can be independent and are often reserved with strangers. The Toy Manchester Terrier was recognized by the AKC in 1958—the only difference between the two breeds beyond size (the Toy weighs less than 12 pounds) is that the Toy Manchester's ears are pointed and erect.

NATURALLY ERECT EARS

LONG, NARROW, WEDGE-SHAPED HEAD

SMALL, DARK, ALMOND-SHAPED EYES

SLIM, SLIGHTLY ARCHED NECK

FIRM, SHORT, SMOOTH, AND GLOSSY COAT

DISTINCTIVE BLACK-AND-TAN COAT

NARROW, DEEP CHEST

MINIATURE SCHNAUZER : GERMANY

The Miniature Schnauzer was developed in Germany at the end of the nineteenth century by crossing small Standard Schnauzers with Affenpinschers, Poodles, and small black spitz-types. The "Mini" was used for ratting on farms and in houses; its compact size made it ideal for urban living. These are bold, lively, intelligent, and gregarious dogs that can be inclined to bark. They make excellent watchdogs and will sound a vigorous alarm. Although they can be stubborn, they are relatively easy to train and make a great family pet.

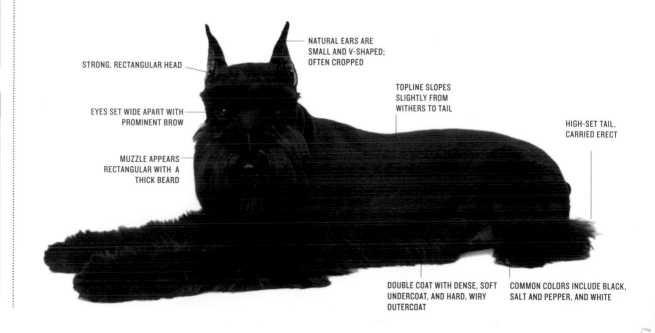

STRONG, RECTANGULAR HEAD

NATURAL EARS ARE SMALL AND V-SHAPED; OFTEN CROPPED

TOPLINE SLOPES SLIGHTLY FROM WITHERS TO TAIL

EYES SET WIDE APART WITH PROMINENT BROW

HIGH-SET TAIL, CARRIED ERECT

MUZZLE APPEARS RECTANGULAR WITH A THICK BEARD

DOUBLE COAT WITH DENSE, SOFT UNDERCOAT, AND HARD, WIRY OUTERCOAT

COMMON COLORS INCLUDE BLACK, SALT AND PEPPER, AND WHITE

NORFOLK TERRIER : ENGLAND

The Norfolk Terrier is one of the smallest working Terrier breeds, but its lack of height is more than compensated for in sheer gameness of spirit. These small terriers are fearless and determined hunters, matching their dedication with a superb temperament that is cheerful, tough, and charismatic. They were developed in Norfolk, England by Frank "Roughrider" Jones. His tenacious terriers were recognized by the English Kennel Club in 1932 and called Norwich Terriers. In 1964 the English Kennel Club separated the terriers into two breeds: the Norwich with its pricked ears, and the Norfolk, whose ears drop forward at the tip. Both breeds have different standards and exhibit their own characteristics.

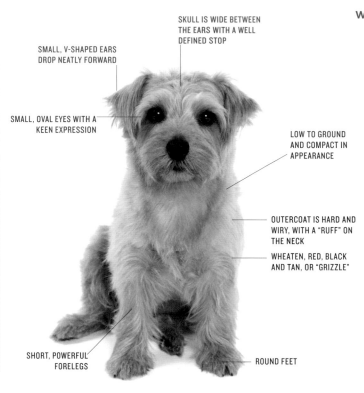

SMALL, V-SHAPED EARS DROP NEATLY FORWARD

SKULL IS WIDE BETWEEN THE EARS WITH A WELL DEFINED STOP

SMALL, OVAL EYES WITH A KEEN EXPRESSION

LOW TO GROUND AND COMPACT IN APPEARANCE

OUTERCOAT IS HARD AND WIRY, WITH A "RUFF" ON THE NECK

WHEATEN, RED, BLACK AND TAN, OR "GRIZZLE"

SHORT, POWERFUL FORELEGS

ROUND FEET

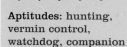
NORWICH TERRIER : ENGLAND

The Norwich Terrier shares the same early history as the Norfolk Terrier. During the nineteenth century, it became fashionable for Cambridge students to keep terriers, and several bought dogs from local dealer Charles Lawrence. The dogs became known as Trumpington Terriers, since Trumpington Street was home to many students. These small, rugged terriers are thought to have had Irish Terrier in them. A union between a brindle Scottish terrier-type and a long-haired red terrier (on Trumpington Street) led to a puppy named Rags, a wire-haired terrier with pricked ears and great hunting instincts. He went on to be a prolific sire and stamped his mark on his progeny; he is generally held as the foundation of the breed. Norwich Terriers are spirited, bold, enduring dogs. They are affectionate, loyal, entertaining, and often independent.

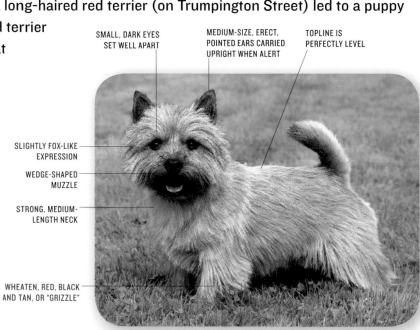

SMALL, DARK EYES SET WELL APART

MEDIUM-SIZE, ERECT, POINTED EARS CARRIED UPRIGHT WHEN ALERT

TOPLINE IS PERFECTLY LEVEL

SLIGHTLY FOX-LIKE EXPRESSION

WEDGE-SHAPED MUZZLE

STRONG, MEDIUM-LENGTH NECK

WHEATEN, RED, BLACK AND TAN, OR "GRIZZLE"

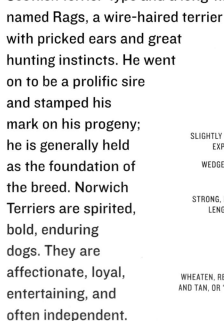

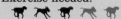

TOY FOX TERRIER : UNITED STATES

The Toy Fox Terrier was developed in the United States during the first decades of the twentieth century through breeding small Smooth Fox Terriers with a variety of toy breeds, including Miniature Pinschers, Italian Greyhound, Chihuahuas, and Manchester Terriers. The breed has a great personality: they retain the terrier qualities of liveliness, intelligence, and hunting instinct, but in a moderated form. They also make excellent companions for active homes and love to be at the center of attention. They have a tendency to bark and dig, though, and have a high small prey drive.

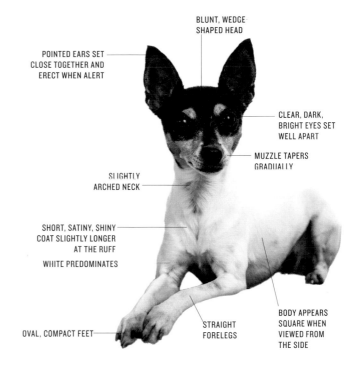

BLUNT, WEDGE-SHAPED HEAD

POINTED EARS SET CLOSE TOGETHER AND ERECT WHEN ALERT

CLEAR, DARK, BRIGHT EYES SET WELL APART

MUZZLE TAPERS GRADUALLY

SLIGHTLY ARCHED NECK

SHORT, SATINY, SHINY COAT SLIGHTLY LONGER AT THE RUFF

WHITE PREDOMINATES

STRAIGHT FORELEGS

BODY APPEARS SQUARE WHEN VIEWED FROM THE SIDE

OVAL, COMPACT FEET

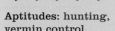

TEDDY ROOSEVELT TERRIER : UNITED STATES

This American breed developed from a variety of small terrier-types and other breeds brought to the United States mostly by working class English immigrants. Their dogs—which included Manchester Terriers, Smooth Fox Terriers, Bull Terriers, Whippets, and Beagles—were widely used for ratting on farms, in factories, in harbor areas, and at industrial sites. Eventually a terrier of uniform characteristics began to emerge and became known as the Rat Terrier based on its hunting propensities. There were two clear types of Rat Terrier, one with long legs and one with shorter legs. The shorter-legged variety became known as the Teddy Roosevelt Terrier based on the president's affection for the breed.

SMALL, PROMINENT EYES, SET OBLIQUELY

BROAD, SLIGHTLY DOMED SKULL

NECK BLENDS SMOOTHLY INTO WELL LAID BACK SHOULDERS

TAIL CARRIED IN AN UPWARD CURVE

FORELEGS TURN SLIGHTLY INWARD

SHORT, DENSE, MEDIUM-HARD TO SMOOTH COAT

VARIED COLORS, INCLUDING SOLID WHITE, BICOLOR, AND TRICOLOR

LOW-SET HOCKS

AT A GLANCE

Size: medium-small

Exercise needed:

Grooming needed:

Aptitudes: hunting, vermin control, agility, watchdog, companion

Height: 17–20 in.

Weight: 33–40 lb.

Average life expectancy: 12–15 yrs

AKC: terrier

CHARACTER

Affection

Playfulness

Friendliness to dogs

Friendliness to strangers

Ease of training

✚ HEALTH ✚

Although generally healthy, some health problems include dermal and epidural cysts, progressive neuronal abiotrophy, eyelid disorders, spiculosis, and hip dysplasia.

KERRY BLUE TERRIER : IRELAND

"Kerries" are exceptionally versatile dogs that have been used on farms in rural Ireland for many years. They have excellent hunting instincts; prey on a range of small game, vermin, and birds; and will retrieve from land and water. In addition, the Kerry has been used for herding livestock and is a vigilant watchdog. These dogs have clearly defined personalities and are highly intelligent. The Kerry is generally relatively easy to train, good humored, curious, bold, and loyal to its entire family. They may be aggressive with other dogs and pets, though, and can be reserved with strangers.

SMALL, ROUND, DARK EYES

LONG HEAD WITH FLAT, CLEAN CHEEKS

STRONG UNDERJAW

SKIN ON NECK IS TIGHT WITH NO DEWLAP

UPPER FORELEG IS LONG, FORMING 90-DEGREE ANGLE WITH SHOULDER BLADE

COMMON COAT COLORS

The Kerry Blue Terrier can be any shade of blue-gray.

BLUE-GRAY

COAT CLOSE-UP

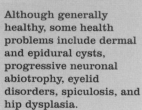

Single coated, soft, wavy, dense, and medium length

MEDIUM

Kerry puppies are born black, with their blue coloration not appearing until they are between nine months and two years old.

BUTTON EARS CARRIED
CLOSE TO CHEEKS, TOP
FOLD SLIGHTLY ABOVE
LEVEL OF SKULL

SHORT, LEVEL BACK

SHORT, POWERFUL
LOINS WITH SLIGHT
TUCK-UP

HIGH-SET TAIL,
CARRIED STRAIGHT

LOW-SET HOCKS

HISTORY

The Kerry Blue is most associated with the mountains of Kerry and around Lake Killarney where they are thought to have developed. There are many colorful stories surrounding the breed's history but no truly substantiated accounts. One of the more exotic tales relates how a blue dog from either a Russian ship or one of the Spanish Armada swam ashore from a shipwreck in Tralee Bay and bred with local dogs, giving rise to the Kerry Blue. What is more likely, is that the breed was developed by farmers who bred local terrier-types, possibly crossed with Irish Wolfhounds, to produce a robust, hardy, and versatile dog that was allegedly favored by poachers. Kerries were first shown as a breed in Ireland around 1916 and by the 1920s accounted for 25 percent of all registrations with the Irish Kennel Club. They were first seen at Crufts in 1922, and the same year, the breed made an appearance at the American Westminster Dog Show.

PATTERDALE TERRIER : ENGLAND

The Patterdale Terrier traces to the Lake District of northern England where the steep, rocky terrain and often harsh climate necessitated a tough, enduring breed. These dogs were used by fox hunters on foot and generally worked in pairs with a pack of Foxhounds; the Patterdale was used to access the foxes in tight crevices and holes and to follow the animals when they retreated down holes. The breed was developed from Fell Terrier types, bred chiefly by J. Bowman, an Ullswater hunter, Cyril Breay, Frank Buck, and Brian Nuttall, and has been described as being "tough as nails." Although primarily a working terrier breed, Patterdales can also make good companions for active homes.

POWERFUL, WEDGE-SHAPED HEAD

TRIANGULAR EARS FOLD TIGHTLY

HIGH-SET TAIL

COMMONLY BLACK; CAN BE RED, LIVER, BLACK AND TAN, OR BRONZE; ALL EITHER SOLID OR WITH SOME WHITE MARKINGS ON CHEST AND FEET

EYES SET FAIRLY WIDE APART

FIRM BUT FLEXIBLE CHEST

SHORT, STRAIGHT FORELEGS

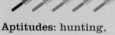
RAT TERRIER : UNITED STATES

This American breed developed from the various small terrier-types brought to the United States by English immigrants at the end of the nineteenth century. These dogs are believed to trace primarily to Manchester Terrier and Smooth Fox Terrier crosses and were highly rated for their rat-killing abilities. The Rat Terrier was used for vermin control, but also for the sport of rat catching and was deemed the most successful breed in this endeavor. At some point, Whippet or Italian Greyhound was added to the mix to increase the Rat Terrier's speed and raciness, and Beagle to improve its hunting skills. President Theodore Roosevelt kept a number of Rat Terriers and did much to popularize the breed. These dogs are said to have two personalities: their dedicated and relentless hunting character, and their soft, affectionate, playful nature in the home. They make wonderful companion animals and generally get along with other dogs.

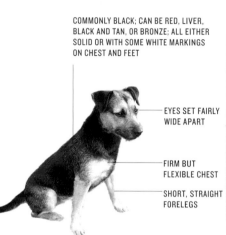

SMALL, PROMINENT EYES

BROAD, SLIGHTLY DOMED SKULL

POWERFUL JAWS, HINGED WELL BACK

LONG, SLIGHTLY ARCHED NECK

TAIL CARRIED STRAIGHT UP WHEN ALERT

SHORT, DENSE, SMOOTH COAT

COMMON COLORS INCLUDE SOLID WHITE, BLACK, SHADES OF TAN, SHADES OF CHOCOLATE, BICOLOR, OR TRICOLOR

COMPACT, OVAL FEET, TWO MIDDLE TOES ARE LONGER THAN THE OTHERS

AT A GLANCE

Size: small

Exercise needed:
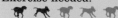

Grooming needed:

Aptitudes: hunting, vermin control, watchdog, companion

Height: 10–12 in.

Weight: 18–20 lb.

Average life expectancy: 12–14 yrs

AKC: terrier

CHARACTER

Affection

Playfulness

Friendliness to dogs

Friendliness to strangers

Ease of training

SEALYHAM TERRIER : WALES

The Sealyham Terrier was developed by Captain John Edwardes at his Sealyham Estate in Haverfordwest, Wales, between 1850 and 1891. He wanted to breed a dog that was brave and agile enough to hunt badger, otter, and fox, and based his new breed on a mix of terrier types, including Dandie Dinmonts, Fox Terriers, and West Highland Whites. Sealyhams were used for digging prey out of holes and accompanying Otter Hounds. The breed was recognized by the English Kennel Club in 1910 and by the American Kennel Club in 1911. The Sealyham is a loyal and devoted companion that can be independent and aggressive to other dogs. The breed is also wary of strangers and retains a high prey drive.

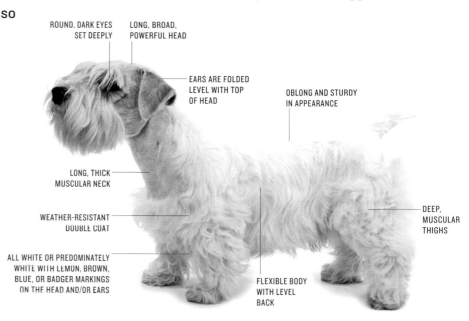

ROUND, DARK EYES SET DEEPLY

LONG, BROAD, POWERFUL HEAD

EARS ARE FOLDED LEVEL WITH TOP OF HEAD

OBLONG AND STURDY IN APPEARANCE

LONG, THICK MUSCULAR NECK

WEATHER-RESISTANT DOUBLE COAT

DEEP, MUSCULAR THIGHS

ALL WHITE OR PREDOMINATELY WHITE WITH LEMON, BROWN, BLUE, OR BADGER MARKINGS ON THE HEAD AND/OR EARS

FLEXIBLE BODY WITH LEVEL BACK

AT A GLANCE

Size: very-small

Exercise needed:

Grooming needed:

Aptitudes: vermin control, hunting, watchdog, companion

Height: 9–10 in.

Weight: 25–40 lb.

Average life expectancy: 12–14 yrs

AKC: terrier

CHARACTER

Affection

Playfulness
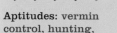

Friendliness to dogs

Friendliness to strangers

Ease of training

SKYE TERRIER : SCOTLAND

The Skye Terrier developed on the Isle of Skye off of northwestern Scotland and, tracing back 400 years, is one of the oldest of the Scottish terrier breeds. Interestingly, while most breeds have seen great changes over the last hundred years, the Skye Terrier is pretty much the same. These dogs developed their long coat to protect them from prey and weather, and are highly skilled hunters, taking on fox, badger, otter, rats, and any other vermin that crosses them. They were widespread during the nineteenth century, partly due to the influence of Queen Victoria, but are seen less often today. Skye Terriers are affectionate and loyal dogs that are fearless hunters and make good watchdogs. They may be aggressive with other dogs and are wary of strangers.

LONG, POWERFUL HEAD

FEATHERED EARS EITHER PRICKED OR DROPPED

COLORS INCLUDE CREAM, BLACK, BLUE, GRAY, AND FAWN

STRONG MUZZLE WITH LEVEL JAWS

SOFT, WOOLLY UNDERCOAT; LONG, FLAT OUTERCOAT HANGS STRAIGHT ON EITHER SIDE OF BODY

GRACEFULLY ARCHED NECK CARRIES HEAD HIGH AND PROUDLY

LONG, FEATHERED TAIL, NOT CARRIED ABOVE LINE OF BACK

FORELEGS CURVE SLIGHTLY ROUND THE CHEST

AT A GLANCE

Size: small

Exercise needed:

Grooming needed:

Aptitudes: hunting, vermin control, watchdog, companion

Height: 9–11 in.

Weight: 18–22 lb.

Average life expectancy: 11–13 yrs

AKC: terrier

CHARACTER

Affection

Playfulness

Friendliness to dogs
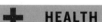

Friendliness to strangers

Ease of training

✚ HEALTH ✚

Although generally healthy, problems can include Scottie Cramp, von Willebrand's disease, Cushings syndrome, hypothyroidism, epilepsy, craniomandibular osteopathy, and cerebellar abiotrophy.

SCOTTISH TERRIER : SCOTLAND

Also known as the "Scottie," or "Diehard" on account of its tenacious character, the Scottish Terrier is a distinguished and rather glamorous member of the Terrier family. This has been a relatively recent transition since the historic Scottie was bred as a working, hunting terrier and was different in appearance to today's breed. Scotties retain their innate hunting instinct and are determined and single minded. They are totally fearless and always ready for action, be it a game or a hunt. They can be aggressive to other dogs but are devoted, loyal, and affectionate to their families.

MUZZLE TAPERS SLIGHTLY TO NOSE

LONG HEAD

SMALL, PRICKED EARS

SMALL, DARK, BRIGHT EYES WITH PIERCING EXPRESSION

HIGH-SET TAIL, CARRIED ERECT

STRONG, THICK BODY

LEVEL TOPLINE

SQUARE, POWERFUL JAW

FORECHEST EXTENDS IN FRONT OF FORELEGS

SHORT, STRONG LEGS

BROAD, VERY DEEP CHEST

HISTORY

Scotties were bred in the Scottish Highlands and used by gamekeepers for hunting and ridding large estates of foxes, badgers, stoats, otters, rats, and any other vermin that crossed their paths. The modern history of the breed traces to nineteenth-century Aberdeen, where there was a population of specific terriers, the Aberdeen Terriers. Early breeder Captain Mackie took his Aberdeen Terriers south to England in the 1870s, where he bred them to type. This coincided with the formation of the Kennel Club in 1873 and a debate over what constituted a "Scottish Terrier." A standard was drawn up in 1880, with Mackie's terriers, now called Scottish Terriers, winning many shows—one champion, Dundee, was recognized as one of the foundation dogs of the breed. There have been many revisions to the Scottie standard through the last century on both sides of the Atlantic.

COMMON COAT COLORS

BLACK

WHEATEN

WHITE

Black, wheaten, white, or brindle of any shade.

COAT CLOSE-UP

MEDIUM

Double coat with soft, dense undercoat and hard, wiry, medium-length outercoat

Scotties are extremely independent and can be difficult to train. Start puppies young, and keep a good sense of humor at all times!

STAFFORDSHIRE BULL TERRIER : ENGLAND

The Staffordshire Bull Terrier has its foundation in the early Bull and Terrier breeds that were bred for dog fighting and animal baiting, which had reached an ascendency in the early nineteenth century. These dogs were characterized by their bravery and fierceness while fighting, but their gentleness with their handlers. The Staffordshire was named after the area in England with which the dogs were most associated and was recognized by the Kennel Club in 1935. Despite their bloody heritage, Staffies, or Nanny Dogs as they are often called, have superb temperaments and are noted for their affection for children—hence the "Nanny" nickname. They have a reliable, loyal, and devoted nature and are generally good with other dogs. The Staffy is intelligent, easy to train, dependable, and a fun loving companion—but given their lovely nature, are not very good watchdogs!

SHORT, DEEP HEAD WITH DISTINCT STOP

SMALL, ROSE, OR HALF-PRICKED EARS

FOREFACE IS SHORT WITH STRONG JAWS AND TIGHT LIPS

SHORT, SMOOTH COAT

RED, FAWN, WHITE; BLACK, BRINDLE, OR BLUE; WITH OR WITHOUT WHITE

CLOSE-COUPLED BODY WITH A LEVEL TOPLINE

STRONG FORELEGS SET WIDE APART

MEDIUM-LENGTH TAIL, SET AND CARRIED LOW

GERMAN PINSCHER : GERMANY

By the nineteenth century, the German Pinscher was widespread in Germany and valued as a stable dog for catching rats and vermin, and for guarding properties. Josef Bertha founded the Pinscher Klub in 1895 by, the same year the breed was officially recognized. By the end of World War II, the breed was almost extinct and was saved by the efforts of Werner Jung, who bred his females Kitty V. Bodenstrand and Jutta to some oversized Miniature Pinschers and began to re-establish the type. All German Pinschers today trace back to his lines. These dogs are lively, intelligent, fiercely protective, and devoted. They can be wary of strangers and other dogs, and make good watchdogs.

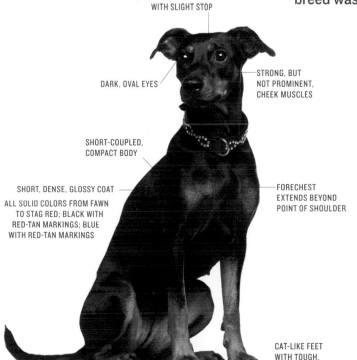

BLUNT, WEDGE-SHAPED HEAD WITH SLIGHT STOP

DARK, OVAL EYES

STRONG, BUT NOT PROMINENT, CHEEK MUSCLES

SHORT-COUPLED, COMPACT BODY

SHORT, DENSE, GLOSSY COAT
ALL SOLID COLORS FROM FAWN TO STAG RED; BLACK WITH RED-TAN MARKINGS; BLUE WITH RED-TAN MARKINGS

FORECHEST EXTENDS BEYOND POINT OF SHOULDER

CAT-LIKE FEET WITH TOUGH, DARK PADS

WEST HIGHLAND WHITE TERRIER : RUSSIA

The West Highland White, or Westie as it is affectionately known, has a relatively short history dating only to the end of the nineteenth century. Yet in that time, it has become a popular breed. Westies are known for their lively, affectionate nature; they are cheerful, outgoing dogs that like to be at the center of everything and will launch into an adventure with great spirit. They can be independent and occasionally stubborn, though, so they require patient training. Westies also like to bark and dig.

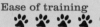

SLIGHTLY DOMED SKULL

SMALL, POINTED ERECT EARS

HEAVY EYEBROWS

WIDE-SET DARK EYES WITH A LIVELY EXPRESSION

COMPACT BODY WITH LEVEL TOPLINE

SHORT, BLUNT MUZZLE TAPERS TO BLACK NOSE

SHORT, HIGH-SET TAIL, CARRIED ERECT BUT NOT CURVED OVER BACK

DEEP, BUT NOT BROAD, CHEST

SHORT LEGS WITH STRONG BONES

ROUND FEET

Westies are born with droopy ears that gradually become pricked by about three months, or in some cases, a little later.

HISTORY

The Westie was first bred for hunting aggressive prey like badger and fox in the Scottish Highlands, and will hunt any kind of vermin. By the seventeenth century, Scotland was home to a range of terrier types that developed regional differences but were all rugged and enduring. Evidence indicates that white terrier types were bred in the western Highlands and on the Isle of Skye. Colonel Edward Donald Malcolm of the Poltalloch Estate was influential in the breed's development at the end of the nineteenth century. At first, his dogs were called Poltalloch Terriers, but he moved to change the name and established the White West Highland Terrier Club in Glasgow in 1905. In 1906 the Kennel Club changed it again to the West Highland White. The first Westies arrived in the United States in 1907 but were called Roseneath Terriers. In 1909 the American Kennel Club adopted the name, West Highland White.

COMMON COAT COLORS

The Westie's coat is always white.

WHITE

COAT CLOSE-UP

Double coated, with hard, straight outercoat approximately two inches long.

MEDIUM

SOFT-COATED WHEATEN TERRIER : IRELAND

AT A GLANCE

Size: medium-small

Exercise needed:

Grooming needed:

Aptitudes: hunting, vermin control, herding, watchdog, companion

Height: 17–19 in.

Weight: 30–40 lb.

Average life expectancy: 12–14 yrs

AKC: terrier

CHARACTER

Affection

Playfulness

Friendliness to dogs

Friendliness to strangers

Ease of training

✚ HEALTH ✚

Although generally healthy, problems can include renal dysplasia and protein-losing diseases.

It is better to get one puppy at a time so that the dog will bond with you rather than with another puppy.

SOFT-COATED WHEATEN TERRIER : IRELAND

This is one of the three long-legged terrier breeds native to Ireland, and despite its long heritage, was recognized as a distinct breed only in the twentieth century. These were developed as all-around farm dogs, and this versatility underlines the breed today. The Soft-Coated Wheaten Terrier is a charming, engaging, and fun companion that is notably gentle and calm for a terrier breed. They are generally accepting of other dogs, and although they can be independent, with patience they are relatively easy to train.

SMALL-TO-MEDIUM EARS FOLD FORWARD

LONG RECTANGULAR HEAD

COMPACT, STRONG BODY WITH LEVEL BACK

ALMOND-SHAPED DARK REDDISH-BROWN OR BROWN EYES

HIGH-SET TAIL; USUALLY DOCKED AND CARRIED AT 90 DEGREES TO BACK

POWERFUL MUZZLE AND LARGE, BLACK NOSE

DEEP CHEST AND WELL-SPRUNG RIBS

HISTORY

This breed traces back several hundred years to a general farm dog that exhibited great diversity in type, but was extremely willing and able in spirit. These dogs were widespread on rural properties and were used for hunting, herding livestock, watching over homes, and companionship. They share the same roots as the Kerry Blue and the Irish Terrier, with all three breeds exhibited in the same class for "Irish Terriers" in Ireland during the nineteenth century. The Soft-Coated Wheaten Terrier was the last of the Irish terrier breeds to be recognized and was accepted by the Irish Kennel Club in 1937. The breed made its debut in the Irish Kennel Club Championship Show on St. Patrick's Day, 1938.

COMMON COAT COLORS

LIGHT WHEATEN

WHEATEN

The coat can be any shade of wheaten.

COAT CLOSE-UP

MEDIUM

Abundant, soft, silky, single coat with a gentle wave.

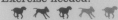
CHARACTER

Affection

Playfulness

Friendliness to dogs

Friendliness to strangers

Ease of training

✚ HEALTH ✚

Generally very healthy, but hereditary problems may include progressive retinal atrophy.

GLEN OF IMAAL TERRIER : IRELAND

Sometimes called the Irish Glen of Imaal Terrier or the Wicklow Terrier, this breed came into existence during the reign of Elizabeth I, who hired French mercenaries to put down civil unrest in Ireland. The soldiers brought with them their low-slung hounds, and those that remained in Ireland bred their dogs with the local terrier stock, eventually resulting in this breed. Unlike many other terriers, these are "strong dogs" rather than "sounders"—they were bred to go silently into dens after their prey, rather than bark to indicate its location. All in all, the Glen was a tough, enduring, feisty breed, a survivor, and retains these characteristics today. They are playful and affectionate with their families, but may be wary of strangers and scrappy with other dogs.

HEAD IS LONG AND WIDE, WITH A PRONOUNCED STOP

BROWN EYES ARE ROUND AND SET WELL APART

SMALL ROSE OR HALF-PRICKED EARS WHEN ALERT

TAIL IS CARRIED UPRIGHT

BODY IS DEEP AND LONG

SHORT, STRONG, BOWED FORELEGS

FRONT FEET TURN OUT SLIGHTLY FROM PASTERNS

HISTORY

The Glen of Imaal is one of four native Irish dog breeds and also one of the oldest. These small, tough terriers developed in the remote valley of Glen of Imaal in the Western Wicklow mountains, an area of harsh terrain and difficult living. They were used to protect rural farms from intruders, guard livestock, and above all, hunt vermin and other predators. They are said to have been used for dog fighting on the side and were known as "turnspit" dogs, running on a wheel to turn meat cooking in kitchens.

COMMON COAT COLORS

WHITE

WHEATEN

White, Wheaten, Blue, Brindle

COAT CLOSE-UP

MEDIUM

Double coat, outercoat is harsh, medium-length and weather resistant

Glens are intelligent and can have a stubborn streak, so consistency and firmness is essential in training puppies.

AT A GLANCE

Size: small

Exercise needed:

Grooming needed:
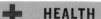

Aptitudes: hunting, vermin control, watchdog, companion

Height: 12–15 in.

Weight: 18–20 lb.

Average life expectancy: 12–14 yrs

AKC: terrier

CHARACTER

Affection
🐾🐾🐾🐾🐾

Playfulness
🐾🐾🐾🐾🐾

Friendliness to dogs
🐾🐾🐾🐾🐾

Friendliness to strangers
🐾🐾🐾🐾🐾

Ease of training
🐾🐾🐾🐾🐾

✚ HEALTH ✚

Generally exceptionally healthy, but hereditary problems may include primary lens luxation.

WELSH TERRIER : WALES

This terrier originates from Wales and may be the oldest existing dog breed in the United Kingdom. It was originally bred for hunting small-to-medium-size prey, including otters and badgers. Welsh Terriers are still valued for hunting, but they are currently on the English Kennel Club's list of breeds that are in danger of dying out, with as few as 300 or so pups registered annually (compared to the nation's most popular breeds that register in the tens of thousands). The Welsh is also one of the calmest, most affable terrier breeds. They are dignified, sensitive dogs that are relatively easy to train.

RECTANGULAR HEAD

SMALL V-SHAPED EARS FOLD JUST ABOVE THE SKULL

SMALL, DARK, DEEP-SET EYES

DEEP, STRONG JAWS WITH FLAT CHEEKS

LEVEL TOPLINE

TAIL SET HIGH, CARRIED ERECT

STRONG, UPRIGHT PASTERNS

SMALL, ROUND, CAT-LIKE FEET

HISTORY

The Welsh Terrier is an ancient breed that was developed in relative geographic isolation in Wales. The breed is probably a descendent of the broken-coated Old English Black and Tan, which no longer exists. The Welsh was specifically bred for hunting and chasing into burrows after game, and is exceptionally brave. These dogs have very good scenting abilities which are an essential part of the breed.

COMMON COAT COLORS

Deep tan with black or grizzle jacket

TAN & BLACK

COAT CLOSE-UP

The Welsh Terrier has a wiry, dense outercoat with wiry furnishings on muzzle, legs, and quarters.

MEDIUM

Maintaining obedience in a Welsh Terrier is an ongoing challenge, and it is important to reinforce training constantly.

COMPANION AND DESIGNER DOGS

BICHON FRISÉ : SPAIN

Dating back to at least the fourteenth century, these small, friendly dogs are particularly associated with the Spanish Island of Tenerife. They were originally taken there by sailors who traded with the islanders. In the sixteenth century, they became favored pets among the French, Spanish, and Italian nobility, and the dogs often appear in artwork from this time. Later, in the nineteenth century, they were used by circuses and vagabonds for performing tricks. Bichons are fun, playful, affectionate dogs, but they can be prone to barking.

AT A GLANCE

Size: small

Exercise needed:

Grooming needed:
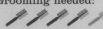

Aptitudes: companion

Height: 9–12 in.

Weight: 10–16 lb.

Average life expectancy: 12–15 yrs

AKC: non-sporting

CHARACTER

Affection

Playfulness

Friendliness to dogs

Friendliness to strangers

Ease of training

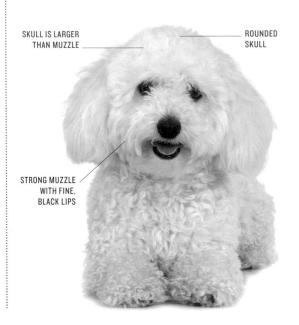

SKULL IS LARGER THAN MUZZLE

ROUNDED SKULL

STRONG MUZZLE WITH FINE, BLACK LIPS

FORWARD-LOOKING, ROUND, DARK EYES

LEVEL BACK WITH SLIGHT MUSCULAR ARCH OVER LOINS

BOLOGNESE : ITALY

The Bolognese is a member of the Bichon family and traces back to the Barbet, historically known as the Barbichon. These dogs are closely related to the Bichon Frisé, but developed in the area around Bologna in northern Italy. They were favored by Italian nobility and were often given as valuable gifts between noble families. Unlike the Bichon Frisé, the Bolognese is a rare breed, which is no reflection on its lovely characteristics. These dogs are intelligent, inquisitive, playful, and affectionate. They bond well with their families, including children, and are good with other dogs, but they can be prone to barking.

AT A GLANCE

Size: small

Exercise needed:

Grooming needed:

Aptitudes: companion

Height: 9–12 in.

Weight: 5–9 lb.

Average life expectancy: 12–14 yrs

AKC: FSS

CHARACTER

Affection

Playfulness

Friendliness to dogs

Friendliness to strangers

Ease of training

LONG, PENDENT EARS

SQUARE MUZZLE WITH A STRONG UNDER JAW

BODY IS SQUARE IN APPEARANCE

FORELEGS ARE STRAIGHT AND PARALLEL

AT A GLANCE

Size: medium-small

Exercise needed:

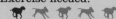

Grooming needed:

Aptitudes: companion, therapy, agility

Height: 15–17 in.

Weight: 10–25 lb.

Average life expectancy: 10–14 yrs

AKC: non-sporting

CHARACTER

Affection

Playfulness

Friendliness to dogs

Friendliness to strangers

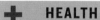

Ease of training

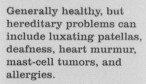

＋ HEALTH ＋

Generally healthy, but hereditary problems can include luxating patellas, deafness, heart murmur, mast-cell tumors, and allergies.

COAT CLOSE-UP

SHORT

The Boston Terrier's coat is short, smooth, shiny, and fine in texture.

BOSTON TERRIER : UNITED STATES

The Boston Terrier is sometimes called the "American Gentleman," and deservedly so due to its dapper appearance and gentle disposition. It is hard to believe that these lovely little dogs were bred from fighting stock tracing back to the American Civil War. Today's Bostons are dignified, loyal, and occasionally cheeky dogs that have won hearts around the world. They are intelligent, inquisitive, and relatively easy to train, although like most terrier breeds they have a tendency to be stubborn at times. Bostons are often used as therapy dogs and enjoy agility.

HISTORY

The Boston Terrier developed in Boston, Massachusetts, at the end of the nineteenth century and traces to British Bulldog and White English Terrier crosses. One dog that greatly influenced the breed development was Hooper's Judge, whose grandson Tom, born in 1877, is considered the first true Boston Terrier type. The breed was recognized by the American Kennel Club in 1893.

SQUARE HEAD, FLAT BETWEEN THE EARS

LARGE, ROUND, DARK EYES SET WELL APART

LEVEL TOPLINE WITH RUMP CURVING SLIGHTLY TO TAIL SET

SHORT, SQUARE, WIDE, DEEP MUZZLE

FORELEGS ARE SET MODERATELY WIDE APART

SMALL, ROUND FEET

COMMON COAT COLORS

BLACK & WHITE   **BRINDLE & WHITE**

The Boston Terrier can be black, brindle, or seal, with white markings usually on the face, chest, and legs.

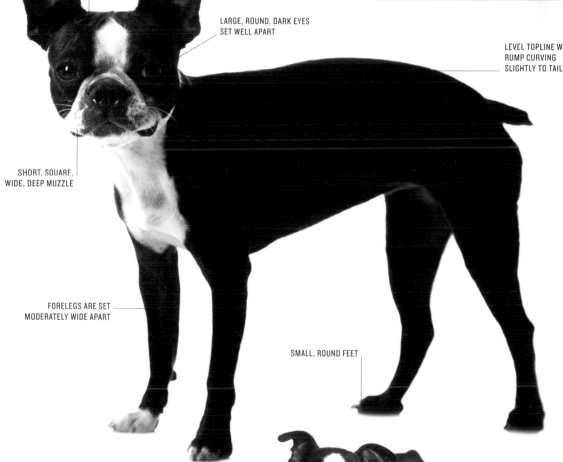

Because of the Boston's large head, they often require Caesarean section to give birth. Litters average just three or four puppies.

AT A GLANCE

Size: very small

Exercise needed:

Grooming needed:

Aptitudes: companion, watchdog

Height: 9–11 in.

Weight: 9–16 lb.

Average life expectancy: 11–14 yrs

AKC: toy

CHARACTER

Affection

Playfulness

Friendliness to dogs

Friendliness to strangers

Ease of training

✚ HEALTH ✚

Although generally healthy, problems can include dry eye, progressive retinal atrophy, bladder stones, ear problems, hernias, diabetes, patellar luxation, and liver shunt.

COAT CLOSE-UP

LONG

Long, dense outercoat, and soft undercoat. Hair grows upward on the bridge of the nose to create the characteristic "chrysanthemum" look.

COMMON COAT COLORS

GOLD & WHITE

CREAM

Any color allowed. Shih Tzuz are often gold and white, black and white, or brindle and white. They can also be solid black, gold, or brindle.

SHIH TZU : CHINA

The Shih Tzu is a cheerful, sparky, and gregarious companion who loves to play and to be the center of attention. They have sweet natures and are kind, gentle, and usually calm around the house. Despite their friendly character, they will vigorously sound the alarm if they feel the need and make excellent, noisy watchdogs.

BROAD, ROUND HEAD

LARGE, PENDENT, HEAVILY COATED EARS

DEFINITE STOP

LARGE, DARK, ROUND EYES

SHORT, SQUARE MUZZLE WITH UNDERSHOT JAW

Shih Tzu puppies, like all puppies, can be easily injured and should never be left unattended with small children.

BODY IS LONGER THAN ITS HEIGHT

STRONG LEGS

HISTORY

This little breed traces to the ancient "Lion Dogs" bred by Buddhist monks in Tibet where they were often kept in conjunction with the much larger Tibetan Mastiff and used to sound the alarm on intruders. The breed became very popular in China, particularly with the Manchu emperors of the Qing Dynasty, and developed differently from those in Tibet—the Chinese type became the Shih Tzu, whereas the Tibetan type developed into the Lhasa Apso. Shih Tzus were bred extensively in the nineteenth century by the empress Cixi who kept large kennels for them, as well as for Pugs and Pekingese. They arrived in England in the late 1920s. They were not imported to the United States in significant numbers until the 1950s, but were already popular there by the 1960s.

YORKSHIRE TERRIER : ENGLAND

Yorkshire Terriers, or "Yorkies," are busy, active little dogs that are somewhat self-important. They like to be the center of attention and to bask in unadulterated admiration. They are self-confident, charismatic, and playful, and have huge personalities. Despite, or perhaps because of, their diminutive size, they can be aggressive toward other dogs and wary of strangers; they are also inclined to bark. Although famous for their coiffed appearance, Yorkies love a good romp outside and retain the terrier instinct to chase small rodents.

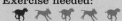

HISTORY

The breed developed in the nineteenth century in Yorkshire and Lancashire, in northern England, from small terrier-types that were favored by mill owners and weavers. The terriers, many of which had emigrated with workers from Scotland were valued for keeping rodent populations at bay. Breeds such as the now-extinct Clydesdale, Waterside, and Old English Toy Terrier are all thought to have contributed to the Yorkie. The most influential early Yorkie was Huddersfield, who won numerous show classes and ratting events. All modern Yorkies trace back to him through his ten sons and one daughter. Yorkies were being exhibited in the United States by 1878 and were recognized by the American Kennel Club in 1885.

SMALL, ERECT, V-SHAPED EARS

HEAD IS FLAT ON TOP

DARK EYES WITH AN INTELLIGENT, SPARKLING EXPRESSION

LEVEL TOPLINE

COMPACT BODY WITH A SHORT BACK

ROUND FEET

COMMON COAT COLORS

BLACK & TAN

STEEL BLUE & TAN

The Yorkie is commonly black and tan or dark steel blue and tan. Kennel clubs are often fussy about the precise color of the Yorkie's coat.

Yorkie puppies are born black. Their tan or blue-and-tan coloring emerges gradually as they mature.

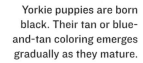

CHIHUAHUA : MEXICO

The Chihuahua is the world's smallest dog breed, but it has an enormous personality. These dogs have also appeared on the big screen in a number of Hollywood blockbusters and are frequently used in advertising. Chihuahuas require sensitive and devoted homes. They do not like being left alone and form strong bonds with their owners but are wary of strangers. Generally Chihuahuas get along well with other dogs, but they may need extra attention because they are small and more vulnerable to injuries than bigger dogs. They need consistent socialization and training, and can be inclined to bark.

AT A GLANCE

Size: very small

Exercise needed:
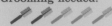

Grooming needed:

Aptitudes: Companion

Height: 6–9 in.

Weight: under 6 lb.

Average life expectancy: 14–18 yrs

AKC: toy

CHARACTER

Affection

Playfulness

Friendliness to dogs

Friendliness to strangers

Ease of training

+ HEALTH +

Generally healthy, but health problems can include patellar luxation, dental issues, hypoglycemia, epilepsy, hydrocephalus, and heart problems.

COAT TYPES

SMOOTH   **LONG**

Two coat types: long—soft, flat, or slightly wavy with undercoat, feathering on ears, feet and legs; short—smooth, soft, close, and glossy.

A Chihuahua puppy's weight will double seven to ten days after birth.

LONG TAIL CARRIED IN A CURVE OR CURLED OVER BACK

SMALL, DAINTY FEET

COMMON COAT COLORS

 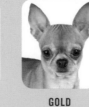 

FAWN   **BLACK & TAN**   **GOLD**   **BLACK & WHITE**

Can be any color including fawn, black and tan, gold, black and white, blue, chocolate, and red.

APPLE-DOME SKULL

SHORT, POINTED
MUZZLE

WELL-DEVELOPED
CHEST

ROUND EYES WITH A
SAUCY EXPRESSION

LARGE, ERECT EARS WHEN ALERT,
FLARING TO THE SIDES AT 45
DEGREES WHEN RESTING

LEVEL TOPLINE

BODY SLIGHTLY LONGER
THAN HEIGHT

HISTORY

This breed traces back to the state of Chihuahua in northern Mexico. Dogs were an important part of early Central and South American life with the Techichi Dogs of the Toltecs and the Xoloitzcuintli of the Aztecs dating back at least 3,000 years. Dogs formed part of the cultures' spiritual life and they were often sacrificed or painted on pottery placed in graves as it was believed that dogs carried the spirits of the deceased to the underworld. Both pottery figurines and remains found in graves resemble the modern Chihuahua. When the Spanish conquistadors arrived in the fifteenth century and plundered the native cultures, the little dogs were abandoned or escaped into the wild. They were rediscovered 300 years later in the 1850s in Chihuahua and slowly began to make their way to the United States and England. They did not become popular until the mid-twentieth century, with their popularity in the United States boosted by Xavier Cugat, a famous Rumba King whose Chihuahuas appeared with him on his weekly television shows.

AT A GLANCE

Size: small

Exercise needed:

Grooming needed:

Aptitudes: companion, therapy, agility

Height: 11–13 in.

Weight: 5–12 lb.

Average life expectancy: 13–15 yrs

AKC: toy

CHARACTER

Affection
🐾🐾🐾🐾🐾

Playfulness
🐾🐾🐾🐾🐾

Friendliness to dogs
🐾🐾🐾🐾🐾

Friendliness to strangers
🐾🐾🐾🐾🐾

Ease of training
🐾🐾🐾🐾🐾

✚ HEALTH ✚

Generally healthy, but problems can include primary lens luxation, progressive retinal atrophy, and patellar luxation.

COAT CLOSE-UP

HAIRLESS   **POWDERPUFF**

The double coat is straight and silky on top, and short and woolly underneath.

CHINESE CRESTED : CHINA

Affectionately known as the "Dr. Seuss Dog" because of its resemblance to characters from the Dr. Seuss stories, the Chinese Crested comes in two varieties, Hairless and Powderpuff. The Hairless has soft, silky hair on its head (crest), tail (plume), and feet (socks). The rest of the body is hairless and the skin is soft and smooth. The Powderpuff is entirely covered with a double, straight, and silky coat. The two types often come from the same litter. They are fun, playful, and affectionate dogs that get on well with children, strangers, and other dogs. Maintenance of the Hairless variety's skin is similar to maintaining human skin and as such it can be susceptible to dryness and sunburn.

HISTORY

Hairless dogs existed in China by the sixteenth century. They became popular with Chinese seafarers and were used for ratting on board ships and were traded as curiosities in ports. These dogs arrived in England in the 1860s as part of a zoological show but were not registered until 1881. They were introduced to the United States in 1880, and the American Chinese Crested Club was founded in 1978.

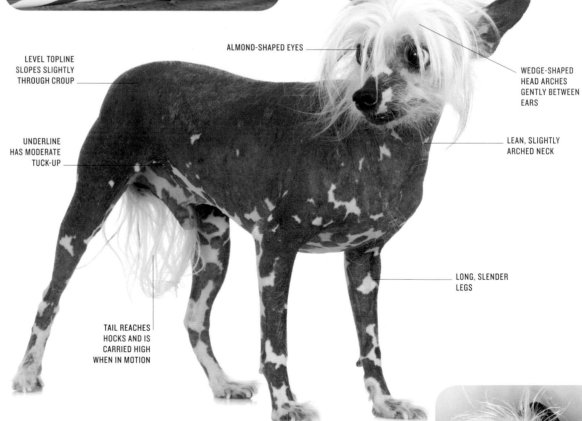

ERECT EARS

ALMOND-SHAPED EYES

WEDGE-SHAPED HEAD ARCHES GENTLY BETWEEN EARS

LEVEL TOPLINE SLOPES SLIGHTLY THROUGH CROUP

UNDERLINE HAS MODERATE TUCK-UP

LEAN, SLIGHTLY ARCHED NECK

LONG, SLENDER LEGS

TAIL REACHES HOCKS AND IS CARRIED HIGH WHEN IN MOTION

HARE FEET

COMMON COAT COLORS

MOTTLED   **SLATE**

The skin of the Hairless comes in a variety of colors, ranging from pale pink to black. The Powderpuff can be any color.

Chinese Crested Dogs are highly intelligent; puppies are always eager to play and learn new tricks.

CHINESE IMPERIAL : CHINA

The Chinese Imperial traces back to ancient China and is a close relative of the larger Shih Tzu. These dogs were bred to resemble miniature lions, a revered symbol of the Buddhist faith, and were also known as Lion Dogs, Foo Dogs, or Sleeve Dogs. Both Chinese Imperials and Shih Tzus share the same wonderful, sweet temperament. The Chinese Imperial is a bold, fun, and playful companion who loves nothing better than curling up on a warm lap. These are people-oriented dogs and need to be with their families. They are very friendly and good with other dogs and children, but given their small size, should never be left unattended with either.

LARGE, ROUND HEAD WITH A HIGH FOREHEAD

LARGE, ROUND, DARK EYES SET WELL APART

WELL-COATED, DROP EARS

WIDE, SHORT MUZZLE

BROAD, DEEP CHEST

SHORT-COUPLED AND STURDY BODY

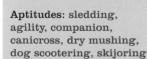

CHINOOK : UNITED STATES

The Chinook is one of just a few all-American breeds and was developed in Wanalancet, New Hampshire, by polar explorer Arthur Treadwell Walden in the early 1900s. Walden made his Chinooks famous through his expeditions and they proved themselves a worthy adversary to other sled breeds such as the Husky and Malamute. Although once kept mainly as a working breed, today Chinooks are chiefly kept as companions. They are best suited to active homes and excel at sledding, agility, and high-octane activities.

WEDGE-SHAPED HEAD

STRAIGHT, LEVEL BACK WITH NO SIGN OF WEAKNESS

SABER TAIL IS WELL COVERED WITH HAIR

DARK MARKINGS AROUND THE EYES ARE DESIRABLE

THICK, DOUBLE COAT; OUTER LAYER IS STRAIGHT, STRONG, AND COARSE

FLEXIBLE PASTERNS ARE MODERATE IN LENGTH

Size: very small

Exercise needed:

Grooming needed:

Aptitudes: companion,
therapy, agility

Height: 8–11 in.

Weight: 4–11 lb.

Average life expectancy:
12–15 yrs

AKC: toy

CHARACTER

Affection

Playfulness

Friendliness to dogs

Friendliness to strangers

Ease of training

✚ HEALTH ✚

Although generally
healthy, some health
problems can include
patellar luxation, dental
issues, and seizures

COAT CLOSE-UP

LONG

The coat is long, fine,
and silky: shorter on
head and front of legs;
longer on chest, fringes
on ears, and back of
forelegs, with "culottes"
of feathering on hind
legs. The feet may have
tufts of hair and tail is
heavily feathered.

PAPILLON : FRANCE

The Papillon takes its name from the French word for "butterfly," and is so named because its large, wing-like ears make its face resemble a butterfly. This is a superb companion breed whose dainty, elegant looks combined with their excellent character make them popular. Papillons are joyful, playful, charming, and affectionate dogs that are devoted to their families. They are intelligent, friendly, and easily trained, making them perfect as therapy dogs, as well as for agility and obedience classes.

HISTORY

The breed traces to a dwarf-spaniel type sometimes referred to as the Titian Spaniel or Toy Spaniel that was popular throughout Europe by the sixteenth century. These small dogs were favored by the nobility and were seen as "comforters," being the modern equivalent of a lap dog. Although France is listed as their country of origin they actually developed all over Europe, including in Belgium, Spain, and Italy. They can be seen in many artworks from these countries from the sixteenth century on. The Papillon became a regular at the French Court and were kept by a succession of French royals. Legend says that Marie Antoinette was accompanied by her Papillon on her way to the guillotine. The breed arrived in the United States in the first decade of the twentieth century—a Papillon named Joujou was the first to be registered with the American Kennel Club in 1915.

LONG TAIL, SET
HIGH AND CARRIED
OVER BACK

SMALL HEAD, GENTLY
ROUNDED BETWEEN
EARS

LARGE, ERECT EARS
WITH ROUNDED TIPS

SLENDER, FINE-
BONED LEGS

UNDERLINE
SHOWS
TUCK-UP

RABBIT-LIKE FEET

COMMON COAT COLORS

BLACK & WHITE

TAN & WHITE

The Papillon's
coat is white
with patches of
any other color.
Symmetry of
facial markings is
desirable.

At two to three weeks
old, Papillon puppies
begin to get their baby
teeth, which should all
be in place by around
eight weeks.

PEKINGESE : CHINA

The Pekingese is a particularly dignified breed that can be a little proud and aloof. They are devoted and affectionate on their own terms and loyal to their families, but they are characteristically not fond of strangers. The "Peke" is independent and does not really believe in the importance of obedience and training! They have enormous personalities, but are not for everyone. Pekes require a special understanding and empathy, but for the right homes, can be quiet, calm, and reserved companions.

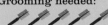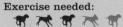
✚ HEALTH ✚

Although generally healthy, some health problems can include brachycephalic airway obstruction syndrome, back problems, eye problems, and patellar luxation.

COAT CLOSE-UP

LONG & COARSE

The outercoat is long, coarse, and straight, with a "mane" around the shoulders and feathering on the ears, tail, legs, and toes; undercoat is softer.

HISTORY

The breed is ancient and closely associated with China's emperors and ruling elite. They were bred specifically to resemble miniature lions—the lion being a revered Buddhist symbol. They became known as Foo Dogs, and statues of them were placed outside Buddhist temples or used as amulets. The dogs were bred in great numbers at China's royal palaces and tended to by eunuchs. In 1860 the British ransacked the Imperial Summer Palace in Beijing, taking five Pekingese dogs among the rest of their loot. These were taken to England and formed the foundation for the breed there. Pekes arrived in the United States in the early 1900s with two gifted by the dowager empress Cixi—one to Alice Roosevelt, wife of Theodore Roosevelt, and one to financier J. P. Morgan.

Pekingese dogs shed a lot and require plenty of grooming, including keeping their facial creases and eyes clean. Get puppies used to this as early as possible so it becomes an enjoyable part of their routine.

WIDE-SET, LARGE, DARK EYES

HEAD APPEARS BROADER THAN IT IS LONG

COMPACT, PEAR-SHAPED BODY

BODY LOW TO THE GROUND

LARGE FRONT FEET ARE FLAT AND SLIGHTLY TURNED OUT

COMMON COAT COLORS

FAWN

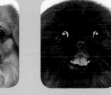

BLACK

The Peke's coat can be any color, but is commonly gold, red, sable, fawn, white, cream, or black; may have a black mask.

COTON DE TULEAR : MADAGASCAR

These rare dogs from Madagascar have been bred for centuries specifically as companions, and this is what they do best. They take their name from the cotton-like appearance of their coat and the town of Tulear. Cotons want to be with their families at all times and, given their friendly nature, will take part in any activity offered. They are bright, trainable, cheerful dogs, but will bark to sound an alarm to a doorbell or stranger. The Coton is a sensitive breed, however, and requires lots of early socialization to thrive.

AT A GLANCE

Size: very small

Exercise needed:

Grooming needed:

Aptitudes: companion, agility, watchdog

Height: 9–11 in.

Weight: 8–13 lb.

Average life expectancy: 12–15 yrs

AKC: FSS

CHARACTER

Affection

Playfulness

Friendliness to dogs

Friendliness to strangers

Ease of training

HEALTH

Although generally healthy, some health problems can include spinal disc disease and eye problems.

COAT CLOSE-UP

LONG

The Coton's coat is cottony in texture, and is dense, profuse, straight, or slightly wavy.

COMMON COAT COLORS

White with slight shadings allowed on ears or body as long as they do not detract from the overall appearance of a white coat.

WHITE

SKULL IS ROUND ON TOP AND BROAD IN RELATION TO ITS LENGTH

HISTORY

Many colorful tales of shipwrecks and heroics tell how the Coton first came to the island of Madagascar. In truth, the breed most likely developed from small Bichon-type dogs that were popular with sailors and sea merchants. Bichons trace back to the fifteenth or sixteenth century when Tulear, in Madagascar, was a thriving port. Once on the island, the different Bichon-types bred and, over time, a distinct type developed that was unique to the island. Cotons were given to the Malagasy royals and nobles as gifts, and by the seventeenth century, the breed had been adopted by the ruling "Merina" dynasty, only royalty could own them. Cotons became known as the Royal Dog of Madagascar and are now the official dog of the island.

Coton puppies start to get their adult coats between seven and twelve months of age.

ROUND, DARK, BRIGHT, AND LIVELY EYES

RECTANGULAR BODY WITH SLIGHTLY CONVEX TOPLINE

AT A GLANCE

Size: medium

Exercise needed:

Grooming needed:

Aptitudes: watchdog, companion

Height: 18–24 in.

Weight: 48–77 lb.

Average life expectancy: 10–14 yrs

AKC: not recognized

CHARACTER

Affection

Playfulness

Friendliness to dogs

Friendliness to strangers

Ease of training

ELO : GERMANY

The Elo is the result of a German couple's experiment to create the perfect pet in terms of behavioral characteristics and temperament, rather than looks. The experiment, which began in 1987, involved several breeds. As a result, the Elo's appearance is even more varied than the other modern "designer" breeds. They tend to have some distintive spitz-type traits, however, including erect ears and curly, bushy tails. The experiment has been successful in that the Elo is generally affectionate, loyal, and lively.

TRIANGULAR, PRICKED EARS WITH ROUNDED TIPS

WEDGE-SHAPED HEAD

BODY IS SLIGHTLY LONGER THAN IT IS TALL

MEDIUM-SIZE, DARK EYES WITH A LIVELY EXPRESSION

DOUBLE COATED WITH DENSE UNDERCOAT. OUTER COAT SEEN IN TWO LENGTHS, LONG OR MEDIUM

STRONG NECK

AT A GLANCE

Size: very small

Exercise needed:

Grooming needed:

Aptitudes: companion

Height: 8–11 in.

Weight: 3–7 lb.

Average life expectancy: 12–16 yrs

AKC: toy

CHARACTER

Affection

Playfulness

Friendliness to dogs

Friendliness to strangers

Ease of training

POMERANIAN : GERMANY

The Pomeranian is a member of the Spitz family and traces its ancestry to the Arctic. The breed as we know it today, however, was developed in Germany and is the smallest of the German Wolfspitzen. Queen Victoria did much to popularize the breed in England, and a "Pom" called Turi was with her when she died. The first Pom was registered in the United States in 1888, and the dog's popularity increased rapidly. Poms are lively, inquisitive, and playful. They like to live life by their own rules and on their own terms.

SMALL, POINTED, ERECT EARS SET HIGH

WEDGE-SHAPED HEAD, BROAD AT BACK, TAPERING TO NOSE

TAIL SET HIGH WITH EXTENSIVE PLUME, CARRIED ARCHED OVER BACK TO LIE FLAT

SHORT MUZZLE AND A FOX-LIKE FACE

COMPACT BODY

PRONOUNCED FORECHEST

AT A GLANCE

Size: small

Exercise needed:

Grooming needed:

Aptitudes: companion

Height: 12–13 in.

Weight: 13–18 lb.

Average life expectancy:
9–14 yrs

AKC: toy

CHARACTER

Affection

Playfulness

Friendliness to dogs

Friendliness to strangers

Ease of training

✚ HEALTH ✚

Although generally
healthy, problems can
include heart conditions,
patellar luxation, hip
dysplasia, deafness, and
brachycephalic airway
obstruction syndrome.

COAT CLOSE-UP

LONG

The moderately long,
silky coat often has
a slight wave, with
feathering on the
ears, chest, legs, tail,
and feet.

CAVALIER KING CHARLES SPANIEL : ENGLAND

The Cavalier King Charles Spaniel is renowned for its gentle disposition and sweet nature.
These dogs have a lovely temperament, being affectionate, calm, quiet, easy to train, and
playful. They are generally good with other dogs and pets, and are friendly to all, which makes
them unhelpful watchdogs! They are excellent lap dogs, but also love a run in the countryside
and enjoy most activities. They still retain their spaniel instincts and will often flush small game
from undergrowth.

HAZEL OR BROWN
EYES WITH A GENTLE
EXPRESSION

EARS SET LOW, BROAD WITH
ROUNDED TIPS, AND CARRIED
CLOSE TO THE HEAD

HISTORY

These dogs trace their roots back many centuries and share the same early history as their smaller relative the
King Charles Spaniel or English Toy Spaniel, as they are known in the United States. Small spaniel-types appeared
in European paintings from the sixteenth century onward, when they were known as "comforters" and were the
preserve of the aristocracy. They are particularly associated with King Charles I of England whose little spaniel,
Rogue, is said to have accompanied him to his execution. It is from Charles II, the Cavalier King, that the breed
takes its name though. He was besotted with the little dogs who always accompanied him, and decreed they be
allowed entrance into any public building, including public houses and parliament.
The breed did not get its name until 1928, when their standard was drawn up.
This differed considerably from that of the King Charles Spaniel, particularly in
the shape of their heads.

COMMON COAT COLORS

RED & WHITE

TRICOLOR

Common coat
colors include red
and white, known
as "Blenheim,"
and tricolor (black
on white with tan
markings).

Only buy puppies from
recommended breeders,
and always make sure
you visit the puppy in its
home with its mother.

FRENCH BULLDOG : FRANCE

French Bulldogs are often described as the "clowns of the dog world," and they do seem to have a keen sense of humor. These are charming dogs, and although they are small in height, they are solid and muscular in frame. They are exceptionally bright, affectionate, eager to please, and devoted to their families. Although they can be stubborn on occasion, they are generally very amenable and cheerful dogs.

CHARACTER

Affection

Playfulness

Friendliness to dogs

Friendliness to strangers

Ease of training

✚ HEALTH ✚

Although generally healthy, some health problems can include brachycephalic syndrome, von Willebrand's disease, intervertebral disc disease, patellar luxation, hip dysplasia, and entropion.

COAT CLOSE-UP

SHORT

The French Bulldog's coat is fine, smooth, short, and shiny.

LONG, HIGH-SET "BAT" EARS WITH ROUNDED TIPS; CARRIED ERECT

LARGE, SQUARE HEAD

SHORT, LOW-SET TAIL, STRAIGHT OR "SCREWED," BUT NOT CURLY"

SHORT, BROAD, DEEP MUZZLE

BROAD AT SHOULDERS AND NARROWING OVER LOINS

COMPACT, MUSCULAR BODY

SHORT, MUSCULAR FORELEGS SET WIDE APART

Most French Bulldog puppies are born by Caesarean section because their heads are too big for the birth canal. There are just three to five puppies per litter.

HISTORY

The "Frenchie" traces back to Bullenbeissers and British Bulldogs, both of which were used for dogfighting and bull baiting. When this was outlawed in England in 1835, these dogs had to find a new role. Breeders bred them to be smaller, and they became fashionable as companions. In the nineteenth century, many English artisans moved to France and took their small bulldog-types with them. In France these were crossed with the French Bullenbeissers, and a small bulldog-type emerged called the Bouledouge Francais. Some of the French Bulldogs arrived in England in 1893, and in 1902, the French Bulldog Club of England was formed. The breed became established in the United States in the 1880s. At this time, some Frenchies still exhibited rose ears rather than bat ears, and in 1897, the French Bull[dog] America wrote a new standard specifying bat ears, which ha[ve] become a distinctive feature of the breed.

COMMON COAT COLORS

The French Bulldog's coat is commonly brindle, fawn, or white.

BRINDLE & WHITE   **FAWN**

AT A GLANCE

Size: medium

Exercise needed:

Grooming needed:

Aptitudes: companion, therapy, agility, hunting, guarding, military

Height: 19–23 in.

Weight: 40–60 lb.

Average life expectancy: 12–14 yrs

AKC: non-sporting

CHARACTER

Affection

Playfulness

Friendliness to dogs

Friendliness to strangers

Ease of training

✚ HEALTH ✚

Although generally healthy, problems can include deafness, bladder stones, skin problems, and allergies.

COAT CLOSE-UP

SMOOTH

The Dalmatian's distinctive coat is short, dense, fine, and glossy. The coat sheds year round and needs regular brushing.

COMMON COAT COLORS

White with clearly defined black or liver spots distributed evenly.

BLACK & WHITE   **LIVER & WHITE**

DALMATIAN : CROATIA

The distinctive Dalmatian with its striking spotted coat pattern is an instantly recognizable breed. These elegant dogs combine a playful personality with great versatility and historically have been used in a range of roles including as hunters, ratters, farm dogs, watchdogs, circus performers, military dogs, firehouse dogs, carriage dogs, and of course as companions. They are intelligent and trainable, and love to be involved in any activity. They can occasionally be aggressive toward other dogs and are sometimes reserved with strangers.

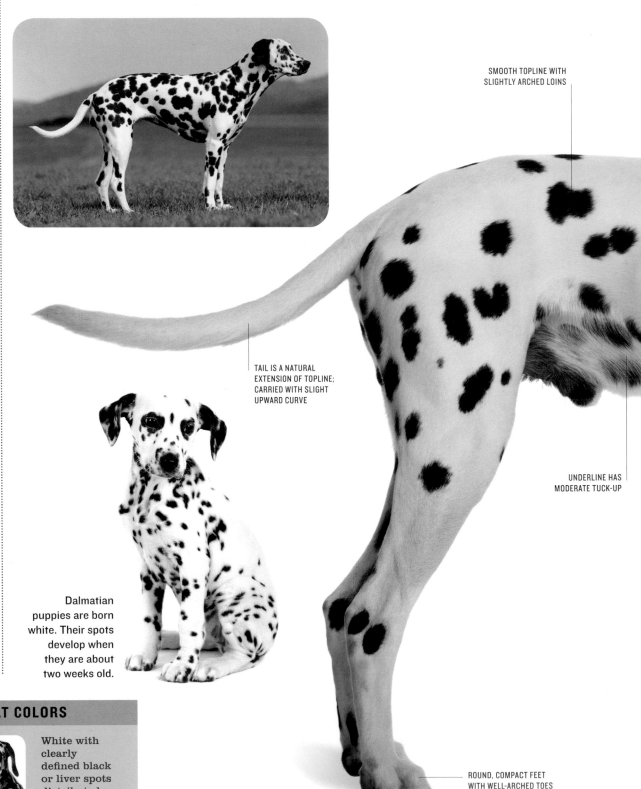

SMOOTH TOPLINE WITH SLIGHTLY ARCHED LOINS

TAIL IS A NATURAL EXTENSION OF TOPLINE; CARRIED WITH SLIGHT UPWARD CURVE

UNDERLINE HAS MODERATE TUCK-UP

ROUND, COMPACT FEET WITH WELL-ARCHED TOES

Dalmatian puppies are born white. Their spots develop when they are about two weeks old.

HISTORY

Spotted dogs appear in Ancient Egyptian art and in Italian Renaissance art. A letter written by sixteenth-century Serbian poet Jurij Dalmatin refers to two spotted Turkish dogs that he then bred—possibly Dalmatians! The dogs are, however, most associated with England and the United States. They were favored as coaching dogs from the sixteenth century onward in England, guarding the coaches and horses when they were unattended, and as a way to deter highwaymen. Dalmatians became known as English Coach Dogs, Plum Pudding Dogs, or Spotted Dicks. In the United States, the Dalmatian accompanied early fire trucks, running alongside them and clearing the way ahead. They became known as Firehouse Dogs, and in 1951 a Dalmatian named Sparky was designated the official mascot by the National Fire Protection Association. This dog's popularity rocketed following the release of Disney's *101 Dalmations* in 1961, and it has remained a popular companion breed ever since.

TOP OF SKULL IS AS WIDE AS IT IS LONG, AND FLAT BETWEEN THE EARS

POWERFUL MUZZLE

BROWN OR BLUE, MEDIUM-SIZE EYES

LONG, ARCHED NECK

HIGH-SET EARS TAPER TO A ROUNDED TIP

DEEP, WIDE CHEST

STRONG LEGS

CHARACTER

Affection

Playfulness

Friendliness to dogs

Friendliness to strangers

Ease of training

✚ HEALTH ✚

Generally healthy, but problems can include cleft palate, syringomyelia, chiari-like malformation, and glaucoma.

COAT CLOSE-UP

ROUGH   **SMOOTH**

Brussels Griffons can be smooth coated (like a Pug) or rough coated (like a Schnauzer).

BRUSSELS GRIFFON : BELGIUM

Also known as the Griffon Bruxellois, this breed is of ancient origin and was perhaps first documented in the fifteenth-century painting *The Marriage of Giovanni Arnolfini*, by Jan Van Eyck. (Although the breed bears a strong resemblance to the little dog in the painting, that image has been cited as the ancestor of a number of other modern breeds as well.) The Brussels Griffon is a fun, plucky companion breed that exhibits many terrier qualities. These dogs are game for any adventure and enjoy long walks, but are equally happy to settle down in an armchair and be a lap dog. They are spirited, bold, outgoing, and friendly, although they can be prone to barking.

HISTORY

Whether or not this is the breed portrayed in Jan Van Eyck's masterpiece, it certainly traces back to a rough coated terrier-type and was popular for many years as a guard dog on horse drawn cabs, as well as a ratter on farms. During the nineteenth century, there was some influence from Pugs, Affenpinschers, and King Charles Spaniels.

SMALL, HIGH-SET EARS

LARGE, DARK, ROUND EYES

SQUARE IN APPEARANCE WITH A THICKSET BODY

SHORT MUZZLE

LOWER JAW PROJECTS TO FORM AN UNDERBITE

SMALL, ROUND, COMPACT FEET

COMMON COAT COLORS

BLACK   **RED**

Brussels Griffons come in four colors: red, "belge" (black-and-reddish brown), black and tan, and black.

Brussels Griffons have been described as "Velcro with four legs" because they like to stick to their owners and hate to be left alone.

HAVANESE : CUBA

The Havanese is the Cuban member of the bichon family and was originally called the Bichon Havanais or Havana Silk Dog. The ancient bichon-type dogs, which are all small with long coats, developed regional variations leading to the different breeds we recognize today. The Havanese is trainable, intelligent, and naturally affectionate, which makes it an ideal family pet. Although a toy dog, it is energetic and requires regular light exercise. The breed's non-shedding coat makes it suitable for allergy sufferers, but the dogs need extensive grooming to keep their coats in top condition.

SKULL IS FAIRLY BROAD, BUT ALWAYS LOOKS REFINED

EARS ARE SLIGHTLY RAISED ON THE SKULL

LARGE, OVAL, DARK EYES

STURDY, MODERATE-LENGTH NECK

FEET ARE SMALL, COMPACT, AND WELL-CUSHIONED WITH SLIGHTLY ELONGATED TOES

DOUBLE COAT IS SOFT AND PROFUSE

JAPANESE CHIN : JAPAN/CHINA

Although called Japanese, this ancient breed actually traces to China and is closely related to the Pekingese. These small companion dogs were dispersed throughout the ancient world via trading along the Silk Road. They made their way to Japan where they became the preserve of the imperial households. The breed was recognized by the American Kennel Club in the late 1888. They are delightful, affectionate, devoted, and playful companions.

SHORT, BROAD, ROUND HEAD WITH AN INDENTED STOP

NASAL BRIDGE IS SHORT AND WIDE

LARGE, DARK, ROUND EYES SET WIDE APART

SHORT, UPRIGHT NECK HOLDS THE HEAD HIGH

BODY IS SQUARE WITH MODERATELY WIDE CHEST

STRAIGHT FORELEGS

KING CHARLES SPANIEL : ENGLAND

Also known as the English Toy Spaniel, the King Charles Spaniel is a close relative of the Cavalier King Charles Spaniel. In the seventeenth century, the breed was a favorite of King Charles II of England and the breed's exceptionally long ears resemble the wigs worn by the aristocracy at that time. King Charles Spaniels are loyal and devoted dogs that adore their families. They are calm, generally quiet, playful, and enjoy a good walk. They are also often independent and stubborn, and can be wary of strangers.

DOMED SKULL WITH DEFINED STOP

LARGE HEAD IN COMPARISON TO BODY

LARGE EYES WITH SOFT EXPRESSION

SQUARE, BROAD, DEEP JAW

LONG, LOW-SET EARS HANG CLOSE TO THE HEAD

COMPACT AND SQUARISH IN APPEARANCE

KROMFOHRLANDER : GERMANY

The Kromfohrlander traces to a stray farmdog named Peter—likely a Grand Griffon Vendéen and Wire Fox Terrier cross—who was adopted by American servicemen in the 1940s in northern France. He ended up in Germany where dog breeder Ilsa Shleifenbaum bred him to a Fox Terrier that produced puppies exactly like Peter. This formed the base for the new breed, which is still rare. The Kromfohrlander was developed as a companion breed and is good-natured, affectionate, and playful.

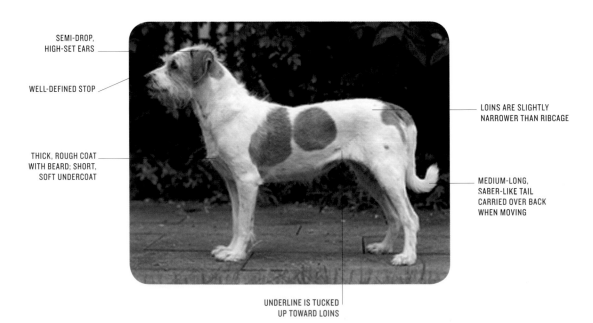

SEMI-DROP, HIGH-SET EARS

WELL-DEFINED STOP

LOINS ARE SLIGHTLY NARROWER THAN RIBCAGE

THICK, ROUGH COAT WITH BEARD; SHORT, SOFT UNDERCOAT

MEDIUM-LONG, SABER-LIKE TAIL CARRIED OVER BACK WHEN MOVING

UNDERLINE IS TUCKED UP TOWARD LOINS

KYI-LEO : UNITED STATES

One of the original "designer dogs," this rare breed was developed in San Francisco in the 1950s by crossing a Lhasa Apso and a Maltese. By 1972 it got the name Kyi, from the Tibetan word for "dog," and Leo, from the Latin for "lion," in homage to the Maltese, which is also known as the Maltese Lion Dog. The breed is recognized by the American Rare Breed Association. These are affectionate, playful dogs that arc devoted to their families but may be wary of strangers. They are lively, can be stubborn, and have unusually dexterous front paws.

HEAD IS COVERED IN LONG HAIR

DROP EARS

WHISKERS AND BEARD ON MUZZLE

THICK, SILKY COAT

ROUND FEET

BLACK AND WHITE PREFERRED; OTHER COLORS ACCEPTABLE

LHASO APSO : TIBET

These ancient dogs developed in remote Tibet relatively uninfluenced by other breeds. They are closely associated with the Buddhist monasteries where they were bred and revered. Their history is entrenched in the myths, legends, and spiritual beliefs of Buddhism; they were considered to be the living incarnation of the mythical Tibetan Snow Lion. The Lhasa Apso is a charismatic, affectionate, playful, and protective dog that can be wary of strangers and, as such, makes a good watchdog

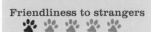

NARROW SKULL, NOT QUITE FLAT

STRAIGHT FOREFACE

HEAD COVERED WITH HEAVY HAIR

BODY IS LONGER THAN ITS HEIGHT

HEAVILY FEATHERED EARS

FRONT AND HIND LEGS ARE COVERED WITH HAIR

LÖWCHEN : GERMANY

Also known as the Little Lion Dog, the Löwchen traces its history at least to the sixteenth century when its likeness began to appear in German paintings. The breed almost disappeared during World War II but was revived through the efforts of Belgian breeder Madame Bennert and German breeder Dr. Hans Rickert. These are cheerful, playful, and eager-to-please dogs that have great personalities, although they can be noisy!

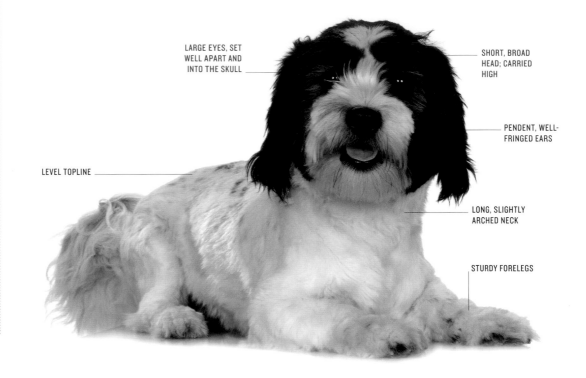

LARGE EYES, SET WELL APART AND INTO THE SKULL

SHORT, BROAD HEAD; CARRIED HIGH

PENDENT, WELL-FRINGED EARS

LEVEL TOPLINE

LONG, SLIGHTLY ARCHED NECK

STURDY FORELEGS

MALTESE : MALTA

This ancient bichon breed was developed from spaniel roots and is indigenous to the island of Malta. It was named by the Romans after its place of origin. The Maltese is distinctive for its long, silky white coat, which for centuries ensured its popularity among the European aristocracy. Although these little dogs are gentle and affectionate, they are also intelligent, lively, and fearless. They are wary of strangers and have a tendency to bark.

SKULL IS AS BROAD AS IT IS LONG

COMPACT BODY

HIGH-SET TAIL IS CARRIED CURVED OVER THE BACK, WITH TIP LYING TO ONE SIDE

MUZZLE IS CHISELED AND LONGER THAN IT IS DEEP

REAR PASTERNS ARE SHORT AND VERTICAL

FORELEGS ARE LEAN BUT STURDY FOR THEIR SIZE

MINIATURE PINSCHER : GERMANY

There is much speculation surrounding the development of this feisty little breed, which is commonly known as the "Min-Pin." They are believed to have developed from German Pinschers crossed with Dachshunds and Italian Greyhounds several hundred years ago; their likeness appears in historic artwork. They arrived in the United States in 1919 and gained American Kennel Club recognition in 1929. Min-Pins are fearless, lively, inquisitive, and self-possessed dogs that can be independent and stubborn.

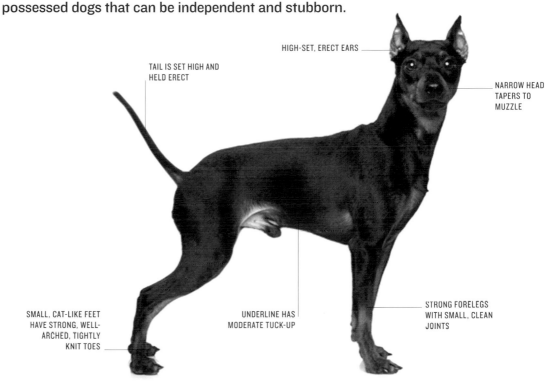

HIGH-SET, ERECT EARS

TAIL IS SET HIGH AND HELD ERECT

NARROW HEAD TAPERS TO MUZZLE

SMALL, CAT-LIKE FEET HAVE STRONG, WELL-ARCHED, TIGHTLY KNIT TOES

UNDERLINE HAS MODERATE TUCK-UP

STRONG FORELEGS WITH SMALL, CLEAN JOINTS

PHALÈNE : FRANCE

The beautiful Phalène is the drop-ear variety of the Papillon, and is not recognized as a separate breed by some kennel clubs. These lovely little dogs trace back to at least the sixteenth century, when they began to appear in paintings. The Phalène is believed to be the older of the two types of Papillon and was once more popular than its prick-eared relative. Their fortunes reversed at the end of the nineteenth century when the Phalène started to disappear. It is only within the last fifty years or so that there has been a concerted effort to reestablish the Phalène, and numbers are now on the rise. The Phalène is a delightful, charming companion, a friend to everyone, playful, sweet, calm, and gorgeous.

SMALL HEAD, SLIGHTLY ROUNDED BETWEEN THE EARS

THE FINE MUZZLE IS NOTABLY THINNER THAN THE HEAD AND TAPERS TO NOSE

STRAIGHT, SLENDER FORELEGS

FEET ARE RABBIT-LIKE, THIN, AND ELONGATED

SMALL GREEK DOMESTIC DOG : GREECE

This ancient breed is also known as the Meliteo Kinidio and for many years was considered a variant of the Alopekis, another small Greek breed. Small Greek Domestic Dogs are now categorized as a separate breed, but are rarely seen or heard of beyond their homeland. These are lively, versatile companions that are as happy on vermin patrol as they are being a lap dog. The Small Greek Domestic Dog also serves as a useful watchdog and will sound a vigorous alarm.

AT A GLANCE

Size: small

Exercise needed:

Grooming needed:

Aptitudes: watchdog, vermin control, companion

Height: 10–15 in.

Weight: 14–26 lb.

Average life expectancy: 12–14 yrs

AKC: not recognized

CHARACTER

Affection

Playfulness

Friendliness to dogs

Friendliness to strangers

Ease of training

DROP EARS ARE SET HIGH, WELL FEATHERED, AND HANG CLOSE TO CHEEKS

LARGE, ROUNDISH EYES ARE DARK IN COLOR

MUZZLE GENTLY TAPERS TO NOSE

BODY IS LONGER THAN ITS HEIGHT

JAPANESE SPITZ : JAPAN

The Japanese Spitz is a big dog in a little dog's body—this tough little dog acts as a house protector and guardian. An enthusiastic watchdog, the Japanese Spitz will alert its family whenever it feels it is necessary, but owners must be sure to say when enough is enough, if the dog starts barking obsessively. The high-spirited Spitz is intelligent, playful, alert, and obedient—he is not difficult to train as long as his owner is consistent. This breed learns quickly and enjoys agility games.

AT A GLANCE

Size: small

Exercise needed:

Grooming needed:

Aptitudes: companion, watchdog, agility

Height: under 10–14 in.

Weight: 10–12 lb.

Average life expectancy: 12-15 yrs

AKC: not recognized

CHARACTER

Affection

Playfulness

Friendliness to dogs

Friendliness to strangers

Ease of training

TRIANGULAR, ERECT EARS

LONG TAIL, COVERED WITH THICK FUR

ALMOND-SHAPED, DARK EYES

THICK, PURE WHITE COAT

MUZZLE GENTLY TAPERS TO NOSE

AT A GLANCE

Size: very small

Exercise needed:
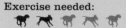

Grooming needed:

Aptitudes: watchdog, companion

Height: 8–10 in.

Weight: 9–15 lb.

Average life expectancy: 12–15 yrs

AKC: non-sporting

CHARACTER

Affection

Playfulness

Friendliness to dogs

Friendliness to strangers

Ease of training

TIBETAN SPANIEL : TIBET

The Tibetan Spaniel developed in the Himalayan Mountains of remote Tibet more than 2,000 years ago, and has a history closely entwined with the Buddhist faith. These dogs were bred by Tibetan monks as "little lion dogs." They were thought to bring good luck and were valued as watchdogs in the monasteries—the little dogs lay on top of the exterior walls and sounded a vigorous alarm when needed. Legend has it that they also turned prayer wheels. The breed arrived in England in 1898, and in the United States in 1966. They are devoted, sensitive, and intelligent dogs that thrive on the companionship of their families.

PLUMED TAIL IS CARRIED IN A CURL OVER THE BACK WHEN MOVING

HEAD IS SMALL AND SLIGHTLY DOMED

DARK, EXPRESSIVE EYES ARE SET FAIRLY WIDE APART

BLUNT MUZZLE WITH DEEP, WIDE BOTTOM JAW

NEAT, RABBIT-LIKE FEET ARE WELL HAIRED

FORELEGS ARE SLIGHTLY BOWED

AT A GLANCE

Size: medium-small

Exercise needed:

Grooming needed:

Aptitudes: watchdog, companion

Height: 15–16 in.

Weight: 18–30 lb.

Average life expectancy: 12–15 yrs

AKC: non-sporting

TIBETAN TERRIER : TIBET

Like the Tibetan Spaniel, the Tibetan Terrier traces back more than 2,000 years with its history closely tied to monasteries deep in the Himalayan Mountains. These dogs were bred in monasteries, earning the name "Holy Dogs of Tibet." They were also used for herding and guarding livestock, for companionship, and for watching over the monasteries. They first arrived in the United States in the 1950s. Tibetan Terriers are eager to please, playful, affectionate, devoted, and gentle, but they can be wary of strangers.

CHARACTER

Affection

Playfulness

Friendliness to dogs

Friendliness to strangers

Ease of training

LARGE, DARK EYES SET WELL APART

HEAD IS WELL FURNISHED WITH LONG HAIR

PENDENT, V-SHAPED EARS

STRONG MUZZLE WITH A WELL-DEVELOPED LOWER JAW

PROFUSE DOUBLE COAT

LARGE, FLAT, ROUND, HAIRY FEET WITH NO ARCH IN THE TOES

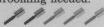
CHARACTER

Affection

Playfulness

Friendliness to dogs

Friendliness to strangers

Ease of training

✚ HEALTH ✚

Although generally healthy, problems can include brachycephalic airway obstruction syndrome, back problems, eye problems, patellar luxation, hip dysplasia, and Pug-dog encephalitis.

COAT CLOSE-UP

SHORT & SMOOTH

Short, fine, smooth, glossy coat. Neither hard nor woolly

COMMON COAT COLORS

Silver, apricot-fawn with black mask, or solid black.

FAWN   **BLACK**

PUG : CHINA

The Pug has often been described as *multum in parvo*, meaning "a lot in a little," which is an appropriate description of this lovely little breed that is packed with personality and charisma. Pugs have a lively, gregarious nature and make superb companions. They are renowned for their sense of humor and are guaranteed to make people laugh. As much as they love to clown around, they can also be dignified and rather regal, depending on their mood. They are eager to please, intelligent, and playful. On the downside, they can be stubborn and are prone to snoring and wheezing.

HISTORY

The Pug is an ancient breed that traces back to at least 400 BCE. Chinese philosopher Confucius (551–479 BCE) wrote about "short-mouthed dogs" thought to refer to the Lo-Chiang-Sze or early Pug types. Pugs were the preserve of China's elite and were treated with lavish care. The breed arrived in England in 1688 and quickly became fashionable among the aristocracy; the dog's popularity then spread to France and Russia. The first Pugs are thought to have arrived in the United States in the mid 1860s and, after a slow start, became popular companions there.

SMALL EARS, EITHER ROSE OR BUTTON

DEFINED WRINKLES ON FOREHEAD

FAIRLY LARGE, ROUNDED HEAD

SHORT, BLUNT, SQUARE MUZZLE

UNDERSHOT JAW

HIGH-SET TAIL, TIGHTLY CURLED OVER BACK; DOUBLE CURL PREFERRED

BROAD CHEST

PROMINENT, LARGE, DARK, ROUND EYES

Pugs love to get on furniture. If you want a dog that doesn't sit on your sofa, a Pug probably isn't for you.

RUSSIAN TOY

AT A GLANCE

Size: very small

Exercise needed:

Grooming needed:

Aptitudes: companion, vermin control, watchdog

Height: 8–11 in.

Weight: 3–7 lb.

Average life expectancy: 12–14 yrs

AKC: FSS

CHARACTER

Affection

Playfulness

Friendliness to dogs

Friendliness to strangers

Ease of training

RUSSIAN TOY : RUSSIA

The Russian Toy, also known as the Russkiy Toy, is a new breed developed in Russia in the mid-twentieth century based on the English Toy Terrier. Breeders began to reestablish once-popular English breeds that had all but disappeared from Russian, but after some years of development, a new type emerged that was later recognized as a distinct breed. The Russian Toy, which is now found in long and smooth coat varieties, is vcry small, but fairly feisty. They have a keen instinct for ratting and are lively and playful with their families. They are wary of strangers though, and make good watchdogs.

THE SKULL IS HIGH AND ROUND, WITH A LEAN AND POINTED MUZZLE

LARGE EARS ARE ERECT AND SET HIGH

SQUARE BODY WITH SLIGHTLY PRONOUNCED WITHERS

EYES ARE LARGE, ROUND, AND PROMINENT

LEGS ARE LONG AND LEAN

AT A GLANCE

Size: small

Exercise needed:

Grooming needed:

Aptitudes: guard dog, watchdog, vermin control, companion

Height: 10–13 in.

Weight: 10–16 lb.

Average life expectancy: 13–15 yrs

AKC: non-sporting

CHARACTER

Affection

Playfulness

Friendliness to dogs

Friendliness to strangers

Ease of training

SCHIPPERKE : BELGIUM

These small, black dogs probably developed from the now-extinct Leauvenaar that was related to the Belgian Shepherd. Schipperkes were widely used for guarding and ratting by farmers, and were popular with boatman on the watcrways of Belgium and the Netherlands. They remained a working-man's dog until 1885 when Queen Marie-Henriette bought one and instantly elevated the breed to high society. Given their compact size and protective tendencies, Schipperke's are lively, bold, and adventurous dogs that are reserved with strangers.

SMALL, DARK, ALMOND-SHAPED EYES WITH A LIVELY EXPRESSION

BROAD, WEDGE-SHAPED HEAD WITH TAPERING A MUZZLE

DOUBLE COAT HAS A HARSH, BRISTLY OUTERCOAT WITH NECK RUFF

SHORT, WIDE, AND SQUARE BODY

STRAIGHT FORELEGS SET RELATIVELY FAR APART

SMALL, ROUND FEET

SCHNOODLE : UNITED STATES

The Schnoodle is one of the many Poodle crosses, this time with a Schnauzer. Both the Schnauzer and Poodle come in a variety of sizes, and so does the Schnoodle. These are highly intelligent dogs that love to be involved in any activity and have lots of energy. They are generally good with other dogs and people, and are very affectionate and playful with their families. The Schnoodle makes a great family companion for an active home and can also be a vigilant watchdog, but can be prone to barking and digging.

HEAD IS WELL FURNISHED WITH HAIR, INCLUDING EYEBROWS AND BEARD

EARS HANG CLOSE TO THE HEAD

BODY IS SLIGHTLY LONGER THAN ITS HEIGHT

MUZZLE IS STRONG AND SQUARE

COAT VARIES IN TEXTURE BETWEEN SOFT AND WAVY TO LOOSELY OR TIGHTLY CURLED

PARENTS

MINATURE SCHNAUZER · MINATURE POODLE

COCKAPOO : UNITED STATES

Cockapoos are a mix of the American Cocker Spaniel or English Cocker Spaniel and Poodle and are one of the older "new breeds." They were first developed in the United States in the 1950s, and have since become a popular hybrid. As with most hybrids, there is great variation in appearance dependent on the bloodlines of the parents. Poodles, for example, come in three different sizes, and there is a great difference between English and American Cocker Spaniels, and between those of working or show background. In general terms, Cockapoos make lovely companion dogs and are noted for their outgoing, friendly temperament.

LARGE, ROUND, WELL-SPACED EYES WITH A SOFT EXPRESSION

MODERATELY ROUNDED SKULL

FEATHERED EARS HANG CLOSE TO HEAD

NECK IS SLIGHTLY ARCHED AND CARRIED HIGH

SINGLE, LOW-SHEDDING COAT

PARENTS

COCKER SPANIEL · POODLE

TOPLINE IS LEVEL TO SLIGHTLY SLOPING TO HINDQUARTERS

TAIL IS SET IN LINE WITH BACK AND CARRIED UPRIGHT

PUGGLE : UNITED STATES

Puggles result from cross breeding Pugs with Beagles. They have become a popular designer breed based on their cheeky personalities and compact size, which makes them suitable for urban living. The Puggle is friendly, affectionate, and playful, but independent and can be a little harder to train than some. They generally get along well with other dogs and people, and are relatively calm in the house. There is no breed standard for them.

HISTORY

Puggles dates back to the 1980s, when breeders in the United States experimented with creating new dogs. By 2000, Puggles were being sold commercially to pet owners wanting to own a different, distinctive dog. Like many "designer" breeds, the Puggle may have originally emerged as the result of an accidental breeding that produced a particularly endearing mutt.

WRINKLES OFTEN PRESENT ON FOREHEAD

MUZZLE NORMALLY LONGER THAN THAT OF THE PUG

LARGE, DARK EYES

HIGH-SET, VELVETY, HANGING EARS

SOLID AND THICK-SET BODY

LEG LENGTH VARIES GREATLY IN THIS BREED

COMMON COAT COLORS

The most common color is fawn, but it can be also be red, black, parti-colored, or lemon and white.

FAWN

PARENTS

PUG   BEAGLE

Pugs love to get on furniture and the Puggle may well expect similar comforts.

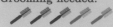

GOLDENDOODLE : UNITED STATES

The Goldendoodle is bred by crossing a Golden Retriever and a Poodle, and was developed in North America in the 1990s. This cross has proven to be popular, particularly in the United States, Australia, and England. Goldendoodles have a low-shedding, low-dander coat that makes them more suitable for allergy sufferers. They are intelligent, gregarious, friendly, playful, and make wonderful companions. They are human-oriented dogs and tend to develop a strong bond with their owners. Although calm and easygoing, they need a lot of exercise.

LONG TAIL MAY CURL UPWARD

EARS HANG CLOSE TO HEAD

STURDY BODY

GENTLY DOMED SKULL

HISTORY

The Goldendoodle followed swiftly on the heels of the Australian Labradoodle and first appeared as a deliberate hybrid crossbreed in the early 1990s. Having seen the successful breeding of smaller hybrid crosses with Poodles, Golden Retriever breeders decided to create a larger, but similar, dog by crossbreeding to Standard Poodles.

Goldendoodle puppies go through several coat changes before they develop their adult coats at about one year of age. Their shaggy eyebrows and beards begin forming as puppies and are noticeable, but take some time to develop fully.

COMMON COAT COLORS

CHALK   CHOCOLATE   GOLD

Common colors include chalk, chocolate, cream, gold, red, black, blue, silver, and coffee.

PARENTS

GOLDEN RETRIEVER   POODLE

AUSTRALIAN LABRADOODLE : AUSTRALIA

Labradoodles are the result of Labrador Retriever and Poodle heritage. They combine the best qualities of both breeds and have won peoples' hearts in a relatively short amount of time. These lovely dogs combine a largely non-shedding, low-dander coat with great personalities, high intelligence, and good trainability. They are energetic but generally calm, with those from a Standard Poodle cross exhibiting particularly good temperaments. The Labradoodle is bred in three sizes: miniature, medium, and standard.

CHARACTER

Affection

Playfulness

Friendliness to dogs

Friendliness to strangers

Ease of training

✚ HEALTH ✚

Although generally healthy, some issues can include skin problems, ear problems, progressive retinal atrophy, epilepsy, diabetes, hip dysplasia, elbow dysplasia, and hypothyroidism.

COAT CLOSE-UP

LONG   WOOL   FLEECE

There are three coat types: long—a shedding coat in a range of textures; fleece—very soft, non-shedding, similar to angora, can be straight, wavy, or spirals; or wool—a non-shedding coat that can be thickly curled, loosely curled, or thick, dense, and straight.

PARENTS

LABRADOR
RETRIEVER

POODLE

BROAD, SCULPTED HEAD WITH
WELL-DEFINED EYEBROWS

EYES ARE ROUND,
LARGE, AND
EXPRESSIVE

PENDENT EARS ARE SET
FLAT AGAINST HEAD
AND LEVEL WITH EYES

STRONG CHEST

BODY APPEARS
COMPACT AND
SQUARE

HISTORY

The development of the Labradoodle is credited to Wally Cochran of the Royal Guide Dogs in Victoria, Australia, in the late 1980s. He was approached by a blind woman from Hawaii, whose husband was allergic to dogs and who hoped Cochran could produce a guide dog that would be suitable for her home. Cochran's breeding program was extremely successful with a large percentage of his dogs becoming guide dogs, and ensuing media coverage saw an explosion in the popularity of the new hybrid breed. These animals are now found all over the world, and although they are not yet officially recognized as a breed by the various Kennel Clubs, it seems likely that they will be in the future.

Puppy coats do not typically trigger allergies in people, but when the adult coat comes in, it might. While Labradoodle coats (fleece and wool type) are more suitable for allergy sufferers, they are not "non-allergenic."

COMMON COAT COLORS

CHALK   CHOCOLATE   GOLD   BLACK

Common colors include chalk, chocolate, cream, gold, red, black, blue, silver, and cafe.

CHEAGLE : ENGLAND/UNITED STATES

The friendly, playful Cheagle is a combination of Chihuahua and Beagle. As with all mixed-breed dogs, looks can vary enormously—especially when combining a hound with a toy breed! The Cheagle tends to be smaller than the Beagle, but retains that breed's speed and agility. It can also inherit some of the Chihuahua's feistiness and fondness for barking. Although each dog will be unique, Cheagles are generally courageous, loving, loyal, and protective. They are outgoing dogs that need plenty of exercise but minimal grooming.

LONG, PENDENT EARS

ROUND, DEEP-BROWN EYES

COAT IS USUALLY A COMBINATION OF BLACK, WHITE, AND BROWN

THE CHEAGLE OFTEN HAS AN OVERBITE INHERITED FROM THE CHIHUAHUA

WELL-DEVELOPED CHEST

SHORT, SMOOTH COAT

PARENTS

CHIHUAHUA | BEAGLE

GOLLIE : ENGLAND/UNITED STATES

The Gollie, sometimes called the Golden Collie, is a mix of Collie and Golden Retriever. These dogs are extremely intelligent, alert, active, responsive, good with all family members, and easy to train. They often retain the Golden Retriever's soft mouth and love of water, but they will also have the Collie's instincts to herd—including other pets. They can be any color but are often cream or shades of red-brown or black. They are calm indoors, active outdoors, and suitable for urban living only with sufficient exercise.

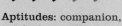

ALMOND-SHAPED EYES

EARS VARY BUT CAN BE SEMI-PRICKED OR PRICKED WHEN ALERT

MUSCULAR HINDQUARTERS

MUZZLE IS LONG AND NARROW

COAT IS TYPICALLY LONG WITH FEATHERING ON TAIL, CHEST, LEGS, AND EARS

PARENTS

GOLDEN RETRIEVER | COLLIE

JACK-A-BEE : ENGLAND/UNITED STATES

The Jack-a-Bee is blend of Beagle and Russell Terrier. These small- to medium-size dogs are loyal, energetic, and fun-loving. They tend to keep their noses to the ground and sniff everything during their walk—a Beagle-inherited trait. The Jackabee's instinct to follow a trail and their terrier's tenacity can make them oblivious to recall commands when exercising off lead in wooded areas, so care should be taken. They are intelligent, sociable dogs that require consistent obedience training.

AT A GLANCE

Size: small-medium

Exercise needed:

Grooming needed:

Aptitudes: companion, agility

Height: 10–14 in.

Weight: 11–28 lb.

Average life expectancy: 13–15 yrs

AKC: not recognized

CHARACTER

Affection
🐾 🐾 🐾 🐾 🐾

Playfulness
🐾 🐾 🐾 🐾 🐾

Friendliness to dogs
🐾 🐾 🐾 🐾 🐾

Friendliness to strangers
🐾 🐾 🐾 🐾 🐾

Ease of training
🐾 🐾 🐾 🐾 🐾

MEDIUM-LENGTH EARS ARE INCLINED TO FALL AHEAD, FLAT TO THE CHEEK

FLAT HEAD WITH LITTLE WIDTH BETWEEN THE EARS

TAIL SET HIGH AND CARRIED UPRIGHT WHEN MOVING

LEG LENGTH CAN VARY DRAMATICALLY BETWEEN INDIVIDUAL DOGS

PARENTS

RUSSELL TERRIER | BEAGLE

JACK-A-POO : ENGLAND/UNITED STATES

The Jack-a-Poo is a Russell Terrier and Toy or Miniature Poodle mix. This is a fairly new hybrid, which means its appearance will not "settle" for several more generations. However, these are generally loving, cheerful, happy, and family-oriented dogs that make good pets. Despite their scruffy looks and carefree nature, Jack-a-Poos are intelligent, active, and playful and need regular exercise, both physically and mentally. They are highly trainable and enjoy learning tricks—a classic example of a big character in a small package.

AT A GLANCE

Size: small

Exercise needed:

Grooming needed:
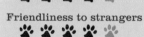

Aptitudes: companion, agility

Height: 10–15 in.

Weight: 12–18 lb.

Average life expectancy: 13-15 yrs

AKC: not recognized

CHARACTER

Affection
🐾 🐾 🐾 🐾 🐾

Playfulness
🐾 🐾 🐾 🐾 🐾

Friendliness to dogs
🐾 🐾 🐾 🐾 🐾

Friendliness to strangers
🐾 🐾 🐾 🐾 🐾

Ease of training
🐾 🐾 🐾 🐾 🐾

TAIL LENGTH VARIES

COAT CAN BE WIRY, CURLY, WAVY, BROKEN, OR SHORT

LEG LENGTH WILL VARY

ROUND OR ALMOND-SHAPED DARK EYES

CAN HAVE PROMINENT EYEBROWS AND A BEARD

PARENTS

RUSSELL TERRIER | MINIATURE POODLE

CHARACTER

Affection

Playfulness

Friendliness to dogs

Friendliness to strangers

Ease of training

✚ HEALTH ✚

Generally healthy, but they can suffer from epilepsy, progressive retinal atrophy, shaker syndrome, and patellar luxation.

COAT CLOSE-UP

LONG

The coat is usually long and wavy or curly, harsh, and dense.

MALTIPOO : UNITED STATES

The adorable Maltipoo is a cross between a Maltese and a Toy or Miniature Poodle, and is an ideal companion for families who want to devote themselves to their dogs. The Maltipoo likes nothing better than being at the center of attention, and will settle for nothing less. These little, fluffy dogs are not happy being left alone and will bark. Sometimes Maltipoos take time to accept strangers, and can be aloof, but they are devoted and affectionate to people they know and trust. Similarly, they do not always accept other dogs at first, and time should be taken to properly socialize them. Despite their small size, Maltipoos like to get out and about and enjoy a good walk and a lively play session.

SKULL IS SLIGHTLY ROUNDED

MEDIUM-LENGTH, PENDENT EARS

FORWARD-LOOKING, DARK, ROUND EYES

SOFT, WAVY COAT

Maltipoo puppies are difficult to distinguish from adult dogs, as they retain their "puppyish" looks throughout their lives.

PARENTS

MALTESE | MINATURE POODLE

HISTORY

The Maltipoo was developed as a small companion dog more suitable for allergy sufferers than some other breeds due to their low-shedding coat. Dogs produce different levels of allergens in their saliva, which is transferred to the coat when they groom themselves—this, and skin cells (dander), may cause allergies.

COMMON COAT COLORS

APRICOT

BLACK

The Maltipoos coat can be any color, but is commonly white, black, cream, or apricot.

MAL-SHI : AUSTRALIA/UNITED STATES/ENGLAND

Also known as the Malti-Zu and Malt-Tzu, this is one of the few popular "designer" breeds that is not founded on a Poodle cross. This hybrid "breed" was developed in the 1990s through crossing Maltese and Shih Tzu in an attempt to produce a low-shedding companion breed. Mal Shis are gregarious, happy, intelligent, and affectionate little companion dogs that love to be the center of attention. They make excellent family dogs and are also vigilant watchdogs. They can be prone to barking if left on their own.

SKULL IS SLIGHTLY ROUNDED

FORWARD-LOOKING, DARK, ROUND EYES

EARS ARE MEDIUM LENGTH AND HANGING

SOFT, WAVY COAT

STURDY LEGS

PARENTS

MALTESE | SHIH TZU

POM-CHI : UNITED STATES

The Pom-Chi—a Pomeranian and Chihuahua cross—was developed in the United States as a very small companion breed. Pom-Chis are affectionate and playful with their families, but can be wary of strangers and need to be consistently socialized from a young age. Given their size, they are suitable for apartment living, but still enjoy a walk and a play outside. They make good watchdogs but can also be prone to nuisance barking and do not like to be left alone.

LARGE, ERECT EARS

MODERATELY SHORT, SLIGHTLY POINTED MUZZLE

SMALL, DAINTY FEET

COAT VARIES FROM MEDIUM LONG TO SHORT AND FROM STRAIGHT TO WAVY

COMPACT BODY

PARENTS

POMERANIAN | CHIHUAHUA

AT A GLANCE

Size: very small

Exercise needed:

Grooming needed:

Aptitudes: companion

Height: 9–14 in.

Weight: 9–16 lb.

Average life expectancy:
13–15 yrs

AKC: not recognized

CHARACTER

Affection
🐾 🐾 🐾 🐾 🐾

Playfulness
🐾 🐾 🐾 🐾 🐾

Friendliness to dogs
🐾 🐾 🐾 🐾 🐾

Friendliness to strangers
🐾 🐾 🐾 🐾 🐾

Ease of training
🐾 🐾 🐾 🐾 🐾

SHIH-POO : UNITED STATES

The Shih-Poo is a cross between a Poodle and a Shih Tzu. The Shih-Poo is one of many Poodle crosses, bred in an attempt to combine the high intelligence and low-shed coat of the Poodle, with the desirable traits of another breed. The Shih-Poo may have the curly coat of a Poodle or the long, straight coat of a Shih Tzu. The size varies, too, depending on whether the Poodle parent is a toy or miniature breed. But this dog always has an alert expression, a sturdy body, and an affectionate and playful character. Shi-poos are a joy to train.

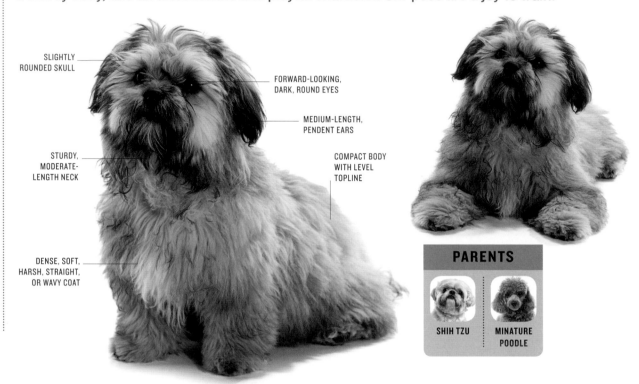

SLIGHTLY ROUNDED SKULL

FORWARD-LOOKING, DARK, ROUND EYES

MEDIUM-LENGTH, PENDENT EARS

STURDY, MODERATE-LENGTH NECK

COMPACT BODY WITH LEVEL TOPLINE

DENSE, SOFT, HARSH, STRAIGHT, OR WAVY COAT

PARENTS

SHIH TZU | MINATURE POODLE

AT A GLANCE

Size: medium-small

Exercise needed:

Grooming needed:

Aptitudes: companion, watchdog

Height: 10–18 in.

Weight: 25–45 lb.

Average life expectancy:
12–14 yrs

AKC: not recognized

CHARACTER

Affection
🐾 🐾 🐾 🐾 🐾

Playfulness
🐾 🐾 🐾 🐾 🐾

Friendliness to dogs
🐾 🐾 🐾 🐾 🐾

Friendliness to strangers
🐾 🐾 🐾 🐾 🐾

Ease of training
🐾 🐾 🐾 🐾 🐾

SIBORGI : UNITED STATES

The Siborgi, or Horgi as they are sometimes known, is one of the less common crosses and an unusual looking dog. They were developed by crossing the Corgi with the Siberian Husky and are normally short but solid dogs that have a high exercise requirement. The Siborgi can be difficult to obedience train and should be consistently socialized from a young age. They are very playful and affectionate with their family but can be wary of strangers and prone to barking and digging.

LONG, LOW-SET, BUSHY TAIL

ERECT, HIGH-SET EARS

LONG, LEVEL BACK

ALMOND-SHAPED EYES CAN BE TWO DIFFERENT COLORS

NARROW HEAD TAPERS TO MUZZLE

PARENTS

SIBERIAN HUSKY | CORGI

TACO TERRIER : UNITED STATES

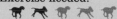

The Taco Terrier was developed primarily in the United States by crossing Chihuahuas with Toy Fox Terriers to produce a very small but sporty companion dog. Tacos combine the best of both parent breeds and are generally easy to train and obedient. These dogs can get along well with other dogs but do need to be carefully and consistently socialized from an early age. Tacos are normally outgoing, playful, and affectionate dogs that, given their small size, are suitable for apartment living. However, they do enjoy a good walk or play session outside and often retain terrier-like instincts for hunting and digging. The Taco is a good watchdog, but can also be prone to barking if left alone for long periods.

HIGH-SET, ERECT EARS

NARROW HEAD TAPERS TO MUZZLE

STURDY MUSCULAR BODY

FORELEGS HAVE STRONG BONE AND SMALL, CLEAN JOINTS

UNDERLINE HAS MODERATE TUCK-UP

PARENTS

CHIHUAHUA | TOY FOX TERRIER

YORKI-POO : UNITED STATES

Originating in the United States, the Yorkie-Poo—a Yorkshire Terrier and Toy Poodle cross—was created to be a trainable lapdog. Although Yorki-poos are active and energetic, they don't need a lot of exercise. These perky little characters make good watchdogs and will bark to alert their families when a stranger is near. They are eager to please and relatively trainable for a terrier type. Above all, Yorkie-Poos are affectionate and love to be with people; they are not happy being left alone for extended periods of time.

BODY IS ATHLETIC AND SLIGHTLY LONGER THAN ITS HEIGHT

EARS VARY AND CAN BE BUTTON, PENDENT, OR SEMI-PRICKED

LARGE, BRIGHT EYES

MUZZLE IS STRONG AND SLIGHTLY TAPERED

COAT VARIES IN TEXTURE BETWEEN SOFT AND WAVY TO LOOSELY OR TIGHTLY CURLED

PARENTS

YORKSHIRE TERRIER | MINATURE POODLE

No dog book would be complete without paying homage to the mutt—the dog of uncertain heritage that dominates many cultures. Mutts come in all shapes and sizes, but by looking at them, breeders and other dog experts are able to guess at their origins. The dogs on the following pages represent common mutts, and each section includes the various breeds "in the mix" that contribute to the dogs' temperament, intelligence, and so on. There are also photos to show the original breed characteristics (the large paws of a Golden Retriever, for example, or the wiry coat of a Border Collie) that show up in the mutt's appearance.

Mutts are unpretentious dogs, not concerned about dog shows or breed registration. They're also less likely than purebred animals to be susceptible to genetic disorders and hereditary health problems. As a result, many people consider the humble mutt to be the uncrowned king of the dog world.

MUTTS

IN THE MIX

Lakeland Terrier

Soft-Coated Wheaten Terrier

Wire Fox Terrier

Airedale Terrier

SOFT-COATED TERRIER MIX

This dog is a mix of terriers, which accounts for his forward-folded ears, tousled coat, and slightly curved tail. The color of his coat suggests that his ancestry includes some Soft-Coated Wheaten Terrier. He has a rectangular, powerful muzzle and a broad nose, a look that is particular to terriers. The other terriers in this dog's background provide his long legs and fuzzy face. This endearing character will have the curious and alert nature that is typical of terrier breeds; he will also have a strong small-prey drive and a tendency to dig.

THE EARS ARE FOLDED DOWN AND V-SHAPED, SET HIGH AND WIDE ON THE HEAD

A BROAD NOSE, AT THE END OF A LONG, RECTANGULAR MUZZLE

TAIL IS THICK AND SHORT LIKE A SOFT-COATED WHEATEN'S. IT'S ALSO SET HIGH ON THE BACK AND CURVED LIKE A LAKELAND TERRIER

THE YELLOW-GOLD COLOR AND SOFT COAT COME FROM THE SOFT-COATED WHEATEN

PAWS AND LEGS

THE ROUND, COMPACT FEET COME FROM THE WIRE FOX TERRIER, AND THE STRAIGHT FRONT LEGS ARE A GENERAL TERRIER TRAIT

COAT

WELSH/MANCHESTER TERRIER MIX

IN THE MIX

Welsh Terrier

Manchester Terrier

Wire Fox Terrier

Airedale Terrier

This is another dog of terrier descent. She shares some of the classic traits exhibited by most terriers: the squarish muzzle with a beard underneath, the wiry coat, the strong back and chest, and a short but not stubby tail. This terrier is young, but already showing signs that she will grow into a solid frame. Her head narrows slightly toward the muzzle, and her coat is wiry and thick. Her background of Manchester Terrier tends toward a sleek and slender frame, but the composition of her coat and color come from a mix of many other dogs. She will need consistent obedience training to curb her instincts to dig and hunt.

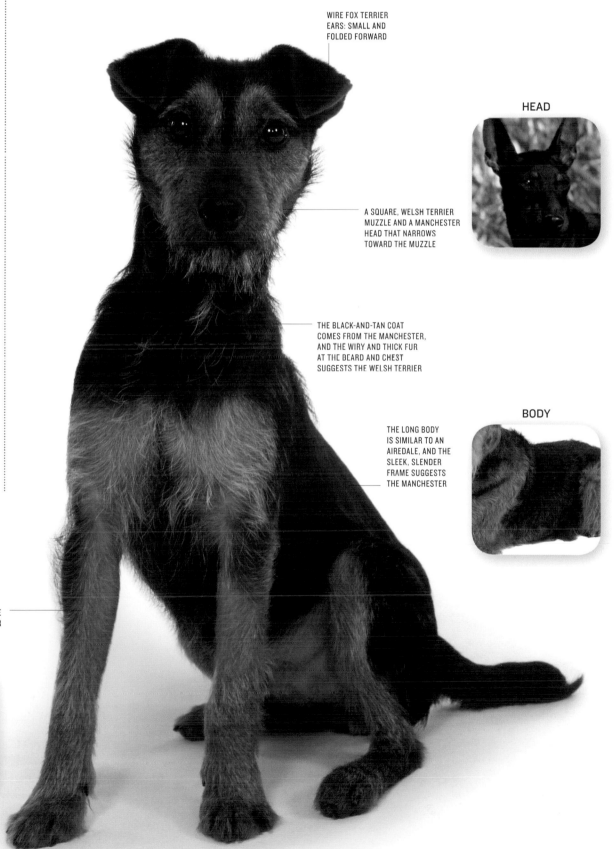

WIRE FOX TERRIER
EARS: SMALL AND
FOLDED FORWARD

HEAD

A SQUARE, WELSH TERRIER
MUZZLE AND A MANCHESTER
HEAD THAT NARROWS
TOWARD THE MUZZLE

THE BLACK-AND-TAN COAT
COMES FROM THE MANCHESTER,
AND THE WIRY AND THICK FUR
AT THE BEARD AND CHEST
SUGGESTS THE WELSH TERRIER

BODY

THE LONG BODY
IS SIMILAR TO AN
AIREDALE, AND THE
SLEEK, SLENDER
FRAME SUGGESTS
THE MANCHESTER

THE HEIGHT OF AN AIREDALE, WITH THE
LONG, STRAIGHT LEGS OF A MANCHESTER

PAWS AND LEGS

IN THE MIX

Beauceron

Malamute/Finnish Lapphund

Australian Shepherd

Irish Terrier

BEAUCERON/NORDIC MIX

Coming from a mixture of several herding breeds, this dog is large, powerfully built, and alert. His ancestry is scattered far and wide, with a background of Australian, Finnish, and Irish dogs. His tail is reminiscent of many Nordic breeds, well-furred and held in a curl. His coat, however, takes its length from the Australian Shepherd and its color from the black-and-tan Beauceron. This dog was built for herding sheep. He has powerful, well-muscled legs and large, rounded paws, as well as a broad chest and generally sturdy frame. This mutt would make a loyal and protective companion for an active family.

EARS

FOLDED OVER THE TOP OF THE SKULL, SET HIGH ON THE HEAD

WELL-FURRED AND CURLED LIKE THE TAILS OF MANY NORDIC DOGS, BUT LONG AND THICK LIKE A BEAUCERON

THE SAME POWERFUL BUILD AND BROAD CHEST AS THE BEAUCERON AND THE NORTHERN BREEDS

PAWS AND LEGS

THE MALAMUTE AND THE BEAUCERON SHARE THE LARGE, ROUNDED PAWS AND WELL-MUSCLED LEGS

THE BLACK-AND-TAN BEAUCERON COAT, WITH THE MEDIUM LENGTH OF THE AUSTRALIAN SHEPHERD AND THE THICKER SIDES OF THE LAPPHUND

COAT

IN THE MIX

Collie

Malinois

Golden Retriever

Whippet

COLLIE/RETRIEVER MIX

This dog has a little of everything. Her background includes the Collie, Malinois, and Golden Retriever. The tucked-up stomach also suggests some Whippet in her heritage, and her elongated neck and long, slender legs may mean that she has some sighthound blood in her genes. Overall, though, she seems to take most of her physical characteristics from the Collie and the Malinois: the Collie's tail, muscular thighs and padded feet; and the Malinois' powerful jaws, long body, and strong and straight forelegs. Her coat is weather-resistant, and needs little grooming to maintain its appearance.

THE POWERFUL JAWS SUGGEST THE MALINOIS, WHEREAS THE SLIGHTLY NARROWED MUZZLE COMES FROM THE COLLIE

THE SEMI-PRICKED EARS RESEMBLE THOSE OF A COLLIE

EARS

THE DARK EYES HAVE AN INTELLIGENT EXPRESSION

THE RICH FAWN-TO-MAHOGANY COLOR AND WHITE CHEST COME FROM THE MALINOIS, THOUGH THE THICK AND WAVY COAT ITSELF IS CLEARLY GOLDEN RETRIEVER

PAWS AND LEGS

THE STRONG, STRAIGHT FORELEGS AND CAT-LIKE FEET SUGGEST THE GOLDEN RETRIEVER

THE TUCKED-UP UNDERLINE IS A TRAIT OF THE WHIPPET, AND THE LONG BODY AND POWERFUL CHEST COME FROM THE MALINOIS

BODY

THE TAIL INDICATES A COMBINATION OF COLLIE AND RETRIEVER WITH ITS THICK BASE, SLIGHT CURVE, AND HEAVY FEATHERING

IN THE MIX

Bearded Collie

Petit Basset Griffon Vendeen

Border Collie

BEARDED COLLIE/PETIT BASSET GRIFFON VENDEEN MIX

This scruffy looking dog is most directly related to the Bearded Collie, but also shares some genes with the Petit Basset Griffon Vendeen and the Border Collie. Her long, wiry coat with a thick, insulating undercoat is typical of the Bearded Collie, though the black-and-white pattern is closer to the color of a Border Collie. The large feet, rounded rib cage, and ears set far back on the head are all suggestive of the Petit Basset Griffon Vendeen (or PBGV, as it is also commonly known). She will be an intelligent and biddable companion, but will need a great deal of physical and mental exercise to keep her healthy and happy.

EARS

ANOTHER FEATURE SHARED BY BOTH THE PBGV AND THE BORDER COLLIE, EARS ARE SET FAR BACK ON THE HEAD AND HANG DOWN

THE SKULL AND MUZZLE, BROAD AND SQUARE, BOTH SUGGEST A BEARDED COLLIE AND A PBGV

BODY

A LITTLE LONGER THAN IT IS TALL, MEDIUM-SIZE, WITH A ROUNDED RIB CAGE. SUGGESTIVE OF BOTH THE PBGV AND THE BORDER COLLIE

PAWS AND LEGS

COAT

THE BEARDED COLLIE AND PBGV PROVIDE A LONG, WIRY COAT, AND THE BORDER COLLIE PROVIDES THE BLACK AND WHITE COLOR

THE BORDER COLLIE IS VISIBLE IN THE SHORTER HAIR ON THE LEGS AND PAWS, WHILE THE PBGV PROVIDES THE DOG'S LARGE FEET

IN THE MIX

Akita

Golden Retriever

Norwegian Buhund

Tervuren

AKITA/RETRIEVER MIX

This dog is an example of a more elegant style of mutt, with a lush, golden-red coat, a beautiful head, and bright eyes. She is a mix of Akita, Golden Retriever, and Norwegian Buhund, with just a hint of Tevuren. Her Akita blood shows itself in her long, broad, level back; her pricked ears set wide and well-furred at the base; and her overall strong body. She gets her furry, low-held tail and her long, straight, golden coat from the Golden Retriever. The Tervuren and Norwegian Buhund show up mostly in the coloring and length of her coat. This highly intelligent mutt would make a good companion for an active family.

EARS

BRIGHT, ROUND EYES, WITH A POINTED MUZZLE AND A LONG, ELEGANT HEAD

WELL-FURRED, WIDE-SET, PRICKED EARS

THE TERVUREN AND THE GOLDEN RETRIEVER BOTH HOLD THEIR FURRY TAILS LOW, WITH A GENTLE CURVE

THE TERVUREN PROVIDES THE FEATHERING ON THE TAIL, NECK, AND CHEST. WHEREAS THE COAT IS LARGELY SUGGESTIVE OF THE GOLDEN RETRIEVER, LONG AND GOLD, THE BUHUND GIVES THE COLOR A DEEPER RED

COAT

THE STRONG BODY OF AN AKITA OR RETRIEVER, WITH A LONG, BROAD, LEVEL BACK

BODY

IN THE MIX

German Shepherd

Rottweiler

Malamute

Tervuren

SHEPHERD/ROTTWEILER MIX

This dog is a classic example of a working breed, descended from dogs built for physical labor. Her head shape reflects a cross of Rottweiler and German Shepherd, whereas her color and build are that of a German Shepherd. The density of her coat also makes it likely that there's some Alaskan Malamute in the mix. She shares most of her traits with the German Shepherd and the Rottweiler, namely in her strong, broad body; black-and-tan coloring; and large, folded ears, which are a cross between the two. This formidable mutt will need consistent obedience training and will have powerful guard-dog instincts.

A SLIGHTLY ROUNDED CROWN AND LARGE MUZZLE HINT AT MALAMUTE BLOOD

EARS

WIDE-SET, LARGE, V-SHAPED EARS THAT FOLD FORWARD, A CROSS BETWEEN THE GERMAN SHEPHERD'S PRICK EARS AND THE ROTTWEILER'S DROP EARS

BODY

THE LONG BODY AND STRAIGHT BACK OF A GERMAN SHEPHERD, AND THE BROAD, DEEP CHEST OF A ROTTWEILER

A COMBINATION OF THE TERVUREN AND MALAMUTE CREATE A LONG, THICK COAT, AND THE PATTERN AND COLORING COMES FROM THE BLACK-AND-TAN GERMAN SHEPHERD

COAT

PAWS AND LEGS

THE LARGE, COMPACT FEET SUGGEST THE MALAMUTE, AND THE STRONG, STRAIGHT, PARALLEL LEGS BELONG TO THE TERVUREN AND MALAMUTE

IN THE MIX

Whippet

Ibizan Hound

Manchester Terrier

WHIPPET/IBIZAN MIX

This dog is of sight-hound descent, with heritage consisting largely of Whippet and Ibizan Hound. There is also a possibility that the Manchester Terrier appears in this dog's history, particularly in his slightly arched neck and straight, muscular front legs. His low chest and concave stomach are characteristic of the Whippet, while the large, pointed ears suggest the Ibizan Hound. His coat is short and stiff, also a trait of the Ibizan hound, but lies smoothly against the body in the style of the Whippet. This attractive mutt will be an energetic dog with a strong small-prey drive.

EARS

THE EARS ARE LIKE THOSE OF AN IBIZAN HOUND, LARGE AND POINTED, GIVING THE DOG AN ALERT APPEARANCE

THE LONG, SMOOTH MUZZLE WITH A SLIGHT ROMAN PROFILE SUGGESTS AN IBIZAN, WITH THE LARGE, DARK EYES OF A WHIPPET. THE HEAD IS SLENDER, IN THE STYLE OF ALL SIGHTHOUNDS

PAWS AND LEGS

THE STRAIGHT FORELEGS, MUSCULAR THIGHS, AND POWERFUL HINDQUARTERS REFLECT THE WHIPPET, MANCHESTER, AND IBIZAN.

THE WHIPPET'S DEEP CHEST, RAISED STOMACH, AND GRACEFULLY ARCHED BACK

SHORT AND STIFF LIKE AN IBIZAN'S COAT, SMOOTH AND SLEEK LIKE A WHIPPET. THE COLOR AND PATTERN ARE THE DOG'S OWN, THANKS TO ITS MIXED HERITAGE

COAT

Greyhound

Ibizan Hound

Whippet

GREYHOUND/IBIZAN MIX

While clearly descended from Greyhounds, this dog's build is made stronger and stockier by adding Ibizan Hound to the gene pool. Her long, level back; chestnut-and-white coat; and long, tapering tail are all signs of Ibizan Hound blood. The Greyhound is still the most prominent, though, noticeable in the deep chest, tucked-up underline, and classic Greyhound muzzle. However, this dog is smaller in stature than either the Greyhound or Ibizan Hound, which may indicate the presence of some Whippet blood. Either way, this elegant mutt will have a strong small-prey drive.

BODY

THE TUCKED-UP STOMACH AND DEEP CHEST ARE CLASSICALLY GREYHOUND, AND THE LONG, LEVEL BACK IS LIKELY OF IBIZAN STOCK

THIS DOG'S HEAD CLEARLY INDICATES ITS SIGHTHOUND HERITAGE, PARTICULARLY IN THE PIERCING, INTELLIGENT EXPRESSION

THE SHORT, SMOOTH COAT OF A HOUND

COAT

LONG, TAPERING, AND SLIGHTLY CURVED TAIL, HELD LOW TO THE GROUND

PAWS AND LEGS

THE TOES ARE LONG AND WELL ARCHED REFLECTING THE GREYHOUND, WHIPPET, AND IBIZAN HERITAGE

IN THE MIX

Scottish Deerhound

Labrador Retriever

Irish Wolfhound

German Shorthaired
Pointer

DEERHOUND/LAB RETRIEVER MIX

This wirehaired dog shares traits with the Scottish Deerhound and the Labrador Retriever. To a lesser extent, he also inherited some genes from the Irish Wolfhound and German Shorthaired Pointer. He has a wiry, tousled, blue-gray coat, which comes directly from his hound roots. The strong jaws and bearded muzzle are traits of the Deerhound and Lab, respectively, and his angular head comes from the German Shorthaired Pointer. This is a large dog, with a powerful build that he inherits from his hound ancestry, but he will likely have a loving and gentle nature.

A GERMAN POINTER'S ANGULAR
HEAD, A SCOTTISH DEERHOUND'S
BEARDED MUZZLE, AND A
LABRADOR'S STRONG JAWS

BODY

A LAB'S THICK, TAPERING TAIL,
BUT WELL-FURRED LIKE A
DEERHOUND'S

THE STANCE OF A DEERHOUND, WITH
THE BROAD, DEEP CHEST OF THE
GERMAN POINTER

PAWS AND LEGS

LONG, POWERFUL LEGS,
TYPICAL OF DEERHOUNDS
AND WOLFHOUNDS

THE BLUE-GRAY, WIRY,
TOUSLED COAT IS A
COMMON CHARACTERISTIC
AMONG HOUNDS

COAT

BORDER COLLIE/WHIPPET MIX

This dog gets most of her traits from the Border Collie, seen in the shape of her head, which is relatively flat between her ears; her tapering muzzle; and black-and-white coat. She also has a few characteristics of Whippets and Collies mixed in, such as her wide-spaced ears, slender forelegs, and narrow body. This dog has a bright eyed, energetic look, and her hunting and herding background gives her a lot of energy. This endearing mutt will make a loyal companion for an active family.

IN THE MIX

Border Collie

Whippet

Collie

HEAD

THE HEAD IS ENTIRELY BORDER COLLIE:
A MEDIUM-LENGTH, TAPERING MUZZLE,
RELATIVELY FLAT SKULL, AND BRIGHT,
INTENSE EYES

THE COLLIE PROVIDES SEMI-PRICKED
EARS, BUT THEY ARE SPACED FAR
APART LIKE A WHIPPET'S

THE SLENDER FRAME IS
MOST LIKE A WHIPPET

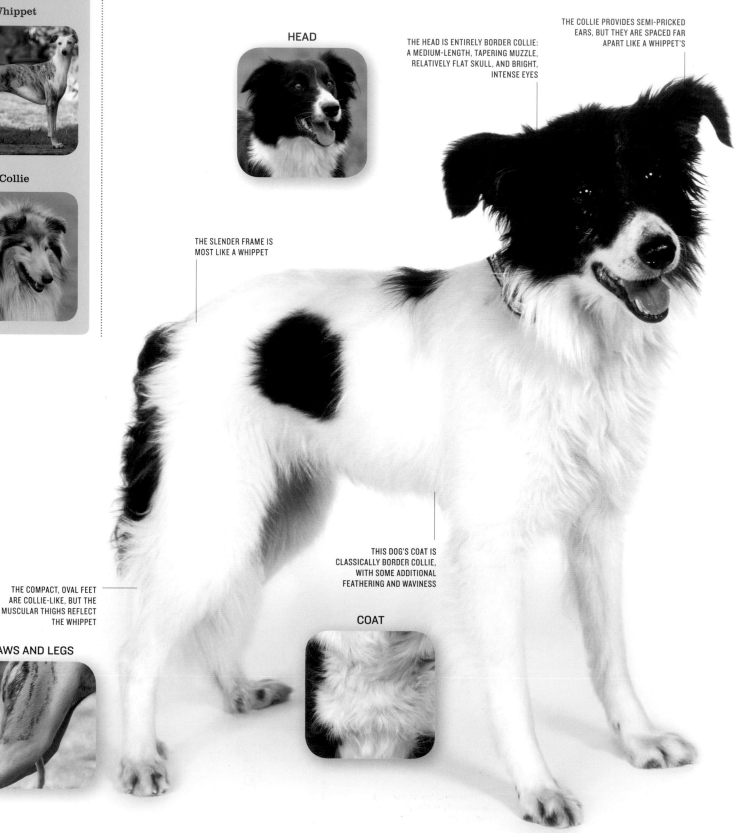

THIS DOG'S COAT IS
CLASSICALLY BORDER COLLIE,
WITH SOME ADDITIONAL
FEATHERING AND WAVINESS

COAT

THE COMPACT, OVAL FEET
ARE COLLIE-LIKE, BUT THE
MUSCULAR THIGHS REFLECT
THE WHIPPET

PAWS AND LEGS

IN THE MIX

Scottish Deerhound

Greyhound

Borzoi

Saluki

DEERHOUND/GREYHOUND MIX

This dog's long, wiry coat; strong frame; and tapering muzzle all indicate the Scottish Deerhound in his heritage. The increased size and bone structure also suggest this background. He has a lot of Greyhound in his blood, too, most notably in his deep chest and high stomach. The Borzoi and Saluki make a few appearances in his paws, nose, and coat. This dog is built for sprinting, thanks to his Greyhound background, and his deep chest provides good lung capacity for running.

EARS

THE SMALL EARS, FOLDED BACK AT REST AND SEMI-PRICKED AT ATTENTION, ARE GREYHOUND AND DEERHOUND TRAITS. THE DARKER COLOR IS A BORZOI CHARACTERISTIC

THE LARGE NOSE, TAPERING MUZZLE, AND STRONG JAWS REFLECT THE BORZOI AND DEERHOUND INFLUENCE

THE TUCKED-UP UNDERLINE AND DEEP CHEST COMES FROM THE GREYHOUND AND BORZOI, THE WIDE HIPBONES FROM THE SALUKI, AND THE LARGE BONE STRUCTURE SUGGESTS THE DEERHOUND. THIS DOG IS SHAPED LIKE MOST SIGHTHOUNDS

THE COAT IS SOFTER THAN THE DEERHOUND'S NORMALLY HARSH, WIRY FUR, THANKS TO THE DOG'S SALUKI HERITAGE. THE SALUKI AND BORZOI CONTRIBUTE EXTRA FEATHERING ON THE LEGS, SHOULDERS, AND EARS

COAT

PAWS AND LEGS

THE LONG, WELL-ARCHED, STRONG TOES ARE TYPICAL OF SIGHT-HOUND BREEDS LIKE THE BORZOI, DEERHOUND, AND SALUKI

IN THE MIX

Corgi

Brittany

Dachshund

SPANIEL/DACHSHUND MIX

This mix of Corgi, Brittany, and Daschund has a fluffy, red-brown and white coat that is relatively straight and long, with feathering on his legs and tail. The shape of this dog's body could come from either a Corgi or a Daschund—as could the low-carried, long-haired tail. The color, pattern, and downward-folded ears all come from his Brittany genes. Because of a background of spaniels and herding dogs, this dog has the potential to be extremely energetic, and would make a loyal companion and good watchdog.

BODY

THE TAPERING MUZZLE SUGGESTS A DACHSHUND, WHEREAS THE SMALL HEAD WITH A BROAD FOREHEAD COMES FROM A CORGI

BRITTANY EARS, FOLDED DOWN AND SET HIGH ON THE HEAD

BOTH THE DACHSHUND AND THE CORGI SHOW THE LONG BODY, SHORT LEGS, AND SLIGHTLY ARCHED LOINS THAT THIS DOG EXHIBITS

TAIL

LONG-HAIRED TAIL IS CARRIED LOW LIKE A CORGI'S OR BRITTANY'S

COAT

CHESTNUT WITH WHITE PATCHES, MEDIUM LENGTH WITH SLIGHT FEATHERING

IN THE MIX

Pomeranian

Chihuahua

Swedish Lapphund

Pug

POMERANIAN/CHIHUAHUA MIX

This small dog takes her traits from all the classic toy breeds: the Pomeranian, Chihuahua, Swedish Lapphund, and Pug. The dog gets her coat—fluffier than a Chihuahua but shorter than a Pomeranian and Lapphund—from this mix of dogs. The Pomeranian and Chihuahua are most clearly visible, especially the Chihuahua's small head and pointed ears. The compact, square body and broad chest suggest the Pug, providing a sturdier frame for this dog than that of the Chihuahua or Lapphund. This little mutt is bound to have a strong, playful character and plenty of energy.

THE DOG HAS A SMALL, DOMED HEAD, ANOTHER FEATURE THAT IS DIRECTLY INHERITED FROM THE CHIHUAHUA, BUT A POINTED POMERANIAN OR LAPPHUND MUZZLE

THE POINTED AND ERECT EARS RESEMBLE A POMERANIAN OR LAPPHUND, BUT ARE DISTINCTLY CHIHUAHUA IN THEIR SIZE

TAIL

A TIGHTLY CURVED TAIL LIKE A PUG'S, ALSO SIMILAR TO THE POMERANIAN OR LAPPHUND

BLACK LIKE A LAPPHUND OR PUG, WITH SHORT, SMOOTH FUR THAT IS A MIDDLE GROUND BETWEEN BOTH THE SHORT- AND LONG-HAIRED DOGS IN ITS GENE POOL

COAT

THE LEVEL BACK SUGGESTS A CHIHUAHUA, BUT THE COMPACT FRAME AND BROAD CHEST BELONGS TO A PUG

BODY

IN THE MIX

Pointer

Great Dane

English Setter

POINTER/GREAT DANE MIX

Although this dog clearly has some Pointer blood, he also shares several traits with the Great Dane. He has the long, straight forelegs and short, sleek coat of the Pointer, and is as long as he is tall, which is a trait the Pointer and Great Dane share. His ears and the shape of his head are more Dane-like than Pointer, however, and his possible English Setter genes present themselves in his coat and paws. This handsome mutt will need lots of exercise.

EARS

A GREAT DANE'S EARS: LARGE, FOLDED OVER, AND SET HIGH AND BACK ON THE HEAD

THE POINTER AND GREAT DANE BOTH CONTRIBUTE TO THIS DOG'S RECTANGULAR MUZZLE AND BROAD HEAD

HEAD

THE BLACK-AND-WHITE COLORING LIKELY COMES FROM A GREAT DANE, AND THE SHORT, SLEEK COAT IS A POINTER TRAIT. THE ENGLISH SETTER ADDS A LITTLE LENGTH TO THE COAT

COAT

BODY

ANOTHER TRAIT SHARED BY THE POINTER AND GREAT DANE, THIS DOG IS AS TALL AS IT IS LONG

THE TIGHT, STRONG FEET AND SPECKLED LEGS BELONG TO THE ENGLISH SETTER, BUT THE LONG, STRAIGHT FRONT LEGS SUGGEST POINTER

IN THE MIX

Golden Retriever

Collie

German Shepherd

Chesapeake Bay Retriever

RETRIEVER/SHEPHERD MIX

At first glance, this dog appears to be largely Golden Retriever. And even though that ancestry does have a significant hand in his appearance, his herding-dog heritage is also apparent, especially in the shape of his head, which is slightly Collie-like, and his muzzle, which hints at German Shepherd. This attractive dog has the body shape of the Chesapeake Bay Retriever, without sharing that breed's distinctive coat. The coat is clearly that of the Golden Retriever. This dog is likely to be highly intelligent and biddable, but will need plenty of physical and mental exercise.

HEAD

THE GERMAN SHEPHERD IN THIS DOG'S BACKGROUND PROVIDES A STRONG, TAPERING MUZZLE AND A LARGE, WEDGE-SHAPED HEAD

BODY

EARS ARE FOLDED AT THE TIPS IN THE MANNER OF A COLLIE, BUT TRIANGULAR AND HIGH ON THE HEAD LIKE A GERMAN SHEPHERD

A RETRIEVER'S CLASSICALLY LONG, STRONG BACK, SLIGHTLY ROUNDED AT THE REAR

THE WAVY, GOLDEN COAT OF A RETRIEVER, WITH HEAVY FEATHERING AROUND THE STOMACH AND TAIL

PAWS AND LEGS

THE DOG'S RETRIEVER BLOOD SHOWS ITSELF IN ITS STRONG LIMBS AND LARGE PAWS

GLOSSARY

A

Abdomen The underside between the chest and the hindquarters.

Agility trials An organized competition at which dogs negotiate a series of obstacles and jumps in classes of increasing difficulty.

Agouti A color used to describe Siberian Huskies, with alternating bands of light and dark along each hair in the coat.

AKC (American Kennel Club) A registry of purebred dog pedigrees in the United States, which promotes and sanctions major dog shows, including the Westminster Kennel Club Dog Show.

Albinism A relatively rare, genetically recessive condition resulting in white hair and pink eyes.

Ankle See *hock.*

Ankylosis Abnormal immobility and fusion of a joint, which is noted as a cause of faulty tails in the German Shepherd standard.

Apple head A round-shaped skull.

Apricot A dull, medium-saturated orange, that is primarily used to describe Afghans, Pugs, Mastiffs, and Poodles.

Apron Longer hair below the neck on the chest; also called the frill.

Arm The area of a dog's body between the shoulder and the elbow. Sometimes called the *upper arm.*

Assistance dog A dog trained to aid a person with a disability.

B

Back The area of a dog's body extending from the withers to the croup.

Badger A grayish-brown color that may be mixed with a few dark hairs, primarily used to describe Great Pyrenees and Sealyham Terriers.

Bandy legs Legs that bend outward.

Barrel A rib area that is round in cross section.

Barrel hocks Hocks that turn out, causing the feet to turn in. Also called *spread hocks.*

Bat ear An erect ear with a broad base, rounded at the top, with the opening facing forward.

Bay The prolonged bark or "voice" of a hunting hound.

Beard Long, thick hair on the lower jaw.

Belly The underside of the abdomen.

Bird dog A sporting dog bred to hunt game birds.

Biscuit A combination of light gray, yellow, and brown primarily used to describe Pekingese and Samoyeds.

Bitch A female dog.

Bite The relative position of the upper and lower teeth when the mouth is closed. Bite positions include level, scissors, undershot, or overshot, depending on the breed.

Blaze A white stripe running up the center of the face, usually between the eyes.

Blenheim Red-and-white parti-color used to describe the Cavalier King Charles Spaniel.

Blue A blue-gray color primarily used to describe the Kerry Blue Terrier.

Blue merle A color pattern of black blotches or streaks on a blue-gray background primarily associated with Border Collies and Australian Shepherds.

Bobtail A dog born without a tail, or a dog with a tail docked very short. Often used as a name for the Old English Sheepdog.

Body length Distance from the front of the breastbone to the posterior.

Bone Informally used to describe the strength and thickness of limbs in proportion to the overall size of the dog.

Breastbone The sternum.

Breed A domestic race of dogs (selected by humans) with a common gene pool, function, and characteristic appearance.

Breeder A person who breeds dogs.

Breed standard A detailed written document from a specific breed club describing how the perfect dog of a breed should look, move, and behave.

Brindle A layering of black hairs in regions of lighter color (usually, fawn, brown, or gray) producing a tiger-striped pattern, used to describe a wide range of breeds, including Great Danes, American Bulldogs, and Boxers.

Broken-haired A rough, wiry coat.

Brows The ridges formed above the eyes by frontal bones.

Brush A bushy tail, heavy with hair.

Bullbaiting An ancient blood sport in which dogs were trained to attack a bull.

Bull neck A heavy, muscular neck.

Button ear A small, neat ear with the flap folding forward to cover the opening.

C

Cafe au lait A pale-coffee color primarily used to describe Poodles.

Candle-flame ears An erect ear that curves slightly inward at the base with a slight pinch on the outer edge to resemble the shape of a candle flame, characteristic of the English Toy Terrier.

Canid A family (Canidae) of carnivorous animals including dogs, wolves, coyotes, foxes, and jackals.

Canines All dog-like species belonging to the Canidae family of mammals. Also refers to the two upper and two lower large, pointed teeth toward the front of the jaws.

Cap Dark color pattern on the skull of some breeds.

Cape Long, thick hair covering the shoulders.

Cat foot A neat, round foot, with well-arched toes set closely together.

Chest The part of the body or trunk that is enclosed by the ribs.

Chestnut Rich, reddish-brown color primarily used to describe Irish Setters and Pharaoh Hounds.

Chiseled Clean-cut features in the head, as opposed to bumpy or bulging lines.

Cinnamon Yellowish-brown color, primarily used to describe Chow Chows.

Clip The method of trimming the coat in certain breeds.

Close-coupled Of the dog's body, indicates a relatively short distance between the last rib and the hindquarters.

Coat The dog's hair. Most breeds have two coats: a topcoat and an undercoat.

Cobby Compact, with a short body.

Collar Markings around the dog's neck, usually white. Also, a neck band to which a dog's leash is attached.

Companion dog A dog used to provide companionship for humans.

Conformation The form, structure, and shape of an individual dog in conformance with its breed standard.

Copper A bright, brownish red, primarily used to describe Siberian Huskies.

Coupling The part of the body between the ribs and the hindquarters; the loin.

Coursing The blood sport where small, fast prey animals are pursued by sighthounds.

Cow-hocked Hocks turning in, causing the rear feet to turn out.

Crank tail A tail carried down and resembling a crank in shape.

Cream Light to medium yellow or yellowish-white color, which varies depending on the breed.

Crest The upper, arched portion of a dog's neck.

Cropping The controversial practice of cutting or trimming a dog's ear leather to encourage the ear to stand erect.

Crossbreed A dog whose parents are two different breeds.

Croup The region of the pelvic girdle formed by the sacrum and surrounding tissue.

Crown The top part of the head.

Cry The baying or "music" of the hounds.

Culotte The longer hair on the back of the thighs.

Cur A dog of mixed breed; a mongrel.

Cynology The scientific study of canines.

D

Dam The female parent.

Dapple A mottled or variegated coat color pattern.

Deadgrass A dull straw color primarily used to describe Chesapeake Bay Retrievers.

Dentition The dog's forty-two adult teeth.

Depth of chest An indication of the volume of space for the heart and lungs. A deep chest extends below the dog's elbow.

Dewclaw A functionless extra claw on the inside of a dog's leg.

Dewlap Loose, pendulous skin under the throat and neck.

Dish-faced A slight concaveness of face when viewed in profile.

Docking The controversial practice of removing a portion of a dog's tail.

Domed Evenly curved topskull.

Double coat A weather-resistant, protective topcoat together with an undercoat of softer hair for warmth and waterproofing.

Drop ear An ear in which the leather folds over; not erect or pricked.

E

Elbow The joint between the arm and forearm.

Entropion A complex genetic condition that causes the upper or lower eyelid to turn in, often resulting in corneal ulceration.

Even bite See *level bite*.

Ewe neck A neck in which the topline is concave rather than convex.

F

Fawn A brown, red-yellow with hue of medium brilliance associated with a wide range of breeds.

FCI (Federation Cynologique Internationale) An international federation of kennel clubs based in Belgium, which licenses international shows in its 72 member countries, including the famous annual World Show.

Feathering Long fringes of hair on the ears, legs, tail, and body.

Flank The side of the dog's body between the last rib and the hip.

Flush To drive birds from cover; to spring.

Forearm The portion of the forelimb between the arm and the wrist.

Forequarters The frontal area of the dog's body from the shoulder blades down to the feet.

Foundation stock The first generation of a particular breed.

Foxy Sharp expression; pointed nose with short foreface.

Frill See *apron*.

Fringes See *feathering*.

Frontal bones The anterior bones of the cranium forming the forehead.

FSS (Foundation Stock Service) A breed registry of the American Kennel Club in which breeders can record the parentage of a breed they are working to establish in the United States. These dogs provide the *foundation stock* from which an AKC fully recognized breed might result if sufficient numbers of individual dogs are registered.

Furnishings The long hair on the extremities (including the head and tail) of certain breeds.

Furrow A slight indentation down the center of the skull to the stop.

G

Gait Any of the various foot movements of a dog, such as a trot, canter, or gallop.

Game Hunted wild birds or animals.

Gaskin The lower or second thigh.

Grizzle A mixture of black or red hairs with white hairs. Frequently, a bluish-gray or iron-gray color primarily associated with some terrier breeds.

Groom To brush, comb, trim, or otherwise tidy a dog's coat.

Groups The divisions used to facilitate judging, which varies from one kennel club to another. The seven AKC groups are sporting, hound, working, toy, terrier, non-sporting, and herding.

Gun dog A dog trained by a hunter to find or pursue game.

H

Harlequin Patched or pied coloration, usually black or gray on white, primarily used to describe Great Danes.

Height Vertical measurement from the withers to the ground; also called *shoulder height*.

Herding group Group of dogs bred to help shepherds and ranchers work livestock.

Hindquarters The rear area of the dog, including the pelvis, thighs, hocks, and paws.

Hip dysplasia Abnormal formation of the hip joint.

Hock The bones of the hind leg that form the joint between the second thigh and the metatarsus; the dog's true heel.

Hound group Group of dogs used for hunting game by scent or sight.

I

Incisors The six upper and six lower front teeth between the canines. The point of contact forms the *bite*.

Interbreeding The breeding together of dogs of different breeds.

J

Jowls Flesh of the lips and jaws.

K

Knee See *stifle*.

L

Leather The flap of the ear.

Lemon Used to describe pointers, this color is a brilliant, medium-saturated yellow. Color definitions may vary by breed. Always check the breed standard for the definitive color description.

Level bite When the front teeth (incisors) of the upper and lower jaws meet exactly edge to edge. Also called *pincer bite* or *even bite*.

Litter The puppy or puppies of one whelping.

Liver A deep reddish-brown color, from light to very dark, used for a wide range of breeds.

Loin The lumbar region of the lower back and sides of the dog's body.

Lure coursing Organized events for sight hounds, in which the hounds chase an artificial lure over a course.

Luxation Dislocation of a bone from a joint.

M

Mahogany A dull reddish-brown used to describe several breeds.

Mandible The lower jawbone.

Mane Long, thick hair on the top and sides of the neck.

Mantle Dark-shaded portion of the dog's coat on the shoulders, back, and sides.

Markings Contrasting color or pattern in a dog's coat.

Mask Dark shading on the dog's face.

Merle A marking pattern characterized by a marbling effect of dark patches against a lighter background of the same color, primarily used to describe Shetland Sheepdogs, Collies, Great Danes, and Australian Shepherds.

Molars The posterior teeth used to grind food, with two on each side in the upper jaw and three on each side in the lower jaw of an adult dog.

Mongrel See *crossbreed*.

Mottled Pattern of dark roundish blotches on a lighter background, used to describe several breeds, including the Peruvian Inca Orchid.

Mustard A dull brown-yellow color, primarily used to describe Dandie Dinmont Terriers.

Muzzle The front region of the head, including the nasal bone, nostrils, and jaws; foreface. Also, a strap or wire cage attached to the foreface, generally employed to prevent a dog from biting.

Muzzle band White marking around the dog's muzzle.

N

Non-sporting group AKC division containing a "group of dogs that may share attributes, but don't fit into the mold of other groups."

Nose The dog's olfactory organ. Also describes the ability to detect by means of scent: a hot-nosed hound follows a fresh trail at speed, whereas a cold-nosed hound follows an older trail at a steady pace.

O

Occiput The posterior region of the skull.

Otter tail Thick at the root, round, and tapering, with the hair parted or divided at the underside, as seen in the Labrador Retriever.

Out at the elbows Elbows turning out from the body as opposed to being held close.

Overshot The incisors of the upper jaw projecting beyond the incisors of the lower jaw.

P

Pack Several hounds kept in a single kennel, and used to hunt prey over large distances, often accompanied by hunters on horseback. A mixed pack comprises males and females.

Pads Tough, shock-absorbing projections on the underside of the paws.

Parti-color Two or more definite colors, one of which must be white.

Pedigree A written record of a dog's genealogy of three generations or more.

Pelvis Hip bones.

Penciling Black lines dividing the tan on the toes.

Piebald Coat with patches of two colors, especially black and white.

Pincer bite See *level bite*.

Pinto Marked with white and some other color, primarily used to describe Akitas.

Plume A long fringe of hair on the dog's tail.

Point The stance of the hunting dog indicating the presence of prey.

Pointing breeds Term commonly applied to breeds that point birds.

Pompon A rounded tuft of hair left on the end of the tail when the coat is clipped.

Pricked ear (or Prick ear) Ear that is carried erect and usually pointed at the tip.

Pump handle A long tail, carried high.

Puppy A dog under 12 months of age.

Purebred A dog whose sire and dam are the same breed.

R

Racy Tall, and of comparatively slight build.

Rear pastern The region of the hind leg between the hock and the foot.

Red sesame Red with a sparse black overlay, primarily used to describe the Shiba Inu and Shikoku.

Register To record a dog's breeding particulars with a national kennel club.

Registries Organizations that keep official records of purebred dogs for tracking lineage.

Retrieve The act of bringing game back to the hunter. Also, an exercise in some obedience classes.

Retrieving breeds Term commonly applied to those sporting breeds that typically return birds to the hunter.

Rib cage The collection of bones and cartilage that define the thoracic region.

Ring tail A tail that is carried in almost a complete circle.

Roach back A convex curvature of the back.

Roan The fine mixing of colored hairs with white hairs that often produces a blue- or iron-gray. For example, a blue roan is a coat comprised of black and white hairs.

Roman nose Where the bridge of the nose forms a slightly convex line from the forehead to nose tip, characteristic of the Borzoi. Also called *Ram's nose*.

Rose ear A small drop ear that folds back at the midway point.

Ruby A rich mahogany red (English Toy Spaniel). Color definitions may vary by breed. Always check the breed standard for the definitive color description.

Ruff Thick, longer hair growing around the neck.

Rule book(s) Both the *Rules Applying to Registration & Discipline* and the *Rules Applying to Dog Shows* as well as various sets of obedience and field trial rules. There are also a number of rule books relating to specific events.

Rust Used to describe several breeds, this color is a medium-brilliant reddish-brown. Color definitions may vary by breed. Always check the breed standard for the definitive color description.

S

Saber tail Carried in a semicircle.

Sable Coat color produced by black-tipped hairs on a background of silver, gold, gray, fawn, or brown.

Sacrum The region of the vertebral column that consists of three fused vertebrae that articulate the pelvic girdle.

Saddle Markings in the shape of a saddle over the back. Color definitions may vary by breed. Always check the breed standard for the definitive color description.

Saddle back Overlong back, with a dip behind the withers.

Sandy Used to describe several breeds, this color is a dull yellowish-gray of medium saturation. Color definitions may vary by breed. Always check the breed standard for the definitive color description.

Scent hound A hound that hunts primarily by scent rather than sight.

Scissors bite A bite in which the outer side of the lower incisors touches the inner side of the upper incisors.

Screw tail A naturally short tail twisted in a spiral formation.

Seal Almost black with a red cast when viewed in the sun or bright light, primarily used to describe the Boston Terrier.

Second thigh The part of the hind leg from the stifle to the hock.

Sedge A light chocolate color, primarily used to describe Chesapeake Bay Retrievers.

Semi-prick ears Ears carried erect with just the tips leaning forward.

Sickle hocked Inability to straighten the hock joint on the back reach of the hind leg.

Sight hound A hound that runs or courses game by sight rather than scent.

Sire The male parent.

Skeleton Descriptively divided into axial (skull, vertebrae column, chest) and appendicular (forequarters, hindquarters) portions.

Slab-sided Flat ribs with too little spring from the spinal column.

Sled dogs Dogs worked, usually in teams, to pull sleds.

Sloping shoulder The shoulder blade set obliquely or *laid back*.

Smooth Short hair, close lying.

Snipy A pointed, weak muzzle, lacking breadth and depth.

Solid color (self color) One color, or one color except for lighter shadings.

Soundness The state of the dog's physical and mental health.

Speak To bark.

Spectacles Dark markings around the eyes or from the eyes to the ears.

Spike tail Straight, short tail that tapers rapidly along its length.

Splashed Irregularly patched; color on white or white on color.

Splayfoot A flat foot with toes spreading; open-toed.

Sporting group AKC division of dogs that were originally bred to assist the hunter to hunt birds, both on land and in the water.

Spread hocks Hocks pointing outward.

Spring See *flush*.

Spring of ribs Curvature of ribs for heart and lung capacity.

Square body A dog whose measurements from withers to ground equals that from forechest to rump.

Squirrel tail Tail carried up and curved over the back.

Stag red Deep red (almost brown) with intermingling of black hairs, characteristic of the Miniature Pinscher.

Standard See *breed standard*.

Sternum Breastbone.

Stifle The joint of the hind leg between the thigh and the second thigh; the dog's knee.

Stop The step up from the muzzle to the back of the skull.

Swayback Concave curvature of the spine between the withers and the hip bones.

Symmetry Pleasing balance between all parts of the dog.

T

Tail set How the base of the tail is set on the dog's rump.

Tawny Sandy yellow color, primarily used to describe Ibizan Hounds.

Terrier group AKC division of generally small dogs used originally for hunting vermin.

Thigh The hindquarter from the hip to the stifle.

Ticked Small, isolated areas (smaller than spots) of black or colored hairs on a white background. Color definitions may vary by breed. Always check the breed standard for the definitive color description.

Tongue The barking or baying of hounds on the trail, as to give tongue, to open or speak.

Topknot A tuft of longer hair on top of the head.

Topline The dog's outline from just behind the withers to the tail set.

Toy dog Small purebred dogs bred to be companions or lap dogs.

Toy group AKC divison of small dogs bred to be companions or lap dogs.

Trail To hunt by following ground scent.

Tricolor Three colors in the coat: white, black, and tan.

Trim To groom the coat by plucking or clipping.

Trousers Long hair at the back of the thighs.

Tuck-up Characterized by a markedly shallower body depth at the loin compared to the depth of the chest; small-waisted.

Tulip ear An ear carried erect with edges curving in and forward.

Type Sum of qualities that distinguish dogs of one breed from others.

U

Undercoat Coat concealed by a longer topcoat.

Underline The combined contours of the sternum and the abdominal floor.

Undershot The front teeth (incisors) of the lower jaw overlapping or projecting beyond the front teeth of the upper jaw when the mouth is closed.

Upper arm The humerus or bone of the foreleg, between the shoulder blade and the forearm and associated tissues.

V

Variety A division of a breed (which may not be approved by all kennel clubs). In the AKC there are nine breeds that are divided into varieties: Cockers, Beagles, Collies, Dachshunds, Bull Terriers, Manchester Terriers, Chihuahuas, English Toy Spaniels, and Poodles.

Veil Part of the dog's coat hanging straight down over the eyes or partially covering them.

W

Walleye An eye with a whitish iris; a blue eye, fisheye, or pearl eye.

Webbed toes Toes connected by a membrane; often found in water-retrieving dogs.

Wheaten Pale yellow or fawn color, characteristic of several terrier breeds.

Wheel back A marked arch of the thoracic and lumbar vertebrae.

Whelping The act of birthing puppies.

Whip tail A tail carried out stiffly straight and pointed, also called a "rat tail," characteristic of the Irish Water Spaniel.

Whiskers Hairs on the sides of the muzzle; vibrissae.

Wirehair A dense coat of crisp, wiry texture.

Withers Highest point of a dog's shoulders.

Wolf sable Silver or gray with black tips, primarily used to describe Pomeranians.

Working group AKC group of dogs used primarily for manual labor or sentry duties.

Wrinkle Loose, folding skin on the face.

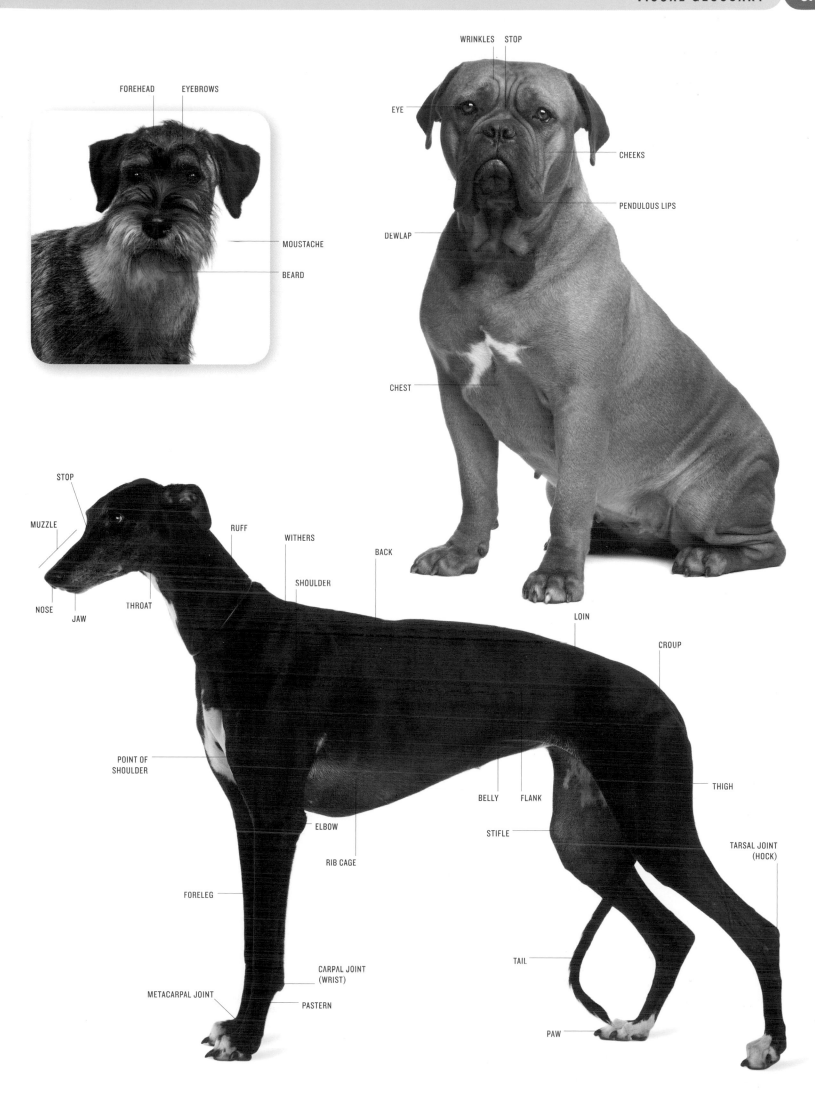

FOREHEAD   EYEBROWS

MOUSTACHE

BEARD

WRINKLES   STOP

EYE

CHEEKS

PENDULOUS LIPS

DEWLAP

CHEST

STOP

MUZZLE

RUFF   WITHERS

BACK

SHOULDER

NOSE   JAW   THROAT

LOIN

CROUP

POINT OF
SHOULDER

THIGH

BELLY   FLANK

ELBOW   STIFLE

TARSAL JOINT
(HOCK)

RIB CAGE

FORELEG

CARPAL JOINT
(WRIST)

TAIL

METACARPAL JOINT

PASTERN

PAW

INDEX

ACKNOWLEDGMENTS

Key: b=below,c=centre, l=left, r=right, t=top

1 Lisa A. Svara/Shutterstock 2 Eric Isselee/Shutterstock 3 Alexia Khruscheva/Shutterstock 7 JPagetRFPhotos/Shutterstock 8 Zuzule/Shutterstock 9 otsphoto/Shutterstock 10tl Rita Kochmarjova/Shutterstock 10tr Dimedrol68/Shutterstock 11bl Rita Kochmarjova/Shutterstock 11bc Abramova Kseniya/Shutterstock 11br David Pegzlz/Shutterstock 12 Oleg Golovnev/Shutterstock 13bl tristan tan/Shutterstock 13br Neftali/Shutterstock 14 U.S. Air Force/Staff Sgt. Stacy L. Pearsall 15 PHB.cz (Richard Semik)/Shutterstock 16-17 DragoNika/Shutterstock 18t Vivienstock/Shutterstock 18b Oldsingerman20 19t Alexandra Baranova, Hodowla Samorodok Hanaana www.ruscanaan.ru 19b Saving Carolina Dogs 22t Pat028 22b Futuristicpals 23t, bl Marina Jay/Shutterstock 23br Magdalena Szachowska/Shutterstock 23bl AnetaPics 23bl Marina Jay/Shutterstock 23bl Nikolai Tsvetkov/Shutterstock 24t Tracy Morgan/Dorling Kindersley/Getty Images 24bl Debra Bardowicks/Oxford Scientific/Getty Images 24br Tracy Morgan/Dorling Kindersley/Getty Images 25t Eric Isselee/Shutterstock 25b Tracy Morgan/Dorling Kindersley/Getty Images 26tl Magdalena Szachowska/Shutterstock 26tr Markus Gann/Shutterstock 26cl cynoclub/Shutterstock 26bl Laila Kazakevica/Shutterstock 26bl Liliya Kulianionak/Shutterstock 26bl Eva Miliuniene/Shutterstock 26bl Eric Isselee/Shutterstock 27t Eric Isselee/Shutterstock 27b Laila Kazakevica/Shutterstock 28t, bl Linn Currie/Shutterstock 28cl, br Utekhina Anna/Shutterstock 28bl Christina 28bl Lilly M 29tr, c, bl Jagodka/Shutterstock 29cl Lenkadan/Shutterstock 29bl Gelpi JM/Shutterstock 29bl Shchipkova Elena/Shutterstock 30r, bl Eric Isselee/Shutterstock 30cb, bl Utekhina Anna/Shutterstock 30bl Skabarcat/Shutterstock 30bl Vivienstock/Shutterstock 31t Eric Isselee/Shutterstock 31cr Rita Kochmarjova/Shutterstock 31br Makushin Alexey/Shutterstock 32t, bl Pleple2000 32br kallerna 33t Erik Lam/Shutterstock 33b Pleple2000 34t APPMGC 34c, bl Caronna 34bl, bc, br Pleple2000 34br Sally Wallis/Shutterstock 35t DragoNika/Shutterstock 35b Pleple2000 36t, b Tatiana Katsai/Shutterstock 36cl, b Anke van Wyk/Shutterstock 36b Elisabeth Hammerschmid/Shutterstock 36b Eric Isselee/Shutterstock 36b, 37r nancy dressel/Shutterstock 37l Elisabeth Hammerschmid/Shutterstock 38tl Eric Isselee/Shutterstock 38bl Capture Light/Shutterstock 38bl Vivienstock/Shutterstock 38bl Lilly M 39t Eric Isselee/Shutterstock 39b f8grapher/Shutterstock 40c, bc, bl Eric Isselee/Shutterstock 40bcl dogboxstudio/Shutterstock 41t Tracy Morgan/Dorling Kindersley/Getty Images 41b Kuznetsov Alexey/Shutterstock 42-43 Glenkar/Shutterstock 44t WilleeCole Photography/Shutterstock 44bl Liliya Kulianionak/Shutterstock 44bl Ksenia Raykova/Shutterstock 44bl Eric Isselee/Shutterstock 44bc Lenkadan/Shutterstock 44br steamroller_blues/Shutterstock 45tl Jagodka/Shutterstock 45br Africa Studio/Shutterstock 47t Ysbrand Cosijn/Shutterstock 47b David Brian Williamson/Shutterstock 48t Tracy Morgan/Dorling Kindersley/Getty Images 48b Eric Isselee/Shutterstock 49t Tracy Morgan/Dorling Kindersley/Getty Images 49b Paris Match via Getty Images 50t Tracy Morgan/Dorling Kindersley/Getty Images 50cl Craig Pemberton/Caronna 50cl, cr, bc Eric Isselee/Shutterstock 50c, bl Andrew Williams/Shutterstock 50br Eric Isselee/Shutterstock 51t George Makatura 51r Erik Lam/Shutterstock 51c Zuzule/Shutterstock 51cl Keith Rousseau 51bl Alens/Bigstock 51br Zuzule/Shutterstock 52t Lenkadan/Dreamstime 52b Eric Broeksma 53t, bl In Green/Shutterstock 53cl Pleple2000 53c Jesus Keller/Shutterstock 53bl PardoY/Shutterstock 53bl Tadas_Naujokaitis/Shutterstock 53bl Eric Isselee/Shutterstock 54t Томасина 54tr Alexey Stiop/Shutterstock 54b Dorling Kindersley/Getty Images 55t Eric Isselee/Shutterstock 55bl Eric Isselee/Shutterstock 56t Capture Light/Shutterstock 57t Erik Lam/Shutterstock 57b Tracy Morgan/Dorling Kindersley/Getty Images 58t Zuzule/Shutterstock 58b Dorling Kindersley/Getty Images 59t, bl Steffen Heinz 59bl, bc, br Nancy Dressel/Shutterstock 60t, br, cb Eric Isselee/Shutterstock 60cb Eric Isselee/Shutterstock 60bl Tracy Morgan/Dorling Kindersley/Getty Images 60bc fotosearch/Getty Images 61t f8grapher/Shutterstock 62-63t, br Lisa A. Svara/Shutterstock 62cb Anna Furman/Shutterstock 62bc, 63br Lisa A. Svara/Shutterstock 64t Tracy Morgan/Dorling Kindersley/Getty Images 64b, 65t Pleple2000 65b Tracy Morgan/Dorling Kindersley/Getty Images 66t Stefan Petru Andronache/Shutterstock 66br Glenkar/Shutterstock 66bl Luis Miguel Bugallo Sánchez 66bl Vadim Eddy/Shutterstock 66bc Pleple2000 67t L. Nagy/Shutterstock 67b Lee319/Shutterstock 68-69 ARTSILENSE/Shutterstock 68cb Hans Surfer/Getty Images 68bl, 69br Eric Isselee/Shutterstock 68bl Mila Atkovska/Shutterstock 68bc Luis Alvarez/Getty Images 68br, 69cr Ysbrand Cosijn/Shutterstock 69t Vivienstock/Shutterstock 70t Erik Lam/Shutterstock 70bl Ivonne Wierink/Shutterstock 70br Rob van Esch/Shutterstock 71t Eric Isselee/Shutterstock 71b Nina 72t, bl Erik Lam/Shutterstock 72cb Zuzule/Shutterstock 72bl Ysbrand Cosijn/Shutterstock 72br Eric Isselee/Shutterstock 73t, b Pleple2000 74tl, bl, cb, r Magdalena Szachowska/Shutterstock 74bl Lilly M 74bc, 75crb TheDaringDuke 75tr Fir0002/Flagstaffotos.//gnu.org/licenses/fdl.html 76t Alephalpha 76b Pleple2000 77t, bl Pleple2000 77bl Susan Schmitz/Shutterstock 77bc Ron Armstrong 77br Lee319/Shutterstock 77crb cynoclub/Shutterstock 78t Eric Isselee/Shutterstock 78bl Ysbrand Cosijn/Shutterstock 78bl, 79tcr Nikolai Tsvetkov/Shutterstock 78bl Eric Isselee/Shutterstock 78bc momo_leif/Shutterstock 78br VitCOM Photo/Shutterstock 78br, 79tl Jagodka/Shutterstock 79tcl, bl Chin Kit Sen/Shutterstock 79tr Jagodka/Shutterstock 79c, bc Eric Isselee/Shutterstock 80t Capture Light/Shutterstock 80bl Julia Remezova/Shutterstock 80br AlexussK/Shutterstock 81t DanielV27 81b Ing. Urban Michal 82t Eric Isselee/Shutterstock 82b Lokal_Profil 83t avarand/Shutterstock 83b Timberdoodle Kennels, Ron & Pat Rosinski 84cl Eric Isselee/Shutterstock 84-85, 84bl Margo Harrison/Shutterstock 84bl, 85tl Michelle Milano/Shutterstock 85tr, bc Eric Isselee/Shutterstock 86t Barna Tanko/Shutterstock 86cl Zuzule/Shutterstock 86br, bl otsphoto/Shutterstock 86bl Barna Tanko/Shutterstock 86bc otsphoto/Shutterstock 87t Erik Lam/Shutterstock 87b cynoclub/Shutterstock 88-89 belu gheorghe/Shutterstock 90t Erik Lam/Shutterstock 90b Shutterstock 91b Alapaha Connection Kennels 92tr, tl, bl, br Erik Lam/Shutterstock 92cl Glen Jones/Shutterstock 92bl Lars Christensen/Shutterstock 93tr Eric Isselee/Shutterstock 93br Makarova Viktoria/Shutterstock 94t Alias Studiot Oy/Shutterstock 94b Wendy Hodges 95t Erik Lam/Shutterstock 95bl Elisabeth Hammerschmid/Shutterstock 95clb Wolf Avni/Shutterstock 95bc cynoclub/Shutterstock 95br, bl Eva holderegger walser 96-97t, 96br Eric Isselee/Shutterstock 96bl David Ward/Dorling Kindersley/Getty Images 96clb, br, 97br, tr Eric Isselee/Shutterstock 96tl, bc Bonnie van den Born, http://www.bonfoto.nl. GFDL of CC-BY-SA-2.5-NL 98t Eric Isselee/Shutterstock 98b Pleple2000 99tl, br Eric Isselee/Shutterstock 99tr, bc Kazlouski Siarhei/Shutterstock 99cl Eric Isselee/Shutterstock 99bl Eric Isselee/Shutterstock 100tr, tl, b Erik Lam/Shutterstock 101t Rolf Klebsattel/Shutterstock 101cl Denis Tabler/Shutterstock 101cr cynoclub/Shutterstock 101bl Wim Harwig 101bc cynoclub/Shutterstock 101br cynoclub/Bigstockphoto 102tr Eric Isselee/Shutterstock 102tl, bcRolf Klebsattel/Shutterstock 102cl Andraž Cerar/Shutterstock 103tl, bc Wicker1 103tr Erik Lam/Shutterstock 103bl, br Tallmantz 104tl, tr, cl, bl, 105t Eric Isselee/Shutterstock 105b TrueBlueLacys 106tl, bl Degtyaryov Andrey/Shutterstock 106tr, br, bcr, bcl Eric Isselee/Shutterstock 107t Pavel Shlykov/Shutterstock 107br, bl Bulda/Shutterstock 108t, b Eric Isselee/Shutterstock 109t Angelo Giampiccolo/Shutterstock 109b Sanne vd Berg Fotografie/Shutterstock 110tl Isselee/Dreamstime.com 110tr Mikel Martinez/Shutterstock 110bl Francesco Scotto di Vetta/Shutterstock 110bl Erik Lam/Shutterstock 110br Ysbrand Cosijn/Shutterstock 110br, 111br Makarova Viktoria/Shutterstock 111tl, bl Eric Isselee/Shutterstock 111tr Lee319/Shutterstock 112t, bl, br Roman Zhuravlev/Shutterstock 112cl Suzi Nelson/Shutterstock 112cr Linn Currie/Shutterstock 112bl Jana Behr/Shutterstock 112br Markus Gann/Shutterstock 113tr, br iofoto/Shutterstock 113cl Picture-Pets/Shutterstock 113crb Eric Isselee/Shutterstock 113bl Patrick Johnson/Shutterstock 113bl, br GK Hart/Vikki Hart/Getty Images 113bc Eric Isselee/Shutterstock 114t Pleple2000 114b paulinux/Shutterstock 115t, br Eric Isselee/Shutterstock 115cr, cl, cb, bl Inna Astakhova/Shutterstock 116tl Claudio Domiziani 116tr, cl Eric Isselee/Shutterstock 116cb cynoclub/Shutterstock 116bl, bc Eric Isselee/Shutterstock 117t Jose Luis Alves/Shutterstock 117b Tracy Morgan/Dorling Kindersley/Getty Images 118t Pleple2000 118b Ionete 119tr Steffen Heinz 119tl Isselee/Dreamstime.com 119b DRS Photography/Shutterstock 120t, cl Vivienstock/Shutterstock 120cb Liliya Kulianionak/Shutterstock 120bl Pleple2000 120bl Eric Isselee/Shutterstock 120bl Elisabeth Abramova/Shutterstock 120br Liliya Kulianionak/Shutterstock 121t TatyanaPanova/Shutterstock 121cr Sergieiev/Shutterstock 121bl Lenkadan/Shutterstock 121bl Annette Shaff/Shutterstock 121br Jeffrey Ong Guo Xiong/Shutterstock 122t Томасина 123b Margo-CzW 124t Dorling Kindersley/Getty Images 124b Eric Isselee/Shutterstock 125t Erik Lam/Shutterstock 125bl StBrecht 125bc Pleple2000 125br Ermolaev Alexander/Shutterstock 126tl kazenouta/Shutterstock 126cb PozitivStudija/Shutterstock 126bc, 127cr cynoclub/Shutterstock 126r Eric Isselee/Shutterstock 127t Kerioak - Christine Nichols/Shutterstock 128t Erik Lam/Shutterstock 129t Pleple2000 129b Traceywashere 130t, b Eric Isselee/Shutterstock 131t cynoclub/Shutterstock 131bl visceralimage/Shutterstock 131bc Erik Lam/Shutterstock 131br Roman Zhuravlev/Shutterstock 132bl Jagodka/Shutterstock 132bc Thierry Pirsoul/Shutterstock 132br, r steamroller_blues/Shutterstock 133tr Eric Isselee/Shutterstock 133br Marina Jay/Shutterstock 134t Flaxphotos/Shutterstock 134b Andreas Wolber 135t Isselee/Dreamstime.com 135bl Lilly M 135bcl Agnes Cartier Millon 135bcr Striatic 135br deniss09/Shutterstock 136cb Erik Lam/Shutterstock 136bl Pleple2000 136bc KIKKUZZO88 137t Pleple2000 137b bikeriderlondon/Shutterstock 138cb David Huntley Creative/Shutterstock 138bl 139tr Eric Isselee/Shutterstock 138bc Vtis/Shutterstock 138br, 139bl Eric Isselee/Shutterstock 138r Vivienstock/Shutterstock 139br Liliya Kulianionak/Shutterstock 140t Isselee/Dreamstime.com 140b Tracy Morgan/Dorling Kindersley/Getty Images 141t Erik Lam/Shutterstock 141b Jezzabell 142t Eric Isselee/Shutterstock 143t Buffy1982/Dreamstime.com 143b Summer06 144t Erik Lam/Shutterstock 145t Isselee/Dreamstime.com 145b, 146tl, tr, bl Eric Isselee/Shutterstock 146cr, bc Serge Vero/Shutterstock 146bcl, br cynoclub/Shutterstock 147t, bcr Isselee/Dreamstime.com 147br Tad Denson/Shutterstock 147bl Eric Isselee/Shutterstock 147bcl pixshots/Shutterstock 148t Eric Isselee/Shutterstock 148b Lee319/Shutterstock 149t WilleeCole Photography/Shutterstock 149b Steffen Heinz 150t, b Tracy Morgan/Dorling Kindersley/Getty Images 151t Lilly M 151b Pleple2000 152t Isselee/Dreamstime.com 152b Erik Lam/Shutterstock 153t absolutimages/Shutterstock 153b Eric Isselee/Shutterstock 154tl Zuzule/Shutterstock 154bcl, br, 155tr Eric Isselee/Shutterstock 154bcr SheltieBoy 155l steamroller_blues/Shutterstock 155br Rita Kochmarjova/Shutterstock 156t Pleple2000 156b Brindis320 157tl Dora Zett/Shutterstock 157tr, bl, br Jagodka/Shutterstock 157crb, bc JStaley401/Shutterstock 158t, c Tracy Morgan/Dorling Kindersley/Getty Images 158cl, br Photobac/Shutterstock 158bl Dorling Kindersley/Getty Images 159tl, bl, br Eric Isselee/Shutterstock 159cr Julia Remezova/Shutterstock 159crb, bc Liliya Kulianionak/Shutterstock 159bcl pavelmayorov/Shutterstock 159bcr Vasiliy Khimenko/Shutterstock 160t Capture Light/Shutterstock 160br alarich/Shutterstock 161tr, bl Fedor Selivanov/Shutterstock 161tl, br f8grapher/Shutterstock 161crb Galen D./Shutterstock 162tl, bl, bcr Vivienstock/Shutterstock 162tr, br Divedeeper 162bcl Jonathan Oakley 163tl, bl Andreas Gradin/Shutterstock 163tr, bcr Erik Lam/Shutterstock 163br leli/Shutterstock 163bcl Erik Lam/Shutterstock 164tl, tr Exhaustfumes 164bl Maja H./Shutterstock 164br fotoivankebe/Shutterstock 165t Artem Kursin/Shutterstock 165b Zbynek Jirousek/Shutterstock 166-167 Bildagentur Zoonar GmbH/Shutterstock 168c, cl, bl Tracy Morgan/Dorling Kindersley/Getty Images 169t Pleple2000 169b, 170b Eric Isselee/Shutterstock 171t, b Tracy Morgan/Dorling Kindersley/Getty Images 172t, cl Susan Schmitz/Shutterstock 172c Sean MacLeay/Shutterstock 172cr, br Eric Isselee/Shutterstock 172bl Annette Shaff/Shutterstock 173t Pleple2000 173br Tracy Morgan/Dorling Kindersley/Getty Images 174t, br PardoY/Shutterstock 174c, cl MaraZe/Shutterstock 174bl, 175bc Erik Lam/Shutterstock 175r Jagodka/Shutterstock 176t Steffen Heinz 176bl Hillary Kladke/Getty Images 176br Zachary Boumeester/Getty Images 177bl Nicaise 177br Tracy Morgan/Dorling Kindersley/Getty Images 178tr, cl, br Pleple2000 178r, 179r Erik Lam/Shutterstock 180t Tracy Morgan/Dorling Kindersley/Getty Images 181br Oleg Golovnev/Shutterstock 183tr Tracy Morgan/Dorling Kindersley/Getty Images 184t Makarova Viktoria/Shutterstock 184bl, bc, 185tr, bl Eric Isselee/Shutterstock 184bcr Serega K Photo and Video/Shutterstock 185bl Erik Lam/Shutterstock 186t, cl Dave King/Dorling Kindersley/Getty Images 186cb verityjohnson/Shutterstock 186bc Steve Shott/Dorling Kindersley/Getty Images 186br, 187t, bl Tracy Morgan/Dorling Kindersley/Getty Images 187br Alephalpha 188tl Dave King/Dorling Kindersley/Getty Images 188tr Sanne vd Berg Fotografie/Shutterstock 188b Tracy Morgan/Dorling Kindersley/Getty Images 189b Marc Henrie/Dorling Kindersley/Getty Images 189t dooziedog.com 190t Marc Henrie/Dorling Kindersley/Getty Images 190b, 191br, bl Tracy Morgan/Dorling Kindersley/Getty Images 192t Cynoclub/Dreamstime.com 193bl Tracy Morgan/Dorling Kindersley/Getty Images 193br Dieter Nagl/AFP/Getty Images 193t Bjørn Konestabo 193b Mirta12 194t Tracy Morgan/Dorling Kindersley/Getty Images 194b bikeriderlondon/Shutterstock 195b Joanna Zembrzuska CC-BY-2.5 196b, 197bl, br Tracy Morgan/Dorling Kindersley/Getty Images 198t Pleple2000 199t f8grapher/Dreamstime.com 199b Tracy Morgan/Dorling Kindersley/Getty Images 200t Canarian 200br Tracy Morgan/Dorling Kindersley/Getty Images 201t Yann Arthus-Bertrand/Corbis 201b Sandra Russell/Dorling Kindersley/Getty Images 202t sajat keszites 203t Frédéric Duhayer/Royal Canin 203b Volbu1 204-205 Vivienstock/Shutterstock 207tl Eric Isselee/Shutterstock 207tr AnetaPics/Shutterstock 207br Nancy Bauer/Shutterstock 207bl Exhaustfumes 208t AnetaPics/Shutterstock 208bcl Eric Isselee/Shutterstock 208bl otsphoto/Shutterstock 208br, bcr Eric Isselee/Shutterstock 208bc Anna Matheis 209br, bl, tl Jagodka/Shutterstock 209tr Caro108 209bc Peter Baxter/Shutterstock 210t Liliya Kulianionak/Shutterstock 210b Tracy Morgan/Dorling Kindersley/Getty Images 211t Eric Isselee/Shutterstock 211b steamroller_blues/Shutterstock 212tl Eric Isselee/Shutterstock 212tr Anna-Mari West/Shutterstock 212b Jagodka/Shutterstock 213t Eric Isselee/Shutterstock 214t Podius/Dreamstime.com 214bl Iliyan Kirkov/Dreamstime.com 214bcl, br Robert Southworth 214bcr, 215t Jack Cronkhite/Shutterstock 216t Tracy Morgan/Dorling Kindersley/Getty Images 217t Veronika Druk/Dreamstime.com 217bl Photomika-com/Shutterstock 217br GLYPHstock/Shutterstock 218b Dorling Kindersley/Getty Images 219b Eric Isselee/Shutterstock 220t Karen Faljyan/Shutterstock 221tl jcsmilly/Shutterstock 221tr Prwstd/Dreamstime.com 222tl, bcl Toloubaev Stanislav/Shutterstock 222bl Nata Sdobnikova/Shutterstock 222bc Eric Isselee/Shutterstock 222bcr Four Oaks/Shutterstock 222br, r Eric Isselee/Shutterstock 223tr ingret/Shutterstock 223cr Utekhina Anna/Shutterstock 223br Marcel Jancovic/Shutterstock 224t, bc steamroller_blues/Shutterstock 224bl Pleple2000 224bcl Lilly M 224br Ewa Studio/Shutterstock 225t, cl Erik Lam/Shutterstock 225cb, cbr Jagodka/Shutterstock 225bl Marina Jay/Shutterstock 225br Alister G Jupp/Shutterstock 226-227 Roman Zhuravlev/Shutterstock 228bl Zuzule/Shutterstock 228br Eric Isselee/Shutterstock 229tl Andreas Gradin/Shutterstock 229tr Margo Harrison/Shutterstock 229b Przykuta 230bl Robynrg/Shutterstock 230br Eric Isselee/Shutterstock 231t Jagodka/Dreamstime.com 231b Eric Isselee/Shutterstock 232t Dmitry Kalinovsky/Shutterstock 232b Eric Isselee/Shutterstock 233tl vrihu/Shutterstock 233tr dezi/Shutterstock 233b Dorling Kindersley/Getty Images 234t Eric Isselee/Shutterstock 234b otsphoto/Shutterstock 235tl Eric Isselee/Shutterstock 235tr Capture Light/Shutterstock 235b Torsten Dickmann/Fotomann.de 236t Erik Lam/Shutterstock 236bl, br Piotr Pietryka 237t Tracy Morgan/Dorling Kindersley/Getty Images 237bl Eric Isselee/Shutterstock 237br Vtls/Shutterstock 238t Medvedev Andrey/Shutterstock 238b Eric Isselee/Shutterstock 239t Tracy Morgan/Dorling Kindersley/Getty Images 239b Linn Currie/Shutterstock 240t, bcl Erik Lam/Shutterstock 240cl, br Fotomicar/Shutterstock 240cr Marina Jay/Shutterstock 240bl, bcr, 241t, bl cynoclub/Shutterstock 242t, br, cl, bl Eric Isselee/Shutterstock 242bcl Erik Lam/Shutterstock 242bcr, 243t cynoclub/Shutterstock 243b Alfredo J. Correa/Shutterstock 244t violetblue/Shutterstock 244b Capture Light/Shutterstock 245t Verena Matthew/Dreamstime.com 246t Ysbrand Cosijn/Shutterstock 246b, br, l, 247t, br Marlonneke Willemsen/Shutterstock 248tr Capture Light/Shutterstock 248b Susan Schmitz/Shutterstock 249t Linn Currie/Shutterstock 249b Eric Isselee/Shutterstock 250t Linn Currie/Shutterstock 250bl, bcr eAlisa/Shutterstock 250bcl Pavel Shlykov/Shutterstock 250br Robynrg/Shutterstock 251t cynoclub/Shutterstock 251b, 252t Eric Isselee/Shutterstock 252cl SergiyN/Shutterstock 252b Eric Isselee/Shutterstock 252cb Condor 36/Shutterstock 253t, bl, bcr Eric Isselee/Shutterstock 253cl Picture-Pets/Shutterstock 253bcl, br Natalia V Guseva/Shutterstock 254t, bcr Tracy Morgan/Dorling Kindersley/Getty Images 254cl Radomír Režný/Dreamstime.com 254bl Brand New Images/Getty Images 254bcl Tracy Morgan/Dorling Kindersley/Getty Images 254br Ray Nolan 255t, bl, bc Robynrg/Shutterstock 255cl Joy Prescott/Shutterstock 255br Robynrg/Shutterstock 256-257 cynoclub/Shutterstock 258tr Editor at Large 258b Erik Lam/Shutterstock 259tr Takingpics/Bigstock 259c, cl, bl iofoto/Shutterstock 260tl, bl Viorel Sima/Shutterstock 260tr, br Eric Isselee/Shutterstock 260cl Carlos Restrepo/Shutterstock 261cr tandemich/Shutterstock 261bl Vicente Barcelo Varona/Shutterstock 261tl, bc Eric Isselee/Shutterstock 261br Konstantin Gushcha/Shutterstock 262tl Andrey Starostin/Shutterstock 262r, cl, bcl Ewa Studio/Shutterstock 262cl, bl Eric Isselee/Shutterstock 262bcr Sergey Lavrentev/Shutterstock 262br phloxii/Shutterstock 263tr Nikolai Tsvetkov/Shutterstock 263br Eric Isselee/Shutterstock 264t Ron Armstrong 264c, bl Eric Isselee/Shutterstock 265t Debraljensen 266t Pleple2000 266c Furmananna/Dreamstime.com 266br, bl Jay Kim/Shutterstock 266bc cat4wisson/Bigstock 267t PardoY/Shutterstock 267cl Linn Currie/Shutterstock 267br, bl Eric Isselee/Shutterstock 267bc Jagodka/Shutterstock 268t, cl, bl, br Eric Isselee/Shutterstock 269t Hjb 269b Toloubaev Stanislav/Shutterstock 270t otsphoto/Shutterstock 270cl, bl Pieter Bregman/Shutterstock 270bc elaine hudson/Shutterstock 271t Eric Isselee/Shutterstock 271c Jagodka/Shutterstock 271bl Ysbrand Cosijn/Shutterstock 271cl Robert Neumann/Shutterstock 271br Jagodka/Shutterstock 272t AnetaPics/Shutterstock 272cl, bl, 273 br Jagodka/Shutterstock 272c Julia Remezova/Shutterstock 272bc Maja H./Shutterstock 272r Eric Isselee/Shutterstock 274r Isselee/Dreamstime.com 274br, cl, bl Eric Isselee/Shutterstock 274cl Pleple2000 274bc Nikolai Tsvetkov/Shutterstock 275t Eric Isselee/Shutterstock 275b Andrey Perminov/Shutterstock 276t otsphoto/Shutterstock 277tl Tracy Morgan/Dorling Kindersley/Getty Images 277tr Cristian labrin 277b Isselee/Dreamstime.com 278b Eric Isselee/Shutterstock 279t Jagodka/Shutterstock 279b JP Chretien/Shutterstock 280t Hook5966 280b Templario2004/Dreamstime.com 281t, bl Erik Lam/Shutterstock 282t, c, cl, br Eric Isselee/Shutterstock 283tl, tr Pavel Sazonov/Shutterstock 283br Lee319/Shutterstock 284t Scott Bolster/Shutterstock 284bl, bc RTImages/Shutterstock 285tr, cl, tl, bl Rick's Photography/Shutterstock 285br Stuart Monk/Shutterstock 285bcl Eric Isselee/Shutterstock 285bcr Jagodka/Shutterstock 286tr, bcl Ryhor M Zasinets/Shutterstock 286tl, cl, bcr Ron Chapple/Dreamstime.com 286cr Hannamariah/Shutterstock 286bl Lee319/Shutterstock 286br Lisa A. Svara/Shutterstock 286br Eric Isselee/Shutterstock 287tl Hans Surfer/Getty Images 287tl, tr, bcr Eric Isselee/Shutterstock 287tc, bcl, bl, br Erik Lam/Shutterstock 288tr steamroller_blues/Shutterstock 288tr Jagodka/Shutterstock 289br, cl Eric Isselee/Shutterstock 289br Chin Kit Sen/Shutterstock 289cl Jagodka/Shutterstock 290tr, cl, bc Jaime Staley-sickafoose/Dreamstime.com 290c Eric Isselee/Shutterstock 290c Chin Kit Sen/Shutterstock 290br Rob Hainer/Shutterstock 291tr, tl Eric Isselee/Shutterstock 291crb Toloubaev Stanislav/Shutterstock 291crb steamroller_blues/Shutterstock 292tl, tr Kozzi2/Dreamstime.com 292cr, bl Eric Isselee/Shutterstock 292cr Chin Kit Sen/Shutterstock 292bl Sergieiev/Shutterstock 293tl steamroller_blues/Shutterstock 293clb Jaime Staley-sickafoose/Dreamstime.com 293bl Vicente Barcelo Varona/Shutterstock 293bl Chin Kit Sen/Shutterstock 293br Rob Wiss 294-295 Richard Chaff/Shutterstock 296cl, 297cl, cr vnlit/Shutterstock 298tl, bl Eric Isselee/Shutterstock 298clb, tc Orange Snowman 299tl, cra Waldemar Dabrowski/Shutterstock 299cla Laila Kazakevica/Shutterstock 299cl, bl Lisa A. Svara/Shutterstock 300tl, tc Eric Isselee/Shutterstock 301cla, br Lisa A. Svara/Shutterstock 302cla, cr Rhonda Odonnell/Shutterstock 303tl, 304clb, bl Laila Kazakevica/Shutterstock 305tl, br Eric Isselee/Shutterstock 305cla Johanna Goodyear/Shutterstock 305clb, tc Gibason/Bigstock 306tl, tc Andraž Cerar/Shutterstock 306cl Laila Kazakevica/Shutterstock 306clb Waldemar Dabrowski/Shutterstock 306br Isselee/Dreamstime.com 307tl, bc Eric Isselee/Shutterstock 307clb AlexAnin/Bigstock 308tl digitalphotonut/Bigstock 308cl, bl Kuzma/Shutterstock 309cla cynoclub/Bigstockphoto 309clb, br Ferenc Szelepcsenyi/Shutterstock 309br, 310cl, bl, tc Eric Isselee/Shutterstock 311tl, tc, bl Lisa A. Svara/Shutterstock

All other images wiki-AM